Short OF
THE Glory

The Fall and Redemption
of EDWARD F. PRICHARD Jr.

Tracy Campbell

THE UNIVERSITY PRESS OF KENTUCKY

Publication of this volume was made possible in part by a grant
from the National Endowment for the Humanities.

Editorial and Sales Offices: The University Press of Kentucky
663 South Limestone Street, Lexington, Kentucky 40508-4008
www.kentuckypress.com

08 07 06 05 04   5 4 3 2 1

The Library of Congress has cataloged the hardcover edition as follows:

Campbell, Tracy, 1962–
    Short of the glory : the fall and redemption of Edward F. Prichard, Jr. / Tracy
Campbell.
        p.   cm.
    Includes bibliographical references and index.
    ISBN 0-8131-2073-X (alk. paper)
    1. Prichard. E.F. (Edward Fretwell) 2. Politicians—United States—Biography.
3. United States—Politics and government—1933–1945. 4. United States—Politics
and government—1945–1953. 5. Political corruption—United States—History—20th
century. 6. Kentucky—Politics and government—1951– 7. Educational change
—Kentucky—History—20th century. I. Title
E748.P88C36   1998
973.91'092—dc21
[B]   98-29859

Paper ISBN 0-8131-9096-7

This book is printed on acid-free recycled paper meeting the requirements
of the American National Standard for Permanence in Paper for Printed Library
Materials.

Manufactured in the United States of America.

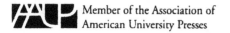

Member of the Association of
American University Presses

To Leslie and Alex

Contents

Photos follow page 150

Acknowledgments

IN the course of writing this book, I have received support and encouragement from a host of wonderful people and organizations. Faculty enrichment and renewal grants from Mars Hill College were indispensable in beginning and finishing the research. The Mellon Foundation provided a fellowship for 1994-95 and an additional summer fellowship that allowed me to devote an entire year to research and writing. The Bingham Foundation, through a James Still Fellowship, provided much-needed research funds. I wish to especially thank Dorothy Graddy and the staff of the Faculty Scholars Program at the University of Kentucky for helping make my stay there so productive. A grant from the Kentucky Oral History Commission made the transcriptions of my oral history interviews possible. I also am indebted to Earl Leininger, Dean of Mars Hill College, and my colleagues in the history department for their support. While other members of the Prichard family declined to discuss this project in any way, Henry Prichard was open and generous.

Terry Birdwhistell, James Klotter, Jim Lenburg, and Don Ritchie each read various drafts of the manuscript. I thank them for challenging me to dig deeper into the complex persona of Ed Prichard. Any remaining errors or weaknesses, of course, are mine and mine alone. I am indebted to the staff of the University Press of Kentucky for supporting me from the very beginning of this project. This book, it must be noted, could not have been undertaken without the work of Terry Birdwhistell at the University of Kentucky library. Terry conducted numerous interviews in the 1980s with dozens of Prichard's contemporaries, all in case someone should decide to do a Prichard biography. Those interviews now comprise the Prichard Oral History Project. Terry's good humor and constant encouragement made the process of researching Prichard's life a much easier task. My thanks also to Jeff Suchanek and other members of the oral history project at the University of Kentucky library for expediting the transcription of my interviews.

I am grateful to the crucial assistance provided by the staffs of numerous archives and libraries throughout the country: the Library of Congress; the National Archives; the King Library, University of Kentucky; Eastern Kentucky University; the Pogue Library, Murray State University; the Southern Historical Collection, University of North Carolina at Chapel Hill; the Columbia University Oral History Collection; the staffs of the Roosevelt, Johnson, Kennedy, and Truman presidential libraries; the Harvard Law School Archives; the Wisconsin State Historical Society; Mars Hill College; the Lexington Herald-Leader; the Louisville Courier-Journal library; and the Filson Club Library. My thanks as well to the Princeton University Alumni Records Office. John Dawahare located tapes of various Prichard television appearances housed at Kentucky Educational Television. I am also grateful to Professor Athan Theoharis of Marquette University for his advice on conducting research within the FBI.

Philip Ardery of Louisville generously allowed me to examine his own FBI records pertaining to the vote fraud investigation. William Stone also provided some private documents, including Prichard's FBI file, that proved very helpful. Judge Sara Combs opened up her home to me on two occasions to study her collection of Gov. Bert Combs's papers. The late Mary Bingham granted me permission to examine her family's papers at the Filson Club. Katharine Graham graciously allowed me to peruse her private papers, and the papers belonging to her late husband, at her home in Georgetown. I also wish to thank Evelyn Small, Mrs. Graham's researcher, for taking time to help me with the Graham papers.

As before, my wife, Leslie, made writing this book a joy. She patiently tolerated the persistent presence of a certain Kentuckian in our household and kindly listened to endless stories about our sometimes overbearing boarder. She and our son, Alex, made it all worthwhile. It is to them that this book is lovingly dedicated.

Introduction: A Christmas Funeral

THE holiday season of 1984 was a painful one for the friends and family of Ed Prichard. Since Thanksgiving, he had been in a Lexington, Kentucky, hospital and had twice undergone major surgery. His doctors were increasingly pessimistic of his chances for survival. The end finally came on December 23. Then, two days after Christmas, they gathered at Christ Church Episcopal in Lexington to pay their final respects. Some of those present were relieved that the physical suffering Prichard had endured for years was now over. Others came to acknowledge a legacy of considerable achievement. Still others simply wanted to say farewell to a beloved friend. But through it all, there was the unspoken but heartfelt sadness of what might have been.

They came to honor a complex and tragically ironic man. Though he possessed a photographic memory and had graduated from the Harvard Law School and clerked at the U.S. Supreme Court, Ed Prichard had only recently earned a significant living as a practicing attorney. Though known as a political prodigy who had held a series of significant posts within the Roosevelt and Truman administrations, he had never held any elective office. Despite that, for days following his death, major national newspapers ran lengthy obituaries of the "former FDR Brain Truster." The *Washington Post* described him as "an intellectual prodigy" whose "admirers envisioned him in the White House some day." In Kentucky, the major daily papers' headlines proclaimed the death of the eminent political adviser, and subsequently ran lengthy articles concerning his life in the days leading to his funeral. The *Louisville Courier-Journal* editorialized that "his intellect bedazzled, bemused, entertained, and often inspired those around him from early childhood until his final illness." The *Lexington Herald-Leader* proclaimed that his was "a story of pride before a fall, of wisdom gained through suffering, of redemption through service to others."[1]

The 350 people attending Ed Prichard's funeral included a litany of powerful and distinguished people that only hinted at the breadth of his life's impact: the current governor of Kentucky and three former governors; *Courier-Journal* owner Barry Bingham; a congressman and several mayors; two college presidents; several state and federal judges; and even a few Washingtonians such as civil rights attorney Joseph Rauh. Many of them shared a political philosophy that was already beginning to seem dated. "This," as one observer noted, "was the last roundup of liberal Democrats."[2]

Both before and after the services, friends gathered in small groups and relieved their grief by retelling humorous stories of their fallen friend. Their memory was of a man who was abnormally large in every sense of the word—large in his girth, which sometimes swelled to over 300 pounds; large in his intellect; large in his prodigious appetite for both food and politics; and, lastly, large in his flaws.

After the funeral, another service was held to allow more people to mourn him properly. This remarkable event, organized by Katharine Graham, owner of the *Washington Post,* was held in the nation's capital. Speakers such as Mrs. Graham, Joseph Rauh, and Arthur M. Schlesinger Jr. spoke at the service and later went to Graham's office for further stories and memories. Remembered with such fondness were Prichard's intimate relationships with some of the leading luminaries of the century: Felix Frankfurter, Eugene Meyer, Philip Graham, Fred Vinson, Sir Isaiah Berlin, and Lyndon Johnson. But permeating the remembrance was the certain air of tragedy that all who knew him felt. This was, after all, the man whom Katharine Graham once described as no less than "the most impressive man of our generation, the one who dazzled us most"—perhaps, *the* best and brightest of the World War II generation.

They all knew about the amazing rise of Ed Prichard: his early love of county politics; his extraordinary academic career that made him a legendary figure at Princeton and Harvard Law School; his year as clerk to Justice Felix Frankfurter at the U.S. Supreme Court; and his impressive résumé of jobs within FDR's administration in World War II—all before he reached the age of thirty. They also knew that when Prichard came home to Kentucky in 1945, it was *assumed* by his admirers that he would be governor within a short time. Indeed, it was not out of the question that one day Ed Prichard would be president.

All of these expectations came crashing down in the general election of 1948. That particular election is best remembered as the one in which Harry Truman scored the political upset of the century by defeating Republican Thomas Dewey. In the small region of Bourbon County, Kentucky, that election is today even better known as the one that ended the career of Ed Prichard. When 254 fraudulent ballots were discovered in the voting boxes before the polls opened, a federal investigation ensued. Within months, Ed Prichard and his law partner were indicted. In July 1949, a dramatic courtroom admission sealed Prichard's fate. After his conviction and months of unsuccessful appeals, the wunderkind of the later New Deal took his cell in a federal prison. Thunderstruck friends and colleagues were left to ask simply: Why did a man with such promise throw it all away on 254 ballots in a statewide race?

In late 1950, after obtaining presidential clemency, Prichard returned to Kentucky a disgraced felon rather than the darling of the New Deal. For two decades, Prichard toiled in virtual anonymity in central Kentucky, serving in various statewide political campaigns and gubernatorial administrations, all without public recognition or compensation. Prichard's personal tragedy was compounded in the late 1960s when his diabetic condition produced both chronic kidney failure and eventual blindness. Out of these bouts with illness, Prichard somehow climbed back into the political arena by the 1970s, becoming Kentucky's most persuasive and eloquent voice for education reform. When he died, a whole generation within his home state knew little of Prichard's checkered past. For them, he was synonymous only with enlightened reform. Others, however, could only remember what one woman in Bourbon County asked when confronted with Prichard's name: "Wasn't he the one that went to the pen?" Somewhere in between is a singular American story.

Most political biographies concern those who have reached a certain visible plateau from which they receive significant attention or exercise power. Stories of those like Ed Prichard, who self-destructed before obtaining such prominence, are usually dismissed. Moreover, their stories are often too difficult, if not impossible, for historians to recover. The usual remnants of an active political life, such as collections of an individual's papers and correspondence, memoirs, monographs, or dissertations, are not to be found when examining Ed Prichard's life. He left no public papers; is seldom, if ever, mentioned in books or articles on the New Deal or Kentucky history; and even his own oral histories have been sealed by his widow. Such imposing research impediments often reminded me of why it is much easier to write about the well known, who leave behind them more paper trails for the historian to examine.

But, as I soon discovered upon embarking on this book, the historical trails of people such as Ed Prichard exist in more remote places. Although he kept no papers, his correspondence with many others who deposited their materials in various libraries remains. Moreover, oral history has been vital to recovering Prichard's life. Through my own interviews and other oral history collections, the rich saga of Prichard's life began to take shape. Lastly, sources such as declassified FBI files and other records revealed the undercurrents of Prichard's life in ways I could never imagine when I began my research.

As the numerous episodes of American political scandal—both historical and contemporary—remind us, Ed Prichard's saga is not unique. American history is replete with examples of political corruption and stories of brilliant and promising figures who recklessly self-destructed in public. What is special about Prichard is the exaggerated nature of the heights he quickly reached and the depths to which he fell, as well as the methods by which he acquired power and the tactics that were used to bring him down. Few politicos have possessed Prichard's vast intellect, and fewer still were ever imprisoned for such a crime.

But there is more to Prichard's story than merely an individual who was somehow morally flawed. His flaws did not emerge or grow in a vacuum. Prichard was the product of a political culture, at both the local and the national level, that tolerated and quietly encouraged the type of behavior that eventually consumed him. This subterranean world existed layers beneath the surface of visible political activity. It is where power is exercised in its most naked form but is rarely exposed. Prichard's complex life allows us a revealing glimpse into that world and sheds light on a culture that was essentially paradoxical—while devoted to a political ethos that sought to enhance certain democratic principles, it was also comfortable resorting to tactics that were anything but democratic. Prichard reflected this culture, and this culture was, in many ways, a reflection of him.

Finally, this is not just a book about Prichard's sudden rise and fall from grace. In his later life, while beset with a new assortment of imposing challenges, Prichard fought valiantly to overcome the demons that had so long haunted him. Ultimately, the saga of Ed Prichard demonstrates some of the most basic elements of the human condition—of cowardice and courage, hubris and humility. His story is as timeless as a Greek tragedy.

These were just some of the items surrounding the services for Prichard that December day in 1984. The following morning, his cremated remains were buried in a private service in the Prichard family plot. The cemetery was located in the beautiful Kentucky town of Paris, where it had all begun almost seventy years before.

Part I
Star Rising

My son, paradoxically enough . . . being a Southerner and . . . of course a Democrat you will find yourself in the unique position of choosing between (a) those ideals implanted as right and proper in every man since Jesus Christ . . . and (b) ideals inherent in you through a socio-economic culture over which you have no power to prevail; consequently I strongly urge you my son always to be a good Democrat but to be a good man too if you possibly can.

—William Styron, *Lie Down in Darkness*

1 The Political Education of "Sonny" Prichard

ON a typical sultry summer afternoon in the early 1920s, the pulse of activity at the county courthouse in Paris, Kentucky, decreased as surely as the heat and humidity escalated. By the late afternoon, the men often gathered in the first-floor office of Pearce Paton, the popular county clerk of Bourbon County. In such a milieu, one of the most treasured folk rituals of American politics was practiced—stories were endlessly exchanged of past elections, rumors were originated and circulated about every prominent person in the county, and predictions were offered on upcoming political contests. Amid the roar of the fans and the tobacco smoke, a visitor to the clerk's office at any time in the 1920s would likely have found seated next to Paton a chubby, wide-eyed young boy named Edward "Sonny" Prichard. For Sonny, the courthouse was a temple. After hearing the lawyers argue their cases in the county and district courts, Sonny often read every law book in the judge's chambers in incessant curiosity before strolling into Paton's office. Sonny's attendance in the building did not end when school started in the fall. After his classes, Sonny raced not to a favorite watering hole or a playground like other youngsters did. Instead, he returned to the courthouse. The Bourbon County courthouse, in short, was Sonny's first schoolroom, and he faithfully committed to heart its sundry lessons.

For a young boy in the 1920s, Bourbon County, Kentucky, was an idyllic place. No other county in the state, in fact, fit the stereotype of Kentucky bluegrass gentility as well as Bourbon County. It stood in a world of lush rolling hills of bluegrass, where the world's finest horseflesh roamed comfortably in regal luxury. Their owners lived in an antebellum world seemingly light-years from the Appalachian coalfields just a few counties away. Here resided various traditions steeped in southern romantic folklore. Columned mansions adorned the countryside, with sprawling estates neatly encased in seemingly endless white wooden fences.

The county's association with bluegrass was more than geographical. In the 1920s four manufacturing facilities in the county packaged most of the world's bluegrass seed. Long one of the richest per capita counties in Kentucky, Bourbon County in 1920 had 194,000 acres of farmland valued at more than

$52 million, making it the second-ranking county in the commonwealth in land values. Some of the world's most opulent horse farms were located in Bourbon County, and numerous Kentucky Derby winners had been—and would be—foaled or retired here. Later, in the 1970s and 1980s, the county's most noted resident was Secretariat, the famed Triple Crown winner. Many of the major routes, traditionally called "pikes," were gently hugged by rugged gray rock fences. Bourbon is a county that one Kentucky journalist wrote "could be located only in Kentucky. It wouldn't fit anywhere else."[1]

Sonny Prichard was enamored with the history of his home county, and there was much to interest the young political animal. Bourbon County's political history was steeped in rich tradition and Kentucky folklore. Its very name derives not from the liquor, but from the colonists' desire to honor the royal house of Bourbon, which had aided the American revolutionaries in their war against Great Britain. By the late 1700s, the county seat, Hopewell, was renamed Paris to accentuate the French flavor. On the eve of the Civil War, Bourbon County had the second highest number of slaves of any county in the state. Bourbon's allegiance, then, mostly went to the Confederacy, and Republicans found little fertile soil in Bourbon after the war. Population growth did not occur in that era, however, for Bourbon's numbers deviated little in the century following the antebellum era—in 1860 the population totaled almost fifteen thousand. By 1930, that figure had barely reached eighteen thousand. The county exhibited other qualities that made it unique. In the 1920s and 1930s, it contained nearly five thousand African-Americans, one of the largest per capita populations of any Kentucky county, at just over 26 percent.[2]

At the center of the county's political activities stood the imposing courthouse, located in the town square in Paris. Constructed between 1902 and 1905 and designed by a Washington, D.C., architect, the impressive building, some hoped, would attract the state capital away from Frankfort. It never did, but the building dominated the city, and its location atop a slight bluff in the northern part of town allowed virtually anyone in Paris to peer at its dome. The first floor, built from South Carolina granite, housed the offices of the county clerk and judge, the county sheriff, various license and tax offices, and the county courtroom. Inside, the sweltering heat of the central Kentucky summers was somewhat alleviated by the high ceilings and expansive windows, with large wooden shutters to block the summer sun. A grand marble staircase in the center of the building led to the second story. Built of bedford stone, the upper floor contained the circuit court offices and courtroom, an impressive amphitheater-like expanse that could hold more than two hundred people in wood-backed seats.[3]

The Paris courthouse was significant, however, for more than its architecture. In Bourbon County, as in virtually every county in Kentucky, political power has been located historically in the "courthouse rings" that dominate the county political landscape. The state contains 120 counties, more than any other state in the union except Texas and Georgia. The nominal reason for creating so many small county units was to provide proximity to the county seats. Since mountain residents had to traverse miles of treacherous hills and streams to arrive at the county seat, new counties were created to save them long and arduous journeys. The real reason for so many counties, according to a noted journalist, "was that county governments afforded splendid and multitudinous opportunities to get close to the public trough."[4] Each county election consequently witnessed a healthy number of officeholders seeking to become clerk, sheriff, jailer, coroner, commissioner, or school board member. The tie that residents had with their home county was pervasive—even some urban dwellers in Lexington or Louisville identified themselves principally as inhabitants of their county.

Political corruption has a long-standing history in many of these counties. In the early nineteenth century, county offices such as clerk, deputy sheriff, and constable were effectively sold to the highest bidder. By the middle of the century, according to a historian of Kentucky counties, "the sale of office gave way to the sale of votes," and the state's constitution mandated that voting be done by voice, making corruption much easier. As other methods were employed, voting fraud became a complex procedure. Those wishing to sell their votes would often wait until late in the day, when anxious candidates and their assorted cronies raised their offering prices in a close election.[5]

Patronage was also distributed from the governor's office in Frankfort to the county through the medium of the "courthouse rings." Every administration had a designated representative in each county who handled patronage matters and was expected, in the words of the ring, to "deliver" the county for the administration on election day. In this context, "delivering" meant more than simply engaging in philosophical debates or going door to door canvassing prospective voters for one's favorite candidate. It implied winning an election by whatever means necessary. Precinct captains and election officers played significant roles in delivering their counties in a variety of ways, thus ensuring their own jobs and the jobs of the other ring members.

Often such tactics included holding up the final vote tally until campaign headquarters informed the election officers of the number of votes needed to ensure victory; purposely counting a properly marked ballot improperly; or "stuffing" the boxes with ballots of people whose names did not appear on the registration lists or with those on the list who did not vote. One survey revealed that in over a century's worth of voting returns, it was not uncommon for some counties to return more than 110 percent of its potential vote. Buying votes, which could be as easy as waiting outside the precincts to hand out five and ten dollar bills to arriving voters, remained common. "Chain ballots" have been skillfully employed as well. As historian Thomas D. Clark explained: "A local boss secured a blank official ballot, maybe from someone sacrificing his vote; the ballot was marked and traded all day for unmarked ones. The venal voter got a dollar for his vote, but only if he fetched out a blank ballot to keep the chain continuous."[6] In such ways, courthouse rings ruled elections, dispensed jobs, and maintained power. "Voting irregularities" were an accepted part of such a political culture.

The creation and maintenance of Kentucky's "little kingdoms" of counties and their contingent rings played a significant role in the state's political, social, and economic history. Not only did such powerful, entrenched rings destroy democratic forms at the local level, but the resources thus poured into the maintenance of county governments took precious funds away from badly needed areas and perpetuated the cycles of poverty. Numerous attempts to consolidate counties, and in the process make county governments less costly and more efficient, had been—and would be—thwarted by courthouse rings at every turn. And the rings had several powerful allies in opposing reform. As historian Robert Ireland stated, legislators and administrations in Frankfort have usually vehemently opposed county reform since their power has been "often derived from these cliques and usually dependent upon them in large degree for reelection and political support."[7]

Bourbon County was in no way immune to such abuses. As the county's Democratic party faced new challenges to local offices after Reconstruction, new methods were employed to ensure Democratic victories. Election officers and precinct workers signed fraudulent ballots and made voting more difficult for the opposition by strategically changing voters' assigned precincts at the last minute. After all, the first rule in vote cheating is not to "get the vote out," but to decrease the voting pool by as wide a margin as possible. On one occasion in 1901, the incumbent Democrats simply refused to recognize a Republican victory by throwing out the election results altogether in a manner reminiscent of a banana republic. One Bourbon resident stated that after World War II it was no more than a game to see "how many dead darkies" could be voted in after the election in the basement of the courthouse.[8]

Political power at the county level in Kentucky was often handed down from one family member to another. In fact, one's connection with a certain family could be all the requirement necessary for victory. One candidate in the mountains once went so far as to declare that he was "descended from the best people in the mountains on my wife's side at least."[9] In Bourbon County, a handful of families either operated or benefited from the maintenance of the courthouse ring for many decades.

No discussion of Bourbon County's political makeup can occur without a proper understanding of the role that selected families have played in the county's history. Today, the inside door of the county clerk's office bears the faded photographs of some Democratic party icons—Woodrow Wilson, Franklin Roosevelt, and a member of a prominent local family, Judge William Breckinridge Ardery. His father, William Porter Ardery, was a man of means who owned three separate farms throughout the county and had served as Bourbon County sheriff and the first president of the People's Bank of Paris.[10] His only son was born in 1887 and graduated from nearby Centre College in Danville in 1909. The following year, Ardery married Julia Hogue Spencer. Ardery was admitted to the Kentucky bar in 1909, and he practiced law in Paris and served as editor and publisher of the *Paris Democrat*. In 1938, the Arderys moved to a beautiful family home named Rocclicgan, located on the Lexington Pike.

In addition to his law practice, Ardery raised tobacco and cattle and, like his father, was heavily engaged in the Democratic party. In 1923, voters elected Ardery to the Kentucky General Assembly, where he hoped to use the platform of the state legislature to stump for higher office. He sought the party's nomination for governor in 1931, but at the state Democratic convention in Lexington held that summer, Ardery's bid failed. It would be his last try at statewide office. After serving as commonwealth's attorney in the early 1930s, Ardery was elected Fourteenth Circuit district judge in 1935, whereupon he launched one of the state's most noted judicial careers. In 1954, Judge Ardery was named the state's most outstanding circuit judge, and three years later he received a gold medal for distinguished service to the state. Ardery died in 1967, having served as circuit judge for more than three decades. Julia Ardery became one of the county's best-known and best-loved volunteers, and her genealogical studies of the county were widely popular. The Arderys, along with their children, occupied a unique position within the county hierarchy.[11]

The Clays were another prominent local family. With nominal ties to former presidential candidate Henry Clay, the family in Bourbon County traced its lineage to Gen. Green Clay, the first deputy surveyor of Kentucky. In 1807 he became speaker of the Kentucky Senate and later commanded more than three thousand Kentucky troops in the War of 1812. One of Green's sons, Cassius, became a well-known emancipationist. Another, Brutus, settled in Bourbon County and became one of the county's wealthiest farmers. Elected to Congress in 1862, Brutus eventually served as chairman of the House Committee on Agriculture. Brutus's only son, Cassius, graduated from Yale in 1866 and returned to live in Paris, where he took over the management of his father's farms. A staunch Democrat, he was elected to the Kentucky General Assembly in 1871 and to the state senate in 1885. In 1889, Bourbon County named Cassius as a delegate to the Kentucky Constitutional Convention, and that body made him its presiding officer. Under Clay's leadership, the convention successfully wrote and adopted Kentucky's fourth and current constitution. Like Judge Ardery, Cassius Clay sought higher office but failed to get the nomination for governor in 1891 and 1895. His son, Cassius M. Clay III, was born in 1895. Among other pursuits, Cassius III wrote several books on the regulation of public utilities and farming.[12]

Many other families left their mark within the Democratic ranks of Bourbon County as well. Not all sought elective office. The Brannon family, longtime owners and publishers of the Paris Democratic newspapers, did not seek office but held considerable political clout. After World War II, Paul Brannon, a fiery partisan Democrat, acquired the *Paris Kentuckian-Citizen* and ran it as a functioning component of the local Democratic machine.[13]

The Patons were another mainstay of Paris courthouse politics. Edward Drane Paton was a longtime county clerk in the courthouse until his death in 1906. He began his political career by winning an election for coroner in 1877 and eventually succeeding to the position of clerk. The man chosen to succeed him after his death was the deputy clerk and Paton's son, Pearce. For more than thirty years, the popular Pearce was reelected county clerk and was opposed for the office on only two occasions. In 1909 he defeated his Republican opponent in the general election by a vote of 1,418 to 1. When he died in 1942, he was eventually succeeded in office by his son, Ed Drane Paton. For almost a half century, then, three successive Patons held the post of Bourbon County clerk.[14]

These families occupied something approaching the top of the political hierarchy in Bourbon County for several decades, owning some of the county's most prestigious homes and occupying some of its most important political offices. They often worked in concert with the powerful acknowledged king of Bourbon County Democratic politics, Judge W. G. McClintock, who shared many traits with his counterparts in other Kentucky counties. According to one student of such leaders, the prototypical county boss performed a variety of duties attendant on his post: "It was his policy to know every man and boy in his bailiwick, and he virtually did know every male in the county by his first name. It was his pleasure to always be of service to the community. If you needed a recommendation, or a job, or a loan, you could always get assistance. That is, if your politics was right."[15] On the other side of the equation were families who did not inherit the social and political status enjoyed by the Clays or the Arderys. One such family was the Prichards of Houston Avenue.

The patriarch of the Prichards, Andrew Jackson Prichard, had served two terms in the Kentucky legislature in the late 1850s before he joined the Confederacy. His son, Thomas Jackson, married Mariamne Fretwell, daughter of a prominent Bourbon County family, and they moved to Huntington, West

Virginia, where he was a prosperous physician and coal mine operator. In 1891, Mariamne gave birth to a son christened Edward Fretwell Prichard, who attended the Millersburg Military Academy in Millersburg, Kentucky, before enrolling at Centre College in nearby Danville, where he graduated in 1912. One of his Centre classmates and varsity football and baseball teammates was future chief justice Frederick M. Vinson.[16]

"Big Ed" Prichard, otherwise known as "Prich" in Bourbon County, was an imposing physical specimen, standing six feet four inches and weighing more than two hundred pounds. He was athletically built, with broad, muscular shoulders and strong, meaty hands. After graduating from Centre, he married Allene Bashford Power, the daughter of one of the county's most successful wholesalers, and they lived in Paris. Allene was a gentle, beautiful, and intelligent woman who had attended Wellesley—those who knew her consistently used the word "lovely" to describe her. She read widely, possessed a superb soprano singing voice, and often displayed a robust sense of humor.[17]

Allene's gracious refinement vividly contrasted with her husband's gruff worldliness. Big Ed dabbled in owning a Buick dealership, real estate, farming, and a host of other assorted business ventures. He became a horse breeder and owned a prized thoroughbred named Tannery. In 1930, in fact, Tannery was a local favorite to win the Kentucky Derby but finished eighth in a field of fifteen to Gallant Fox. Prichard also engaged in a variety of risky business ventures, making and losing significant amounts of money. Ed and Allene lived in a rather modest one-story brick house at 131 East Seventh Street in Paris, which they had purchased in 1919. Located in a small, working-class neighborhood, the Prichards could walk next door to the county public library.

On January 21, 1915, Allene gave birth to a son, Edward Fretwell Jr. Two years later, a second son was born, Henry Power, who was named for her father. The two Prichard boys were raised amid some affluence. By 1920 Prichard employed more than forty people on his farm in Bourbon County. Four years later he had become enough of a financial success that he sold his house on Seventh Street and moved his family into a two-story red brick home on Houston Avenue, located at the end of a road of other large, expensive homes. From the front porch, the Prichards could easily see the clock on the courthouse dome, just one block away.[18]

Big Ed also earned another reputation among some within the county, one best summarized by one county resident: "Big Ed Prichard was supposed to be a crook. Just what he exactly did, I don't know, but that was the impression." Throughout the 1920s, Prichard avoided the agricultural depression sweeping the southeast primarily by raising thoroughbred horses; then, with the fall of prohibition in 1933, Prichard turned to owning a beer distributorship located in Lexington and a dairy farm in Bourbon County. In the words of John Ed Pearce, "Big Ed" Prichard "loved sports, hunting, good whisky and horse racing," a suitable Kentucky and Bourbon County combination.[19] In addition to these enterprises, he also had one other love—politics.

Throughout the early 1900s, Big Ed could often be seen at the county courthouse. He was also a man on the move seeking political office. Working diligently within the Democratic party of Bourbon County, he came to know all the right people. But there was more to working within the party than shaking the right hands. Having been a precinct officer, Big Ed understood the voting procedures not taught in government classes at Centre College. Big Ed was expected to "control" his Paris precinct, and he did so with some skill. Prichard dispensed political favors and, on one occasion, earned some valuable chits when counting the votes in an election involving Judge Ardery. As one observer recalled, when the election seemed too close for comfort, Big Ed simply stuffed the ballots afterward in order to ensure victory for Ardery. Such political experience paid off in 1937, when Prichard was elected to the Kentucky House of Representatives, taking the seat once held by Judge Ardery. As the saying goes, "politics is local," and Big Ed Prichard was an expert, in every sense of the word, on what constituted "politics" in Bourbon County in the early 1900s.[20]

Ed and Allene Prichard were thus, in many ways, opposites. Like many couples of the era, they inhabited separate spheres—she in the home and church, and he in his business and the courthouse. Allene may not have been privy to her husband's growing political contacts, nor to the tactics he used to enhance his own political star, but she was not barren of her own deeply held political views. Years later, when the Daughters of the American Revolution refused to permit Marian Anderson to sing at a DAR event, Allene promptly resigned from the DAR in protest. Such was the political and social environment in which the Prichard boys were raised.[21]

The young Ed Prichard combined his mother's love of reading, languages, and history with his father's love of politics. It was a potent combination. People in Paris quickly understood that this was no ordinary toddler. During his earliest years, while his father conducted business in one office of the courthouse, little Ed Prichard began to roam the halls of the capacious building, taking in all the sights, smells, and unique personalities it had to offer. "From the time I was about nine years old," Prichard recalled, "I was a constant habitué at the courthouse."[22]

A story that the younger Prichard often told relates to his childhood, his relationship with his father, and the cynical political environment in which he was raised. When he was a young boy, the smaller Prichard was with his father in the courthouse on an election day. On this particular afternoon, news came that a Bourbon County farmer named Squire Lowry had died that morning. Big Ed recognized Lowry's name as one who was usually added to the voting list, or "voted in," late in the afternoon by a precinct worker in order to sway a tight election or to swell a victory margin. Big Ed told his son to run over to the precinct and inform the election officer not to vote Lowry in, since any later examination of the voting list might prove troublesome. The young boy ran as fast as he could to the precinct, and when he arrived he told the precinct worker the news. The officer seemed somewhat irritated, as if he had already voted the man in. After pausing, the election officer told the boy, "You go back and tell that sonofabitch the last thing the squire did before he died was to cast his vote."[23]

Prichard recalled another amusing and telling situation, one that occurred in the 1935 gubernatorial primary. The "boss" of the Bourbon County Democratic party, W.G. McClintock, gave a precinct worker $500 to buy votes. Later that day, the worker came back to McClintock complaining, "The sentiment's against me." McClintock replied, "You silly sonofabitch, that's what the money's for—to combat sentiment."[24]

Politics became Prichard's boyhood passion. He went with his father whenever he could to Frankfort and listened attentively to all the state office-seekers who campaigned in Paris. But the youngster also loved the daily anecdotes that floated around the courthouse. Prichard copied the speaking and debating skills of Paton and other local politicians. He carefully watched how to use language effectively and how to persuade others with an effective combination of humor, bravado, and brains. He also acquired the ability to tell a story in the most captivating way. Neither Paton nor Big Ed sought to hide any of the seamier sides of politics from the young pol.

Little Edward, or "Sonny," as most of Bourbon County knew him, shared his father's size but not his athletic prowess. He had no interests in sports and quickly grew overweight, a trait he would never lose. Other children, in fact, regarded him as effeminate, or a "sissy." "He certainly wasn't the most masculine person in the world. He had no interest in masculine pursuits," said one female classmate. If his physical presence made him so unlike the other children, early on it was apparent Sonny Prichard also possessed an extraordinary mind. "He was so superior in his intellect," recalled a childhood friend, and "that was one of the things that caused other boys to stand apart from him." His classmates and teachers soon found that Sonny's intellect was backed by a photographic memory. Consequently, he had great difficulty relating to children his own age. As one childhood acquaintance recalled, "He was pretty much of a loner."[25]

To many of the other children in Paris, Sonny Prichard was nothing short of a physical and intellectual anomaly. "He was not popular with his peers," recalled a former classmate. "He didn't even like to do the same things the rest of us did."[26] Instead of venturing to a local playground with other children at every available opportunity, Sonny spent his recreational moments at the courthouse. "Soon as I'd get out of school," Prichard related, "I'd go down and listen to the trials. I guess it was the drama that appealed to me." He watched court sessions, visited the offices of all the county officials, and listened to the speeches of visiting politicians in the courthouse square. All the while, the young Prichard "looked forward to one day being a participant." Another classmate remembered that Sonny "would go to the judge's office there and go through his law books and just study them from one end to the other."[27] He also read voraciously books on Kentucky and national politics, storing what he read in his remarkable memory. Possessing an insatiable mind, coupled with total recall, Prichard had a love of books and reading, particularly of politics and history, that became an important component of his young life.

As Sonny began schooling, he attended a small private school in Paris run by Fanniebelle Sutherland. Sutherland was known as a stern taskmaster, and her school on Main Street attracted many of the city's wealthier children— and Prichard's parents spared no expense for their gifted son. One student, however, remembered Sonny at this time primarily for his love of food. "I remember him trying to talk everyone out of their sausage biscuits." During lunch, in fact, Sonny could most often be found in the kitchen imploring the cook to allow him additional food. Beginning in his youth, Sonny's eating habits were prodigious, and he soon grew overweight.[28]

Because of his adultlike brain, many of his classmates at Sutherland's school simply could not relate to Sonny Prichard. "We always felt sort of inferior around him," remembered one such student, who felt Sonny's teachers "always thought he was just perfect." After three years, when Sutherland's school closed, Sonny attended the city schools of Paris. Because of his impressive scholastic ability, he was promoted two grades. A former teacher remembered: "They had to do it. He was too bright to be held back." To add to Sonny's already awkward social status—his obesity and his precocious mind—now he was fully two years younger than the other children in his class. He later understated the case: "Being the youngest member of the class, I tended to be a little backward socially." Prichard's uncommon brilliance, in short, produced a profound loneliness. As he matured, no one could challenge him intellectually in the confined world of Bourbon County, with the lone exception of the courthouse politicians, who were prepared to teach the young Prichard the earthy side of acquiring and exercising power.[29]

Sonny's love of politics was no accident. Firstborns are inclined, in Frank J. Sulloway's terms, "to align his or her interests with those of the parents, adopting the parents' perspective" in order to maximize parental investment and attention. By imitating his father's love of politics, Sonny quickly carved out his own niche within the family. Sonny and his father were never as close as they were when Sonny accompanied Big Ed to the courthouse or when they discussed political issues. His parents' approval of his growing enthusiasm for his father's political world brought Sonny his greatest sense of security and love. Not surprisingly, his younger brother, Henry, or "Power," as he was known in the county, sought a different avenue within the family that did not compete with his older sibling. While Sonny emulated his father's political pursuits, Power's interests turned to music, one of his mother's great loves. "I was never jealous of him at all," Power later said, noting that no sibling rivalry existed since he had few "overlapping interests" with his older brother.[30]

When he was eleven years old, Sonny accompanied his father to Frankfort to watch his first meeting of the Kentucky legislature. It was a singular memory in his life. The young man soaked up all he could of the sights and sounds of the Kentucky General Assembly, basking in the myriad personalities and political conflicts. He later acknowledged that it was common knowledge throughout the capital that the Assembly was blatantly corrupt. "You could have taken $100,000," Prichard remembered, "and repealed the Ten Commandments" in the 1926 Kentucky General Assembly.[31]

With his intellectual curiosity, Sonny Prichard was fortunate to find himself in the Paris city school system of the 1920s. Considered one of the finest in the entire state, it had been given the highest possible rating by the Southern Association of Colleges and Secondary Schools. The system's reputation resulted from two factors. First, the per capita wealth of the city allowed it a tax base that far exceeded that of similar-sized areas throughout the state. With such sources of revenue, the Paris city system hired teachers and bought books and equipment at a rate rivaled only by the systems in Louisville and Lexington. Second, Dr. Lee Kirkpatrick, the superintendent of the city schools, was one of the most progressive and far-sighted educational administrators in the entire state. In fact, those who remember this period in Paris school history tend to refer to it as "the Kirkpatrick era." The eighteen teachers employed at the city high school all possessed college degrees, a rare exception to the rule in Kentucky high schools in the 1920s. Dr. Kirkpatrick even encouraged his teachers to attend summer school and obtain graduate degrees, and he was especially interested in the methods of teacher training taught at Columbia University, where he sent several of his teachers. Kirkpatrick stuck to the basics in designing the school's curriculum, insisting that students master the classics and learn languages like Latin and Greek. Paris, Kentucky, schools could provide as thorough an education as any public system in America.[32]

Sonny's transition from private to public schools, academically speaking, came easy. To his teachers, Sonny Prichard presented a singular academic prospect. One such teacher, Marion Mitchell, later reflected that "in all of my teaching years, I do not think I knew any young person as interested in knowing things." During the eighth grade, Sonny was enthralled by a series of workbooks entitled "Ask Me Another." Unable to interest other students in the workbooks, Sonny began visiting Mitchell's boarding room after school to implore her to ask him questions in the books. She did so, but often had to remind him to leave when the dinner hour arrived.[33]

Prichard was not the only bright student in the school. Among others was Judge Ardery's son, Philip Pendleton Ardery. He stood out academically among his peers in ways eclipsed only by Sonny. In just about any other school district in the state, Phil Ardery would probably have been the county's premier student and valedictorian, but he was unfortunate in being in the same class with Sonny Prichard. "I was one of the top people in the class but Prich was always well ahead of me," commented Ardery, who found himself in that role in grade school, high school, and even law school. But academic rivalry also brought them together as friends. On some occasions, Sonny visited Rocclicgan and he would "get out and do the things he hadn't done before like shoot a .22 rifle we had or hunt rabbits," said Phil Ardery.[34] Sonny also found time to talk politics with Phil's father on every available occasion.

Sonny's friendship with Phil Ardery was a rare exception in his young social life. He continued to grow well beyond his years intellectually and amazed members of the "courthouse gang" with his prodigious memory and political acumen. Sonny's eagerness to learn all about county politics delighted Pearce Paton, who served as Sonny's first political mentor. Longtime county attorney William T. Baldwin stated that Paton taught Sonny "everything there was to know about county government." Sonny delighted in hearing Paton swap stories with and about other county and state politicians. Paton, in turn, enjoyed being the recipient of such interest by the young prodigy. Sonny, however, did not confine his courthouse education to Paton's musty clerk's office. He would even "sit on the bench with the county judge when he heard cases," recalls Baldwin. By the time he was in high school, Sonny "had read every document in the place," and proceeded "to know every politician in the county."[35] Before he could even vote, Sonny was intimately involved with the Bourbon County courthouse gang.

To Sonny's beloved high school English teacher, Zerelda Noland, this experience was a double-edged sword: "He grew up in that courthouse," she recalled, but added that the men in the courthouse were not always a "good influence" on the young man. "The men, you know how they do, they told stories about their tricks and shady dealings at election time. He absorbed that" just as he absorbed everything else, she noted.[36] The political education Sonny received in Bourbon County had a profound impact. Here he internalized the art and the intricacies of local politics. Sonny not only basked in the excitement of campaigns, political stump speeches, and the heady expectation of election night, but also understood the process by which political power was sought and maintained. In observing his father's political activities and spending hour upon hour with Pearce Paton and the local courthouse crowd, an eager Sonny Prichard found this Machiavellian world a classroom. Prichard understood, in detail, how things like election fraud were, in his own words, "As common in Bourbon County as chicken-fighting, and no more serious. I never really paid much attention to it, thought of it as something you did for fun." By his teenage years, Sonny had learned that such activity was nothing more than "second nature."[37]

As he progressed in Paris High School in the late 1920s, Noland became Prichard's favorite teacher and he, in turn, her most prized student. Their first encounter revealed Prichard's penchant for the dramatic. He walked into her class on the first day of school wearing a broad-brimmed Panama hat, attempting to personify, even then, the stereotypical image of a Kentucky colonel. "The first day he came into my class," Noland remembered, "he swept off his hat and put his head on the desk." Not impressed, Noland reprimanded him: "'Edward, you're in this class now, and you'll hold up your head.' And he did." Noland was a widely popular teacher who taught demanding courses, and she quickly saw Sonny's precocious nature: "I learned he could seem asleep and absorb knowledge faster than anyone else." Prichard often closed his eyes when concentrating on a particular subject, and some of his teachers naturally mistook this trait as either a case of inattentiveness or sleepiness. Noland was also an adept observer of the dynamics surrounding Prichard and his classmates. "He was inclined to make fun of others," she said, adding that he did so "possibly to gain stature, but that didn't make for friendships." Admitting that Prichard's already profound intellect kept her "on her toes," Sonny did not hesitate to challenge her in class, a trait he carried throughout most of his life. On one occasion, Noland took Sonny out of the room and scolded him in the hall for correcting her on a minor point in class.[38]

Of all areas of student activities, none engaged Sonny's interests as much as the Paris High debate team, where he could match wits with other students and master the oratory he heard so often in campaign speeches. Sonny's debating team partner in high school was often Phil Ardery. Their first competition was a microcosm of the relationship that developed between Phil and Sonny. Attempting to memorize a speech rather than the points of a debate, Ardery tensed up in their first contest and momentarily froze. Prichard came to his rescue and "pulled the whole thing out," Ardery admitted. Professor W.R. Sutherland of the University of Kentucky judged Paris High's team the winner based on Prichard's ad hoc performance. "Prich won that debate because I was a dismal failure," Ardery later admitted.[39]

The debating team of Prichard and Ardery developed steadily and their victories mounted. Opponents sometimes attempted to divert Prichard's attention—an obvious target was his physical size. One member from a team in Scott County called Sonny "Tightpants Willie" before a match, much to Prichard's great anger. Among the more challenging debates in which Prichard participated was one in which he argued in the affirmative regarding "equalizing education in Kentucky." He contrasted the public education students received in better-funded counties like Bourbon with those of the poorer mountain counties.[40]

On the trips the debating team took throughout the region, Naomi Isrig, a third member of the team, remembered that "the fascinating thing was [Sonny] knew a story about everybody in every house that we passed. He knew all the interrelationships among all the people and," she added, "he loved to talk scandal."[41] Prichard's vast reading and his endless questioning of people and their family relations proved to be a lifelong interest. Perhaps because he developed so few close personal relationships, Sonny seemed obsessed with talking about people and learning their family history. And, as Isrig observed, family scandal was a favorite topic. By this time in his life, Prichard startled people he had never previously met by knowing many of their intimate family details.

Throughout his high school years in the late 1920s, Sonny continued to impress his teachers with his absorptive mind. Although Phil Ardery managed to keep up with Sonny in areas such as physics and chemistry, no one could match him in areas such as English, history, and languages. Phil acknowledged the incipient rivalry he had with Sonny—"I wished to hell I could beat him in class but I never could."[42] While Prichard continued to score at the top of his class, he grew even more alienated from his classmates, continued to eat, gain weight, and fail miserably in athletic contests. Not surprisingly, Sonny attracted little female companionship. One classmate recalled, "I never knew him to have a girl. I don't remember him having a date in school." Noland lamented that "he was not what you might call romantically adept. He liked the girls, but they tended to overlook him."[43] Physically awkward and socially something approaching an intellectual freak, Sonny devoted little attention to the opposite sex, or they to him. Cursed with overwhelming brilliance, Prichard found no one in his class who could measure up to his curiosity, his memory, or his passion for politics. He increasingly turned to books, politicians at the courthouse, and food to fill an ever-gaping hole in his young life.

Schoolwork could not contain all of Sonny's energies. By his early teens, he was already beginning to sow his own political oats. A charter member and officer of the Bourbon County Young Men's Democratic Club, the sixteen-year-old enthusiastically supported William Ardery's 1931 bid for governor.

Along with the nominal promises of balancing the state budget, not raising taxes, and voicing support for the tobacco industry, Ardery had also promised to support organized labor, a courageous stance that appealed to the young Prichard. During the convention, Prichard served as chief page to Frederick A. Wallis, the convention's presiding officer. When the convention threw its support from Ardery to Ruby Laffoon, Wallis selected the young Prichard as a member of the committee who notified Judge Laffoon. By this time, the friendship between Sonny and William Ardery had developed into one that Phil Ardery later described as a father-son relationship. When the Democratic convention gave its nod to Laffoon, the *Lexington Herald* noted the young Prichard's disappointment but added, "Prichard bowed to the will of the majority and, like all good Democrats, is actively espousing Laffoon's cause."[44]

In this same year, when he was just sixteen years old, Prichard was already in his senior year at Paris High School and preparing for college. Invariably, his intellectual prowess began to attract serious attention. In May, he was awarded the highest honor in a two-day achievement contest sponsored by Centre College, his father's alma mater. Sonny received the highest marks among other selected students from all over the state in French and history, and he was awarded forty-five dollars for winning the highest overall scores. For the fourth consecutive year, he won the state history contest and also won the Kentucky State General Scholarship contest, which was sponsored by the University of Kentucky. In graduation ceremonies at Paris High, Sonny received the Georgetown College cup for "outstanding scholarship, character, and leadership in school activities."[45]

Sonny's intellectual and political development coincided with the end of Republican "prosperity" and the beginnings of the Great Depression. In Kentucky, the effects of the Depression were well evident by the time Sonny graduated: 245 businesses in the state had gone bankrupt in 1930, followed by increasing numbers in the next two years. In 1930, the National Bank of Louisville, the largest and oldest bank in the city, failed. One of the bank's depositors was the Commonwealth of Kentucky. Since state deposits were bonded, the state narrowly averted financial disaster. Across the state, in industries such as tobacco and coal mining, jobs disappeared and frustration and hunger grew. The growing economic and political turmoil throughout the country came just as Prichard's personal politics took shape.[46]

If proof was needed that Sonny Prichard was not just a local intellectual phenomenon, it came later in the summer of 1931. Prichard was invited to take a national intelligence test with more than one hundred thousand other students from across the country. The Central Press Association sponsored the first-time event and promised an all-expense-paid trip to Europe for the top six winners. On July 20, Sonny received a phone call from a reporter with the

Lexington Herald informing him that he had been selected as one of the national winners and that he would be promptly flown to New York for his cruise. "Well, that's good," proclaimed Prichard. The newspaper delighted in the young prodigy's response that betrayed his sixteen years. When asked if he could go, Sonny stated, "I don't know. I guess I could go." After a slight pause, he shouted, "I know darned well I can go."[47]

For the remainder of the summer, as most of the country's teenagers coped with the Depression, Sonny sailed from New York to Europe, visiting along the way such places as Lisbon, Cannes, and several locations in Greece. The bulk of the time was spent in Italy, where he toured Milan, Naples, Florence, and Rome. Prichard sent Phil Ardery a postcard that read: "Well, here I am in Italy where even the children speak Italian." All expenses were underwritten by the Italian Tourists Bureau, which served as a propaganda arm of Benito Mussolini's government. Mussolini himself gave Prichard an autographed picture. Far from having his young head turned by *Il Duce*, Sonny soon thereafter tore up the photograph because he found Mussolini's fascist philosophy so repugnant.[48]

Prichard's heady summer excursion ended in September. Having been marked as one of the six brightest students in America, he returned home from his European tour ready for college. The choice of which college he would attend was not an easy one. After all, finances were an increasing concern in the early days of the Depression. He could have attended the University of Kentucky, as Phil Ardery chose to do, and remained close to home. Or he could have attended his father's alma mater, Centre College, which was already aware of his intellectual ability firsthand.

In the end, Sonny chose neither option close to Paris. For any young man wishing to obtain the highest academic challenge in 1931, no school in Kentucky or, for that matter, the entire South, could meet his requirements. State universities, not only in Lexington but also in Chapel Hill and Charlottesville, were hard hit by the Great Depression. Private southern institutions like Duke, Emory, and Vanderbilt would have to wait another decade until they acquired national reputations. Consequently, Sonny looked elsewhere and enrolled at Princeton. Considering that yearly expenses at Princeton exceeded one thousand dollars, the costs involved would be severe, but his father was doing relatively well, especially with his horses.

Armed with a cache of academic awards, Prichard headed off to begin his freshman year at Princeton in September 1931. His first sixteen years, spent in the confines of Paris and Bourbon County, had left a lasting impression on his young psyche. Despite what was ahead and the elite group in which he would find himself, the political education he had obtained from his father and the courthouse gang of Bourbon County left an indelible mark on

Prichard. He would not return to live in Kentucky for fourteen years. By the time he did, the world—and Sonny Prichard himself—had undergone dramatic and profound changes. But the political and social culture of Bourbon County remained essentially the same as the day when Sonny first accompanied his father to the Paris courthouse.

2 Banishment to Paradise

WHILE the Great Depression exacted a terrible price from American institutions of higher education in the early 1930s, the schools of the Ivy League were relatively untouched. Princeton, in fact, rose in prominence during these years, staying afloat financially and thriving academically. Located in a tranquil village northeast of Trenton, Princeton's gothic campus retained its small-town charm and peaceful, scholarly atmosphere in the 1930s while other Ivy League schools such as Harvard and Penn were surrounded by growing urban sprawls. The university and its surrounding environs of tree-lined streets and picturesque homes made it an idyllic refuge from a world beset with economic collapse. When Albert Einstein arrived in Princeton in 1932 to join the newly created Institute for Advanced Study, he told a friend it was like a "banishment to Paradise."[1]

When sixteen-year-old Ed Prichard arrived at Princeton in the fall of 1931, it was already known as "the northernmost university in the South" because of the large number of southerners who attended Princeton. At that time, Princeton was quite different in its class makeup from what it would be later. The entering class in the early 1930s was limited to 600—and they were all white men. Princeton's elitist and admittedly segregated makeup was a time-honored tradition that would die slowly. When the university grappled with the issue of admitting African Americans during World War II, the *Princeton Herald* concluded that since southern whites were so much a part of the Princeton campus and would, therefore, be offended by the presence of blacks on campus, integration "was a noble idea whose time had not yet arrived."[2]

For a gifted mind, one that required constant intellectual challenges as well as the freedom to pursue political interests outside the classroom, Princeton presented a remarkable opportunity. For young Ed Prichard, as it was for Einstein, Princeton was a certain paradise in the economic cataclysm of the later Hoover years.

Yet at first, Prichard felt somewhat awkward in his new setting. "I was, again, younger than the others, and I had gone to a public school," he recalled. "Most of my classmates had gone to private schools and had their own way of dressing, talking," and in Prichard's memory, even "their own body language." Once in the Ivy League, Prichard left one aspect of his Bourbon County life behind—he would not be known again as Sonny. Instead, his classmates began referring to him as "Prich," which was one of his father's nicknames. Now, in his own right, the younger Prichard took on his father's mantle. But in his academic work, he seemed to have picked up where he had left off in Paris High School. Prichard was never awed or intimidated by the Ivy League. Although he considered courses in the sciences and math to be "fairly hard," he found his courses in English, political science, and history to be "the easiest time in the world." Early on, Prichard's photographic memory became a campus sensation. During a course in Professor Willard Thorpe's freshman English class, Thorpe grew irritated as Prichard kept his eyes closed during class. Professor Thorpe, not aware that this was Prichard's unique way of listening carefully, publicly reprimanded him for falling asleep in class and missing the details of the professor's lecture. Whereupon, Prichard proceeded to recite Thorpe's lecture verbatim to a stunned classroom.[3]

Prichard's four years at Princeton were marked by far more than academic achievement and acclaim. Princeton offered the young Kentuckian numerous stimulating outlets that he craved. One was the debating team. On campus fewer than five months, Prichard was the only freshman nominated to compete in the annual Class of 1876 Prize Debate. The topic selected for the contest was whether the Hoover administration "deserves the confidence of this House." Prichard, true to his Democratic roots, argued in the negative. He opened the debate by proclaiming that there were essentially two items on which an administration should be properly judged: whether it had fulfilled its preelection promises and whether it successfully met unforeseen crises. President Hoover, Prichard urged, had done neither. While his opponents proclaimed that the Hoover administration "will go down in history because of its excellence," Prichard refuted such claims by laying the blame for the nation's economic crisis squarely at the Republican president's feet. While Prichard did not persuade the judges of the merit of his argument, he nonetheless caught their eye and they awarded him an honorable mention. It was an auspicious beginning to Prichard's political and debating efforts in the Ivy League.[4]

In his freshman classes, Prichard earned a place on the honor roll. He majored in history and also took courses in economics and English. Certainly not one to spend long hours pining away in the library, he took an active role in the Whig-Clio club his freshman year. The club sponsored numerous speakers, including some who took issue with the socialist tenets of Princeton alumnus Norman Thomas, who had appeared on campus only weeks before. Even in an atmosphere as conservative as Princeton, hearty discussion occurred in Prichard's freshman year on some of the fundamental aspects of capitalism, socialism, and democracy. Such discussions were not limited to the halls of academe. "In 1931," commented historian Arnold Toynbee, "men and women all over the world were seriously contemplating and frankly discussing the possibility that the Western system of Society might break down and cease to work." With bank failures and soup lines increasing every day, the basic question of what type of society would be created out of the Great Depression was discussed and debated by freshmen at Princeton and all around the country with increasing frequency.[5]

Prichard's first years in college coincided with a presidential election. Since he was only seventeen, Prichard could not vote, but he found the campaign to be one that consumed his energies, both on campus and off. A sign of things to come occurred in a model political convention in April 1932 organized by the student Democrats of Princeton. The students picked their own slate of candidates, drew up a party platform, and established policy committees along the same lines as the real convention that would be held later that summer. For this occasion, Prichard was chosen to deliver the keynote address to the model convention. This selection was evidence that the Kentucky freshman had already established himself as one of the campus's leading politicians.

According to the student newspaper, Prichard's keynote address was "enthusiastically received" by the students. Prichard assailed the policies of President Hoover as half-hearted measures that "doctored symptoms rather than the disease itself." On an issue dear to the hearts of Princeton students, Prichard said, "The Anti-Saloon League still holds President Hoover by the nose," referring to the looming issue of Prohibition. Asking for nothing less than a national plebiscite to decide the issue of repealing Prohibition, Prichard thundered his conclusion by calling upon all "forward-looking men and women of America" to rally to the party of Jefferson in the November elections.[6]

Naturally, Prichard became an active member of the Princeton Woodrow Wilson Democratic Club. Shortly after stirring interest on campus with his keynote speech to the model convention, Prichard publicly endorsed former New York governor and 1928 nominee Alfred E. Smith for president. While Smith received nominal support by the Princeton Democrats, the students went through several ballots before deciding upon a bizarre ticket of former war secretary Newton D. Baker and Virginia senator Harry Byrd. Prichard, who had lobbied a state convention the previous year for Judge Ardery, worked the student delegation in support of Al Smith. Not surprisingly, as the ballots progressed, so did the number of those voting for the former New York governor. At seventeen, Prichard already displayed formidable and aggressive lobbying skills.[7]

Perhaps the reason Smith won Prichard's support early in the 1932 race was his promise to repeal Prohibition, a topic that had engaged Prichard in the final debate of his freshman year. Chosen by his class to compete for the Hope Debating Prize, Prichard asserted that Prohibition should be immediately repealed. He claimed that the effort to restrict alcohol had been an enormous failure and that allowing the voters to decide the issue themselves was simply the democratic thing to do. Prichard won first place in extemporaneous speaking and second place overall.[8] As he left for home following his freshman year, Prichard enjoyed quite an auspicious start in the Ivy League: honor roll, memberships in the Democratic and Whig-Clio clubs, and a growing reputation as one of the most formidable debaters and orators on campus.

Preparing to return to New Jersey in the autumn of 1932, Prichard observed with great interest as the real Democratic convention convened that summer to nominate Franklin D. Roosevelt. Unknown to Prichard, the decision to select the New York governor would have a singular impact—not only on the nation, but on the political career of Ed Prichard himself. The foremost thing on young Prichard's agenda as he began his second year at Princeton was helping Franklin Roosevelt win in November. Here Prichard's ravenous political appetite was most apparent. He made frequent trips to Trenton, New Jersey, working at the Democratic party headquarters on FDR's campaign. Prichard spoke twice before sizable crowds in Trenton in late October on FDR's behalf.[9]

Back on campus, the extent to which Prichard's political cast was not shared by his classmates was revealed in a campus mock election. Out of more than 2,400 votes cast, Herbert Hoover received 1,528 to Roosevelt's 500 and Norman Thomas's 385. Interestingly enough, the employees of the university, including the staff and the physical plant, voted decidedly in favor of FDR in their own informal election.[10] For the sons of America's elite, shielded from the ravaging effects of the Depression, the promise of the New Deal was not one they welcomed with open arms.

Prichard finished the 1932 campaign in high style. He sat on the same platform with Newton Baker and various local, county, and state Democratic candidates at a large party rally in Trenton on November 2. Prichard then returned to Princeton in time to debate a team from Yale on the upcoming election. Prichard and a fellow sophomore, Edmund A. Gullion, spoke on behalf of Roosevelt while the Yale team proclaimed the merits of the Republican administration. The debate was held without judges and therefore no decision was rendered. While the Yale team discussed the election primarily on the basis of personalities, comparing Roosevelt's "inexperience" with Hoover, Prichard and Gullion took a different tack. Gullion discussed the upcoming election as a referendum on policies, not personalities, and in particular hammered away at the Republican stand on the tariff and Prohibition. Prichard, who spoke last, discussed political philosophy. He "struck out boldly" for FDR and, specifically, "the control and planning of industry to the end of industrial democracy, rather than the allowance of a liberty of special privilege."[11]

If public speeches and debates were not enough, Prichard wrote a lengthy article that appeared in the Princeton literary magazine, the *Nassau Lit,* which drew even more campuswide attention. Titled "Balancing the Political Budget," Prichard's essay assailed Republican economic policies and specifically Hoover's inability to alleviate the current economic crisis. The article generated heated rebuffs in the *Daily Princetonian,* which asked, "What was Mr. Prichard doing in the days before the depression? Crying his awful warnings of the approaching catastrophe . . . or does his present anger against Hoover's blindness spring from the fact that he was busy buying stock?" The letter's author obviously underestimated the extent of Prichard's commitment to the election of FDR, while also imposing some class dynamics on the Kentuckian that simply did not fit. "In spite of Mr. Prichard," the letter continued, "economics remains that science which is not aware of a cause until it has beheld an effect."[12]

While he may not have carried the day among the majority of Princeton students and faculty, Franklin Roosevelt won more than 57 percent of the popular vote on November 8, 1932. For Ed Prichard, he had played his own part in Roosevelt's campaign by campaigning in Trenton and Princeton in FDR's behalf, debating teams from schools such as Columbia and Yale, and writing articles calling for the end of Republican control of the White House. While exuberant Democrats throughout the country looked forward to the patronage that would follow FDR's inauguration, Prichard, of course, had more pressing matters to attend to at school. In mid-November 1932, just as his political campaigning at Princeton ended, another chapter of his Princeton career began when he was named to the News Board of the *Daily Princetonian,* where he soon became an associate editor.[13]

The Princeton student editors obviously saw Prichard's writing and political skills as a considerable asset, and he viewed the opportunity to work on the paper as another outlet for his prodigious intellectual and political talents. He could cover political stories, interview politicians and writers who came to campus, and learn the ropes of editing news stories and editorials on a tight schedule. He later recalled his years on the newspaper in glowing terms. "One of the best experiences of my life. I loved it, just loved it," Prichard remembered. He also acknowledged that the grinding schedules of a daily paper had a beneficial impact: "It got me over a sort of writer's cramp" and "gave me some fluency in writing."[14] Not surprisingly, he handled his various chores at the paper deftly and quickly rose within the ranks of the paper's editorial structure.

Interestingly enough, one area of college life that held little interest for Prichard was campus politics. Just as he had never sought a leadership role at Paris High, he never sought his class presidency or any other campuswide office while at Princeton. Ever the vote counter, Prichard knew that his brand of politics generated many enemies, and it seems questionable whether he could have won in any case. More to the point was a deeper issue: while Prichard could speak passionately for others in a campaign, he consistently avoided the opportunity to be publicly rejected himself. Although he seemed brimming with self-confidence, Prichard was also a teenager with a delicate ego that could have been shaken easily by an election defeat.

These two halves of Ed Prichard—the one side politically ambitious and anxious to display his brilliance, the other deeply insecure and longing for approval—battled each other throughout his life. At Princeton, Prichard selectively met the needs of the former while minimizing the potential damage to the latter. An interesting episode occurred in his sophomore year when he sought to win his class nomination for the second straight year by competing in the prestigious Class of 1876 Prize debate. Eight other students in the class also sought the nomination, including Prichard's friend Edmund Gullion. The routine election was not without a strange twist. When the ballots for the sophomore and freshman classes were tabulated, a large number of suspicious unsigned ballots were discovered. The illegal votes caused the Princeton Undergraduate Council to order a new election wherein no unsigned ballots would be counted. The name of the candidates for whom the unmarked ballots were signed was not disclosed, nor was the culprit, or culprits, who had placed the fraudulent ballots in the boxes ever discovered. The following day, Ed Prichard won the class election to compete in the debate. Whether he brought with him some of the election tactics he had learned in the Paris courthouse to Princeton is a question that was never resolved.[15]

Prichard's teammate in the Class of 1876 Debate was freshman Gordon A. Craig. Craig had already won the Hope Freshman Speaking contest and, like Prichard, was a history major. Craig and Prichard teamed to defend the Reconstruction Finance Corporation's work in Washington. Craig's debating prowess won the day, and he won the overall prize over Prichard. No one was more surprised, however, at the judge's decision than Craig. Having worked with Prichard as a teammate, Craig saw immediately that the young Kentuckian was well ahead of his years. Craig later said that Prichard was the finest debater he had ever heard and that defeating Prichard was no more than "a fluke." At times funny, at other times outrageous, Prichard could often overwhelm his opponents by his total recall. "You wondered where all those facts were coming from," said Craig. Prichard's disappointment in losing the title as Princeton's top debater for the second year was somewhat offset by his election as secretary of the Wilson Democratic Club.[16]

In the fall of 1933, Prichard continued to use the debate team to sharpen his oratorical skills as well as to defend the New Deal. In November, the rather imposing team of Prichard and Craig traveled to Meriden, Connecticut, and defeated the Harvard team by defending the National Recovery Administration. No team in the Ivy League proved the equal of the young Princeton duo.[17]

In order to understand Prichard's evolving mind on a variety of issues, the pages of the *Daily Princetonian* are invaluable. For example, a remarkable letter to the editor in early 1933 displayed some of his early religious convictions. At the time, Princeton still required students to attend chapel services. In one such service, a Princeton official spoke with what some considered to be socialist tendencies in the name of Christ. Responding to criticism that socialist principles did not belong in the chapel and that such offending sermons had no place in such services, Prichard fired back an angry letter. While admitting that the sermon was "socialistic in the sense that it called attention to some of the most glaring anti-Christian aspects of our social system and advocated social reconstruction as a religious necessity," Prichard said, "in no sense was it a piece of propaganda for the Socialist party." Then, in elegant, decisive language, he revealed some of his own ruminations on the issues of religion and politics:

> After all, is not any preaching propaganda? Is not any teaching, in a broad sense, propaganda to a lesser degree? Why are we made to go to Chapel, except to listen to Christian propaganda? And as long as we are going to listen to propaganda, might it not be sensible, enlightening, inspiring, and really Christian, instead of "stuffed-shirt" religion which comforts us with the thoughts that all is well with him who prays regularly, gives his tithe to the Lord and continues to work his employees at sweatshop wages and to sell his customers Bolivian bonds?
>
> After all, we live in a social system which makes it impossible for the average person to be a Christian. We preach chastity and then pay women so little that they must become prostitutes to keep from starving. We preach honesty and then pay clerks so little that they must steal to live. We treat the populace to the spectacle of national wealth impotent in the hands of a few, while millions starve for want of things which we have a plethora. Then we preach the virtue of restraint and tell them like Paul Elmer More once did that the Lord is testing them.

"The simple truth," asserted Prichard, "is that if we are to have a world in which Christianity can be practiced we must change our social order." Those who differed, he concluded, "are oblivious of the fact that most of our schools—and, regrettably, some of our churches—have been effective agencies of propaganda for the capitalist system."[18]

Prichard's emotional response revealed that he was well acquainted with the writings of such Christian socialists as Reinhold Niebuhr and Harry F. Ward. By this time, Niebuhr was a well-known theologian who had also run for a New York Senate seat as a socialist. Combining both radical politics and

Christianity, Niebuhr saw America in the early 1930s on the verge of societal breakdown. If capitalism was not "brought under social control," Niebuhr wrote, "the disinherited, in whom bitter need is bound to generate more passion than circumspection, will make short shrift of the whole of our civilization." Throughout his college career, Prichard returned often to this theme himself. For Prichard, piety in the face of hunger and despair was a false Christianity that mocked the essential teachings of Christ.[19]

Prichard's letter concerning the chapel controversy underscored a growing political dilemma facing him and other Democrats wary of the patrician Roosevelt: whether to abandon capitalism altogether and seek socialist solutions to America's economic collapse or to be allegiant to the Democratic administration's more cautious reform proposals. This paradox had deep roots. While Prichard had been raised as a loyal Democrat, at Princeton he began considering a fundamental reordering of the capitalist system in which Democrats were as involved in the country's collapse as were Republicans. This ideological tension took other forms—while Prichard consistently advocated socialist proposals in his own articles, he also continued to rise within the ranks of the Democratic Club and never attended meetings of the Princeton socialists. Although he may have been hundreds of miles from Bourbon County, the pull of his parents' politics was strong.

In December 1933, Prichard was elected assistant editorial editor of the *Daily Princetonian,* a post from which he would begin writing his own column. Among his activities, as reported by the paper in announcing his position, were his roles in the debate team, the Wilson Democratic Club, "the executive council of Whig-Clio, the International Relations Club, and Court Club."[20]

The new year, 1934, would be remarkable in Prichard's Princeton career. Subsequently, his legend grew among his classmates. In addition to his course work, he wrote weekly columns for the school newspaper, giving him the widest opportunity yet to display his writing ability and provocative political views. He also received the debating honors he had so long sought. But then he found himself immersed in a small scandal that generated attention from even the *New York Times.*

Beginning in February 1934, Prichard began his *Princetonian* editorial column, which came to be titled "Left Turn." In his first column, he analyzed the labor movement vis-à-vis the development of the National Recovery Administration. Prichard applauded the "militancy" of the nascent American labor movement, writing that "it shows that some of the workers are growing class-conscious and are beginning to organize to secure the standards of life which they must have if the economic system is to be sound. And these standards can be attained only by militant action on the part of the workers themselves." Prichard also applauded the creation of the NRA and concluded: "Big units of industrial organization are here to stay, and the road to their control lies not in trying to unscramble the eggs, but in subjecting industry to social discipline." Prichard feared, however, that in time a timid regulatory government would fall under the control of business itself. "If this fear materializes," Prichard added, "there remains only one alternative—social ownership of the basic industries."[21]

Later in February, Prichard was again chosen to represent his class in the Class of 1876 debate contest. He was also teamed yet again with the reigning champion, Gordon Craig. The topic chosen for the debate had yet another New Deal orientation: "Resolved, that the present administration does not deserve the confidence of this house." Prichard's "vehement" defense of the New Deal centered on two newly created agencies, the NRA and the Agricultural Adjustment Administration (AAA). He contended that the NRA had not only raised wages but also abolished sweat shops. The AAA, he added, had prevented the overproduction of commodities such as cotton and wheat. In observing Prichard perform, Craig witnessed a master orator who "watched his audience carefully and knew when to exploit an audience's expression." Craig stated that he easily envisioned Prichard being lifted out of Princeton and placed in the well of the U.S. Senate and not missing a beat. After Craig had discussed New Deal monetary policy, the pair heard two other Princeton upperclassmen attack the New Deal on lines that the NRA did not "give an even break to the common man" and that Roosevelt's monetary policy had produced nothing but instability. The team of Prichard and Craig were judged victorious, and this time Prichard finally took home the overall prize and a check for $100.[22] For the Kentuckian who had not yet turned twenty, the recognition as Princeton's top debater was an extension of the oratorical skills he had first heard at the Paris courthouse and then developed in high school.

In addition to his rigorous debating schedule, Prichard's lengthy *Princetonian* column continued to urge the New Deal leftward. Commenting once again on the NRA, Prichard argued for the removal of the "aristocracy of ownership," putting in its place "a real industrial democracy." His industrial philosophy was underscored in another article he wrote to counter former Democratic presidential candidate John W. Davis's criticisms of Agriculture Secretary Henry Wallace. When Wallace had contended that laissez-faire economics were outdated, Davis chastised Wallace and instead called for what he termed a return to "the original Jeffersonian ideal." Prichard came to Wallace's defense with a historical overview full of historian Frederick Jackson Turner's frontier thesis: "At the time when Jefferson lived, a laissez-faire system best fulfilled this ideal. Nine-tenths of the people were independent, self-sustaining farmers, living upon land which cost practically nothing; and if they

couldn't buy land, there was always the frontier beckoning." Modern industry, in Prichard's estimation, "has made the tools of manufacture—in other
words, capital—so hard to get in large enough quantities that it is practically
impossible for the average man ever to hope to be able to attain economic security through his own efforts." Such sentences reveal that in addition to
Turner, Prichard had also read Marx. In his concluding remarks, he wrote: "In
instituting a policy of social control of wealth, by democratic means, in order
not to deprive the individual, but restore to him the opportunity to express
the best in his personality, the Roosevelt administration is merely returning
to the Jeffersonian ideal." If this proved unsuccessful, Prichard wrote, "there
is left the Marxian ideal—and even Jefferson once said that it would be well
if every twenty years 'the tree of liberty should be watered by the blood of ty-
rants.'"[23] It is obvious that Prichard was no single-minded FDR partisan, that
in fact he obviously looked upon the president with some skepticism. If the
New Deal proved unsuccessful in alleviating the Depression, Prichard was ready
to abandon the Democratic president for socialist alternatives.

Prichard's "Left Turn" column continued to rankle the normally conservative Princeton student body. Items such as industrial democracy, government
ownership of industries, and the redistribution of wealth were themes often
mentioned in Prichard's column. Perhaps his most clearly stated worldview
came in a March 1934 editorial. It was a remarkable statement, considering
its author was all of nineteen:

> Industry will either have to be content with a smaller, but steady return—not on
> watered and fictitious values, but upon capital invested—permitting the major
> share of the national income to go to labor and management in the form of sala-
> ries and wages which make purchasing power, or else they will soon find their
> industrial system taken out of their possession. For the people of this country can
> tolerate no system which permits such monstrous injustices in the distribution
> of wealth as have been revealed during the past few years. No order which denies
> those who do the useful work of society a fair return for their toil, and which
> deflects the fruits of labor into the pockets of avaricious stockholders who per-
> form absolutely no useful function in society, can long exist in the face of the
> growing insistence of the mass of the people upon a social order based upon some
> ethical or moral principle—not upon the law of the jungle.[24]

Likewise, Prichard advocated the passage of the Wagner Act and particularly angered the sons of America's privileged by calling for higher taxes on the
wealthy. As an indication of the extent to which Prichard's column was gen-
erating critical reaction among other undergraduates, beginning in April the
newspaper placed a disclaimer under Prichard's byline saying, "The Princetonian does not necessarily agree with the sentiments expressed in this col-

umn." Years later, the Princeton alumni newspaper referred to Prichard as "the enfant terrible of Princeton journalism." Prichard kept up the pace, calling for increased public works programs to create more demand for heavy goods. If government did not enter the equation, Prichard said, the traditional boom and bust cycles would "leave us exactly where we were in that annus mirabilis Herberti Hooveris, 1929." In examining the role of unions and railroads, Prichard quickly concluded that "the only way that problem of capital structure and debt revision of the railways will be solved is through government ownership."[25]

These were not the impetuous pronouncements of an exuberant teenager. Prichard was not merely hoping to incite angry responses to satisfy an immature ego. Rather, it is obvious that his was a profound mind for one so young. Before he turned twenty, Ed Prichard's worldview had been cast by his upbringing in the Paris courthouse, the county Democratic party, his parents' political activities, and his witnessing the brutal reality of the Great Depression. He grew to intellectual maturity, in fact, during some of the worst years of America's greatest economic crisis, and his political ideology was forever soured on the free market and corporate America. In an age that freely questioned some deeply held notions, Ed Prichard was not afraid to suggest fundamental change and structural solutions to alleviate real and widespread suffering.

Prichard's lengthy columns also revealed a student who was clearly enjoying himself. But even Prichard's enormous energies and talents had their limits. In May 1934, he declined nomination to a position within the esteemed Whig-Clio organization because of the time that his column and other political duties absorbed. After further forbearance, he was elected president of Whig Hall when the two sides temporarily split into liberal and conservative factions.[26]

As the new president of the Whig Club (of course, the Clio Club was the conservative faction), Prichard grandly proclaimed the guiding principles of the organization. In the process, he defined his own political philosophy. He wrote that "it is evident that individual capitalism has broken down." Instead of the right-wing dictatorship that marked Germany and Italy, Prichard wrote that "the great purpose and aim of those who want to save democracy should be to extend democratic principles into the economic sphere, bringing the industrial and financial system under the democratic control of society. This means, of course, that to a great degree the private profit system must be eliminated." Toward the Roosevelt administration, Prichard was ambivalent—he praised the New Deal for its reforms but also revealed a willingness to object to any programs when they veered toward policies that favored corporate interests.[27]

In his circle of Princeton friends, Prichard developed close ties with a number of other extraordinary Princeton students who would each have significant careers of their own. Edmund Gullion, for example, would be appointed an ambassador in the Kennedy and Johnson administrations; Philip Horton later became executive editor of *Reporter* magazine and wrote a biography of Hart Crane; Gordon Craig became a prominent Stanford historian and was elected president of the American Historical Association; Adrian "Butch" Fisher became dean of the Georgetown Law School; John Oakes became editor of the *New York Times* editorial page; and a gifted young man named William DuBose Sheldon seemed headed for greatness before he was wounded in World War II and killed himself in a naval hospital in 1943. Despite their impressive backgrounds, the intellectual and political leader of this remarkable group, as everyone knew, was Ed Prichard.

As he began his senior year, Prichard remained active in campaigning for various local New Jersey Democrats. His involvement in such campaigns was far more than merely rhetorical. In the 1934 off-year congressional elections, Prichard organized "flying squads" of cars with campaign speakers from the Princeton Democratic Club. These cars were sent to surrounding New Jersey rural areas of Mercer and Burlington Counties. While several Princeton faculty were running for local offices, Prichard made it clear "our organization is squarely behind every Democratic candidate from president to constable." Such innovative plans made Prichard invaluable to the Trenton Democrats.[28]

At times, Prichard unknowingly commented in his *Princetonian* articles on individuals in Washington he would soon come to know personally, such as Harold Ickes and Sidney Hillman. Concerning Hillman, a man for whom Prichard would eventually work, Prichard said he was "the outstanding statesman of the American trade union movement." Prichard commented on Hillman in terms he no doubt would have approved if used to describe himself: "His outlook is radical, but he is eminently practical."[29]

While Prichard continued his onslaught of articles, organized his campaign committee of the Democratic Club, and did his part for the debate club (not to mention, incidentally, that he took a full load of courses), an episode in October 1934 brought the Princeton senior to the attention of the national press. Prichard's somewhat bombastic handling of the situation revealed a remarkable political persona ever eager to turn personal scandal into political advantage.

On the night of October 10, 1934, Col. Henry Breckinridge, a candidate for a New York Senate seat on the Constitutional party ticket, came to Princeton for a debate on the New Deal. A native of Kentucky and a distant relative of the Arderys, Breckinridge had graduated from Princeton in 1907 and Harvard Law in 1910. He had also been assistant secretary of war in the Wilson administration, where he had his run-ins with the assistant secretary of the Navy, Franklin D. Roosevelt. Breckinridge had resigned his post in 1916 as a protest against President Wilson's refusal to advocate universal military training. He became a wealthy New York City attorney (with clients such as Anne Morrow) as well as a dyed-in-the-wool conservative. Breckinridge was a firm opponent of the New Deal and sought a Senate seat in an effort "to preserve the American ideals of liberty and justice." As a guest of the Whig-Clio club, Breckinridge agreed to debate a Princeton student on the merits of the Roosevelt administration. Not surprisingly, Prichard was chosen for the task.[30]

The debate centered on the constitutionality of the New Deal and proved a raucous affair. After P.W. Wilson, an editorial writer for the *New York Times* and president of the Cambridge Union of Cambridge University, discussed the Whig-Clio's attempts to develop the oratory of its members, Prichard took the stage. Deferring to the Supreme Court to determine the New Deal's constitutional basis, Prichard noted that the New Deal was firmly "in keeping with the spirit of the constitution and in harmony with constitutional liberty and ordered freedom." Among other accomplishments, Prichard noted that the Wagner Act's recognition of organized labor "meant freedom for millions from industrial serfdom."

Breckinridge countered by criticizing the economic philosophies of New Dealers like Rexford Tugwell and Henry Wallace, who, in Breckinridge's terms, promoted "prosperity through scarcity." Breckinridge seized upon a weakness in New Deal agricultural policy, that of paying farmers to plow under or destroy their crops. This central component of AAA policy at a time of national scarcity had come under fire from a variety of sources, both left and right. The colonel finished by imploring the nation to "stop stirring up class hatred" and "we will go forward in spite of politicians." The two sides then traded barbs and answered questions from the audience, with the younger Prichard more than holding his own. When the audience was polled to determine the debate's winner, Prichard won by a narrow margin.[31]

What happened following the debate drew more attention than the debate itself. To celebrate the victory, Prichard went to the dormitory room he shared with Kelvin M. Fox, the Democratic Club's vice president, and the two threw a beer party for approximately sixty students, including some campus Republicans who, one newspaper noted, "apparently turned Democratic for the occasion." Although beer was barred from Princeton dormitories in 1934, several beer kegs were brought to Fox's room in Northwest Hall. To get the kegs in Fox's room required some daring students to roll the illegal brew within fifty yards of the office of the university proctors.[32]

The next morning, university proctors discovered an empty beer keg in the dormitory's hall and within a short time their questions led them to Fox and Prichard. After they admitted their complicity in the violation, Princeton dean Christian Gauss summarily suspended the two students indefinitely for violating Princeton's alcohol ban. Gauss added that the two could be reinstated if their parents wrote him requesting reinstatement.[33]

Gauss's action implied that Prichard and Fox were not going to be expelled from the university. Gauss understood that, in the words of Gordon Craig, "Princeton, in those days, was not a very dry place."[34] Beer parties were certainly not uncommon events at Princeton, but university rules could not be blatantly violated by students without some visible form of punishment. Seemingly routine matters such as the discovery of an empty beer keg and the temporary suspension of two students were not items that held any great import beyond the confines of the university campus. But Prichard's reaction to Dean Gauss's suspension made news all the way to the *New York Times*.

Prichard took the suspension in audacious fashion, transforming his actions the night before into political gain. His words, however, were not those of a Princeton socialist, but of a Bourbon County pol. "I was merely doing my best for Roosevelt and recovery," Prichard said straightforwardly, "and the Democratic platform calls for the legalization of beer. When the Democratic Party calls," Prichard proclaimed, "I hear no other voice." He then centered his attack on the university itself: "If Princeton is so reactionary as to be behind even Rooseveltian liberalism, then I will be crucified for her backwardness." When asked if he would offer an apology, he answered simply, "I am not conscious of having anything to apologize for." Prichard did admit, though, that Dean Gauss's actions were "not unjust."[35]

The following day, the situation appeared at an end when Dean Gauss approved the petition by the families of Fox and Prichard for reinstatement. But, again, it was Ed Prichard who made the news of the day. The Princeton junior grandly announced that he had offered honorary memberships in the Woodrow Wilson Democratic Club to the three university proctors who had discovered the kegs and to Dean Gauss himself. The four unexplainedly accepted Prichard's offer on the spot, a move that enraged campus Republicans and temperance proponents, who could only mutter "just you wait" when informed of Prichard's grandstanding. One of the proctors confirmed the story but added embarrassingly, "Unlike Prichard, my duty to Dean Gauss and discipline comes before my duty to Roosevelt and repeal."[36]

Prichard's insolence and sheer nerve created a considerable reaction around campus. One student stated that Prichard's willingness to be crucified on behalf of Roosevelt and repeal "is not alone irreverent, but displays a crass boorishness such as one might not expect to find in a college student in his senior year." Mr. Prichard, the student added, "might well find someone else with whose situation he may compare his own. I would suggest Judas." Finding

Prichard's hubris contrary to Democratic principles, the student asked, "I wonder what Mr. Wilson, or Mr. Bryan, or Mr. Jefferson would say or feel should they have happened to see the *Princetonian* and Mr. Prichard's profession of his Democratic ideals and beliefs therein? Thank God they cannot!"[37]

Prichard's oratorical abundance and his melodramatic style produced some polarized reactions around Princeton. Some, like the previous student, found him a boorish, arrogant, intellectual bully. Others, however, found him a sheer delight. "Mr. Prichard's remarks," observed one freshman, "were obviously made with whimsical intent" and therefore deserved no outrage.[38] Such reactions became common long after Prichard left Princeton. Prichard's ability to create such divergent reactions may account for why, in some quarters, he was admired and genuinely beloved, such as in the Whig-Clio and Democratic clubs. Though he had sufficiently high grades, Prichard was never elected to other elite organizations at Princeton such as Phi Beta Kappa, perhaps because of such occurrences as the beer party and his grandstanding reaction.

Prichard did not confine his focus in the "Left Turn" to national politics. Politics at any level received his careful scrutiny. "I am for Upton Sinclair for Governor of California," Prichard proudly declared, "because he is on the left fringe of the New Deal and because his victory will be construed as a mandate for the President to proceed further to the left." In addition to his other duties, Prichard agreed in November 1934 to head the political division of the literary magazine *Nassau Lit.* His friend Edmund Gullion agreed to head the magazine's literary division.[39]

Prichard took interest in another campus organization, the Princeton Anti-War Society, which elected him to its Executive Council. Like many other college students in the mid-1930s, Prichard saw the approaching signs of war in Europe and wanted the United States to avoid another World War I. In this, he was hardly acting in radical fashion. By 1935, in fact, more than 500,000 students, almost half of the American undergraduate population, attended peace rallies throughout the country and participated in anti-war protests. That same year, a national poll found that 81 percent of college students opposed American entrance in a foreign war. Not yet aware of fascism's threat, Prichard in time changed his thinking on the subject of war dramatically.[40]

Prichard found much encouragement in the November 1934 general election. While some of his preferences, like Sinclair, were defeated, Democratic gains in Congress provided clear proof in Prichard's mind that "the individualistic conservative philosophy of the Old Guard has been clearly repudiated." With the victory of such figures as Robert LaFollette in Wisconsin and Governor Floyd Olson in Minnesota, Prichard perceived a leftward tilt in American politics for some time to come. But this tilt was not unalloyed in Prichard's view. "These extremists will also be advocating, along with much that is fine and good, all manner of claptrap measures, like the bonus, free silver . . . and the thirty-hour week." But these were the only tangible chinks in Prichard's socialist armor. "Personally I believe that any income of more than $20,000 a year is of dubious social value. Whenever a man makes much over that amount, his wealth ceases to become the reward of effort and a means of enjoyment and turns into a tool of aggrandizement and economic power." In short, those with such incomes "become too powerful for the good of democratic government."[41] To correct the situation, Prichard called for much more stringent tax hikes on the rich in order to redistribute the nation's wealth.

In one of his more persistent themes, Prichard examined the Supreme Court's ruling that the National Industrial Recovery Act was unconstitutional. By 1935, the Court remained the last barrier to the New Deal, and the majority Republican justices appointed earlier continued to be a thorn in FDR's flesh. In considering how to address this problem, Prichard presciently prescribed a solution that both he and FDR would later regret having advocated. Prichard speculated that Congress could either pass constitutional amendments protecting New Deal initiatives or "it may pack the Court by the addition of a number of new Justices" sufficient to reverse the anti-New Deal rulings. "Either measure would be justified," Prichard wrote, "as an alternative to the chaos and anarchy which would follow any attempt by nine fallible human beings, all of advanced age, to set aside the popular will."[42]

Although Prichard wished to see the redistribution of income and advocated a general leftward turn in Democratic party policies, he was not an admirer of Louisiana senator Huey Long. Calling the senator "an insincere and unscrupulous demagogue," Prichard elaborated on the Kingfish's weaknesses: "He is not above getting whatever he can of the wealth which he, perhaps justly, condemns. He lives in vulgar ostentation and semi-barbarous luxury . . . his methods of gaining power are a dangerous approximation of those used by Fascists." He then elaborated on the real differences between himself and Long:

> I believe that a redistribution of income and a limit on the wealth a person may inherit and acquire are necessary policies, and desirable. But merely to dissipate the fortunes of the multi-millionaires won't do much in that direction. We'll have to start redistributing drastically way below a million dollars a year if we are to gain any real results in increased social security and more income for the lower classes. In addition to this, if any real progress is to be made in reforming the social order, there must be not merely an attack on large fortunes as such, but an elimination of the methods and sources through which these fortunes are accumulated through monopolistic ownership of certain basic industries like transportation and communications or utilities, or through the anti-social exploitation of natural

resources, like coal and oil, and through the manipulation of the credit system of the country. If we are to attack the excesses of capitalism, we must first attack these sources of capitalistic return. And that is what Huey doesn't propose to do.[43]

By early 1935, Prichard began his final semester at Princeton. His last months in college were spent entirely on his senior honors thesis and he attended no more classes. In order to devote the time needed for research and writing, he stepped down from his editorial post on the *Princetonian.* In his notice to his readers, he wrote that "most of those who read it thought of it chiefly as a device for me to vent my own personal spleen. And perhaps they are right; but I have enjoyed it." Prichard thanked the paper for allowing him to do the column and acknowledged the amount of criticism the paper received for the "Left Turn." "For the more violent and intolerant statements which have issued from 'Left Turn,' I should like to apologize, if anyone has been offended. To my one or two readers," Prichard finished, "I should also like to express my appreciation of their appetite for punishment."[44]

Prichard returned to his native state for the topic of his thesis. He focused on the crucial years in Kentucky political history from 1875 to 1900 and examined the various insurgent movements in the state, such as Greenbackism, the Grange, and the national Farmers Alliance, which produced what is termed today the Populist revolt. To conduct the research, Prichard traveled back to central Kentucky, where he sat in on classes conducted by University of Kentucky southern historian Thomas D. Clark. Bedecked in his customary white suit, Prichard engaged Professor Clark in a variety of topics, all the while wiping the sweat from his face and neck. Prichard also spent research time in Washington, D.C. To secure some books and government documents necessary for his research, Prichard visited the office of Kentucky congressman Virgil Chapman, a fellow Paris native. Chapman put his office staff at the young student's disposal, and the Princeton pol no doubt relished his time in the congressman's office. On one occasion, Prichard found himself in Chapman's office when western Kentucky politician Earle C. Clements ventured in, and the two exchanged some polite conversation. Clements, at the time, was managing Thomas Rhea's unsuccessful attempt for the Kentucky governor's race. Though they did not know it at the time, this was the first encounter in a political and personal relationship that would have a profound impact on both.[45]

When he returned to Princeton to finish writing, Prichard could not refrain from participating in more political chores. When the National Student Federation of America held its national convention at Princeton in April 1935, Prichard led the Princeton representatives. He met opposition, however, from other contingents who charged him with sponsoring "complicated, federal bills with no relation or interest to the conference." The *Princetonian* then noted, "Like a cornered bear, Prichard fought against the charges and was eventually successful in having every resolution he spoke for passed."[46]

Earle Clements was not the only figure Prichard met in his final term at Princeton who would later play a seminal role in his political and personal life. To deliver its series of Stafford Little Lectures in 1935, Princeton chose a diminutive professor from the Harvard Law School, Felix Frankfurter. While Frankfurter was already well known as one of the country's most celebrated legal scholars, he was introduced by Princeton president Harold Dodds as "a man who enjoys the close confidence of the President of the United States."[47] Indeed, Frankfurter had been a close associate of then-governor Roosevelt in New York and remained a valued adviser and confidant of the president on personnel and policy matters.

During his stay at Princeton, Frankfurter agreed to an interview with Edmund Gullion for the school paper. Gullion was somewhat intimidated by the prospect of meeting the eminent law professor and asked Prichard to accompany him. Gullion recalled that after he introduced them, Prichard and Frankfurter hit it off immediately. Prichard later remembered: "We immediately got into a relationship where virtually all the barriers were down at once." The twenty-year-old senior had no hesitancy in engaging the Harvard professor in political debate: "He was bouncy, very ebullient and would stride up and down with his short legs, talking and effervescing all the time," remembered Prichard. Prichard insisted that in this meeting, "We screamed and shouted at one another, not in controversy but in agreement and delight." Frankfurter recalled that "before long, [Prichard] was calling me 'F.F.,' thereby anticipating a privilege of intimacy exercised by FDR." Among other topics discussed in this initial encounter was Prichard's thesis. Upon learning that Prichard's post-baccalaureate plans possibly included Harvard Law School, Frankfurter encouraged Prichard to look him up if he decided to come to Cambridge.[48]

While considering such plans, Prichard continued to type away at his thesis. In his final weeks at Princeton, he took one last time for debating when he competed in the annual Lynde Debate Prize contest, which designated the top debater in the senior class. Again, Prichard took the New Deal's side in arguing against the question "that the tendency toward the concentration of authority in Washington is to be deplored." Although an illness almost kept Prichard from competing, his debating skills could not be equaled by anyone in his class, and he was awarded the prestigious Lynde Prize and the $100 check that accompanied it.[49]

An insight into how his Princeton classmates perceived Prichard can be gleaned from a senior class poll taken in May 1935. Prichard finished a dis-

tant third in the "most likely to succeed" category and fourth in "most entertaining." He finished second in two categories; "biggest bluffer" and "biggest
drag with the faculty." In two revealing categories, however, Prichard won. By
a narrow margin, his classmates voted him the man "who talks the most and
says the least." And by an overwhelming margin, Prichard was picked as the
Class of 35's "best politician."[50] Clearly, Prichard's Princeton classmates recognized his hubris and were somewhat wary, while at the same time respect-
ful, of his political skills.

The one remaining task for Prichard was the submission of his senior thesis. In all, it was a remarkable achievement for any twenty-year-old college
senior. Considering Prichard's other duties and interests his senior year, the
completion of his thesis was another testament to his prodigious intellectual
talents. Covering 256 pages, it was a mature, meticulously researched and lyri-
cally written account titled "Popular Political Movements in Kentucky, 1875-
1900." Using a vast array of primary sources, Prichard's account was a deft
analysis of both Democratic and Republican politics in Kentucky after Reconstruction and the third-party and insurgent movements underlying the two
parties. Writing of the "invasion of the State by industry and capital," Prichard
explained: "along with these vested interests came their concomitants: the
workers in the mines and on the railroads, many of them propertyless and
possessing an increasingly small stake in the existing order, in politics these
men were to play two paradoxical parts: as a source of independence upon
political questions, and as a pitiful object of corruption in elections."

Prichard added, "All of these tendencies can easily be exaggerated and
magnified until they become ridiculous. On many occasions they demonstrated their presence only by some perceptible ripple on the surface, at other
times they churned the waves with such mighty force that not even the most
sanguine could ignore their existence."[51]

Writing well before serious monographs existed on recent Kentucky history, and with only limited works regarding American Populism available,
Prichard still managed to portray the nascent movement in ways that were well
ahead of his time. Perhaps this was due to his extensive understanding of Kentucky history and his own Populist sentiments. "If the Greenback movement
did nothing else," Prichard wrote, "it prepared the ground in the popular mind
for the Populist revolt a decade later," an interpretation that would not be accepted by historians for decades.[52] The one item that produced the shockwaves
of third-party and other insurgent efforts, in Prichard's judgment, were declining economic conditions among workers and farmers. Clearly hoping to draw
a parallel between the 1890s and his own time, Prichard's thesis was full of
economic determinism, a certain byproduct of his readings of Marx.

At the end of his narrative, Prichard wrote a final paragraph that is a revealing portrait of his political philosophy at age twenty:

> And so goes the course of social evolution. As the conservative forces in society sow the seeds of their own destruction, the moderates are gradually converted to the demands of the radical fringes, who represent the discontent of the disinherited. Periods of acute adversity speed up this process, and periods of plenty slow it down. But as long as the vitality of the economic system and the adaptability of those in power continue, the process lasts.[53]

Upon submission of his thesis, Prichard graduated in June 1935 with his B.A., one of only two history degrees in the Class of '35 to be awarded summa cum laude.[54]

When Prichard was in Kentucky earlier that spring, Professor Clark felt certain that he was ready to embark on a scholarly career that would produce one of the country's finest historians. Indeed, sixteen years later, when the eminent historian C. Vann Woodward wrote his epic *Origins of the New South,* he cited Prichard's thesis six times in his examination of Kentucky politics and insurgent movements after the Civil War.[55] But academe was not in Prichard's plans. As he had told Professor Frankfurter, the Harvard Law School was preeminent in his mind, and after learning of his acceptance, Prichard decided to attend the nation's premiere law school that fall.

In intellectual, political, and even social terms, Prichard had come into his own at Princeton. His student years left a legacy that, like the rest of his life, was full of the promise and the pitfalls of his complex personality. The examples of his extraordinary potential were abundant: he achieved rarified academic heights in his course work; he displayed in his brilliant thesis a profound grasp of his home state's political currents; his *Princetonian* articles articulated a radical political philosophy that generated considerable attention and revealed an engaging, active mind fused with an increasingly lucid writing style; and he became one of Princeton's finest debaters. On the other hand, there were some disturbing developments; rumors swirled around the fraudulent class debate election; he earned a reputation for being "not the most honest guy in the world";[56] and his humorous yet flippant reaction to his suspension revealed a somewhat overindulged youth who seemed to consider himself immune to the rules that applied to everyone else. Many expected that Prichard would finally receive his comeuppance when he entered the nation's most demanding law school that fall.

3 Harvard Law School

AT Princeton, Ed Prichard had been more than just a student, even an extremely bright one. Because of his casual ability to perform brilliantly in virtually any intellectual activity—his course work, the debate team, the "Left Turn," his senior thesis—and his reputation as a campus politician, Prichard became something of a Princeton celebrity. When he arrived in Cambridge in the fall of 1935, it would seem the twenty-year-old Kentuckian might realize that now was the time to devote himself fully to his studies and delay his other interests until after graduation. To no one's surprise, however, Prichard's years at Harvard Law School were, in many ways, a continuance of his years at Princeton. If he had been a celebrity in college, Ed Prichard became something of a mini-legend at Harvard Law School.

To most first-year students in the famed law school in 1935, the mission in front of them was daunting. The law school followed a rather open admissions policy, whereby excessively large classes of nearly six hundred students were admitted each year. But exams at the end of the grueling first year proved the place where selective admissions actually occurred at Harvard Law. It was not uncommon for fully one-third of a first-year class to flunk out and another sizable number to drop off by the end of the second year. If a student survived until his third and final year, his class had significantly dwindled. Even the brightest of students with the finest academic pedigrees found the competition severe merely to survive Harvard Law School. For exceptional law students like Philip Elman, who made the prestigious *Law Review* and was a clerk at the U.S. Supreme Court, the grind was so intense that he developed an ulcer his first year. "The School to a certain extent," wrote one longtime faculty member, "like an old drill sergeant, tended to pride itself on its rigor." The Law School took special pride in its imposing reputation. A Harvard publication smugly informed first-year students that the law school "has been likened to a huge machine with which the individual of his own effort must keep pace or perish in the attempt." Another faculty member likened the process to pioneers who set out in wagons to settle the West: "The cowards never started and the weak died along the way."[1]

If the "boot camp" reputation was not enough to intimidate an entering student, meeting some of the school's faculty members for the first time would be enough to humble the brightest of students. For example, after the retirement of Dean Roscoe Pound in 1937, the school came under the leadership of Dean James M. Landis, who taught contracts and had been appointed to the chairmanship of the Securities and Exchange Commission by FDR; the legendary Joseph Henry Beale, who had spent over twenty years on his magnum opus, *Conflict of Laws;* Austin Wakefield Scott, who taught trusts and civil procedure and whose name was adopted for one of the school's most prestigious clubs; and Felix Frankfurter, the school's first Jewish professor, who taught administrative law and public utilities, had defended Sacco and Vanzetti, and was a friend and adviser to President Roosevelt.

Perhaps the most imposing of all on the faculty was the venerable Edward H. Warren, who taught the dreaded first-year course on property and was better known among the students as "Bull." His nickname probably came from his early years at Harvard at the turn of the century, when he took special delight in seizing upon an unprepared student and, like a bull in the ring, gouging his matchless prey to death. The patrician Warren admitted that he "never suffered fools gladly," and became legendary in submitting first-year students to the rigors of the Socratic method. Feeling that students "would rather walk two miles than think for three minutes," Warren adopted some hard-and-fast rules in his class: "(1) No student shall speak unless he is called upon by name. (2) No student shall raise his hand seeking opportunity to speak unless I call for volunteers." Students usually sat in quiet foreboding, hoping Bull's scowling gaze would be directed toward another student when calling for a response. The terror he struck in three decades' worth of first-year students, or "One L's," was legendary by the mid-1930s. *Life* magazine had another version as to the origins of the nickname "Bull," saying Warren earned the name because he "looks, walks, and bellows like one." In fact, when reporters for the magazine came to one of Professor Warren's classes to photograph him, Warren threatened to punch them if they dared interrupt him. Not wishing to test the curmudgeonly professor, the reporters resigned themselves to photographing Warren's gloomy portrait outside the classroom. Perhaps the finest example of Warren's tyrannical legacy came in the 1970s. Actor John Houseman, while preparing for his Academy-Award–winning role as Professor Kingsfield in the motion picture *The Paper Chase,* studied the classroom tactics of "Bull" Warren as the primary model for Kingsfield.[2]

For the legions of "One L's" migrating to Harvard Law School every autumn, there was more to overcome than the intense competition, intimidating faculty, and weighty tradition. The nature of the assignments themselves was something most students had never encountered in college. Law students were required to read copious amounts of thick texts on torts, contracts, property, or criminal law that introduced a new language that had to be quickly mastered—terms like *assumpsit,* and *quare clausum fregit.* Three- to four-page cases could take hours to digest for the uninitiated law student, who then had to cope with the stress of the Socratic questioning by the professor in class the following day. If the student was unprepared or could not adequately answer a barrage of questions in class from his professors, he was exposed to quiet humiliation and, at times, outright embarrassment. To students long accustomed to academic success, the imposing process of law school often proved a humbling and even debilitating experience. Within weeks of entering law school at Harvard, "One L's" were savagely introduced to a new academic culture— they had to think like a lawyer if they planned to survive the next three years. If any cocky student entering Harvard Law assumed that its environment would be just slightly more difficult than their baccalaureate days, they were in for a rude awakening.

Ed Prichard spent the weeks leading up to his departure for Cambridge in typical fashion, concentrating on politics. Just as he had immersed himself in the Kentucky gubernatorial election before his freshman year at Princeton, he was heavily involved in the 1935 campaign. The race boiled down to a September Democratic primary runoff election between Thomas Rhea and the lieutenant governor, Albert Benjamin "Happy" Chandler. Prichard had already met Rhea's campaign manager, Earle Clements, earlier that year in Washington but had no other connection with the candidate himself. Prichard was more acquainted with the thirty-three-year-old Chandler. In 1931, Prichard had spoken on behalf of Chandler's quest for the lieutenant governor's seat at the Democratic convention in Lexington.[3] Chandler was already widely known as a rising star in the Kentucky Democratic party who hugged adoring women, kissed babies, and entertained campaign crowds with his hearty rendition of "My Old Kentucky Home." For Prichard, Chandler was simply a much more likely choice to cooperate with New Deal programs than the more conservative Rhea. In late August, before a crowd of more than eight hundred people in Paris, Prichard introduced the candidate to a Bourbon County contingent. When Chandler addressed the crowd by saying, "Now, I appeal to you good people in Bourbon County, where you have honest elections," he was met by a chorus of laughter. Chandler won the runoff election, and the *New York Times* declared that his victory had "saved Kentucky for President Roosevelt."[4] As Prichard began his legal studies, he had a grateful ally in the Governor's Mansion who always remembered favors done in his behalf.

Upon arriving at Harvard, Prichard found a number of familiar faces. Several of his protégés from Princeton had migrated to Cambridge, including William Sheldon and, a year ahead of Prichard, Adrian "Butch" Fisher. The three worked and socialized often over the course of their Harvard careers. Another first-year student who arrived in Cambridge was none other than

Prichard's Paris High School debating team partner and longtime friend, Phil Ardery, who had attended the University of Kentucky, where he had achieved an illustrious academic record himself. Unlike Prichard, Ardery had been elected to Phi Beta Kappa and had been awarded a rare scholarship from the Harvard Law School for his first year.[5]

Just as he had done at Princeton, Prichard made an immediate splash among his classmates and professors at Harvard. While other students attended Bull Warren's first-year property course in abject fear, Prichard sat in smug confidence that irritated the irascible professor and shocked the other students in class. Phil Ardery, for one, took the class with Prichard and admitted that Warren "scared the hell out of everyone" because he seemed to take special pleasure in humiliating students in class. If there was one student who was not intimidated by Warren it was Prichard, who seemed to enjoy his class confrontations with the legendary professor. In one memorable exchange, Warren asked Prichard about a particular assigned case. When Prichard said he could not deliver the right answer, Warren bellowed, "Oh, how the mighty have fallen!" Not to be outdone, Prichard responded, "Sir, it is not stupidity that makes me give the wrong answers, but terror of the monster before me." Once Warren inquired of Prichard if a job awaited him when Prichard became governor of Kentucky. There was indeed, Prichard responded—Warren would be given the task of rewriting Kentucky's statutes.[6]

Warren's reaction to Prichard probably paralleled those of another law professor, Erwin Griswold, who later became the school's dean and U.S. solicitor general. Griswold remembered that Prichard "had kind of an overgrown boy, smart-alecky trend. But overall you liked him." Among the traits that impressed Professor Griswold was Prichard's command of the English language. But Prichard managed to wrinkle Griswold's brow as well. Following a party one evening, Prichard phoned Griswold at his home at 3:00 A.M. The professor, answering the call from bed, was not amused and recalled that Prichard's late call had been made "just to annoy me. He was showing his independence." To even the most pompous professors, Prichard "showed his independence" on more than one occasion. Some found him arrogant and boorish, an overgrown boy with too many brains and not enough discipline. Others delighted in his escapades and moments of uncompromising wit and brilliance.[7]

To the crowd of Princeton graduates he already knew and a new assortment of Harvard students, Prichard's social and intellectual performances were a sight to behold. Prichard had already mastered an ability to mimic other students and professors, down to their voice, mannerisms, and personal idiosyncrasies. At one party, he even mimicked Professor Griswold in front of the professor himself. Prichard's reputation was not limited to law students. As Robert Amory Jr., a law school classmate, recalled, Prichard soon became "Big

Man on Campus" around Harvard Yard and freshmen whispered to one another, "Isn't that Prich?" With a thick patch of dark hair, rosy cheeks, and an
ever-widening girth, Prichard was an unmistakable presence at Harvard. He
augmented his image by often wearing his traditional white linen suits with a
white straw panama hat, usually smoking a cigar. Looking every bit the Kentucky colonel, Prichard also acquired in Cambridge another unique trait—his
accent became decidedly more southern. When he returned home, people
noticed that Prichard's drawl had become more pronounced, taking on a Deep
South dialect that seemed out of place in Bourbon County. While other law
students found their first year in Cambridge a time of relentless stress, Prichard
treated it as he had all the other years of his education—with a minimum of
preparation and an attitude of supreme self-confidence.[8]

As other first-year students burned the midnight oil preparing for the next
day's classes, Prichard often brought large stacks of books into his dormitory
room. The books, it turned out, were not about the law, but about a wide variety of other subjects. In fact, one of his classmates could not recall ever seeing Prichard in the law library. Prichard spent many nights in his dorm room
instead, reading until 2:00 or 3:00 A.M., on subjects such as poetry, history,
and politics, usually devouring a book each day. Astonished "One L's" could
only shake their heads at Prichard's conduct, assuming it would lead to his
expulsion following the first year. His seeming nonchalance underscored a
deeper reason why Prichard made the decision to attend Harvard in the first
place. It would seem, for example, that Prichard would have at least considered attending the Yale Law School. Unlike its Cambridge counterpart, Yale's
law curriculum in the early 1930s attempted to bring the law out of the musty
case-method approach and apply its study to modern-day realities—a practice termed legal realism. Harvard stayed true to its traditional approach that
treated the law as sacrosanct and above political or sociological considerations
of any kind. While some newer professors ventured into the venue of legal
realism, older members of the faculty remained tied to the more traditional
curriculum. Bull Warren's cases in property were so dated that students were
shocked when the professor mentioned a case one day that was only sixty years
old.[9]

Yet Harvard Law School was not just a weary and anachronistic shell of
its past glory. New faces on the faculty like Landis and Frankfurter were indeed pumping their brand of legal realism into the curriculum. Their visible
connections to FDR were certainly not lost on Prichard. The young Kentuckian perceived the Harvard Law School as a stepping-stone to his political
ambitions, whatever they may have been. While he was known tongue-in-
cheek throughout the school as the "future Governor of Kentucky," there was
little doubt in anyone's mind that Prichard had a considerable political future

ahead of him. What better way to earn his way into the corridors of power than by graduating from what some termed the "incubator of greatness"?

In order to graduate, however, a great deal depended on a student's first-year performance. With no midterm exams, students' grades depended entirely on a series of final exams administered in June. Moreover, summer job offers and positions on the prestigious *Law Review* depended on class placements determined by the first-year exams. Prichard's lackadaisical study habits throughout the year seemed destined to haunt him come exam time. But, again, his academic prowess could not be tamed by even the first year at Harvard Law School. On his exams in June 1936, Prichard scored high enough to rank in the upper 10 percent of his class. Despite the intimidating regimen and competition of the Harvard Law School, Ed Prichard seemed to be the exception to the rule even in Cambridge.

When Prichard came home to Paris in the summer of 1936 after his successful first year in Cambridge, he did not attempt to secure an apprenticeship at a law office, as was customary for young law students hoping to pad their legal résumés. Instead, his previous year's work on behalf of candidate Chandler paid off with Governor Chandler in office. Prichard received a summer job working for the Kentucky Department of Revenue for the "munificent" sum of $125 a month.[10] It would be the last favor Prichard would receive from Chandler.

Prichard arrived back in Cambridge in September 1936 to begin his second year at the law school. The rigor of the first year had already taken its toll—of the 565 students in Prichard's class in 1935, only 389 remained by the second year. Having established himself as one of the school's most promising students, he began the year by asking his old friend from Paris, Phil Ardery, to share a room with him at the Episcopal Theological Seminary on Brattle Street in Cambridge. Ardery had narrowly survived the first year, making barely adequate scores that cost him his scholarship for his second year. During the summer, Ardery had served as a law clerk in a Wall Street firm—a position he obtained through Col. Henry Breckinridge, a family friend and, coincidentally, Prichard's debate opponent at Princeton. Ardery agreed to Prichard's offer, and the two became roommates.[11]

Not surprisingly, as the academic year began, Prichard's mind was preoccupied not with his classes but with the 1936 presidential election only two months away. After classes began, Prichard suddenly disappeared from campus for weeks at a time. Worried friends knew full well where he had gone. Throughout the fall, Prichard returned to Trenton, New Jersey, where he had worked for the Democratic machine during his days at Princeton, and spent the bulk of the semester campaigning for FDR in New Jersey. In Princeton, observers remarked that despite his studies, Prichard "couldn't let an election year pass without mixing it up again in local politics." After the election in early November, Prichard returned to Cambridge, where he read other students' notebooks to catch up in his studies. Classmates were astonished with his extended absence from school, which was a surefire formula for disaster. This was, after all, a school that prided itself on its legendary rigor and where some of the country's brightest young students failed with even perfect attendance and constant study.[12]

Prichard's personal political skills at Harvard grew by his second year. When Kentucky senator Alben Barkley came to speak at Harvard during the presidential election in 1936, Prichard asked a fellow classmate, Morton Holbrook, to introduce him to the senator. Prichard just assumed that Holbrook, who came from Barkley's western part of Kentucky, knew Senator Barkley. A disappointed Prichard discovered from Holbrook that not all young law students are on speaking terms with their congressional delegation. That evening, Holbrook went to hear Barkley speak, assuming that Prichard had been unsuccessful in meeting with the future majority leader. To his shock, Holbrook watched as Barkley was led on stage that evening by Professor Frankfurter and Ed Prichard.[13]

During the 1936-37 year, Prichard established two friendships that were to be crucial to his early life: Felix Frankfurter and Phil Graham. Despite Professor Frankfurter's invitation to Prichard to "look him up" at Harvard, Prichard had little contact with Frankfurter in his first year. With Frankfurter's eyes and ears open to the comings and goings of the law school, the elfish professor was keenly interested in continuing the conversation he had started with Prichard back at Princeton. When Frankfurter finally crossed paths with Prichard in 1936, he asked "Where have you been Mr. Prichard? Why haven't you come to see me?" Prichard responded by claiming he wished not to impose upon Frankfurter, and that he had not been asked. "Oh, so you're one of those young men who have to have an engraved invitation from Tiffany's?" asked Frankfurter. The professor then promptly invited the second-year student over to his home the following Sunday for tea.[14]

A remarkable friendship soon developed between Frankfurter and Prichard. Frankfurter enjoyed the company of bright young men who were willing and able to challenge him on judicial and political matters. Having no children of his own, Frankfurter seemed to need "surrogate sons" like Prichard who treated the professor with respect but not with deference. It was not lost on the politically ambitious Prichard that currying favor with Frankfurter might be helpful in the long run. Frankfurter was well known for sending his favorite protégés on to high-profile jobs in Washington. Among those who owed their positions in the Roosevelt administration to Frankfurter were presidential assistants Thomas Corcoran and Benjamin V. Cohen and the State

Department's Alger Hiss. Another student who had just arrived at the school whom Prichard brought to meet Frankfurter was a Floridian named Philip Leslie Graham. Frankfurter described Graham as a "slender, laughing youth who danced into my room" when introduced by Prichard. The three quickly became very close. As David Halberstam writes, "Prich and Phil Graham became [Frankfurter's] surrogate sons. They were bright, but they were outrageous, and that was what Frankfurter wanted." Halberstam notes that the professor "not only tolerated their contentiousness, he seemed to encourage them to argue with him and to shout him down."[15]

Phil Graham and Ed Prichard were a scintillating pair. When Phil Graham walked into a room, David Halberstam writes, he "took it over, charming and seducing whomever he wished. He was the Sun King." If anyone could match Prichard intellectually it was Graham, who would hold the most prestigious student position in the law school, president of the *Law Review*. Harvard law professor Henry Hart said that Graham not only was qualified in 1939 to be *Law Review* editor, but was also ready to be dean of the entire law school. Graham also had political ambitions of his own and hoped to return to Florida one day and run for elective office. Together, Prichard and Graham were two shrewd southerners—brilliant, charming, witty, and Frankfurter's favorites. They also possessed a dark streak—what Joe Rauh called a "self-destructive impulse"—that no one, including Rauh, could see at the time.[16]

One of the highlights of the second year at Harvard Law School was the Ames Competition in Appellate Brief Writing and Advocacy. Begun in 1911, the competition involved volunteer teams who wrote and argued elaborate briefs before teams of judges in the qualifying rounds held in the students' second year. From there, the teams advanced to semifinal rounds and then to finals held early in the students' third year. The finals were—and still are—elaborate affairs, with the judges usually consisting of a Supreme Court justice and judges from the federal circuit court or state supreme courts. Prichard and Ardery, along with six other students, including Stanley Reed Jr., teamed up to represent the Scott club in the Ames Competition. After preparing their case in *Associated Press, Inc. v WKAA, Inc.,* the Scott team chose Prichard and Robert Lassiter Jr. as its chief attorneys. The case itself involved the students acting as counsel for a radio station, which was being sued by a news organization that claimed certain copyrights to news stories that had appeared in print and were later used by the radio station. Prichard and Lassiter argued that "there is no property right in news at all after it has been dedicated to the public, in this case by publication in the member newspapers." Unlike debates at Paris High or Princeton, where Prichard's oratorical flourishes and voluminous recall could win the day, the Ames Competition involved far more than debating skills. The judges paid close attention to the briefs submitted by the individual teams and evaluated them for their clarity and accuracy, particularly in researching precedents. The Scott team failed to advance to the later rounds in the Ames Competition. Phil Ardery later took the blame for the club's performance, claiming his own work for the club was mediocre.[17]

Since their days in Paris, there had been an implicit competition, almost a sibling rivalry, between Prichard and Ardery. The relationship between the two at Harvard grew strained at times. While Ardery struggled to survive the three years of intense study, Prichard seemed to treat it as though he were in Miss Noland's English class—fearlessly challenging his professors, studying the law as a sideline, and enjoying himself in ways that befuddled classmates like Ardery. But there were other matters that drove wedges between them. One day, as Ardery left the dorm on Brattle Street, he saw Prichard in their room. Later that afternoon, as Ardery opened his mail, he discovered small pencil marks inside the flaps of a letter, evidence that the letter had been opened and then poorly resealed. Ardery confronted Prichard, who claimed innocence and then stated that he had not been in the room all day. Ardery deduced that Prichard's story was now dubious, since he had earlier seen Prichard in the room with his own eyes. The letter in question was from Ardery's mother, and Ardery claimed that "Prich had a gnawing desire to know everything going on, including information to be found in my mail." When roommates thirty years later also claimed that Prichard flagrantly snooped into private areas, it became evident that Ardery's discovery was not that uncommon. Prichard's desire to "know everything" included, at times, secretly venturing into private areas where he knew no boundaries.[18]

When Prichard returned home for Christmas 1936, he wasted no time getting immersed again in Bourbon County politics. He sat in while the Bourbon Democrats elected W.D. McIntyre and county clerk Grace Haskins as chairman and secretary. Afterward, Prichard sent Governor Chandler a telegram, informing the governor that both were "your friends" and could be counted on to be "favorable to your administration."[19] This was the type of communication that relayed to a governor which members of a courthouse gang were loyal supporters and could therefore be counted on to dispense patronage matters when necessary.

Prichard's attentiveness to such matters underscored his real interests. At Harvard, Prichard found little in the meticulous study of cases and law that interested and challenged his insatiable political mind. Case studies of property rights or contract violations simply bored him, but classes that involved political matters won his attention. One was Frankfurter's federal jurisdiction course, which Prichard renamed "Felix Frankfurter's View of Current Affairs." Students were assigned to read each week's Supreme Court advance sheets. One legal student related what happened in class: "Frankfurter would bolt through the door each class day and challenge his charges to explain those decisions . . . the seminar was just plain noisy all the time. Ideas flew across the room like sparks, inevitably igniting full conflagrations of intellectual argument and excitement." Prichard thrived in such circumstances, and here the professor and student measured each other more than ever.[20]

Intellectual sparring matches with faculty aside, Prichard also enmeshed himself fully in the social life of the law school. During his second year, he was invited to join the exclusive Lincoln's Inn, the law school's most elite dining club. Here, sons of the bar's most eminent members socialized, such as Princeton alum John W. Kephart Jr., who was the son of the Pennsylvania Supreme Court's chief justice; Kentuckian Stanley Reed Jr., son of the U.S. solicitor general and future Supreme Court justice; and John S. McCook, son of a New York Supreme Court member. Despite such pedigrees, Ed Prichard became the focal point of Lincoln's Inn, the charming and audaciously funny entertainer at parties and other club functions. Phil Ardery commented that "a lot of guys felt it a privilege to eat at the same table with Prich."[21]

Prichard came to view Lincoln's Inn as an outlet in many ways similar to the Woodrow Wilson Club or Whig-Clio at Princeton. And he was determined to be the acknowledged leader of Lincoln's Inn. In 1938 Prichard ran against his partner in the Ames Competition, Robert Lassiter Jr., for the presidency of Lincoln's Inn. Lassiter had been a football star at Yale and despite Prichard's charm, was more popular than Prichard among members of the Inn. Lassiter won the election, and Prichard had to settle for vice president. But there were tensions involved. Lassiter later told club member Phil Ardery that Prichard had tried unsuccessfully to steal the Lincoln's Inn election. Such allegations were unsubstantiated, but coupled with a previous election at Princeton, where fraud was discovered, a trail of stuffed ballot boxes and veiled insinuations seemed to be following the Bourbon County pol.[22]

Prichard's daily contacts with the austere Harvard faculty and the elitist tone of Lincoln's Inn did little to dampen Prichard's overt support of the New Deal or his not-so-hidden socialist tendencies. At the end of his second year at the law school, he wrote an extensive letter that was published in the *New York Times*. Reacting to an editorial calling for a balanced budget, Prichard replied that "we have not even begun to tax incomes that range from $5,000 to $25,000—and even up to $50,000." In addition to increasing tax rates for the wealthy—a policy he had advocated at the *Daily Princetonian*—he also argued for sharp cuts in military spending, which echoed his years in the Princeton Anti-War Society. "In the last five years," Prichard stated, "the expenditures of the War and Navy Departments have increased from something over $500 million to more than $900 million. I do not think that many people

will contend that there is really a need for this vast increase in military out-
lay." Complimenting Neville Chamberlain's progressive tax policies in Great
Britain, Prichard stated simply that instead of taxing the poor, a 25 percent
cut in military spending coupled with higher taxes for the wealthy would balance the federal budget by 1938.[23]

Despite having missed more than six weeks of classes early in the year,
Prichard still managed to score in the upper ranks of his class in his end-of-
the-year exams in 1937. For his academic accomplishments, Prichard was rewarded with a prized position on the *Harvard Law Review* for his final year.
Few accolades at the school did as much for one's résumé as a *Law Review* placement. Considering that roughly 3 percent of an entering class at Harvard make
the *Law Review,* Prichard's appointment was yet another indication of his considerable intellectual powers. While he still regarded politics as his primary
motivation and interest—one that occupied a large portion of his school year—
he nonetheless could accomplish at Harvard with mediocre effort what many
other exceptionally bright, eager young minds could not, even with their optimum effort.

The contingent of editors on the *Law Review* for 1937-38 was led by
Edwin E. Huddleson Jr., who had the highest marks of any student in the Class
of '38. Also on the board were two members of the Class of '39, Philip Elman
and Phil Graham. Prichard's experience on the *Daily Princetonian* gave him a
fine sense of what he could expect at the *Law Review.* As Robert Amory, Jr.,
who was on the *Review* with Prichard, explained: "The Law Review was damn
hard work. You got there after an early supper, and you frequently stopped by
the yard to get a bowl of cornflakes and milk and you'd go to bed between
2:00 and 2:30." But the *Law Review* was not a student newspaper—it was recognized as one of the country's leading legal journals, and the law school itself made sure its reputation was maintained. In addition to their own classes,
Review editors put in long hours researching cases, editing and writing articles,
and soliciting and editing book reviews. Yet for Prichard, Amory remembered,
"You just couldn't overload him. He just stoked the firebox a little hotter and
turned it out and did it right."[24]

It was also during his final year that *Life* magazine came to Cambridge
for a lengthy pictorial article on the law school. Ostensibly covering Dean James
M. Landis's first days as head of the school, the article was really more an attempt to highlight the law school itself. Pictured were the luminary faculty
(with Bull Warren's portrait serving here) and various aspects of life at the
school, such as the eating clubs, the seminars, and the legal aid society. A
memorable photograph of Prichard endures in this article. With Prichard looking up from a chair, hands folded and tongue sticking out in contempt for
another student's argument, the caption reads: "The chubby 'judge' is Edward

F. Prichard Jr., the school politician, who styles himself 'the future Governor of Kentucky.'"[25]

An indication of Prichard's political inclinations came with FDR's "court-packing plan" of 1937. In order to rid himself of an obstinate Court that primarily comprised Republicans, Roosevelt came off his landslide victory in 1936 confident that he could encourage Congress to change the makeup of the Court. Roosevelt proposed that for every justice over the age of seventy, Congress would allow him to appoint another justice, presumably to help with the increased workload. But a reluctant Congress saw it for what it was—a naked power play to coopt the Supreme Court. For his part, Prichard fully supported FDR in this regard and joined law school vice dean Calvert Magruder in debating the merits of the plan with Professor Griswold. Prichard's unabashed support of the court-packing scheme was a decision he later regretted.[26]

By 1938, Prichard's relationship with the flamboyant Governor Chandler soured. Prichard had campaigned for "Happy" in 1935 on the promise that Chandler would be Kentucky's best New Deal representative. Yet Chandler had proven to be much more conservative than Prichard had hoped. As an indication of Chandler's ideology, he looked upon conservative Senator Harry Byrd of Virginia as his political idol. In 1938, the ever-ambitious Chandler made the risky move of challenging popular Senator Alben Barkley—a major Kentucky politico and an ardent New Dealer—in the Democratic primary. When FDR himself came to Kentucky, both Chandler and Barkley met the president at the railroad station in Covington. At a rally later in the day, FDR made it clear that he liked Chandler but stood solidly behind Barkley. Undaunted, Chandler continued his aggressive campaign against Barkley, earning the enmity of New Deal Democrats like Prichard. When Chandler lost the election by a wide margin, he held a grudge against those of his own party who had deserted him. Chandler would get his Senate seat, however. When the other member of Kentucky's senate delegation died just months after the 1938 primary, Chandler resigned as governor and was then appointed to the Senate by the new governor. For the next few years, Chandler proved troublesome to the Roosevelt administration, and the once amicable relationship between Prichard and Chandler was over.[27]

By the spring of their final year at Harvard Law School, most students prepared to take the bar exams and enter the legal profession. For those students on the *Law Review,* offers from some of the most prestigious Wall Street and Washington firms were not uncommon. Considering Prichard's academic record and law school performance, he likely received some of these offers as well. But his own ambitions did not necessarily involve entering the legal profession immediately. In April 1938, he received an offer from the law school to stay an additional year as a research fellow to Frankfurter. The chance to stay in Cambridge with Frankfurter and Phil Graham and work on some exciting projects interested Prichard far more than assuming an entry-level position in some New York law firm, and Prichard gladly accepted the fellowship.[28] In June 1938, he received his LL.B. from the Harvard Law School, graduating magna cum laude.

During the summer of 1938, Prichard again found work of a political nature. Instead of returning to Paris for a summer vacation, he traveled to Washington, where he worked on the staff of the famous LaFollette Committee. The committee, headed by Wisconsin senator Robert LaFollette, was established to investigate violations of civil liberties, and the committee examined troubling events in the South, including the labor wars occurring in Harlan County, Kentucky. Prichard's exposure to the Senate investigation centered around the bloody "Little Steel" strike in Chicago. During a cross-examination of Thomas Girdler, an executive with Republic Steel, Prichard sat on LaFollette's right and conferred with the senator on lines of questioning. The committee's findings laid the blame for the bloodshed squarely at the feet of the steel companies. Years later, Girdler encountered Prichard at a party and remarked, "I still remember you, sitting up in that white suit next to Senator LaFollette, slipping those questions to him to embarrass and humiliate me." In his first foray to Washington, Prichard did not go without proper advance publicity. Joe Rauh, for one, had heard of Prichard from his former professor, Felix Frankfurter, who had told Rauh that the Kentucky prodigy was "incredible in every respect—science, size, appetite, brains, eloquence." When Rauh first encountered Prichard during the LaFollette hearings, he was not disappointed with Frankfurter's assessment: "far from Felix exaggerating, he was all of those things." Prichard "knew everything, forgot nothing, and he was great fun." For Rauh, Frankfurter was "a one-man advertising machine for Prich."[29]

When Prichard returned to Cambridge, the bulk of his year as a research fellow was spent on two projects—a major article he coauthored with Harvard professor Henry Hart Jr. and a book of Frankfurter's writings he coedited with the future Librarian of Congress, Archibald MacLeish. Prichard also aided Frankfurter on an article written about Benjamin Cardozo, and helped him with his course on labor law. The article with Hart discussed the infamous "Fansteel case," in which a series of sitdown strikes at a metallurgical company in Chicago had produced numerous firings of union employees. In a move that disappointed the labor movement, the Supreme Court invalidated a National Labor Relations Board order requiring the company to rehire the fired workers. Throughout the fall of 1938, Prichard researched and wrote rough drafts of the article, which Hart then edited. The article was published in the 1939 edition of the *Harvard Law Review,* which was now edited by Phil Graham. Amid detailed references to statutes and court opinions, some of

Prichard's prose managed to escape from the legalistic article. If the company had simply followed written laws beforehand, the article claimed, "It is unthinkable that so many of its employees, skilled workmen with long records of service, would ever have persuaded themselves to embark upon open warfare with the company and the courts . . . thus a heavy share of moral responsibility for what happened falls upon the company."[30]

Besides his work with Hart, Prichard also collaborated with "Archie" MacLeish on a book of Frankfurter's most important pre-Court writings. Frankfurter had earlier persuaded poet MacLeish to edit a volume of his papers along with Prichard. For several months, Prichard and MacLeish examined the sometimes illegible handwriting of their subject and his published works. During their collaboration, MacLeish informed Frankfurter that he and Prichard were "excited beyond any words of mine to convey the possibilities of the work." Titled *Law and Politics: Occasional Papers of Felix Frankfurter, 1913-1938,* Prichard and MacLeish's book was published in 1939 by Harcourt Brace. Prichard had also spent time researching material for a book by Frankfurter on Oliver Wendell Holmes. In his preface, Frankfurter thanked Prichard and two of his friends, William D. Sheldon and Butch Fisher, for "the drudgery of compiling these materials." [31]

Prichard's intentions after Harvard became clear in 1939 when he returned to Kentucky to take the bar exam (which he passed). After eight years away in the Ivy League, Prichard was preparing to practice law at home and no doubt continue his political involvement. At some point, perhaps, he contemplated his own political career. But events developing in Washington postponed Prichard's return to his home state.

In January 1939 President Roosevelt finally rewarded Frankfurter's service to the New Deal with an appointment to the U.S. Supreme Court. After his confirmation hearings, which Prichard attended, Frankfurter took his seat on the bench to finish out the 1938-39 term. With him, he took Rauh, a former Harvard Law student, as his law clerk. But who would he choose to be his first full-time clerk beginning in October? As David Halberstam writes, the "clerkship was the ultimate cherished prize, even more valued than the editorship of the *Law Review.*" In no uncertain terms, "it announced to the outside world, particularly in New Deal Washington, who was the brightest star of the year." The decision essentially came down to Prichard and Phil Graham. Graham graduated from law school in June and was also finishing his term as president of the *Law Review.* Frankfurter agonized over having to choose. The new justice finally worked out a deal with Justice Stanley Reed, whereby Reed took Graham on as his clerk for the 1939-40 term, and Prichard became Frankfurter's clerk. Frankfurter told Graham he had informed Reed "that you and Prich will be a pool in which he and I will fish through." The following year,

Graham would then come over and clerk for Frankfurter, acquiring the unique experience of serving two years at the Court as a clerk to two separate justices.[32] Frankfurter got his way, essentially getting both without really having to take sides. But in a sense, Frankfurter did indeed reveal his inclination—after all, Prichard was not carted off to clerk for another justice while he waited in the wings for Graham.

For Ed Prichard, the timing could not have been more propitious. He would be working in the nation's capital with his old mentor—a man who was not only a conduit of bright minds to the New Deal but also now one of the justices on the High Court. Prichard would also be working in close proximity with his close friend Phil Graham. During a time of enormous change taking place at home and around the world, clerking for one of the most politically connected men on the U.S. Supreme Court was a singular political and intellectual challenge for the twenty-four-year-old Prichard. Just as he had absorbed all the lessons provided by the classrooms of the Bourbon County courthouse, Princeton, and Harvard, Prichard prepared in the summer of 1939 for the environs of the ultimate political classroom provided by Washington, D.C. Whether this new challenge would finally tame the young prodigy was a question yet to be answered.

4 An Extended Campus

WHEN Ed Prichard arrived in Washington, D.C., in the summer of 1939, the city was still very much a quaint, leisurely paced southern town that also happened to be the capital of the United States. When he left six years later, Washington had been transformed into a bureaucratic colossus that had emerged as the center of the noncommunist world. The war effort spawned a building boom and the migration of thousands of government and military personnel into the overcrowded city. During these years, Washington lost much of its old charm and, in the words of journalist Malcolm Cowley, became a combination of "Moscow (for its overcrowding)" and "Hell (for its liveability)."[1] For a twenty-four-year-old political animal, however, Washington in the early 1940s was a special place to be, and Ed Prichard witnessed the enormous change that occurred within the city from some rather lofty vantage points.

Prichard began his duties as Frankfurter's clerk in the fall of 1939. The duties of a Supreme Court clerk then differed substantially from those of today. The increased caseload, more than anything else, altered the scope of a clerk's assignments. Today, an individual justice may employ three or four clerks, as well as secretaries and messengers. Before World War II, one clerk performed all of these tasks and worked intimately with his respective justice. But even in this capacity, Prichard stood out among the elite group of individuals who served as clerks to the Court. Whereas many clerks arrived at the Court having never met their future bosses, Prichard and Frankfurter had a personal and professional relationship that was far from typical. Prichard's precocious and sometimes audacious behavior, as well as his fearless ability to take on the giants of the Harvard Law School on matters of law and politics, had singularly impressed Frankfurter. The justice came to view both Prichard and Phil Graham as substitute sons and often encouraged their intellectual challenges and verbal sparring matches. People who knew little of this relationship were shocked at the manner in which the three engaged each other in very spirited and rancorous debate. Far from kowtowing to the justice, Prichard often challenged Frankfurter on a proposed brief or a line of argument. In a word, Prichard was bold and completely candid—almost to the point of considering himself Frankfurter's peer—in whatever he told the justice in chambers. Indeed, this was precisely what Frankfurter cherished in his young clerk. In his year as the first full-time clerk to "F.F.," Prichard began a long line of distinguished jurists who served as clerk to Frankfurter, including Graham, Philip Elman, Eliot Richardson, Alexander Bickel, and Richard Goodwin.

While beginning his duties at the Court, Prichard stayed at a rented house at 1913 S Street in Georgetown. Here some fellow members of the Harvard Law class of '38 resided, among them William K. Van Allen, Robert Lassiter, and William D. "Uncle Billy" Sheldon. To accommodate the influx of friends who wanted a room at the S Street residence, Sheldon led an effort to find a more spacious locale for the collection of approximately a dozen bright young Harvard-trained bachelors. Sheldon, John Oakes, and Van Allen soon visited a mansion known as "Hockley" in nearby Arlington, Virginia, a historic house with white columns and a sweeping lawn that overlooked the Potomac. Sheldon arranged a deal to rent the house from its owner, Adm. Thomas Wilkinson, and Prichard moved in with the other men from S Street to form what became a legendary household during the war years.

Within a very short time, Hockley became something akin to the most popular frat house on campus, only this time the campus was none other than Washington, D.C. In the early 1940s, more than ten men lived at Hockley at one time or another. All would later acquire fame and influence in their own right: Phil Graham, who would later run the *Washington Post;* John Oakes, who later edited the *New York Times* editorial page; William Cary, who was appointed to the Securities and Exchange Commission by President Kennedy; Graham Claytor, who had been Louis Brandeis's clerk and was later president of the Southern Railroad; Van Allen, who would become a partner in a large North Carolina law firm; "Butch" Fisher, who became dean of the Georgetown Law School; and Sheldon. Despite the luminary crowd, it was not a matter of how Prichard would fit in with his housemates but, in the words of Van Allen, "it was everybody else fitting in with Prich."[2]

In their new home, the men of Hockley lived in grand style. According to one visitor, the mansion made "Mount Vernon look like a sharecropper's toolhouse." Hockley was the site of numerous lavish cocktail parties and other social functions. The most celebrated events were the Sunday brunches, which were attended by the likes of Frankfurter, James Landis, Walter Reuther, Stanley Reed, Dean Acheson, and young Adlai Stevenson. On one particular Sunday morning, Graham Claytor, who had been called up by the Naval Reserves, told those sitting at a table about a new bomb the Navy had developed that could detonate in the air and rain shrapnel on the enemy. Claytor noticed a shy, very frail-looking man at the table he had never seen before, and he apologized to his guest for speaking about such technical and complicated subjects as weaponry and leaving him out of the discussion. Afterward, amused Hockleyites informed Claytor that the quiet guest was J. Robert Oppenheimer.[3]

With the rent split ten ways, the men at Hockley could afford some other luxuries. They hired a butler named Youter Johnson, who had previously worked for Dean Acheson. Once caught by Mrs. Acheson in "a compromising situation" with a maid, Johnson had been dismissed only to be hired by the men at Hockley. He subsequently attended the needs of the men who lived at Hockley, including pressing their shirts, serving drinks at all functions, and preparing their meals.[4]

Although he had a photographic memory and other intellectual skills, Prichard was unwilling to perform more mundane chores, much to the chagrin of those who knew him. He was, for example, notoriously inept at handling and budgeting money. When Prichard was short of funds, he was not shy about asking friends for a loan—which they soon learned might never be repaid. At Princeton, Sheldon had loaned Prichard close to $900 over several years. Far from becoming angry, "Uncle Billy" simply came to the conclusion that such sums were worth the price of being a close friend of Ed Prichard. At Hockley, in fact, Sheldon served as a banker of sorts to Prichard. Prichard gave Sheldon his paychecks, then went to him on those occasions when he needed spending money.[5]

To add to the fraternity-house atmosphere, a select group of young women—mostly young government employees and the daughters of noteworthy Washingtonians—regularly attended the various functions at Hockley. One was Katharine Meyer, the daughter of *Washington Post* owner and former Federal Reserve chairman Eugene Meyer, who later referred to herself as one of "the house girls" at Hockley. She elaborated that "for a single girl, it was heaven" to spend time at Hockley, because the men there were "all very brilliant, very attractive, very funny." Despite his wit and brilliance, and Katharine's statement that during these years Prichard was the "one who dazzled us the most," Prichard was not known at Hockley as a womanizer. Yet Katharine "deeply resented" the fact that Prichard was more interested in her sister, Elizabeth. Like many others, Katharine Meyer wanted very much to be a part of Prichard's circle of friends—"We were all bewitched by his charm, by his humor, by his brilliance, by his eloquence" she later said.[6]

Prichard pursued the glamorous Elizabeth Meyer, who at the time lived in New York, but with little success. Instead, he had more luck charming her parents. When Eugene Meyer sent "the boys" at Hockley a bottle of wine for New Year's, Prichard responded by describing himself as "the most vocal, and by legal standards, the most authoritative representative of Hockley." Prichard and Eugene Meyer shared a common fondness for fine cigars, and Prichard once told him that the most beautiful and desirable of all the Meyer girls was Belinda, a particular Cuban brand. But Prichard's spell over Eugene and Agnes Meyer did not last long. Katharine remarked that her parents "became impatient with his constant acceptance of their hospitality," while Prichard refused to display "normal civility" and did not perform the subtle requisite tasks such as writing thank-you notes after a dinner party. After his rejection by Elizabeth, Katharine noticed that Prichard "developed a minor and very temporary interest in me." Prichard's efforts to woo Katharine were, by now, futile. In January 1940, she began dating Phil Graham, and they soon fell deeply in love. Prichard, meanwhile, remained a lonely figure among a group of handsome and eligible young Hockleyites.[7]

To anyone visiting Hockley, it was quickly apparent that it was a very special place. As one Hockleyite remembered, "ten or twelve of the brightest guys in the country" lived under one roof. It was also the one place in his life where Prichard lived among equals. He would intellectually dominate every other locale in his life, but not Hockley. In fact, within this remarkable group, no one dominated in an intellectual sense. Yet in other ways, it was an accepted fact that Prichard stood above the rest. At Hockley, all of Prichard's extroverted qualities were best displayed. Foremost was his wit—James McGlothlin labeled Prichard simply "one of the great raconteurs of history." Van Allen recalled that at most parties or other social situations, Prichard often commanded the attention of those in attendance with his rich archive of stories and gossip. He once amazed guests by listening to a John L. Lewis speech on the radio and then re-creating the speech verbatim to his stunned audience, employing his devastatingly accurate impersonation of the labor leader. But Prichard was more than a class clown. Politics was always heavily featured at Hockley and was taken quite seriously. When one of J.P. Morgan's sons once talked of appeasing the Nazis, Prichard and Phil Graham simply left the room. Throughout his college years, Prichard opposed American military involvement in Europe. But by the time he came to Washington, even the most strident pacifists had difficulty arguing that Hitler did not pose a significant threat to democratic government. "All who love democracy," Prichard proclaimed, "follow us." Such examples attracted the likes of young Arthur Schlesinger Jr., who wrote that "Prich was the dazzling center" of Hockley, "exuberant, witty, bursting with legal ideas, political insight, administration, gossip, and intrigue." As Katharine Graham acknowledged, Phil Graham and Prichard "were the two shining lights of that generation." To the proud alumni of Princeton, Prichard was already "the talk of the town" and boldly claimed that he might be "the presidential candidate in 1956 or 1960." For Prichard, the constant attention and the swirl of luminary and powerful people and the camaraderie among the housemates at Hockley made living there "some of the best days of my life."[8]

Prichard's relationship with Frankfurter brought him into the highest circles of Washington political life. In January 1940, in fact, Prichard accompanied the justice to dinner at the White House, where he first met the president and Mrs. Roosevelt. Even on this occasion, Prichard was not intimidated by the surroundings or his dinner hosts. He instead displayed all the unbridled charm, wit, and brilliance before the Roosevelts that had so captivated Frankfurter. When Prichard accidentally spilled some peas on the floor, he feared that when the president was wheeled away everyone would "see this little messy pile of green beans on the floor." Prichard was relieved when "Fala came around to my end of the table and licked them all up." After an entertaining dinner, the president told the young law clerk, "Now, Prich, drop in on me sometime." Prichard could not let that casual comment go by without saying, "Why, Mr. President, if you will tell me how one drops in on the president of the United States, I shall be glad to do it." Prichard noted that this gave Roosevelt a "big kick and it made him laugh." Even with the president of the United States, Prichard exploited every opportunity to charm his host with the powerful combination of brilliance and humor. And as he was wont to do, Prichard sometimes went too far. Upon reflection the next day, he realized that his manners at the White House might have brought delight to the president and Frankfurter, but that Mrs. Roosevelt might have found his behavior boorish. Prichard wrote a thank-you note to her on stationery with "Hockley" letterhead. Prichard's letter read:

My dear Mrs. Roosevelt,

Justice Frankfurter must have been ashamed, I am afraid, on Monday evening to face you before we left the White House—for fear that the hilarity of our "legal" discussion with the President had disturbed you and your other guests. At any rate he was unwilling to interrupt you directly, and I was shepherded away without a chance to tell you good night or to thank you for a most delightful evening.[9]

No doubt, Prichard's "legal" discussion involved outrageous and amusing anecdotes about the Washington political scene. Far from deferring to his hosts, the twenty-five-year-old Kentuckian quickly felt at home entertaining the president of the United States and an associate justice of the Supreme Court over dinner. No doubt, this was precisely why Frankfurter had brought his clerk along to the White House in the first place.

Living in grand style in the Arlington mansion, Prichard enjoyed his growing social life and the ever-widening sphere of talented and powerful friends he was accumulating. It seemed as though his routines had been extended from Princeton to Harvard and then to Washington. A friend succinctly remarked that Prichard simply considered Washington as nothing more than "an extended campus, and behaved accordingly." *Fortune* magazine later captured the habits that Prichard brought with him to Washington: "an intolerance toward his intellectual inferiors," as well as "a marked tendency to show off and shock his acquaintances."[10]

But there was the grinding work of the Court that beckoned, and just as he had done in college and law school, Prichard assumed that his brilliance alone would carry him through in his work for Justice Frankfurter. Not even the Supreme Court could halt some of his Ivy League propensities. In a fashion similar to the episodes in which he left Cambridge to work in political campaigns during the school year, Prichard left Washington on one occasion to follow Elizabeth Meyer to New York. In his absence, Phil Graham finished his assignments. While Prichard held a special place in Frankfurter's esteem, at least one other justice held a somewhat different opinion. Justice Frank Murphy referred to Prichard as merely "the big fat boy" who was little more than Frankfurter's "pet." Frankfurter well understood that his clerk was not one to burn the midnight oil on any assignment, regardless of its significance: "Prichard, you have the judicial temperament," Frankfurter once chided his clerk, "you don't like to work."[11]

On one memorable occasion, Prichard's carelessness cost him dearly. One of the elementary tasks for a law clerk to perform is to check all incoming cases with a manual titled *Shephard's Citations.* This is a brief background check to make sure no cited case has been recently overruled. In the legal lexicon, the process is referred to as "shephardizing." It is a routine matter that all first-year law students must quickly master. On one case before the court involving an Oklahoma litigant, Prichard did not bother to shephardize the case at all and consequently prepared a brief and sent it on to Frankfurter. The justice then issued an opinion without knowing that the case had, indeed, been recently overturned. Shortly thereafter, Prichard was working in his office when the case was returned to the justice's chambers for rehearing. Realizing the embarrassment he had caused Frankfurter, Prichard panicked. He called his friend Joe Rauh and said that he was in deep trouble: "I'm leaving town—maybe forever," he told Rauh. Prichard then disappeared and Frankfurter was soon on the phone all over town trying to learn the whereabouts of his missing law clerk.

Prichard's precocious nature revealed the unmistakable fact that he still retained some very immature traits. His failure to shephardize the case was one thing—as Frankfurter acknowledged, Prichard's "judicial temperament" suggested he hated such mundane legal chores. Just as he had succeeded brilliantly at law school without giving his very best effort, Prichard assumed that clerking at the court would be no different and that he could overcome any problem with his wits. But even more revealing was the reaction to his carelessness. Instead of confronting Frankfurter directly and learning from the episode,

Prichard simply fled from the scene like a frightened child. In later years, friends would call such flights from reality by Prichard "submerging." For those who depended on him, such flights became all too common.

But Frankfurter understood the psyche of Ed Prichard. He called Rauh and asked if he knew where Prichard had gone. Rauh did not but suspected that he had fled to New York. Frankfurter passed the word on to friends to tell Prichard that all was forgiven and he should return. Within a few days, the justice was at work in his chambers when a tearful Prichard appeared at the door. The bulky figure was soon on his knees crawling on all fours to Frankfurter, begging forgiveness. The two embraced in a scene that has probably never been re-created at any time in the history of the U.S. Supreme Court.[12]

While this episode exposed one particular side of Ed Prichard, another more serious event took place that revealed further aspects of his complex and sometimes reckless persona. A case involving a child's refusal to salute the American flag came before the court in Frankfurter's first full term on the bench. Frankfurter's and Prichard's reaction to the case altered their relationship and exposed a certain dangerously compulsive streak in Prichard's personality.

By 1940 Europe was engulfed in war and the United States was in heated debate over its policy toward the embattled countries of Great Britain and France. Stories of Nazi aggression were deeply disturbing, particularly to American Jews such as Felix Frankfurter. They saw in Adolf Hitler a tyrannical racist who was bent on destroying democracy and posed a considerable threat to the United States. While some "America Firsters" wished to avoid war with Germany at any cost, others like Frankfurter became patriotic zealots in favor of "preparedness."

When Frankfurter came on the Court, he was hailed by many as the champion of civil liberties. After all, he had defended Sacco and Vanzetti and was one of the founders of the American Civil Liberties Union. Frankfurter met opposition in his Senate confirmation hearings among conservative senators who were distrustful of his advocacy of individual liberties because they expected the brilliant Harvard professor to support individual rights over the state. Not long after Frankfurter's confirmation, he heard the case of *Minersville School District v Gobitis*.

Lillian and William Gobitis were members of the Jehovah's Witnesses and students in the public school system in Minersville, Pennsylvania. When they refused to salute the American flag one day on religious grounds, they were suspended. Their father subsequently sued, claiming that the school had violated his children's constitutional rights of religious freedom. Gobitis won his case, and the school district appealed the verdict, which eventually made its way to the Supreme Court. The court was asked to determine what lines could be drawn between individual religious freedom and the rights of the state. As onlookers guessed at the situation when the court heard oral arguments, it was assumed by civil libertarians that Felix Frankfurter could certainly be counted on to vote with Gobitis when the decision was reached.

Few would have suspected early on that Frankfurter supported the school district. While he was very much aware of Jewish history and the crucial issue of religious liberty and tolerance, he was also a superpatriot who regularly whistled "Stars and Stripes Forever" as he walked down the corridors of the Supreme Court building. In conference, Chief Justice Hughes stated, "I simply cannot believe that the state has not the power to inculcate this social objective." Frankfurter surprisingly came to Hughes's aid, and the chief justice understood the political coup that conservatives could achieve if Frankfurter wrote the opinion on behalf of a majority.[13]

Perhaps the single most astonished observer who simply could not reconcile the Frankfurter he knew with the proponent of the Pennsylvania school system over the religious objections of two schoolchildren was Ed Prichard. The young clerk was simply beside himself when he read Frankfurter's draft opinion, particularly such passages as: "The preciousness of the family relation, the authority and independence which give dignity to parenthood, indeed the enjoyment of all freedom, presuppose the kind of ordered society which is summarized by our flag. A society which is dedicated to the preservation of these ultimate values of civilization may in self-protection utilize the educational process for inculcating those almost unconscious feelings which bind men together."[14]

When Prichard read the draft, he reacted in a very telling way. Impulsively, he leapt out of his chair and decided he would show the draft to Frankfurter's previous law clerk, Joseph Rauh. The moment he left the court building with Frankfurter's draft, Prichard broke one of the sacrosanct rules of the court— the absolute secrecy of a developing opinion as well as the confidence placed in him by Frankfurter. Prichard arrived panting at Rauh's home and presented Rauh with a draft by saying, "Felix has made a terrible mistake." Rauh read the draft, he later remembered, "with the sinking feeling when your god, Felix Frankfurter, is about to be ungodded." Rauh and Prichard discussed the implications of the decision and were both certain that the court would soon overturn such a ruling (which it did in 1943) and that Frankfurter would be humiliated and embarrassed. "You have to speak with him," Prichard told Rauh, hoping that Frankfurter could be talked out of issuing the opinion altogether.[15]

Rauh seriously considered the possibility of going to Frankfurter and telling him, "This is the end of your leadership of the court. I mean, it's very clear that this is not going to work." But then Rauh confronted Prichard with the crucial issue: "If you want to take the joint responsibility with me," he told Prichard, "I'll tell him that you gave it to me and I accepted it, as we're jointly liable for whatever wrongdoing we have done here." For the first time in the entire bizarre episode, Prichard was confronted with the ethical implications of his actions. Trembling at this moment when he realized the severity of what he had done, Prichard cried, "Oh, God no, Felix must never know that I told you." Rauh later noted that after this exchange, "we both started to laugh, because it was so ridiculous." Rauh looked back on the conversation with amused wonder: "Here we were, two kids in their twenties talking about this great Supreme Court Justice and how we're going to save him from disaster."[16]

Prichard then simply returned to work, and Rauh kept the affair to himself. Prichard's actions were revealing in ways that went far beyond the details of the case itself. Prichard obviously saw his role as a law clerk as more than simply a confidant and assistant to Justice Frankfurter. He saw himself as an advocate of social policy and a protector of Frankfurter's judicial reputation. In smuggling the draft out of the court, he never considered the ethical implications until he was confronted by them in Rauh's living room. Only then, when his own career and relationship with Frankfurter were threatened, did Prichard's scheme end—Frankfurter's wrath and the consequent damage of being exposed for his deeds now superseded the threat to civil liberties that the *Gobitis* opinion implied. This willingness to bend and break sacred rules in the name of the right cause was evident in the mental and moral makeup of Ed Prichard at this early juncture. Rauh could laugh away the incident as an example of a boyish impulse, perhaps even a prank that had not been completely thought out. Eight years later, another similar case of impulsive action by Prichard that was also not carefully considered would have a different outcome.

In the *Gobitis* affair, Frankfurter apparently never learned of Prichard's indiscretions.[17] Frankfurter's opinion spoke for a resounding eight to one majority. Chief Justice Hughes wrote Frankfurter that "you have accomplished a very difficult and highly important task—The Court is indebted to you." The lone dissenter was Harlan Fiske Stone, who wrote a bitter dissent failing to see how "some sensible adjustment of school discipline" would ever present any circumstance "so momentous or pressing as to outweigh the freedom from compulsory violation of religious faith which has been thought worthy of constitutional protection." Shocked by Frankfurter's opinion, protégés such as Benjamin Cohen and Harold Laski wrote letters of commendation, not to Frankfurter, but to Stone. Even the *Christian Century* criticized Frankfurter's "misguided zeal," and lamented that he seemed "more anxious to have a symbol of liberty saluted than to have liberty maintained." Three years later, the Court, as Prichard and Rauh had predicted, overruled the *Gobitis* decision. In the process, Frankfurter's judicial reputation was undermined and his standing among civil libertarians forever damaged.[18]

Prichard was steadfast that the *Gobitis* decision was an unqualified disaster. He later wrote that Frankfurter was "deeply wounded by the torrent of criticism which this decision evoked." Prichard felt that more was involved in Frankfurter's decision than simply the justice's adherence to judicial self-restraint. Frankfurter had long developed "a careful rationalization of the different considerations which might lead to judicial restraint in social and economic matters and yet justify judicial intervention to protect political and religious liberty." Furthermore, as Prichard acknowledged, "the sentimental patriotism of the immigrant boy welling up irresistibly at a moment of national peril" could not be discounted.[19]

With the *Gobitis* decision, a certain change came over Prichard's relationship with Frankfurter. The usual combative relationship between student and professor took on a new light with Frankfurter's placement on the High Court. Lines were now drawn over which none of Frankfurter's famous "hot dogs" could now cross without risking his wrath. At dinners with Graham, Rauh, and Prichard, Justice Frankfurter often found himself in shouting disputes that simply shocked any onlookers. Katharine Meyer felt that Prichard and Graham "were almost condescending of Felix when they disagreed with him." On one memorable occasion, Frankfurter was explaining the reasoning behind an opinion when he saw Prichard slumped over a table holding up some of his fingers in an odd way. "Prich, what are you doing?" the justice asked. "Oh, nothing, Mr. Justice. Just counting your digressions."[20]

Prichard's unique relationship with Frankfurter did not, of course, extend to other members of the Court. A more typical encounter occurred one day after Frankfurter had been home for several days with an illness. Prichard received a message that Chief Justice Hughes wished to see him. Prichard's appraisal of Hughes was an honest one: "Hughes scared me to death. He's one of the few people in the world who ever really scared me." Prichard walked into the chief justice's chambers "shaking in my shoes. I thought, my God, have I said something indiscreet? Have I done something I shouldn't have?" Prichard's well-known proclivity for discussing pending cases with Phil Graham might have been lurking in his mind. Hughes then walked in and told Prichard, "I just wanted you to tell Justice Frankfurter that for those cases where he was not able to hear oral arguments, he need not recuse himself. He may feel himself perfectly eligible to participate in the decision. Thank you very much." The relieved clerk left the chambers thinking that Hughes was "the most godlike person that I ever saw."[21]

Toward the end of Prichard's year as clerk, a more personal revelation took place. One night in the spring of 1940 after a date with Katharine Meyer, Phil returned to the room at Hockley that he shared with Prichard. Graham was giddy and whistling loudly and awoke Prichard. "You son of a bitch, you've got her," was all Prichard could say, sensing that Graham had proposed to Katharine. Prichard was still jealous of Phil's relationship with Katharine and did not greet the news of their impending marriage well. Throughout the engagement, Katharine perceived that Prichard was rather "put out with both of us." Prichard's prolonged sulking did end, however. Phil then asked him to be his best man.[22]

The lavish wedding of Philip Graham and Katharine Meyer took place at Eugene Meyer's Mount Kisco estate in Westchester County, New York, in June 1940. The crowd in attendance knew Prichard all too well and wondered if he would arrive on time, "given his unreliable habits," according to Arthur Schlesinger. But on this one occasion, Prichard showed up on time with the ring. At the wedding luncheon, the Gobitis case came up, which produced yet another shouting match between Frankfurter, the groom, and the best man. Tempers flared when Prichard and Graham accused Frankfurter of betraying the Bill of Rights. Guests were shocked at the manner in which the revered Supreme Court justice was treated by Prichard and Graham. In the words of Joseph Rauh, "I never saw a guy beat up like Felix was" by Prichard and Graham, who "just destroyed Felix's reasoning." Frankfurter grew angry and stated that he would never again participate in a discussion about Court business. The bride noticed "great large tears" rolling down Prichard's face. Frankfurter ended the episode by grabbing Katharine's arm and taking her for a walk. "It really was a turning point in the relationship of the four of us," said Rauh. "We all went home a little crestfallen that the beautiful days of screaming" at each other and with Frankfurter were now over. Everyone recovered their composure in time to attend the elegant wedding ceremony of Phil and Katharine Graham.[23]

Frankfurter's opinions from the High Court continued to disappoint both Prichard and Graham. Although Frankfurter had encouraged his former students to challenge him on pending cases, the behavior of Prichard and Graham got to be too much. Once when Frankfurter was dictating an opinion to Graham, the young clerk simply stopped typing upon hearing of an offensive judicial phrase or reasoning put forth by his boss. Later, Prichard confessed to Interior Secretary Harold Ickes that Frankfurter "was swinging more and more to the conservative side." Prichard's explanation was personal—he told Ickes that "Felix hates [William O.] Douglas so intensely that he just naturally goes into opposition to Douglas in practically all instances." Prichard later told Phil Graham that Frankfurter "has no sense or reason. We are still buddies, simply because I refuse to discuss judicial matters with him." On other issues, Prichard had little use for Frankfurter's lectures. "Felix is an economic idiot," Prichard noted, adding that the justice's "knowledge and information" of economic issues "have been acquired by osmosis rather than actual study."[24]

As Prichard's relationship with Frankfurter soured, his romantic interests did not fare much better. If Prichard lost Katharine Meyer to his best friend, he was not without other romantic interests in Washington. He was also smitten with a secretary in Francis Biddle's Justice Department office, Evangeline Bell. Evangeline was a tall, strikingly beautiful Radcliffe graduate who spoke several languages and would soon go to work for the Office of Strategic Services in London. She later married diplomat David Bruce and became a legendary figure within the diplomatic circles as well as the world of fashion. Arthur Schlesinger Jr. recalled that Prichard was "very much in love" with Evangeline, and the couple dated for a short time. Evangeline was very fond of Prichard, but she was not in love with him, and when she left for overseas Prichard was brokenhearted. As had been the case through most of his young life, Prichard was haunted with loneliness throughout his years in Washington.[25]

By the end of the court's term in the summer of 1940, Ed Prichard possessed one of the sterling résumés of any young lawyer in the country. Instead of using his accomplishments and connections to secure a lucrative position at a New York law firm or return home, he steadfastly sought to stay in Washington in a political position. There was no one better suited to advance Prichard's career in the New Deal than Frankfurter. Long before he arrived on the Court, Frankfurter had skillfully played his role as FDR's confidant. Such crucial New Dealers as Thomas "Tommy the Cork" Corcoran, Benjamin V. Cohen, and Joe Rauh all owed their initial appointments and advancements to the active lobbying of Felix Frankfurter in their behalf. Prichard hoped, in this way, to be no different.

In late 1940, Prichard's hopes were realized when he secured a position in the Justice Department. He was made an assistant to Attorney General Robert H. Jackson and was assigned to the Immigration Division, where he worked at the cumbersome task of processing the thousands of visas and applications from refugees fleeing Hitler. By day Prichard toiled in the attorney general's office, and by night and weekends held court at Hockley.

As the war raged on in Europe, some Americans, such as Eugene and Agnes Meyer, were already deeply committed to aiding Jewish refugees. They sought Prichard's help in his new role in the Justice Department. Eugene Meyer began his correspondence with Prichard by claiming to be a member of the "Cigar Smoking Cooperative and Dissipating Underwriting Syndicate." When Meyer sent Prichard a box of 200 cigars, Prichard responded with characteristic humor: "When my connection with your syndicate seemed to result in considerable profit, with no risk and investment on my part, I came to suspect that I was being placed on the 'Meyer Preferred List' for purpose of enlisting my potent influence as a public official in behalf of many of your sinister interests." Yet within Prichard's humorous letter was a very serious component—Agnes Meyer's personal request to Prichard to help in securing the entrance of thousands of intellectual and literary "refugees" from Germany. Prichard obliged, telling Meyer he hoped they would call upon him again for help with any refugees.[26]

Prichard's new boss proved to be more resistant to the attributes that had so easily won over Frankfurter. Robert H. Jackson was a no-nonsense New Dealer who was just a year away from his own appointment to the Supreme Court. Jackson came from a very different legal environment than Prichard. He did not attend college and spent only one year in law school. After Jackson passed the bar exam, he practiced law in a small office in Jamestown, New York. In 1934 he came to Washington to work for Internal Revenue. Jackson's unswerving loyalty to FDR was rewarded with a number of high-level posts, including solicitor general, before being tapped by FDR to be attorney general.

Jackson and Prichard never grew close. They were at odds both ideologically and in their personalities. Jackson found Prichard "brilliant," but also "somewhat reckless and erratic." The attorney general further described Prichard as "an extreme liberal who felt that ends justified the means." Prichard quickly grew dissatisfied with his new boss. When Jackson refused to allow a particular European refugee who had escaped from a concentration camp admittance to the United States, Prichard sent the attorney general a biting five-page memorandum challenging Jackson's knowledge of existing immigration law. His memo read more like a legal brief aimed at overturning a flawed judicial opinion than a carefully-worded argument designed to persuade his boss to reverse himself. Prichard wrote, "We are defending democracy poorly when we condemn to concentration camps and to be transported back and forth across submarine infested seas those who have loved democracy enough to give up their own homes and their own countries."[27]

Prichard found one ally in the Justice Department in Francis Biddle, the solicitor general. By March 1941, Prichard felt comfortable enough with Biddle to send him a sharply worded memo that sketched out his frustrations with the attorney general and the department itself. Prichard wrote of his "deep anxiety on discovering the distrust and suspicion with which this Department was being viewed by liberal and progressive forces." He went on to list some of the reasons why the department no longer curried favor with "liberal and progressive forces":

The Bridges case, the Attorney General's espousal of wire tapping, the deportation proceedings against Mrs. Browder, the prosecution of Earl Browder . . . the complete uselessness of the Civil Liberties Unit in moving against local attacks upon civil liberties—all these have played their part in arousing deep rooted fear that this Department . . . is in danger of becoming a liberal front for vicious attacks upon civil liberties, the rights of minorities and the freedom of labor.

Prichard was particularly angry at proposed legislation that he felt harmed organized labor and was supported by the attorney general. "Is there not something that can be done to prevent the use of the Department's prestige and influence in promoting the passage of this anti-labor legislation?" Prichard ended by pleading, "I do not mean to intrude into a jurisdiction which is not mine, but a deep personal concern impels me to write you."[28]

Biddle passed the memo on to Jackson, commenting that "there is something in what he says." Jackson, however, was not impressed. On this occasion, Prichard was not speaking with fearless impudence to Bull Warren or even Felix Frankfurter, but criticizing the policy of the Justice Department to the attorney general himself. Jackson found the memo "so insubordinate that it would have amply justified firing him," but Jackson decided against it considering Prichard's youth. Instead, Jackson replied to Biddle, claiming that Prichard's memo revealed how the department was under attack from both "radicals" and those who accused him of "coddling Communists." Regarding memos like Prichard's, Jackson stated that "we must make up our minds in these times that the world is divided into two unreasonable camps. Each will blame us for everything it does not like and will promptly forget everything we do for it."[29] Although Prichard was not fired, his memo set in motion a reaction by the Justice Department that had far-reaching implications for the young Kentuckian.

Less than two weeks later, the FBI compiled a four-page memo regarding Ed Prichard. At whose suggestion the memo was prompted is unknown, but considering Jackson's anger at Prichard's memos, it is reasonable to assume that Jackson himself asked the FBI director, J. Edgar Hoover, for information on the "erratic" staff member in his office. Hoover was already well aware of the new lawyer in the Justice Department. Earlier, the FBI had burglarized the offices of the Washington Peace Mobilization (WPM) and the Washington Committee for Democratic Action (WCDA) to obtain those organizations' membership lists. The WPM was a local chapter of the American Peace Mobilization, which was primarily devoted to avoiding American entry into the war in Europe. The WCDA was a subsidiary of the National Federation for Constitutional Liberties, which sought to protect the constitutional rights of trade unions and African Americans. Prichard had joined both of these organizations when he came to Washington, reflecting isolationist stances he had taken at both Princeton and Harvard. Hoover interpreted membership in either group as disloyalty and solicited the assistant to the attorney general to fire all employees in the Justice Department belonging to such organizations.

Although that request was denied, Hoover was prepared when the call came for further information on Prichard. The bureau compiled an extraordinary memo dated March 19, 1941, that ultimately suggested that Prichard had communist sympathies. Hoover's memo set out a comparison of the WPM's and the WCDA's official platforms with those of the Communist party. By quoting similar general phrases and half-phrases, the FBI implied that Prichard was, for all practical purposes, a communist. For example, the Communist party platform supported the "repeal of the vicious anti-alien and sedition laws." The Peace Mobilization's platform likewise called for the "repeal of the anti-alien legislation." Similar phrases demanding an end to the poll tax, war profiteering, support for national health legislation, and antilynch laws were certified proof, to J. Edgar Hoover and the FBI, of Prichard's latent communism and disloyalty to his government. Hoover dispatched a cover letter to Jackson, accompanying the FBI's findings on Prichard, labeled "Personal and Confidential." Hoover wrote, "There is set out in this memorandum a comparison of the program of each of these organizations with that of the Communist Party, which indicates their aims and purposes are substantially the same." Hoover blandly concluded, "I thought you would be interested in having this information in view of the fact that Mr. Prichard is an employee of the Department of Justice."[30]

Attorney General Jackson's increasing dissatisfaction with Prichard never developed beyond interoffice communications. Just as good timing had helped Prichard when Frankfurter was appointed to the Court in 1939, another stroke of fortuitous luck came Prichard's way in June 1941. Before his anger with Prichard could increase, Robert Jackson was nominated by Roosevelt to the High Court. FDR, in turn, nominated none other than Francis Biddle to take over Jackson's role as attorney general. It seemed as though Prichard would have found much to be pleased with in Jackson's departure, but his dissatisfaction with the Justice Department meant he would not remain long, even to work for Biddle. In his last weeks at Justice, Prichard fired off yet another memo to Biddle, this time a bit less caustic. Prichard returned to the area of labor policy and suggested the United States adopt an idea first proposed by J.M. Keynes to establish an interdepartmental agency for settling labor disputes.[31]

Fortune magazine later described succinctly the problem Prichard had at Justice in saying that his "impatience with incompetence and his complete outspokenness put him at odds with conservative elements in the Justice Department."[32] By September 1941, Prichard jumped at the chance to leave Justice and work in the Office of Emergency Management, where he served as senior attorney at a salary of $5,000 in the office of Oscar Cox. Here Prichard had no less an occasion than to work on some of the details of Roosevelt's lend-lease arrangement alongside Cox and Phil Graham.[33] This post, however, lasted only three months. In December, Prichard went to work for an individual whom he had long admired—labor activist Sidney Hillman. Prichard was hired shortly before Pearl Harbor as an assistant general counsel in the Office of Production Management, an agency created by FDR to prepare a weak economy for the likelihood of war. Perhaps best of all, as Hillman's legal adviser, Prichard's outspoken pro-labor views would not be matters for possible firing and FBI background checks.

Indeed, in Hillman, Prichard now had a boss who was not only a major New Deal policymaker, but also in the vanguard of the American labor movement. A Jewish refugee from Czarist Russia, Hillman had spent his young life as a labor organizer. From his post with the Amalgamated Clothing Workers of America, he was one of the country's leading exponents of a new notion of industrial democracy called the "new unionism." This strategy sought not only improvement in working conditions and wage increases but also other far-ranging reforms such as unemployment insurance, labor cooperatives, and pro-labor banking institutions. Instead of a militant and sovereign labor movement that would challenge the state, Hillman advocated a movement that worked within the confines of the state to achieve various long-sought goals. Through Frankfurter, Hillman became FDR's chief liaison with the labor movement and was appointed to a number of government posts, such as the National Recovery Administration's Board in the 1930s. In late 1941 Roosevelt appointed Hillman to the post of Associate Director of the Office of Production Management (OPM). The OPM was created to gear up America's war production for the Allies, as well as to prepare for the likely entry of the United States into the war itself. Roosevelt took the political step of dividing the OPM's decisionmaking powers between Hillman and William Knudsen of General Motors. This "Knudsenhillman" agency lacked substantive power and was early on forced to negotiate with reluctant business leaders over issues like wages, inflation, and production quotas.[34]

Prichard's disenchantment with the Justice Department's policies soon extended to include the OPM. Soon after France fell to the Nazis, Prichard dropped the isolationism he had maintained since Princeton and became a stalwart supporter of intervening in Europe. Ironically, the same man who had earlier incurred the wrath of J. Edgar Hoover for his professed pacifism suddenly became one of Washington's most aggressive supporters of the war. Along with New Dealers such as Leon Henderson, Donald Nelson, Lauchlin Currie, and Robert Nathan, Prichard was a member of a contingent known as the "all-outers" because of their demand that corporate America cut its civilian production in order to prepare for war. According to historian Steven Fraser, within the OPM "the 'all-outers' were a besieged minority." Fraser writes that the OPM "was more a political arrangement designed to fend off contending social interests—labor, the military, private enterprise, and the 'public'—than it was an administrative agency capable of really steering the economy." Another historian hit upon the reason why business looked upon the "all-outers" with such suspicion. The New Dealers, in the eyes of business, threatened the very essence of "business control of the mobilization process." After Pearl Harbor, Roosevelt abolished the OPM and replaced it with the War Production Board (WPB), and Hillman was demoted to head the new agency's labor division, further increasing the defensive posture of the "all-outers" like Prichard.[35]

Business leaders who worked for the wartime agencies were labeled as the much-heralded "dollar-a-year men," implying that these men endured severe financial sacrifice to support the war effort. Of course, they could afford such arrangements with their salaries and executive bonuses still safely in tow. Hillman was anxious over the massive hirings of such leaders by Knudsen and asked Prichard to investigate such personnel matters. To his astonishment, Prichard wrote: "I have found myself incapable of obtaining any relevant or important information regarding them." Prichard suggested to Hillman that he place an aide in a position to "exercise intelligent control over important administrative functions . . . such as personnel."[36]

The relatively exposed condition of the burgeoning labor movement as America entered World War II found a strong defender in Sidney Hillman, who was aided in this regard by his adviser on labor matters, Ed Prichard. A flurry of strikes throughout 1941 had damaged production in a number of American defense industries. After Pearl Harbor, Congress moved swiftly to pass legislation that sought to outlaw strikes. One such bill, the Smith bill, outlawed closed-shop strikes and imposed a series of penalties, such as denying rights afforded by the Wagner Act to boycotters and union members belonging to the Communist party. While Congress spoke of the danger afforded the national defense effort, the underlying sentiment among some thoughtful observers was that this was an attempt to expunge labor representatives like Hillman from the hierarchies of wartime agencies. It was also accepted by labor organizers that business leaders and their representatives in Washington perceived World War II as an optimum time to destroy the American labor movement.

Prichard prepared a memo for Hillman to be sent to the president on the "vicious" provisions contained in the Smith bill. Prichard's memo urged a different approach—one in which the president could be authorized to impose compulsory arbitration. Hillman met with FDR and told the president that such items as the Smith bill would destroy the spirit of cooperation among the rank and file for the war effort. When the president refused to intervene and oppose the Smith bill, Hillman then relied on his memo from Prichard to encourage the president to take a more moderate approach. These acts, however, failed to overcome the patriotic antiunion avalanche that overcame the nation during the war years. The Smith Act was enacted in 1943 over FDR's veto, and the administration established the National Defense Mediation Board, which subsequently usurped a good deal of labor's collective bargaining muscle.[37]

Prichard also found himself in some compromising positions within his post at the WPB. When a management-labor conference was called shortly after America's entry into the war, Prichard was selected to serve as a secretary to the deliberations. The conference was significant in that it produced labor's famous no-strike pledge for the duration of the war. Columnist Drew Pearson attended and observed the following situation. As one of the sessions approached noon, Prichard was instructed to tell the conferees that they were to be the guests of Labor Secretary Frances Perkins. At the appointed time, Prichard broke into the session and announced, "Gentlemen, if you will take the elevator to the right, you will find cars waiting to take you to the Labor Department for lunch with Miss Perkins." His admonition was not heard above the din of noise, so Prichard repeated his plea louder. Again no one heard. For a third time, Prichard shouted to the audience his admonition for lunch and to please take the elevator. Whereupon an irritated John L. Lewis looked at Prichard and asked, "Young man, are you studying to be a Pullman conductor?" Afterward, Lewis told a delegate, "Some say this Prichard is a Frankfurter man. Others that he is a Hillman man. I don't know which is worse."[38]

Although he may not have commanded the respect of Lewis, Prichard's reputation soared within a growing circle of talented young New Dealers—both inside and outside of the WPB. Along with Nathan, Currie, Rauh, Leon Henderson, and other "young turks," Prichard met every Monday evening in Nathan's 18th Street apartment to discuss the growing influence of industry in the war effort. Nathan described Prichard's mind as "bifurcated" between "knowledge and strategy." In these meetings, Prichard was "a powerhouse" whose greatest strength was planning strategy to implement the economists' suggestions, Nathan recalled. Of all those within the group, Prichard had the best contacts within the Washington press corps. This self-described "goon squad" provided an arena for some of Washington's brightest and most ambitious supporters of all-out mobilization to discuss strategies.[39]

An example of what made Ed Prichard impressive to even a hardened veteran of the labor movement like Hillman came shortly after he hired Prichard. The young lawyer advised Hillman on current labor policy and made some rather prescient suggestions for future action. Prichard stated that "labor's interest demands the formulation of a national policy which will protect the workers' share of the national income and at the same time prevent the disastrous accentuation of inflationary pressure." Prichard then advocated a five-part program that included increased taxes on the wealthy, a rationing program of vital resources, and wage stabilization. Prichard added that he feared workers did not have full confidence in the pledges made in the "no-strike pledge." One of the factors contributing to labor unrest, Prichard claimed, "is the current rise in living costs." No matter how earnestly the leaders of labor attempted to carry out the no-strike policy, Prichard said, "their efforts will not be effective unless the workers themselves are convinced that the results of this policy are fair to them." Otherwise, Prichard concluded, "this will be pictured as a rich man's war but a poor man's fight."[40] Prichard was at his best in such ways—formulating an informed and precise analysis of political realities fused with a genuine concern for basic democratic principles, and finally, a program of creative and bold action.

Unfortunately for Prichard, his memo to Hillman went to an individual whose power and influence to effect the changes he desired was quickly diminishing. Historian Nelson Lichtenstein writes that Hillman's labor division at the WPB had become little more than "a service organization that sought to resolve labor problems created by the production boom." In time, Hillman saw his role within the mobilization process diminished as the role of "dollar-a-year men" increased. Prichard's increasing frustration was palpable, and he looked for better opportunities within Washington. He wrote several speeches for Florida congressman Claude Pepper, and he began hammering out memos to well-placed individuals outside the WPB on the issues he had raised with Hillman. In April 1942 he wrote a four-page memo to Wayne Coy, a man whom *Time* had called one of the "most important men around the president in 1942." Prichard wrote that "the time is ripe for a national policy of economic stabilization." Again, Prichard called for an affirmative rationing policy, a general price freeze, "a tax program based on ability to pay," and additional income taxes, including a 100 percent excess-profits tax. Prichard, echoing Keynes, even suggested a "more radical measure"—compulsory savings. Such a withholding levy would be available after the war as "the President found it desirable to feed new purchasing power into the economy." Such a program, Prichard advised, "would serve two ends: to sterilize purchasing power now, and to provide a 'kitty' for the post-war economy."[41]

Prichard also communicated with another well-placed New Dealer, the assistant solicitor general, Oscar Cox. In a memo labeled "Strictly Confidential," Prichard congratulated Cox on having helped write an executive order establishing the Office of Economic Stabilization (OES). The OES was given extraordinary wartime powers over the national economy. The new OES director, Supreme Court Justice James F. Byrnes of South Carolina, was granted sweeping domestic economic power that had final authority over wages, rents, prices, salaries, profits, and subsidies. Owing to his powerful perch, Byrnes was labeled the "assistant president" by the press, and his biographer writes that by 1942 "Roosevelt by executive order turned over to Byrnes the management of the civilian economy." In writing to Cox, Prichard pitched, once again, his own plans for a tax program and a "rationing of expenditures." Prichard also took time to praise director Byrnes: "I think the new director can render a great service and one which is wholly relevant to his job. Furthermore, it is one for which his talents peculiarly fit him." An impressed Cox replied, "Your letter of yesterday contains some good ideas. I will see what I can do about getting them across."[42]

If Prichard had been writing such memos in hope of being placed in the newly created and powerful OES, his efforts had their Machiavellian effect. In late October 1942, he resigned his post at the WPB and became head attorney in OES Director Byrnes's office. In addition to the well-timed memos and Prichard's growing legal reputation, it was also fortunate that Byrnes's closest friend on the High Court was Frankfurter. Prichard's job description read: "To furnish legal advice to the Economic Stabilization Director . . . and to prepare legal briefs and legal opinions on the most difficult, important, and complex questions and problems arising out of or in connection with the functional programs, operations, and affairs of the OES." Furthermore, he received the princely salary of $7,000 and moved over to Byrnes's office, located in the east wing of the White House.[43]

The prominence of Prichard's new position attracted the attention of Newsweek, which described Prichard as one who "knows everyone in town, and is already famous for his Southern drawl, chain-cigar smoking, anecdotes, and prodigious memory."[44] Prichard was now working in close relation to Byrnes's two assistant directors, Ben Cohen and Donald Russell. Just a little over four years out of law school, Prichard now had a White House office and a job description that suited his ambitious plans. After enduring an obstinate attorney general and a declining figurehead at the WPB, Prichard was now atop the hierarchy of one of the most powerful agencies in Washington and worked for a man whose power came second only to that of the president's. As a boy growing up in Paris, Kentucky, Ed Prichard had envisioned himself one day as a participant in the politics of the county courthouse. Now, as a young man, Prichard was ready to exercise more power than any of the local politicians in Bourbon County had ever imagined. And he was all of twenty-seven years old.

5 The Wunderkind

WHEN Franklin Roosevelt asked James F. Byrnes to leave his seat on the Supreme Court and assume the directorship of the new Office of Economic Stabilization (OES), he did so with the certain knowledge that he would be handing over to Byrnes some of the most sweeping economic power ever given to an appointed individual in American history. The OES's stated mission was to maintain wartime production while "holding the line" on inflation. Unlike many of his other appointments, FDR did not create hierarchic tension or shared power in the OES. Instead, the president placed his full confidence in Byrnes to control the domestic economic front while FDR maintained vigil over the war.

In his new position in the OES, Prichard found himself working with one of the singular southern politicians of the era. James Francis Byrnes came from humble beginnings in Charleston, South Carolina. The son of a seamstress, Byrnes was told by his mother to learn shorthand as a way of escaping poverty. While he acceded to his mother's wishes, Byrnes's real interests were in politics. He rose within his state's, and then the nation's, Democratic party on a scale eclipsed by only a handful of twentieth-century politicians. After serving in the U.S. House, Byrnes was elected to the U.S. Senate in 1930 and became Franklin Roosevelt's principal ally in the mid-1930s in passing crucial New Deal legislation. Byrnes's power in the Senate rested not only on his considerable legislative skills, but also on the financial backing of millionaire Bernard Baruch. Byrnes had presidential ambitions of his own in 1940, but backed off upon FDR's decision to run for a third term. His loyalty to Roosevelt was rewarded in 1941, when the president named the South Carolinian to the U.S. Supreme Court. Although Byrnes had not graduated from college and had no formal law degree, the Senate quickly confirmed one of their own without even conducting hearings. Yet after a dissatisfying first year on the high bench, Byrnes was receptive to Roosevelt's queries concerning the newly minted OES. When Roosevelt offered him the job of directing the executive agency, Byrnes quickly gave up his lifetime court appointment to join the political fray again and, in the process, become a contender for a future Democratic nomination for president.[1]

Byrnes's relatively small staff at OES was a remarkable one. Donald Russell came to Washington after having worked in Byrnes's old law firm in Spartan-burg, South Carolina. Samuel Lubell had worked for Baruch and served Byrnes as a writer and researcher. Clearly, the foremost man in Byrnes's office was Benjamin V. Cohen, the author of some of the New Deal's early legislation. Cohen had graduated Phi Beta Kappa from the University of Chicago after three years of study and then earned a law degree from Chicago and a rare Ph.D. from the Harvard Law School. At Harvard, Cohen became a close as-sociate of Felix Frankfurter, who helped his young protégé obtain employ-ment in FDR's New Deal in the early 1930s. With Thomas Corcoran, Cohen had written the Securities and Exchange Act and the Public Utilities Holding Act. Some in Washington referred to the team of Cohen and Corcoran as "a sort of semi-autonomous fourth level of government." A shy and humble man, Cohen became one of Roosevelt's most trusted aides. In 1941, when writing to Cohen about accepting an important post, FDR made it clear that he saw Cohen as indispensable: "I am not asking you to do this," the president wrote. "I am telling you!" By the time he came to Byrnes's office in 1942, Cohen was one of the most trusted, seasoned, and brilliant legal minds in Washington.[2]

Prichard's entrée into the OES came, of course, through his connections with Frankfurter. Byrnes's closest association while on the Court, in fact, was with "F.F." Thomas Corcoran told Harold Ickes that Prichard's appointment by Byrnes was owed directly to the intervention of Frankfurter, and Prichard likewise echoed this by noting that he owed his position to his old professor. Early on, Corcoran felt Prichard was out of his league in this capacity, to which Ickes agreed, saying that Prichard "was not the person for an executive job." "Besides which," Ickes knew, "he talks too much."[3] In a short time, however, Corcoran came to see Prichard in a more favorable light. Not surprisingly, Prichard and Ben Cohen developed a close friendship that extended well be-yond Prichard's tenure in Washington. The two shared brilliant minds as well as similar political ideologies. The same, however, could not be said for Prichard's relationship with his new boss.

Although Byrnes was devoted to Roosevelt, he was not a fully confirmed New Dealer. In the late 1930s, Byrnes's southern roots took precedence over his loyalty to FDR. He voted against child-labor legislation and had stated on the Senate floor that a proposed antilynch bill was actually "a bill to arouse ill-feeling between the sections, inspire race hatred in the South, and destroy the Democratic Party." But of all issues, Byrnes and Prichard were on record diametrically opposed to each other on the matter of labor. Byrnes had vehe-mently opposed the CIO and introduced a bill in 1937 to outlaw the sit-down strike. The South Carolina senator was an especial enemy of none other than Sidney Hillman, and the two clashed on repeated occasions. In 1944, in fact, Hillman played perhaps the decisive role in aborting Byrnes's vice presidential candidacy and, in turn, keeping him from the oval office upon FDR's death in 1945. If Prichard had had troubles with his former boss, Robert H. Jackson, the same prospects loomed at the OES.[4]

But the Ed Prichard who came to the OES in 1942 was somewhat different from the man who had worked in the attorney general's office almost two years earlier. He had even more political savvy and no longer audaciously sent off biting memos to his boss complaining of the treatment afforded communists. Also, Byrnes would have been even less tolerant than Jackson of Prichard's "reckless" behavior. Prichard's Washington colleagues soon noticed a subtle change. In a magazine article later published on Prichard, friends observed that he was "growing up" since leaving Hillman's office. Byrnes, it was further noticed, objected if his assistants went "to too many cocktail parties" and especially to those who were "inclined to talk too much." Another example of Prichard's changing habits was in attending a nearby clinic in 1942 in a futile attempt to lose weight.[5]

There were other changes on Prichard's horizon. Although he left the Hockley estate in 1942, he did not go for long without yet another brilliant roommate, the British philosopher Isaiah Berlin. Prichard had earlier met Berlin through their mutual friend, Phil Graham, when Berlin worked in the British Embassy. After he moved out of Hockley, Prichard shared a rented Georgetown house with the British political philosopher. In Berlin, Prichard had a roommate who could easily match his brilliance, just as Phil Graham had. Such daily contact with Berlin was the rarefied air to which Prichard grew accustomed. Berlin felt that Prichard was "extremely intelligent, very human, very liberal-minded, and very funny." Berlin also remarked that Prichard held "stern principles" on political matters, and although he remained "left of the New Deal," by this time he had also developed a very strong anticommunist bent. Berlin also remembered Prichard's sense of humor, particularly his impression of Herbert Hoover. "We laughed and laughed and laughed," remembered Berlin about his time with Prichard. The two often attended parties in each other's company. Arthur Schlesinger Jr. was present at one of these parties. He remarked that Prichard and Berlin "sat next to each other on a large sofa, exchanging gossip, witticisms, recondite literary and philosophical allusions, and ruminations about the war and about the future." Schlesinger added that "the rest of us listened in fascination, each set the other off as in one of those fireworks displays where each rocket shoots higher in the sky than the one before and leaves an ever more glittering trail of light and color behind." Schlesinger concluded, "I thought then I had never heard such conversation. Perhaps I have not heard its equal since."[6]

Prichard worked in a heady world, where each day offered its own brand of excitement. One day while at his desk in the White House, he received a call from Frankfurter, who simply said, "You must come up here right away. It's terribly important!" Prichard quickly hailed a cab and made his way up Capitol Hill to Frankfurter's chambers. There, an exasperated Prichard found the justice having lunch with Navy Secretary Frank Knox. Frankfurter told his former clerk he had been telling Knox of Prichard's imitation of John L. Lewis and wondered if Prichard could do it for Knox there on the spot.[7]

Prichard's wit and devastating impressions quickly became known throughout Washington. His wide grasp of Washington politics and his profound memory also never failed to impress ever more people. One outlet for his energies after work was the prestigious Cosmos Club, located off Lafayette Square. Here Prichard often dined with administration insiders such as Cohen, Leon Henderson, Harry Dexter White, and Mordecai Ezekiel. Jonathan Daniels saw Prichard at the Cosmos Club during one of these dinners and described him as a "Falstaff figure of a man." Daniels later sat in awe of the young Kentuckian as he and White discussed African politics in vivid detail over lunch.[8]

Although many young Washingtonians were deeply impressed by the young Kentuckian, he still had a cagey, conservative boss at OES who was not so overwhelmed. There was no doubt in anyone's mind that James Byrnes was in charge at OES. But because of its numerous duties, Byrnes's small staff played significant roles in determining policy and officiating in wage or price disputes. While Cohen was, in effect, the "chief of staff," Prichard managed to find himself sitting in for Byrnes in various meetings. John Kenneth Galbraith, the head of price control, first encountered Prichard at this time when the young attorney represented Byrnes in meetings over price control. Food rationing soon came to occupy much of Prichard's time at OES.[9]

Prichard usually left those he encountered with one of two polarized impressions. Galbraith, for example, found in Prichard "a combination of insight, persuasion, laced with humor and occasional and frequent resort to absurdity." Galbraith remembered that in Washington in the early 1940s it was not uncommon to hear people talking about "what Prich had said the night before." On the other hand, others were not quite so impressed with someone they considered to be an arrogant know-it-all. Eliot Janeway referred to Prichard as a New Dealer who was not interested in ideas alone. In Janeway's estimation, Prichard's only concern with ideas was "in their exploitation." Carl Hamilton, an assistant in the Food Administration office, was also not overly fond of having the young staffer from Byrnes's office sitting in on matters of food policy: "We allegedly rolled out the carpet for him, and he sat there like a stuffed owl, and looked like one a little bit," Hamilton recalled. In an off-handed reference to Prichard's considerable reputation, Hamilton added, "We kind of refused to be impressed with the genius he was alleged to be."[10]

Within the Department of Agriculture, many more officials shared Hamilton's views of Prichard than Galbraith's. In meetings with Prichard over food rationing, in fact, Agriculture Secretary Claude Wickard grew impatient with Prichard. Wickard recalled that Prichard "had the idea that he knew everything, and that anything anyone else suggested should be examined very carefully and with great suspicion." Wickard's objection to Prichard's attendance in agriculture meetings was that "he didn't know anything about farming, but that didn't bother him a bit." Wickard developed a rather intense dislike for Prichard, whom he accused of liking "to see people suffer who opposed him." Chester Davis, who became war food administrator in March 1943, felt Prichard "had much more authority over food policy than I did." Davis added that Prichard had a profound role in determining food policy because "being in the White House, having access to those who had access to the President if not actually exercising it himself, he could cook up programs, policies, decisions which were as good as edicts. We had no chance even to discuss them."[11]

Prichard's behind-the-scenes role in Byrnes's office can be gleaned from a few references made by his contemporaries. Another administrator in the War Food Office, Jesse W. Tapp, labeled Prichard one of the "masterminds" in creating the overall food subsidy program. In another instance, an irritated Claude Wickard accused Prichard of convincing Byrnes to order a ceiling placed on the price of hogs in order to increase demand for corn from meat packers. Wickard fought the idea but lost, seeing no connection between corn prices and hogs. In language often used by Prichard's critics who resented his superior intellect and, above all, his willingness to expose the weaker minds of his adversaries, Wickard displayed a certain resentfulness: "Prichard was always one of these fellows who is always the smart boy, always has all the answers."[12]

But Prichard was not in the OES because of his knowledge of hogs or corn. At bottom, he was a shrewd political adviser. As an example of his powerful perch within the OES, Prichard advised Byrnes concerning a difficult situation arising out of a serious railway dispute that had serious repercussions throughout the economy, and had to be brokered eventually by FDR himself. The chairman of an emergency presidential commission, the National Railway Labor Panel, had urged the OES to approve an eight-cent-per-hour wage increase for railway workers. Considering Roosevelt's presidential order to "hold the line" on inflation, Byrnes denied previous requests from other labor groups for wage increases, incurring the wrath of labor leaders. Prichard told Byrnes that "acceptance of the report would completely destroy the confidence of any labor organization in the national wage policy and would completely undo anything we may have accomplished." Prichard then spelled out in clear lan-

guage the political dynamics involved in making a decision on the wage increase:

> The question, therefore, is what to do about the report. We must not minimize
> the repercussions that will follow from its rejection. Railroad labor is powerful,
> articulate, and politically effective. One million men are involved in this case—
> more than in any other case considered by the War Labor Board since this office
> was set up. There will be a tremendous kickback if this report is rejected.
>
> Acceptance, on the other hand, would court complete disaster for the stabi-
> lization program. With the railroad unions and the miners rolling in gravy, there
> would be no holding back AF of L, CIO, the farm bloc, the retailers.[13]

This memo revealed why Prichard—despite his bombast and relative inexperience—was a significant resource to a man like Byrnes. Suggestions that
Prichard was nothing more than a conduit for the CIO and Sidney Hillman
are evidentially thin in this instance. As counsel to the OES, Prichard was no
labor partisan and presented the political risks, long and short term, involved
for the OES director in making a difficult decision. Byrnes sided with Prichard's
memo and later referred to "the evil precedent" the pay raise would establish
during the war. In his memoirs, Byrnes's analysis of the railway crisis seems
lifted almost out of Prichard's memo: "The crux of the matter was whether
the yardstick to measure wage increases of railway employees should be different from that applied to all other occupations."[14]

But Prichard was certainly not shifting toward the political center. During these months in Byrnes's office, he attended weekly lunches with a group
of young Democrats working in sundry New Deal and wartime agencies
around Washington. Among those dining with Prichard were Lauchlin Currie,
Oscar Cox, and James Rowe. All occupied impressive posts within the administration. Currie, a distinguished economist, was an administrative assistant
to the president. Cox held a series of high-level posts and was very close to
Harry Hopkins, while Rowe had been a law clerk for Oliver Wendell Holmes
and was a personal adviser to FDR. Carl Hamilton referred to the members
of this group as "representing some of the more extreme liberal thinking of
the administration."[15]

Of all the people Prichard met in Washington, the one who emerged as
his chief political mentor was Thomas G. "Tommy the Cork" Corcoran. The
two shared some striking similarities. Both were brilliant students in college—
Corcoran had graduated at the head of his class at Brown University in 1921.
Both had performed spectacularly at Harvard Law School, where they came
under the guidance of Felix Frankfurter. In 1926, Corcoran had clerked for
Oliver Wendell Holmes. Both Prichard and Corcoran even shared the early
nickname of "Sonny." Above all, both loved the intrigue and the drama of

power politics. Corcoran later summarized his years in the White House by saying, "I was always on the edges of things . . . never completely responsible, but always the fellow who tried to fix little things that happened."[16] Such a description could, of course, have been applied to Prichard. Just as Sonny Prichard had attached himself to Pearce Paton to learn the world of the county courthouse, Corcoran had volumes to teach Prichard about the interior dynamics of Washington politics.

In 1933 Corcoran emerged as a central figure in the New Deal, helping write some of the earliest legislation sponsored by FDR. Like Prichard, Corcoran was a skilled speechwriter and had acquired the nickname of "the phrasemaker of the Potomac." Through his access to the White House, Corcoran recruited dozens of other Harvard alumni to staff the various agencies. Corcoran's tactics at times left something to be desired. James Rowe recalled that Corcoran pounded on FDR's desk when the president refused to go along with Corcoran's advice. "No one," Rowe observed, "ever pounded the desk with Roosevelt." By the time of Roosevelt's third term, Corcoran had left the administration to practice law in Washington. Here Corcoran continued to exercise power, using his considerable contacts and connections to serve him as a highly paid lobbyist. Although he had displayed some liberal notions while in the New Deal, he quickly changed following his departure from the government. One historian wrote that "initially claiming to be a proponent of an activist government committed to the public good," Corcoran then spent the remainder of his life "trying to circumvent or exploit for private gain the laws and regulations that government established."[17]

There was also an expressed component of realpolitik in Corcoran that drew parallels with Prichard's own methods. Corcoran once said there was not enough time to persuade others on every possible political issue. By necessity, then, one "must deceive, misrepresent, leave false impressions—even, sometimes, lie—and trust to charm, loyalty, and the result to make up for it." Corcoran ended this admonition by referring to a quote that Prichard knew well—"a great man cannot be a good man." Corcoran exhibited an ends-justify-the-means brand of cynicism that irritated a good many New Dealers. He grew tired of what he termed the "unthinking left," or the members of the New Deal who looked askance at Corcoran's own somewhat ruthless methods. Corcoran described this group as volatile—"If at any moment you're not 100 percent overboard on the immediate 'line' of their ideological semantics," Corcoran claimed, "they are 200 percent against you as a traitor to 'your own ideals.'" In his later years, Corcoran was also not above lobbying the justices themselves for his corporate clients with cases pending before the Supreme Court.[18]

It is interesting to note that at this juncture Prichard had numerous political and intellectual protégés but had chosen only two mentors—Frankfurter and Corcoran. By selecting these two men as his chief political tutors, Prichard made it obvious that ideological compatibility was not his chief criterion, either in Cambridge or in Washington. Several traits were consistent in "F.F." and "Tommy the Cork"—they were both brilliant, politically shrewd, and early devotees of FDR. But one quality, above all, made these men the perfect mentors for Ed Prichard—they knew everyone. While Prichard could have sought out mentors among other powerful people that he knew—Sidney Hillman or Byrnes, for example—he instead chose two men who were both intellectual heavyweights and well-connected political animals. Both of his mentors felt equally at home, like Prichard, in discussing recent appellate court decisions or the latest personal gossip about a State Department official. Not only did they have much to teach Prichard, but both could maneuver their eager young student into virtually any powerful corridor in Washington.

Considering Prichard's inclination to form friendships with those who were essentially well connected and ambitious, it seemed natural he would also become well acquainted with a young Texas congressman, Lyndon Baines Johnson. At the time, many New Dealers saw LBJ as a bright star on the liberal horizon. Joe Rauh, for example, said that the Texan "had a tremendous reputation for liberal leanings" in the early 1940s. At this point in his career, Johnson was a frustrated congressman, having been narrowly defeated for the U.S. Senate in 1940. Always attuned to rising figures within the administration, Johnson quickly latched on to the young Kentuckian working in the White House. In turn, Prichard saw the young Texan as a proper source for congressional information.[19]

Of all the attributes associated with Prichard during his Washington years—raconteur, adviser, wit—the one that caused concern with Byrnes and others was his frequent leaking of news stories to reporters. Claude Wickard remarked that "the first day Prichard ever showed up I wouldn't talk in his presence." Wickard had heard from others that Prichard loved to talk with reporters. Paul McNutt, who was head of the War Manpower Commission, felt so worried about Prichard's leaking stories that he banned Prichard from some high-level meetings. Thomas Emerson felt Prichard talked to reporters "for purposes of creating a backfire, or letting people know what was happening, or for a hatchet job on some person." Many young politicos enjoy the self-importance that comes from serving as a trusted source to a journalist, but Prichard relished the role to a degree that acquired a certain folk image for the Kentuckian in Washington.[20]

Perhaps the most celebrated story about Ed Prichard deals with precisely this point. President Roosevelt was once angered by a leak that had occurred on some pending legislation. He summoned numerous members of the White

House staff to the Oval Office for a thorough tongue-lashing. Prichard related that "he put the fear of God into us." After threatening offending staff members with dire consequences if further leaking occurred, the president then leaned back and said that he understood that there were some discreet times when a well-timed leak could be beneficial. Roosevelt then mentioned a particular item that should be leaked, perhaps to columnist Drew Pearson, in order to understand how various legislators would respond. The president glared around the room and stared at the conspicuous presence of Prichard and said, "Prichard, couldn't you manage to do that?" "Mr. President," Prichard replied, "I already have." Roosevelt "seemed to like that," Prichard remembered.[21]

Even if Roosevelt found Prichard's journalistic indiscretions somewhat amusing, Byrnes did not. Although the two sometimes lunched together at the Cosmos Club, Byrnes and Prichard were never close. Friends had already commented that Byrnes was displeased with staff members who "talked too much" at parties. Prichard's visible links with the left wing of the New Deal also did not endear him to Byrnes. Marvin Jones noted that Byrnes "did not have complete confidence in Prichard's judgment and indicated he was not going to keep him."[22]

Prichard did not always leak material to journalists—he sometimes leaked information to other politicians to manipulate policy decisions. In 1943 he did so in an act that Eliot Janeway termed "the most flagrant act of surreptitious insubordination in the history of the Roosevelt administration." The matter centered around the staffing of Prichard's most recent former employer, the War Production Board. Within the WPB, an internal struggle emerged by late 1942 that pitted two contrasting views concerning the war economy.

One side was espoused by Ferdinand Eberstadt, who wanted to narrow the WPB's authority over allocations. Eberstadt controlled the WPB's raw materials allocation and strongly supported the military's belief that war production should not be pressed too quickly. Carefully controlling the allocation of raw materials, in Eberstadt's view, stabilized production to acceptable levels desired by both the military and private industry. Opposing Eberstadt was former General Electric president Charles Wilson, the WPB's director of production. Wilson supported a broader mission for the WPB that expanded production for the military at levels that worried some profit-minded industrialists. WPB chairman Donald Nelson came down on Wilson's side, and the administration soon had to contend with an ever-broadening debate within the WPB. In essence, the struggle over production within the WPB was a defining moment in the war, asking whether the war economy should be headed by industrialists, who advocated "stable" mobilization, or by "all-outers" in the government, who demanded full and immediate mobilization. At another level, the WPB struggle presented in stark terms the question of whether the WPB would be controlled by civilians or by the military.

Within the highest echelons of the administration, the WPB internecine conflict became a brushfire that needed to be quickly extinguished. Numerous powerful insiders were satisfied that Eberstadt's notions carried the day. An intimidating array of cabinet members and advisers—Navy Undersecretary James Forrestal, Assistant Secretary of War Robert Patterson, Secretary of War Henry Stimson, Navy Secretary Frank Knox, and Byrnes—all counseled the president to fire the hapless Nelson and replace him with financier Bernard Baruch, a staunch conservative who would bring Eberstadt in as his deputy director. Underlying this group's feelings was the notion, best stated by Stimson, that "if you are going to go to war in a capitalist country, you have to let business make money out of the process or business won't work."[23] FDR apparently agreed and had Byrnes deliver the offer to Baruch in New York in early February 1943. After several days of considering the president's offer, Baruch came to Washington to meet with Roosevelt and formally accept the offer.

But before Baruch's meeting with the president on the afternoon of February 17, Nelson shocked knowledgeable Washington insiders by suddenly firing Eberstadt and replacing him with Wilson. Eberstadt's dismissal effectively undercut Roosevelt's plan and left the president with a daunting political challenge. To fire Nelson that very afternoon and replace him with Baruch would now appear a direct repudiation of Charles Wilson and an implicit support of Eberstadt—a man who had once refused to carry out a request from FDR. Bruce Catton wrote that Roosevelt may have been "ready to go along with the elevation of Eberstadt, as part of the general reshuffle, but with Eberstadt out he would not bring him back in."[24] With little time to consider the implications of firing Nelson, and not wishing to appear as simply reacting to Nelson's move, Roosevelt balked. When Baruch arrived for his scheduled meeting that afternoon, the president obfuscated—he rambled on about the Middle East and then quickly excused himself to attend another meeting. A thoroughly befuddled and humiliated Baruch left Roosevelt's office without being offered anything.

What had happened? Administration officials shook their heads at Nelson's newfound political acumen, while journalists could only speculate on who could have masterminded the episode. To Eliot Janeway, however, there was no mystery. In recounting the story, Janeway placed the responsibility for Nelson's actions squarely at the feet of Ed Prichard. After learning of Byrnes's trip to New York and its message, Janeway charged that Prichard leaked the news of Nelson's upcoming dismissal to his friend, Bob Nathan. Nathan then informed Nelson of his imminent firing and suggested that he counteract Roosevelt's plans by firing Eberstadt. That suggestion, according to Janeway, originated from Prichard. While Prichard and other "all-outers" were not overly impressed with the politically inept Nelson, they were more frightened by the prospects of a Baruch-Eberstadt cabal heading the WPB. In Janeway's estimation, Prichard's behind-the-scenes manipulations revealed the workings of "a Machiavellian genius" who "dared to bluff the president" and, in turn, embarrass Baruch and "betray" Byrnes.[25]

Prichard's actions concerning Nelson saved the WPB chairman's job temporarily. A frustrated Roosevelt—who told Nelson later that day that "he was not dissatisfied" with Nelson's performance—soon thereafter outflanked any more moves within the WPB. On May 28, 1943, Roosevelt signed an executive order that created a new war agency that superseded the WPB entirely, the Office of War Mobilization (OWM). Roosevelt gave the job of directing this new superagency to Byrnes. The South Carolinian now held authority over all civilian manpower matters, including the power to settle disputes between military branches over procurement. Byrnes also managed to persuade the president to allow his office to remain in the east wing of the White House, while the OES was transferred to the Federal Reserve building. In a revealing move, Byrnes had his entire staff at OES transferred to OWM, including his stenographer and chauffeur, with the notable exception of Ed Prichard.[26]

Byrnes's decision to leave Prichard behind seemed to end the young prodigy's bureaucratic rise to power. But again, propitious timing saved Prichard. When Roosevelt named Kentuckian Fred Vinson to succeed Byrnes at OES, it allowed Prichard a certain reprieve. For Vinson, the appointment was the first in a series of promotions that would lead to the chief justiceship of the Supreme Court. The rather obscure Vinson had been born in Louisa, Kentucky, in 1890, the son of the town jailer. Vinson later liked to tell the story of the chief justice who was born in a jail. He received a law degree from Centre College in Danville, Kentucky, where he played on the varsity baseball team with Prichard's father. In fact, after shortstop Vinson played well in the field during a game in 1909, the local newspaper wrongly attributed his performance to Big Ed. After practicing law, he won a seat in the U.S. House in 1924. During the 1930s, Vinson had been a faithful New Dealer, cosponsoring the Guffey Coal Act and strongly supporting Social Security and various wage bills. Vinson had also acquired considerable political dexterity in sitting on the all-powerful House Ways and Means Committee. In 1938 Roosevelt appointed Vinson to the Court of Appeals in Washington. Vinson was then named the chief judge of the U.S. Emergency Court of Appeals, which heard cases involving price-control disputes. He had been a judge for seven years when Roosevelt, as he had done with Byrnes, asked him to leave the lifetime security of the bench and direct OES.[27]

For the next two and a half years, Vinson and Prichard forged a close professional and personal relationship. The new director promoted Prichard to the position of general counsel of OES, thus increasing Prichard's prominence in the agency. Although Byrnes had never extended broad power to Prichard, Vinson allowed the young Kentuckian much wider latitude. Prichard would therefore be at the center of some of the country's most pivotal economic decisions during the final months of World War II. More so than any other single individual in Washington, Fred Vinson was responsible for placing Prichard in his most powerful assignments. Vinson later said that Prichard "had the brightest mind of anybody I was ever exposed to." In short, the New Deal wunderkind blossomed under the brooding eyes of Fred Vinson.[28]

Before Prichard could firmly establish himself in Director Vinson's office, another matter imposed itself on Prichard's career—military service. In the summer of 1943, a manpower shortage threatened America's military capability. The twenty-eight-year-old Prichard had been rejected for military service earlier because of his weight, but was reclassified and eligible for the draft by the summer of 1943. Eliot Janeway, however, interpreted Prichard's draft notice as punishment for the Nelson-Baruch imbroglio. Prichard was inducted into the U.S. Army at Fort Custer, Michigan, as a buck private on August 18, 1943. Before he left town, Prichard made a well-known quip about his role in the manpower shortage that delighted Washingtonians and made *Newsweek* magazine. "They've scraped the bottom of the manpower barrel," Prichard remarked, "now they've drafted the barrel!"[29]

But underlying the humorous self-deprecation was the reality that Prichard's physical condition was very poor for a twenty-eight-year-old. He quickly realized the degree to which he could not handle the simplest physical rigors of military service. By the end of his first day, he confessed to Phil Graham, "I was in anguish." After a conditioning hike, Prichard needed an army truck to come to his aid after running the first mile. "They didn't even ask Christ to go the second mile," he later quipped. By the third day, Prichard added, "my top sergeant divined the depths of my incapacity and took me to the medicos for probing." Prichard was diagnosed with a back ailment and was subsequently hospitalized. "Never again shall I impeach the truly democratic character of our citizen army," Prichard said. "Think of it, two colonels looking out for the health of a mere private. It couldn't happen anywhere but the United States." Whatever the nature of his injury, Prichard's bedridden month in the U.S. Army was mercifully cut short when he was given a medical discharge on September 20, 1943, whereupon he promptly returned to Washington and resumed his duties for OES.[30]

Prichard's military stay may have benefited him in other, indirect ways. Marvin McIntyre, President Roosevelt's secretary, complained to Jonathan Daniels in the fall of 1943 of continuing damaging leaks within the administration. McIntyre confessed that he had previously been certain Prichard was ultimately responsible, but since the leaks continued while Prichard was away in the service, the young Kentuckian was off the hook, at least temporarily.[31]

The task confronting the OES in 1943 was a daunting one, and Vinson desperately needed the talents of the young but cagey politico. Roosevelt's "hold the line" order was being pushed to the limits by organized labor, which advocated higher wages, and by business, which wanted higher prices. The administration opposed both for fear of inflation. Considering its no-win situation, the OES was a highly powerful, yet at the same time unpopular, agency. Furthermore, sensitive disputes involving the National War Labor Board and the Office of Price Administration (OPA) were ultimately decided by Vinson's office. Vinson considered FDR's "hold the line" order nothing short of a papal bull and was adamant in keeping inflation under control. Little wonder, then, that in time Vinson came to be known as the "most hated man in America."[32]

Vinson delegated a number of matters to his staff, and Prichard enjoyed the influence he had on the present director, something he certainly had not had with Byrnes. But Prichard's influence with Vinson was a matter of resentment among many other agencies and individuals in Washington. Chester Davis remarked that he did not mind having to accept the decisions of Vinson, but he hated the notion that Prichard was making a number of the decisions for his distracted boss. "He just could not accept decisions by Prichard," claimed Marvin Jones of Davis, since Prichard "made most of the decisions as to agriculture." The topic of corn prices, which had irritated Claude Wickard, now came under Prichard's domain more than ever before. Prichard convinced Vinson to approve a directive to lower price ceilings for corn. Such seemingly mundane matters should not be quickly dismissed. For American farmers, such actions had profound effects, and they waited anxiously for OES directives on prices. These directives, on numerous occasions, came originally from the desk of the young general counsel to Vinson.[33]

Prichard impressed more than just his boss. Thomas Emerson, who was at OPA and later worked in the OES, described Prichard as "a person of amazing intellectual capacity," someone who "comprehended the implications of problems, piercing through the surface of issues and understanding what was actually occurring in practice." On the other hand, Emerson knew Prichard "did not refrain from advancing audacious ideas." But when the time came to work on a policy, Prichard was no rigid ideologue: "He was entirely reasonable," remembers Emerson, "and was extremely effective on the whole."[34]

In one of the first decisions made by Vinson at OES, Prichard's influence was mightily felt. Shortly before leaving office, Prichard had discussed with Byrnes the matter of raising wages for railway workers. Now with Vinson at

the OES helm, Prichard renewed his battle to veto the panel's recommendation in spite of its political costs. Vinson followed Prichard's advice, although
it is doubtful that he had to have his arm twisted. The railway workers were
angered by Vinson's actions and threatened a nationwide strike. The railway
union's leader, William Leiserson, met unsuccessfully with OES staff, and before Christmas, Roosevelt himself became involved in negotiating a settlement
with Leiserson and the OES. When some within the railroad union refused
to heed Roosevelt's negotiations, the president directed Secretary of War Henry
Stimson to seize the railroads and operate them under emergency war powers. The use of troops facilitated a satisfactory arbitration.[35] But the impact
such young bureaucrats as Prichard were having on wartime America became
a touchy topic around Washington, and Congress and the cabinet seemed
unable to do anything about it. The *Louisville Courier-Journal* uncovered a
good deal of resentment in Washington toward Prichard, who, in the words
of one critic, "never carried a precinct." Prichard responded by claiming that
lawmakers' disputes with him and OES had nothing to do with correcting "a
bad personnel condition in government, but it is to stop government from
attempting to do a necessary job." The young counsel admitted that "the ideal
bureaucrat" would have both lengthy college and business experience, but also
stated that young college-trained men who chose public service were more
"than likely to become efficient public servants."[36]

While working within the administration, "Prich" seldom consulted with
the president. Prichard's status and power derived from the latitude extended
him by Vinson and not from Roosevelt. He described his encounters with the
president as occurring only "from time to time." But Prichard's limited contact with FDR left a lasting impression. Years later, Prichard remarked that the
single most impressive aspect of the president was his overall "magnetism."
Roosevelt and Prichard had similar preoccupations—both enjoyed political
gossip. Prichard remembered Roosevelt as someone who "loved to know everything that was going on . . . he liked to pick up little tidbits about people."
Few in the White House could keep abreast of Washington gossip as well as
the young Kentuckian.[37]

Despite the weighty matters of national importance that regularly came
across Prichard's desk, political issues back home in Kentucky sometimes called.
When the Kentucky General Assembly met in January 1944, the first bill introduced in the House was sponsored by Prichard's father. The bill sought to
repeal the Kentucky state income tax. Upon learning of the bill, the younger
Prichard was said to be "in a perfect swivet, threatening to take the first train
home to set his father right." After Vinson convinced the young man of the
uselessness of such an act, Prichard was reconciled that his father did not really wish to remove the state tax but rather "wanted to force the Republican

governor to make a decision between the state's fiscal needs and campaign speeches."[38] However this father-son dispute was settled, it indicated the degree to which Prichard still had Kentucky economic and political matters on his mind. No matter where he went, it seems, the overriding passion of Kentucky state politics never escaped Ed Prichard.

Prichard's evolving relationship with his boss, meanwhile, was also well-serving to the young pol. Vinson placed great confidence in his general counsel as well as in another Kentuckian who was now working with him, Paul Porter. *Fortune* magazine commented that Prichard "has a passion for the low-down and the dirt and sits in at more discussions and conferences all over the government than seems possible." While Vinson's hands were tied attending to various chores, he often received memos from Prichard on strategic moves he should take. "I think you should sit tight on strawberries," Prichard admonished Vinson, adding that "if you make him sweat it out, it will be interesting to see what Chet's reaction will be." "Chet," in this case, was Chester Bowles, the head of the Office of Price Administration. Prichard also called attention to the criticism the administration was facing with FDR's seizure of Montgomery Ward facilities in Chicago on behalf of striking workers. "I think you should call Justice Byrnes and tell him how important it is for somebody to defend the Montgomery-Ward seizure on the hill," wrote Prichard, adding that if the matter were left unchecked, "it will come back to harm us in the campaign again and again." In the same memo is another interesting suggestion: "I suggest you talk to Justice Byrnes and Judge Rosenman about Lyndon Johnson. It would be a most excellent move." From casually making the OPA director "sweat it out" to seeking an expanded role for an up-and-coming Texas congressman, Ed Prichard was in his element as a growing bureaucratic power broker.[39]

To those Washington insiders who could only guess at the true extent of Prichard's power within OES, evidence that he did, indeed, enjoy the complete confidence of his boss is revealed in a telegram he sent Vinson while the OES director was away attending the Bretton Woods international monetary conference. Since War Food Administrator Marvin Jones postponed a rationing order for ten days until Vinson's return, Prichard acted in the director's absence, informing him later that "I sent him a letter this morning which is on way to you. He probably thinks I read it to you, but situation was urgent."[40] Prichard knew that his influence rested squarely on the shoulders of Vinson, while Vinson's power resided ultimately with the president. For the time being, Prichard's power was secure, at least until the war was over or until a new president was in office.

From the shadows of power, Prichard continued to exercise a certain influence over some matters of profound political importance. In February 1944, for example, he was in the middle of a political crisis that pitted the president against the majority leader, Kentucky senator Alben Barkley. When Roosevelt called for a tax increase on excess profits to fund a national service plan he supported, conservative members of the Senate refused to go along with the president's tax plan that would raise $10.5 billion. Instead, the Senate proposed an emasculated bill that exempted numerous industries from excess taxation and ultimately would raise only $2 billion in revenue. The president, according to Byrnes, in deciding whether to veto the legislation supported by Alben Barkley, relied heavily upon the advice of Fred Vinson. Vinson and Prichard strongly opposed the Senate bill and came to Byrnes's office at OWM to give him a veto message that they wished the president to deliver. Eventually, the president did indeed side with Vinson, who was joined in opposition to the bill by Byrnes and Treasury Secretary Morgenthau. On February 22, Roosevelt issued a stern veto message that included a passage that infuriated Senator Barkley. The Senate bill, according to FDR, suggests "that I should give approval to this bill on the ground that having asked Congress for a loaf of bread to take care of this war for the sake of this and succeeding generations, I should be content with a small piece of crust." The president continued, saying that the bill supported by Barkley provided relief "not for the needy, but for the greedy." Feeling personally betrayed by the unusually bitter veto message, Barkley urged Congress to override the veto and promptly resigned. Barkley then called the White House to voice his anger with the president directly to Prichard. In the Senate, Barkley was quickly unanimously reelected as majority leader, and both houses of Congress quickly overrode the presidential veto.

Barkley never knew that the offending speech had been written by Ben Cohen and Prichard. Barkley later said he was told the speech was coined simply by a member of Byrnes's staff. Byrnes, however, said he simply did not know if that was the case because "I did not pay too much attention to the memorandum" that came out of his office to accompany the one presented by Vinson and Prichard. Samuel Rosenman, Roosevelt's chief speechwriter, commented that the president delivered the speech "pretty much in the form in which it came to him" from Byrnes's office. Prichard naturally kept his role in the imbroglio hidden from Barkley. In retrospect, the rift between Roosevelt and Barkley produced by the veto message had, perhaps, even greater significance than anyone realized at the time. Later that summer, Roosevelt dismissed the popular Barkley as a possible running mate because he was "too old." Instead, Roosevelt acquiesced in the selection of Missouri's Harry S Truman, who was all of six years younger than Barkley. Barkley's reaction to the tax bill veto message no doubt weighed heavily on Roosevelt's mind. What became clear only months later was that Prichard's and Cohen's strongly worded veto message may have played a decisive role in selecting the thirty-third president of the United States.[41]

The power exercised by Prichard at OES was not without its costs. Despite the prominence of his office and his growing reputation, the young Kentuckian was still lonely. He dated only on rare occasions and had developed no sustained relationships with women. Also, as one of the remaining progressive New Dealers in the administration, Prichard felt increasingly in the minority. The pressure was vented in a variety of ways. He could always slice up his political enemies with his razor-sharp wit. But there were other times when his frustration took other forms. After reading an editorial in the *Washington Post,* Prichard dashed off an angry telegram to none other than Eugene Meyer, the paper's owner. Prichard accused the *Post* as being corrupted by the "political preferences of those who run it." Weeks later, Prichard apologized, telling Meyer his telegram "reflected the heat of a lonesome and agitated New Dealer."[42]

Prichard's closest friends continued to worry about his more troublesome habits. Phil and Katharine Graham, for example, met occasionally with other Hockleyites for the sole purpose of discussing Prichard's "irresponsibilities"—specifically, his inability to control his personal finances and his increasingly troublesome habit of not finishing his work, which would usually be covered for him by Phil Graham or Bill Sheldon. Katharine Graham recalled that these meetings had little effect on Prichard's behavior. Instead, his friends continued to spend "a lot of time covering up" for Prichard's growing carelessness. In doing so, Prichard's coterie of friends did him no favor. Rather, they simply put off the time when Prichard would have to take full responsibility for his actions. Despite it all, his friends were steadfast—"Still we loved him," said Katharine Graham. "Somehow one couldn't help it."[43]

By the fall of 1944 Prichard's frustration with the direction of the administration mounted. He began to contemplate leaving Washington altogether. He had several options. One he considered was to open a law firm in Chicago with Paul Porter, who had worked in both the OPA and OES during the war. Prichard also considered a request from Phil Ardery to return to Kentucky after the war and practice law back home. Prichard told Phil Graham that he liked the Porter option better, for no other reason than they could "probably afford to hire some drudge to do the work." But the lure of Washington was strong. Wayne Coy admonished Prichard to stay at OES but added that for old New Dealers "the frustration here seems to grow each day."[44]

In addition to his work at OES, Prichard spent a good part of 1944 working on behalf of Franklin Roosevelt's reelection. His role in the campaign was considerably more prominent than the one he had played twelve years earlier as a Roosevelt supporter at Princeton. Prichard wrote campaign material for

Democratic party chief Bob Hannegan and Interior Secretary Harold Ickes. In preparing Ickes for a speech to a "foreign-born group," Prichard suggested that Ickes "call attention to the dastardly attempt of the Republicans to arouse prejudice against Sidney Hillman by calling him 'Russian born.'" To Prichard, this was a cheap effort to "stir up anti-Semitic and anti-foreign prejudice" and should be countered by declaring that "millions of Russian-born soldiers shed Russian-born blood during the last four years in our common cause—and thereby saved millions of American born boys from the same heroic fate." On one memorable evening, Prichard told his brother that he collaborated on a Roosevelt speech with the Hollywood wunderkind Orson Welles. Prichard also accompanied the president on a fateful trip through a freezing rain in New York, when it first became apparent to Prichard that the president "was a dying man." But rationalizing that a "dying Roosevelt was better than a healthy Thomas Dewey," Prichard remained committed to the man who had given life to the New Deal and provided the anchor for Prichard's power base in Washington. Prichard guardedly celebrated FDR's reelection in November 1944, but knew that a full term for the ailing president was unlikely.[45]

Just as he had learned at the Paris courthouse as a boy, Prichard thrived in the intrigue and the machinations involved in the art of politics. Yet since he often worked behind the scenes, the substance of his work went undetected. An instructive example of Prichard's foray into Washington politics was revealed in a series of moves that he exerted in behalf of his friend Ben Cohen. It is also a useful window to view how high-level appointments sometimes revolve around some very human emotions.

When Cordell Hull announced his resignation as secretary of state in late 1944, Byrnes was considered a strong favorite for the post. In the days leading up to the president's appointment, Byrnes discussed the likelihood of the appointment and of his plans to name Cohen as state department counselor. Both men's hopes, however, were dashed when Roosevelt named Edward R. Stettinius to fill Hull's post. Cohen continued to lobby for the counselor position, but no offer came from Stettinius. Harry Hopkins, hearing of Cohen's disappointment, suggested naming him an assistant legal adviser, which Cohen considered an insult.

Stettinius learned of Cohen's displeasure and told him that he simply had not known of his ambition and promised to take the matter up with the president. When Cohen discovered that Roosevelt disapproved of the appointment, he dashed off a letter of resignation to the president. On the night he wrote the letter, Cohen had dinner with Prichard and told him of the recent developments. Afterward, Prichard went to see Frankfurter and told the justice of Cohen's impending departure. Frankfurter agreed that Cohen was simply too valuable to lose and told Prichard that he would endeavor to get Cohen appointed solicitor general.

But Prichard did not stop there. Next morning, he went to see Tommy Corcoran, who voiced displeasure with FDR and also vowed to help Cohen secure the solicitor generalship. Meanwhile, when Roosevelt received Cohen's letter, he called and asked Cohen to come to see him. In the interim, it seems, the president changed his mind. The president expressed profound regret and told Cohen that he had opposed the appointment as counselor on a mere technicality and would easily agree to the position upon seeing Cohen's letter of resignation. But Roosevelt's charm did not assuage Cohen's hurt feelings, and he again wrote the president tendering his resignation. Cohen added that even if the position were offered, he could not accept it under such circumstances, as it would look as though "I had brought pressure to bear." This time, FDR accepted Cohen's letter, saying that "I am losing one of my most trusted advisors."[46]

Prichard deeply respected and admired Ben Cohen and worked desperately, through Frankfurter, Corcoran, and even Vinson, to lobby the president to keep him in Washington. In the process, the maneuvering revealed Prichard's machinations at the highest levels. It also reveals how, in many instances, matters of ego and wounded pride can be the controlling political imperative, even among close political allies.

Prichard's political fortunes took an unexpected twist in March 1945 when Vinson was appointed head of the Federal Loan Agency. As an indicator of how indispensable Vinson saw Prichard, he took the young attorney with him and made him deputy administrator. Vinson relied on Prichard to help administer the finances of the lending agencies grouped under the Reconstruction Finance Corporation. For Vinson and Prichard, the move was a considerable change from the highly charged atmosphere at OES. Prichard was about to be appointed general counsel of the Reconstruction Finance Corporation in late March, but events soon turned that appointment into a moot issue. On April 2, 1945, Byrnes stepped down as head of what was now known as the Office of War Mobilization and Reconversion (OWMR). Roosevelt called upon Vinson to succeed Byrnes. After less than a month at the Loan Administration post, Vinson and Prichard were back on their way to real power, heading an agency with even more political clout than the OES.[47]

The law creating the reconversion agency has been called "the broadest delegation of authority ever granted by Congress to an executive agency." The agency was given wide parameters to formulate reconversion plans after the war was over, as well as to "determine which war agencies should be simplified, consolidated, or eliminated." The "superagency" had been designed, in effect, to have authority over all other wartime agencies and was guaranteed a postwar role in supervising reconversion from a military to a civilian economy. Once again, Vinson and Prichard assumed offices in the east wing of the White House.[48]

The White House office presented, in clear detail understood by all, that the OWMR was the foremost wartime agency with its direct access to the Oval Office. But before Vinson could begin occupying a more daily role in Roosevelt's agenda, the president took off to spend time at the "Little White House" in Warm Springs, Georgia. On April 12, 1945, a stunned world heard the news that also fundamentally changed the world of Ed Prichard—Franklin Delano Roosevelt had died.

The fears that Prichard had expressed during the 1944 campaign concerning the president's health were also widely felt throughout the higher echelons of the Democratic party. That is precisely why the nomination of the vice presidential candidate at the Democratic Convention the preceding summer had been so crucial. While southern conservatives refused to support Vice President Henry Wallace, labor leaders such as Sidney Hillman lobbied hard against Byrnes. While other names, such as Supreme Court Justice William O. Douglas, were floated around the convention floor, the compromise candidate who emerged to claim the nomination was moderate Missouri senator Harry S Truman. The man from Independence, in both political and personal ways, stood in stark contrast to Roosevelt. His succession to the presidency in mid-April 1945 was coldly greeted by young New Dealers like Prichard, who felt that Truman was not only too conservative but also lacked the basic abilities to be president. For the remainder of his tenure in the Oval Office, Truman had a tenuous relationship with New Dealers. Truman's rise to power subsequently had a profound impact on the careers of both Fred Vinson and Ed Prichard.

Harry Truman was well aware of his standing among the New Dealers, and the new president was not one to endure very long what he considered to be disloyalty. Truman was also not one to treat leaks originating from within the administration in the manner that Roosevelt had. Truman was indeed furious when he read of leaks of telegrams he had received from Harry Hopkins in Moscow. During the first weeks of his presidency, Truman's avowed distrust of New Deal liberals, coupled with his intense desire to stop further news leaks, set in motion a chain of events that are still somewhat vague. On April 23, just eleven days after assuming the presidency, Truman received a secret report from FBI director J. Edgar Hoover. Hoping to curry favor with the new president, Hoover's memo concerned the political activities of some members of the White House staff. The president read Hoover's report "with much interest" and then asked the FBI director to conduct a "survey" on all White House employees. One of the targets of this highly classified original memo and the "survey" was an east-wing staff member, Edward F. Prichard Jr.[49]

In the eyes of the FBI, Prichard had several strikes against him—he had already been the target of J. Edgar Hoover's memo in 1941 implying that he was a communist. Prichard was also a very visible member of the cadre of left-leaning New Dealers who remained distant to the new president, and he was widely known as one who was disposed to talk with reporters, particularly Drew Pearson. In the late spring of 1945, just as he seemed headed for even greater prominence in Washington as the right-hand man of Fred Vinson, Prichard became the subject of an intense FBI investigation that had approval from the new president himself.

All of this covert activity, of course, was unknown to the thirty-year-old general counsel of the OWMR, and he continued in his duties for Vinson unimpeded by the knowledge that the president and J. Edgar Hoover had placed him under surveillance. An example of Prichard's influence at OWMR came when he persuaded Vinson to bring in Robert R. Nathan as deputy director for reconversion. Nathan was one of Prichard's protégés among the original "goon squad," and Nathan saw the task of reconversion as one in which general economic planning was necessary in order to forestall a return to the Great Depression. A number of New Deal critics stated that at war's end the government should allow the free market to once again reign, therefore advising the removal of all wage and price controls and government planning. Prichard felt such moves would prove economically disastrous and worked within OWMR to see that Nathan was given a wide berth.[50]

Luck, it seemed, followed Prichard throughout his Washington career. First, the timing of Frankfurter's appointment to the Supreme Court came just as Prichard prepared to leave Cambridge. Then, after making waves at the Department of Justice, Prichard found a position working for Sidney Hillman in the WPB. As the WPB's power waned, Prichard moved on to the powerful OES staff with Byrnes, and upon Vinson's appointment, Prichard clung to Vinson's coattail for a heady ride up the power ladder in wartime Washington. With the death of Franklin Roosevelt, Vinson's political fortunes increased. One historian concluded that during Truman's presidency, Vinson became "the president's most esteemed companion." When Truman accepted Henry Morgenthau's resignation as treasury secretary in July 1945, he quickly named the OWMR director to fill this prized cabinet post.[51]

The Senate quickly confirmed Vinson and he assumed his new duties at Treasury on July 17, 1945. He of course brought Prichard along with him as assistant to the treasury secretary. Just as the war wound down, Congress could be expected to eliminate virtually all of the wartime agencies that had once been so powerful. Luck, it appeared, was again working on Prichard's behalf, as Vinson's appointment elevated young Prichard now to assisting a Cabinet member who oversaw one of the most crucial postwar departments in Washington.

But luck was in fact running out on the thirty-year-old wunderkind. The FBI report on the president's desk in the spring of 1945 launched a series of events that targeted the young aide in Fred Vinson's office. In retrospect, Prichard knew his role in Washington was extraordinary. "I guess it was a heady wine," he later recalled. "I loved it and it was certainly exciting and a challenge." But Prichard also knew that his success had another side—"I think maybe it was too much," he said, adding with ironic candor, "I got to feeling that I was bigger than I was, that the rules didn't always apply to me."[52]

6 "Corrective Steps"

EARLY on May 8, 1945, President Harry S Truman announced that Germany had unconditionally surrendered and that the war in Europe was over. V-E Day was finally at hand. The largest radio audience ever recorded to that time huddled in their living rooms and kitchens to hear the president say:

> This is a solemn but a glorious hour. I only wish that Franklin D. Roosevelt had lived to witness this day. General Eisenhower informs me that the forces of Germany have surrendered to the United Nations. The flags of freedom fly over all Europe.
>
> For this victory, we join in offering our thanks to the Providence which has guided and sustained us through the dark days of adversity.
>
> Our rejoicing is sobered and subdued by a supreme consciousness of the terrible price we have paid to rid the world of Hitler and his evil band. Let us not forget, my fellow Americans, the sorrow and the heartache which today abide in the homes of so many of our neighbors—neighbors whose most priceless possession has been rendered as a sacrifice to redeem our liberty.[1]

Like millions of others around the world, Ed Prichard had listened intently to the president's speech. He was naturally elated at the news, but he listened for a more personal reason. Later that evening, he called Justice Frankfurter at 9:35 P.M. What Prichard did not know was that on that same day, the FBI had installed an electronic listening device on his White House telephone. All of Prichard's phone conversations were subsequently recorded by the FBI. Thus began a series of steps that effectively ended Prichard's Washington career and launched what has been termed one of "the most extensive partisan political wiretaps instigated by any postwar President."[2]

The FBI's wiretap of Prichard began on a historic night and, in the process, revealed Prichard's unique contribution to the day's proceedings. After exchanging pleasantries, Prichard was anxious to know Frankfurter's reaction to Truman's speech. A coy Prichard waited several minutes to tell Frankfurter the real reason behind the phone call:

> FRANKFURTER: . . . we thought it was good, [referring to Truman's speech] . . . who did it? Colonel Vaughan?

PRICHARD: No.
FRANKFURTER: McKim?
PRICHARD: No.
FRANKFURTER: You?
PRICHARD: Yeah . . . *ipsisimis nobis* [by our own very selves] . . .
FRANKFURTER: Well, I thought it was very good. [aside to his wife] Pritch did
   that . . . .
PRICHARD: . . . I feel rather bad now that I didn't say "Advance Columbia" [imi-
   tating Churchill] . . . God Save Pendergast . . .
FRANKFURTER: [laughing] . . . you must be the Charlie McCarthy of this admin-
   istration.
PRICHARD: The Edgar Bergen![3]

The origins of the FBI wiretap on Ed Prichard grew out of a series of events in the White House shortly after Truman assumed the presidency. The "White House survey"—the FBI investigation of the loyalty of the White House staff to President Truman—was concluded on August 13. In the interim, however, steps had already been initiated against Ed Prichard. A nervous J. Edgar Hoover, feeling unsure of where he stood with the new president, wished to prove at the outset that he could be of considerable use to Truman and saw an opportunity in the figure of young Prichard. Hoover's desire to destroy Prichard's chances of further rising in Washington were well connected with Truman's desire to rid the White House of leakers and left-wing New Dealers. Although the full contents of the "White House survey" remain classified, it is certain that Prichard's past outspokenness coupled with his well-known tendency to leak information to reporters drew the close inspection of both the FBI director and the president. At whose direction the wiretap was installed is unknown, but on May 23 Hoover provided Truman's FBI liaisons, Edward McKim and Harry Vaughan, with a "Personal and Confidential" report on Prichard. Included in the report were the transcripts of the conversation between Prichard and Frankfurter on May 8 and with columnist Drew Pearson on May 13. McKim then sent the report on to the president. For over a week, the FBI awaited Truman's reaction.

On June 2, McKim called FBI Inspector Myron Gurnea and asked him to come over to the White House. The two men met in the empty Cabinet room, and McKim opened by saying, "First of all, I want to personally compliment the Director and the Bureau for the hell-of-a-swell job you fellows did" concerning an early report on the White House survey. McKim added, "Both the president and I were particularly impressed with the report and the detailed manner in which the information was set out." McKim described the material contained in Prichard's "technical log" as "unbelievable"—"I was afraid to show it to the President until they were on the boat and out in the river," said McKim, alluding to the presidential yacht, which Truman frequented. Prichard's comments, McKim remarked, were nothing short of "treasonable." Gurnea, however, wanted to know the real issue—Would Truman authorize continuing the wiretaps? McKim relayed that the president had found the Prichard wiretap transcript "the damnedest thing I have ever read," and that the president wished to keep the tap on Prichard's phone. "Incidentally," McKim told Gurnea, "for your confidential information, we are taking corrective steps."[4]

For the remainder of Prichard's stay in Washington, even as he moved to the Treasury building, his phone was wiretapped and the transcripts of his conversations were delivered to presidential assistants McKim and Vardaman, who passed the material on to Truman. Another tap was authorized for the phone of Thomas Corcoran, but a nervous Hoover intervened to stop a tap being placed on Drew Pearson's phone. Considering the legalities of initiating wiretaps, Hoover's anxieties were well founded. Electronic surveillance had been banned by Prichard's old boss, Attorney General Robert Jackson, in 1940, but President Roosevelt had secretly approved a directive allowing the FBI to wiretap individuals suspected of "subversive activities against the Government of the United States," provided that the attorney general approved the taps on a case-by-case basis. Although Truman later claimed that he strongly disapproved of FBI wiretaps, both the president and Hoover did not inform Attorney General Tom Clark of the Prichard wiretap and only informed Clark of the Corcoran wiretap five months after it was initiated. Clark Clifford, one of Truman's most trusted advisers, noted that while the president may have disliked Hoover and the methods of wiretapping, he "was not immune to the attraction of inside information." Truman approved the Corcoran wiretap, according to the FBI, because he wished to ensure that Corcoran's "activities did not interfere with the proper administration of government." The wiretaps subsequently ushered in a new era of domestic political intelligence. The FBI made it clear it was very nervous about such activity, as Hoover himself was advised that "if it became known that we were investigating these people, it would be incumbent upon both the president and [White House aides] to deny that any such investigation had been ordered."[5]

What exactly was so "treasonable" about Prichard's conversations? The wiretaps reveal no evidence worthy of such hyperbole. In Prichard's May 8 conversation with Frankfurter, the references to Truman as a ventriloquist's dummy seemed the extent of Prichard's "treasonable" remarks. There was only scant evidence of leaks originating from Prichard's office. On one occasion, Prichard informed Frankfurter that Assistant Secretary of State Nelson Rockefeller would urge that Argentina be admitted to the United Nations, provided a radical labor leader was discredited, and would therefore ask that

$2 million be allocated for "propaganda." Frankfurter exclaimed, "I'm almost persuaded to have you tell that to Drew." Prichard replied, "I think's that's being done, or will."[6]

Prichard's reference to the infamous Pendergast machine of Kansas City politics also rankled the new president, who owed his political origins to the support of Tom Pendergast's political apparatus. If the president needed proof that Prichard was close with Drew Pearson, Prichard's conversations with the columnist were more than enough to disturb Truman. Perhaps most revealing was the relationship that Frankfurter evidently had with the newspaperman. In all, if the new president wished to gain access to one of the best sources for Washington insider gossip, there was no better place than Prichard's telephone. While Prichard was unaware of FBI activities against him in 1945, he learned of the wiretap on his phone shortly before he died in 1984. Prichard called the affair "a damned outrage," noting that it was "illegal as hell." Prichard suspected that the reason he was singled out was because he had expressed a "dim view" of the "numskulls" Truman brought into the administration. He also did not rule out the possibility that Truman had ordered the tap, because "sometimes people do things that are out of character."[7]

The lengthy transcripts provided by the Prichard wiretaps shed light on the hidden machinations of the FBI director and a somewhat insecure president. They also allow a remarkable glimpse inside the heady world that Prichard occupied in Washington near the end of the war. He regularly conversed with the likes of Frankfurter, Cohen, Lyndon Johnson, Abe Fortas, and Bob Hannegan on an assortment of issues. The cumulative impact of the wiretaps was, no doubt, somewhat disappointing to Truman and the FBI. While he had a few brief conversations with journalists like Drew Pearson, there is no indication from the wiretaps themselves that Prichard regularly fed the Washington news bureau with crucial information, nor did he offer any further derogatory remarks about the president.

The bulk of the Prichard wiretaps are not necessarily the stuff of presidential wrath. For example, Truman took note of Frankfurter's almost juvenile conversational tone with Prichard, as well as his incessant curiosity about Washington politics, of which Prichard kept him abreast. The most common factor throughout Prichard's telephone conversations was the no-holds-barred analysis of administration politics. For example, in August, Corcoran called Prichard to suggest he lobby to obtain a Circuit Court of Appeals appointment for Abe Fortas. Corcoran added that Fortas could help Vinson: "He could protect the interests of the Security Exchange through which all those appeals go." Prichard agreed to work on Fortas's behalf, and Corcoran responded: "I just wanted to put the seed in your ear. I know it will germinate and grow and bear fruit." Prichard agreed to talk with Lyndon Johnson about the nomination and later told Fortas that he was Fortas's "campaign manager" in attempting to have him nominated to the Appeals Court. Though the nomination for Fortas never came, such dynamics reveal the corridors of power that Prichard regularly walked. Perhaps even more important was the degree to which someone with as many contacts as Thomas Corcoran came to rely upon the young Kentuckian.[8]

On one occasion, while Prichard was out of the office, his secretary phoned him that he had received calls that day from the following individuals: Leon Henderson, Bob Hannegan, Mrs. Abe Fortas (who had invited Prichard to a party for Professor Max Radin of the University of California), Tex Goldschmidt at Interior, and Gardiner Jackson. On another day, Bob Hannegan called and asked Prichard's opinion of naming Beanie Baldwin as his executive assistant in the Democratic party hierarchy. Prichard replied, "I think that would be splendid" and strongly endorsed Baldwin. Hannegan then made Prichard promise not to "say anything about it to anybody because I would want to talk to Truman later."[9] In other words, while the president, as the leader of the party, would ultimately make such decisions, the groundwork was prepared by Hannegan and Prichard.

As an example of the gossip in which Prichard reveled, the following conversation between Prichard and an unidentified man that the FBI referred to as "Al" took place on July 15. The caller suggested that Wayne Coy, former FDR assistant and *Washington Post* assistant editor, be named to head the OWMR upon Vinson's nomination to Treasury. Prichard replied that he did not think "the head man will do it." The caller suggested that Prichard contact Bob Hannegan on Coy's behalf, to which Prichard agreed. The FBI report stated: "AL asked what the judge [Vinson] thinks of Wayne and when Prichard said the judge likes him alright, Al said, 'Well, hell, between the judge and the justice [Byrnes] he can get a lot of backing . . . Al said he thinks Hannegan should propose the thing rather than the judge because 'this business of selecting a successor is always psychologically bad.' Prichard said he'd see what he can do."[10] Perhaps alerted by the FBI wiretaps, Truman warded off Prichard and Hannegan's draft for Coy by instead naming a conservative Missouri banker, John Snyder, to the post of War Mobilization and Reconversion head.

When Isaiah Berlin called to report on a conversation he had had with journalist Marquis Childs, both Berlin and Prichard agreed that Childs was "a complete dope, but a nice dope." "Berlin said Childs was hostile to some people, people who 'pressed the button.' Prichard said 'What about Vinson?' Berlin said 'No, nothing against him. Nothing against Byrnes.' Berlin wanted to know if 'he'd' drive out Archie [MacLeish, assistant secretary of state] and Prichard thought not, but thought Archie would go."[11]

During the first months of the Truman administration, New Dealers in various positions began an exodus out of Washington. Many were simply disillusioned with the new president, whom they saw as a poor substitute for FDR and his domestic politics. It has long been assumed that Ed Prichard was also anxious to leave Washington and return to Kentucky to begin his own political career. The FBI wiretaps, however, reveal that Prichard had other ambitions on his mind in the summer of 1945.

In early July, he informed his mother that his "status" was the same and he would "move on" with Vinson. Later that month, he told Corcoran that Attorney General Tom Clark and Lyndon Johnson had discussed with him the possibility of moving back to the Justice Department, perhaps to head either the antitrust division that had been overseen by Thurman Arnold, or the lands division. "I'm sure you should not now go to the Department of Justice," Corcoran advised, adding, "I think it's awfully important that you stay" with Vinson. Prichard agreed, then the two discussed where the best place would be for him. Prichard told Corcoran that he wished to remain with Vinson at Treasury, but that he wanted something more than the general councilorship, and that several "assistant to the secretary" positions were nothing more than "flunky jobs." Instead, Prichard wanted Vinson to name him as Treasury undersecretary, a more powerful position that required Senate confirmation. Corcoran stated that he was attending a dinner that evening at Lyndon Johnson's home, where he would see Tom Clark and Vinson. Corcoran told Prichard that he would lobby on behalf of Prichard's being nominated as an undersecretary, boldly adding, "I will force them to put you in there."[12]

While Prichard was a loyal and devoted Vinson appointee, he did not look upon Vinson in the way he did Frankfurter. Despite the fact that Vinson was a shrewd politician and as well connected as anybody within the administration, he lacked one essential ingredient in order to serve as a proper mentor to Ed Prichard—intellectual brilliance. Prichard respected Vinson's political abilities and knew how the secretary had commanded the admiration of both Roosevelt and Truman. But Vinson simply could not engage Prichard in the kind of intellectual discourse he was accustomed to with mentors such as Corcoran and Frankfurter, or even friends like Isaiah Berlin or Phil Graham. But Vinson certainly had his usefulness.

For more than two years, Ed Prichard had functioned as Fred Vinson's right-hand man and had occupied a series of posts, each a considerable elevation in power and prestige. By the time Vinson had reached the treasury secretary's office, Prichard assumed that his climb would continue. He had, after all, accumulated a glowing résumé and political experience and seemed destined, considering Vinson's confidence in him, for bigger and better things. But in the late summer of 1945, Prichard learned that Vinson had cooled somewhat toward naming his assistant to any higher posts within the administration. In a conversation with Bob Hannegan, the postmaster general and Democratic party chieftain, Prichard decided to broach the subject:

PRICHARD: Bob, something I was going to ask you, oh, have you ever heard anything more about that business over at Justice?
HANNEGAN: About you?
PRICHARD: Yeah.
HANNEGAN: No I was waiting—you see, I talked to the Judge [Vinson].
PRICHARD: What did he say?
HANNEGAN: Oh, he wants you to stay there with him but he don't want to make you Secretary.
PRICHARD: That's right.
HANNEGAN: He says you don't want—he says he knows you better than anybody in the world . . . And he said it would be the wrong thing. He said he just wants to maneuver around just free-lance around. He said now I know him and that wouldn't be the thing to do . . .
PRICHARD: I was afraid he would say that. I can't make out whether he really thinks I don't want it or whether he don't want . . .
HANNEGAN: No, it's not that. . . . . He thinks that is the best thing for you.[13]

Prichard was somewhat taken aback by Vinson's reluctance and was further irritated by the secretary's refusal to offer him even the position of general counsel of the Treasury Department. In a telephone conversation with Lyndon Johnson, the Texas congressman suggested that Prichard attempt to obtain Vinson's endorsement for such a move. Prichard replied that Vinson had plenty of time to offer the post but had decided against it. Prichard's confusion was then clearly expressed to the young LBJ: "Fred has thought of all kinds of reasons for me to go to Kentucky."[14]

What had occurred so quickly to cool Vinson on Prichard, even to the point of suggesting that his young assistant leave Washington and return to Kentucky? Here, it seems, the full dimension of what the FBI had earlier termed "corrective steps" can be better understood. Vinson and Truman saw each other regularly, and Vinson became one of the president's most trusted confidants. At some point in the summer of 1945, either the president or, perhaps, McKim or Vardaman relayed to Vinson the commander in chief's reaction to the FBI's report on Prichard and even some of the wiretaps that had angered Truman. Vinson later told Prichard that he had, indeed, seen transcripts of Prichard's telephone conversations. While not wishing to go so far as to fire Prichard, Vinson certainly was not willing to place his name in consideration for an undersecretaryship or even to the nominal position of general counsel. In other words, considering the extent to which Truman was distrustful of his young aide, Vinson simply *could not* keep Prichard around any longer. At the same time, the new treasury secretary could obviously not fully reveal the reasons behind his new attitude. Vinson's repeated suggestion that it would be best for Prichard to return to Kentucky belies a certain understanding that a powerful appointment no longer existed for the young Kentuckian in Truman's administration.[15]

But Prichard was not through making one last mark on Washington. One of the primary goals of the remaining Roosevelt supporters in Washington was to secure the passage of a full-employment bill. FDR had made the implementation of the bill one of the hallmarks of his "Economic Bill of Rights" in 1944 and had restated his conviction for the necessity of the bill in his last State of the Union address in January 1945. That month, the legislation was introduced in the Senate, where it faced an uphill struggle for passage. The bill, as introduced, had several significant provisions. It declared that "all Americans able to work and seeking work have the right to a useful and remunerative job"; responsibility was placed on the president to see that the national economy was analyzed at regular intervals and to measure economic trends in anticipation of economic downturns; and the federal government was committed to increasing spending and investment to maintain full employment if necessary. The bill provided no specifics as to how government spending would be used to create jobs and was careful not to seriously threaten business interests. Despite these limitations, labor leaders and New Dealers embraced the bill and saw the 1944 election as an endorsement of the principle of government-guaranteed full employment.[16]

Conservatives objected to what they considered the bill's radical provisions of centralized economic planning in peacetime. After a series of Senate hearings, the bill needed some redrafting in order to assuage some nervous senators. But more important, some early supporters of the bill, particularly the National Farmers Union, needed assurance that progressive economic principles would not be taken out in order to obtain the backing of conservative senators. In late August and early September 1945, the bill underwent extensive rewriting. To craft the new version, the bill's original author, Bertram Gross, turned to Leon Keyserling. Gross was a New Deal economist who had been made a special assistant to the Senate Banking and Currency Committee; Keyserling had been general counsel of the National Housing Agency and was an adviser to Banking Committee Chairman Robert Wagner. As two key Senate staffers, Gross and Keyserling had been vital participants in the full-employment bill from its very beginning. But to piece together the revised draft at this crucial juncture, Gross also obtained the services of Ed Prichard at the Treasury Department. The move to bring in Prichard to craft the revised Senate bill reflected just how highly Prichard's political acumen and legal drafting skills were prized, even outside of the administration and on Capitol Hill. In what became his final major undertaking in Washington, Prichard worked to secure what has been termed "the last great battle for the New Deal." The threesome hammered out nine different drafts before submitting their final product to Senator Wagner, who introduced the revised bill to a Senate Banking subcommittee in September. This draft smoothed out some of the technical language of the earlier bill and included new sections on agricultural labor. The draft maintained that "all Americans have a right to opportunity for work" and that the federal government had a responsibility to ensure that this right was adequately protected, but backed off any federal guarantees of underwriting full employment. The bill soon easily passed the Senate 71 to 10. When it was sent to the House, Texas congressman Wright Patman exuberantly called the legislation "the most constructive single piece of legislation in the history of this nation."[17]

Prichard worked in other ways on behalf of the full-employment bill. In his capacities at the Treasury Department, Prichard wrote a letter from Secretary Vinson to Congress supporting the full-employment bill. An earlier draft had been submitted to Vinson that Prichard considered "too long and too technical," and the young assistant assured his boss that he would "work out something a little livelier and more in true Vinson style." But neither Prichard's work on the bill nor Vinson's letter could persuade the House to pass the Senate bill. The language was simply too much for the conservatives in the House. Months after Prichard left Washington, a compromise bill was finally passed that significantly watered down its earlier versions. No longer was "full employment" the goal. Indeed, the bill's title was changed from the Full Employment Act to merely the Employment Act. A more lukewarm phrase had been substituted that stated simply that the government would attempt "to promote maximum employment" in a manner "calculated to foster and promote free competitive enterprise." With the definition of full employment thus altered, and with no expressed commitment within the legislation to maintain full employment levels through government spending and investment, conservatives were delighted with the final emasculated version signed into law by President Truman in 1946.[18]

Despite their close relationship, it became obvious to Prichard during the late summer that something had changed in Vinson's demeanor toward his assistant. The treasury secretary's standoffish behavior toward Prichard had the desired effect. Prichard was convinced by late summer of 1945 that he had reached his heights in Washington and had no choice but to return to Kentucky. The first indication of his plans came when he told Oscar Cox on August 23 that he was leaving Washington. His plans involved, naturally, setting up a law practice. His earlier option to open a practice with Paul Porter fell through. Porter remained in Washington, where he later formed one of the city's most powerful law firms. Prichard instead turned to his old Paris friend and law school classmate, Phil Ardery. Ardery, unlike Prichard, had a distinguished service record during the war, winning numerous medals for his aviation record as a bomber pilot. Ardery led one of the bomb wings at the Normandy landing on D-Day, and upon his return to the states, Ardery was a wings operations officer in Orlando. Sensing the sea change in his political fortunes before leaving for the Treasury, Prichard began considering his future possibilities and called Ardery at a base in Florida to ask him to come to Washington to discuss possibly starting a law practice. Ardery flew to Washington and took a taxi to the White House, where he was escorted into Prichard's office. Ardery recalled that he saw "Prich behind Vinson's desk with a big black cigar sticking out of the corner of his mouth. His feet were on the top of the desk and he had the look of a man who was ruling the world." Ardery added that, in such surroundings Prichard "looked more imposing than the president." The two then discussed the possibility of starting a law practice in Kentucky.

The move seemed a good step for both Prichard and Ardery. In Ardery, Ed Prichard would be getting a war hero and a popular local figure who might help his entrée into certain corners of the local Democratic party. In Prichard, Ardery was getting one of the best-connected young lawyers in Washington, who was sure to draw some attractive clients. Before leaving Washington, Prichard was offered a retainer from the Kentucky State Federation of Labor. More, it seemed, was sure to follow. Since Ardery had made a start in Frankfort before the war, he said he wanted to remain there, while Prichard expressed his desire to have an office in Lexington. The two agreed to have separate offices, and the firm was to be named Prichard and Ardery. Ardery also agreed to find secretaries and to inquire of the law school dean at the University of Kentucky for outstanding recent graduates who might be brought into the firm as associates.[19]

While Ardery returned to Kentucky to begin putting the office together, Prichard submitted his letter of resignation to Vinson on September 29. "I can never forget the stirring times through which it was my privilege to work under the inspiration of your guidance. Nor shall I ever fail to remember the kindness and generosity which you have extended in and out of season," wrote Prichard. Vinson replied that "there are few of your generation who have had equal opportunity to serve their government during the trying times of the recent past, and, I can say with confidence, there is no one who could have made a greater contribution had a comparable opportunity been afforded him." Vinson added: "The Government service needs men like you. My sadness at your leaving is in part alleviated by the conviction that not only will your zeal for public service manifest itself in your every act in the private practice of the law, but also will inevitably result in your return to public life, seasoned as only contact with Kentucky politics can season."[20]

Time magazine reported Prichard's Washington departure and his imminent return to Kentucky. Having trimmed down to 210 pounds, Prichard struck a confident pose for the magazine's photographers. Saying that reports he would someday be governor of Kentucky were "a base canard," Prichard admitted that he intended to "run for something" within a short time. When asked about his prospects, he replied, "My ears are to the ground, but I don't hear any popular clamor yet."[21]

Prichard's exit from the Washington stage did not go unnoticed by the local press. Reporter Al Friendly of the *Washington Post* wrote glowingly that in Prichard's wake "is a saga, several unauthorized anthologies of his epigrams and a record of mighty toil in the vineyards of the New Deal." Friendly summarized Prichard's Washington years: "In the course of his operations he gained the reputation for sitting in more conferences, picking up more lowdowns, fingering more pies and working his own brand of Kentucky-seasoned Harvard liberalism than any man in Washington." Among some of the epigrams attributed to Prichard by Friendly was one where Prichard described a sourly disposed and skinny Cabinet member—"If you could cut out his gall bladder," Prichard chuckled, "he wouldn't weigh 20 pounds."[22]

On October 1, 1945, Ed Prichard left Washington and came home to Paris to live with his parents and begin his law practice in Lexington. He spent the last days of his tenure at Treasury at farewell get-togethers with the likes of Ben Cohen, Paul Porter, Don Russell, and Lyndon Johnson. The FBI summarily ended its surveillance upon Prichard's departure, but continued to monitor his oft-made calls to Tommy Corcoran's Washington office.

Ed Prichard had been in Washington for more than six years and had served a litany of notables—Frankfurter, Jackson, Hillman, Byrnes, and Vinson. During one of the most crucial periods in American history, he had worked in a variety of key agencies in planning the wartime economy and peacetime conversion. The wunderkind had held numerous Washingtonians spellbound with his memory, political acumen, anecdotes, raw humor, and lavish oratory. He had dined with the Roosevelts, roomed with the likes of Phil Graham and Isaiah Berlin, and been subjected to the intruding ears of the FBI. He became lifelong friends with Lyndon Johnson, Arthur M. Schlesinger Jr., Ben Cohen, and Katharine Graham—and a bitter enemy of J. Edgar Hoover. In all, he possessed one of the most accomplished résumés of any thirty-year-old lawyer in the country. For a man with his own political ambitions, he was off to quite a start. To those who knew him, the possibilities for Ed Prichard in 1945 seemed endless. Some, in fact, held the notion best expressed by Joseph Rauh, who commented: "We all felt then that of all of them, the two men most likely to succeed, to become President of the United States, were Philip Graham and Ed Prichard."[23]

In retrospect, such sentiments, which were widely shared by other Washingtonians, ignored too many other factors. While Prichard did indeed possess a remarkable mind and lofty political ambitions, his years in Washington revealed certain traits that threatened to undermine any chances of political power in his own right. Prichard's penchant for arrogant audacity amused and amazed his compatriots, but it bitterly angered his enemies. His "means justify the ends" mentality too often skirted danger. His awkward attempt to sabotage Frankfurter's *Gobitis* opinion, for example, was not the type of careful maneuvering that a Tommy Corcoran would have utilized. His 1941 letter to Robert Jackson, which Jackson described as "insubordinate," was also not the kind of letter that a more ambitious and calculating student of power, like Lyndon Johnson, would have written. Robert Nathan understood that the Ed Prichard he knew did not even want the power that so many had in mind for him. "Prich would rather have been an assistant to the attorney general, rather than attorney general," Nathan suggested. Katharine Graham substantiated that Prichard "wanted the influence but he didn't want the responsibility." Despite his boast to "run for something" upon his return to Kentucky, Prichard was far more at home with appointed positions. Running for elective office offered too many opportunities for public rejection. At bottom, Prichard's deeply hidden insecurities made him more comfortable in the shadows of power, where he could manipulate policies and people without direct public responsibility.[24]

By the time he left Washington, Prichard's political personality was already fully formed. What had started in Bourbon County and blossomed at Princeton and Harvard had now fully matured. While parts of it may have been borrowed from Pearce Paton, "Big Ed," Frankfurter, and Corcoran, the sum of it was entirely Prichard's. In an astonishing way, he managed to combine a certain cynical realpolitik with an almost childlike exuberance that at times was reckless and shortsighted. This potent mixture found a legion of beloved admirers, but it also created a healthy number of lifelong enemies and, unless it could be rechanneled, was not necessarily the stuff that future presidents, senators, governors, or even county judges are made of.

7 A Lukewarm Reception

ALTHOUGH Prichard had passed the Kentucky state bar exam in 1939, in the seven years since he had graduated from Harvard Law School the young attorney had never practiced a single case by the time he arrived home from Washington on October 1, 1945. As some of his critics had earlier suggested, the Paris pol had "never carried a precinct" despite his political experience. On both accounts—practicing law and pursuing his political ambitions—Ed Prichard wished to quickly rectify his perceived weaknesses.

He wasted no time in getting straight to work at the newly minted firm of Prichard and Ardery. As he had promised in their meeting at the White House, Phil Ardery assumed the task of getting the firm started. Both partners needed associates in their respective offices, and Ardery visited the nearby University of Kentucky law school concerning recommendations. The dean of the law school suggested the name of a recent graduate, Alvarado Erwin Funk Jr., the son of the Kentucky attorney general. While the dean said that Funk was one of the finest recent graduates of the school, his political connections were not lost on the fledgling partners. Ardery hired Funk to assist Prichard in the Lexington office.[1]

In his new duties, Prichard obviously wished to use his considerable contacts to bring lucrative clients to the firm. Within days of returning home, he was already attempting to twist the arm of his old boss, Fred Vinson. Prichard wrote to the treasury secretary on behalf of the Franklin County government to seek Vinson's help in locating a 750-bed Veterans' Administration hospital in Frankfort. Prichard wrote that "naturally, anything which helps build up the community will benefit our struggling law firm. If there is anything you can do to help out on this, Phil and I will be most grateful." Prichard also inquired if it was possible for the secretary's office to "mail me copies of the *London Times* . . . nobody in the office ever read them except me."[2] Prichard soon learned that merely picking up the phone or writing a personal letter to a well-placed Washington insider was not always the necessary formula for success. The hospital was eventually located in Lexington. Ironically, Prichard died in this same hospital almost forty years later.

Those of his New Deal friends who remained in Washington sorely missed Prichard. In early 1946, as Lyndon Johnson and Thomas Corcoran discussed a possible cabinet appointment for Supreme Court Justice William O. Douglas, Corcoran replied that Douglas had the most secure job in the world. A nervous LBJ responded, "This security thing is out, by God, with Hiroshima. You haven't got it anymore unless you've got friends." The two then bemoaned the political situation facing party chief Bob Hannegan in keeping the New Deal intact. Johnson mentioned that Hannegan was desperate for help—"he's just looking for any of them, Landis, Prichard—just anybody. He wants to go back and try to get somebody with some brain." Corcoran asked if Prichard's continuing trips to Washington meant he might return. Johnson replied, "No, but it gets him up here every two or three days."[3]

Prichard was indeed in close touch with Hannegan, who also wanted the Kentuckian to return to Washington. In early 1946, Hannegan offered Prichard the job of Democratic National Committee general counsel, a key full-time post. In addition to any legal duties the job entailed, Hannegan also wanted Prichard to help secure passage of President Truman's legislative package, which included a sixty-five-cent minimum wage and the full-employment bill. Prichard, however, did not wish to leave Kentucky. The extent to which Hannegan wanted him in the job was revealed when he agreed to allow Prichard to assume the post and remain at home. Prichard's appointment also underscored a subtle shift in how President Truman regarded the former New Dealer. The fact that Hannegan received Truman's approval before accepting Prichard's terms indicates that, while the president was angered by Prichard's earlier remarks to Frankfurter, he also understood that Prichard was devoted to the Democratic party and to his own legislative agenda. Truman was pragmatic enough not to stand in Prichard's way. In news stories reporting the appointment, Prichard denied he had any intention of running for Congress if Sixth-District Democratic incumbent Virgil Chapman left the House to run for the Senate.[4]

While his professional prospects seemed promising, Prichard's personal life remained marked by intense loneliness. Following a Christmas party in 1945, a somewhat dispirited Prichard wrote to Katharine Graham, informing her that although his law practice was doing well, the energies required for running a law office left him little time for politics. While Prichard adopted the public posture of distancing himself from political matters, he shared with such intimates as Katharine Graham the fact that politics remained his only true devotion. The practice of law, to no one's surprise, was not something that fully engaged his mind. Working in the fledgling firm also left no room for a social life, and a depressed Prichard told Graham he longed for "someone to whom I can let my hair down every night." Despite the activity of his law office and his varied political duties, Prichard missed those who remained in Washington who had come to mean so much to him. In a melancholy letter to Frankfurter, he related what he had told someone when asked "If you don't believe in God, what do you believe in?" Prichard responded "The Frankfurters and the Grahams."[5]

The immediate political task at hand was the upcoming 1946 Democratic primary for the U.S. Senate. The race was on the mind of one *Louisville Courier-Journal* reader, who described himself as a "World War Veteran" from Ashland. Writing that "what I want is a man who is brilliant, honest, and energetic," the veteran claimed that he also wanted someone "who has that quality of magic which is required to make a statesman." After surveying the field, the letter concluded:

> I would like to cast my vote for Edward Prichard Jr. of Paris. His brilliance is such that his opponents can get little but embarrassment by a comparison of intellects. His honesty has never been and can never be challenged. His energy is clearly manifest by his record. He is a veteran and a Legionnaire who served in uniform as long as his country would let him. He is a man with no friends who are enemies of public welfare. He is a prospect that the Democratic party in its present danger cannot afford to bypass.[6]

Before Prichard could consider such possibilities or begin his work with the national party, he found himself involved in a delicate situation that threatened to undermine any political ambitions. W.A. Stanfill, a Republican appointed by Kentucky governor Simeon Willis to fill the U.S. Senate seat vacated by Happy Chandler when he became baseball commissioner, claimed that Prichard had paid no state income taxes when he was in Washington. Throughout his years in Washington, Stanfill learned, Prichard had maintained Kentucky as his official residence and was required to pay taxes in the state. Stanfill also knew of Prichard's growing political ambitions, as well as his adamant opposition to repealing the state income tax. Stanfill couched his attack in very partisan tones: "There is a wide contrast between the program of fiscal economy on the part of our Republican Governor and the 'tax and tax, spend and spend, elect and elect' theory of the New Dealers, as represented by Prichard." The senator went on to add that "Prichard evidently believes in the income tax—he wants it to remain in effect for all Kentuckians except himself." Prichard was in New York when Stanfill's charges were raised. Phil Ardery, acting as Prichard's counsel, defended his partner by saying that he was in the process of paying all taxes that the Department of Revenue deemed outstanding.[7]

The following day, Prichard's tax problems were emotionally discussed on the floor of the Kentucky House of Representatives. Democratic Representative John Y. Brown Sr. of Lexington defended Prichard, calling Stanfill's charge a "smear" campaign, and wanted to know how the senator obtained confidential tax records from the state Department of Revenue. Brown called Prichard a "brilliant, honorable, young man" who had come home to "cast his lot with us and I believe he is entitled to a fair start." After Brown finished, Ed Prichard Sr. took the floor. "Big Ed" had been a member of the Kentucky House since 1944 and defended his son in the strongest terms, to the point of challenging anyone who wrote anonymous critical letters in the newspapers to face him on the floor of the House. "I'd be right here," said Prichard, "ready to meet him any time." No one doubted Big Ed's threat—he had once punched an eastern Kentucky Republican on the House floor over a political squabble.[8]

When Ed Jr. returned home from New York, he responded himself to Stanfill's charge. His reply pulled no punches: "In November 1945, I was informed that if I publicly opposed repeal of the state income tax bill," Prichard claimed, "Mr. Stanfill would give me some unpleasant publicity. This was the first time any question of income tax liability was brought to my notice. I declined to submit to Stanfill's threat." Prichard added that he then received a notice from the Revenue Department asserting that he owed back taxes. The young attorney noted he had paid taxes to the state of Virginia from 1939 to 1945 and did not pay state income taxes to Kentucky for those years because he felt he was not required to by law. "Despite a real doubt as to the validity of the claim," wrote Prichard, "I expressed an immediate willingness to pay." The possible candidate-to-be did not want to spend months involved in legal battles, all the while with the label of "tax dodger" around his neck.

In what would become a recurring problem, Prichard's inattention to his personal finances resulted not only in tax problems but in political embarrassment as well. He therefore agreed to pay the taxes, and was indignant over the ensuing affair sparked by Stanfill. The young man who had honed his powers of ridicule and scorn in the Paris courthouse, Princeton, and Harvard, took direct aim at Stanfill:

> It seems passing strange that, with national and international problems crying aloud for statesmanship, Mr. Stanfill, up to now a senatorial mute, has found time to play Sherlock Holmes with my tax returns. Evidently he regards me as a more urgent menace than either domestic strife or international discord.
>
> The reason for this is plain. It is Mr. Stanfill's purpose to finance his senatorial campaign by punishing Kentucky's teachers and her children, her sick and her aged, her crippled and her blind. That is the real issue. The question is not whether I paid my tax on time. The question is whether Kentucky needs the income tax . . . . Here is an issue which vitally affects Kentucky and its future. If Mr. Stanfill has the courage to debate that issue, I challenge him to meet me before any appropriate forum in Kentucky. If he also desires to debate matters of a more personal character, I am willing to throw those in for good measure. And I guarantee to get for him a larger audience than he has ever had before.[9]

Prichard became heavily involved in the U.S. Senate race of 1946, but not as a candidate himself. Rather, he became a critical player in the Senate campaign of his law partner, Phil Ardery. With a glowing war record and a well-known name, Ardery revealed that he hoped "to try to cash in on that name recognition" and win a wide-open Democratic primary. Ardery's chief opponent was Rep. John Y. Brown, the same man who had so ardently defended the younger Prichard on the floor of the Kentucky House of Representatives.[10]

Prichard's duties within Ardery's campaign involved calling his numerous party contacts and enlisting their support for Ardery. But Prichard seemed torn over his loyalties in the heated race. Obviously, he had to support his law partner—"I am going to pitch in and do everything I can to help him," he admitted. From the beginning of Ardery's announced candidacy, Prichard worked behind the scenes, "arranging the initial financing, getting a most receptive conference with Barry Bingham," and "obtaining the active help of Fred Vinson." Reports that Prichard had also lobbied Senate Majority Leader Alben Barkley in Ardery's behalf were denied by Barkley. In all, despite his war record, Prichard knew Ardery had an uphill fight in dynamics that were rooted in courthouse politics. "While everyone else has dawdled, conferred, and played footsies," Prichard related to Earle Clements, Brown "has made hay—especially in Louisville and in eastern Kentucky . . . . Phil, on the other hand, must build up an organization from the ground up."[11]

Ardery of course depended heavily on Prichard's political skills to build his organization. The necessary ingredient in organizing a statewide campaign was money, and as he had done so often in the past, Prichard turned to Thomas Corcoran in Washington. Prichard mentioned his growing frustration with the trickle of funds that came into Ardery's campaign coffers and asked Corcoran to see Harold Ickes and other party heavyweights about securing more funds. He also sent Lyndon Johnson a copy of Ardery's opening campaign speech in hope of broadening Ardery's support. After several days had passed, an anxious Prichard again reached Corcoran, who admitted he had had little luck in securing any additional money for the Ardery campaign. Prichard replied that he was not surprised, but that the campaign was "giving me hell . . . they're all scared they won't have enough money to keep their headquarters open." Corcoran replied, "Well, Christ all mighty, they got a hell of a lot of nerve looking a gift horse like you in the mouth." Prichard indicated that the Arderys felt he could raise the necessary money if only he really tried. Corcoran then advised his young protégé: "Well, Prich, that's happened to you in your million years of political life as many times as it happened to me. . . . You see Prich, I've lived through so goddamned many of these that sometimes I haven't had enough to keep it going for an hour. Don't ask me, Prich, to be worried about the nervous tension of Kentucky. . . . The bother is whether the candidacy can keep going."[12]

Although Ardery felt Prichard was supporting his candidacy, he also knew that Prichard's support was lukewarm. "I don't think Prich knocked himself out," Ardery later said about Prichard's commitment to his campaign. The tension that existed between the two law partners intensified when Ardery lost the election to Brown.[13] The stresses of the campaign eventually ruptured the relationship the following year, when Ardery and Prichard found themselves on different sides of the political fence in another race.

Despite his burgeoning legal career and political prominence, Prichard's mood at this time could also be rather dark. "Men flounder hopelessly in the mud of moral confusion," he told Frankfurter, "or else seek refuge in the intellectually contemptible proposition that there must be a Church even if there is no God." Politically, Prichard sometimes grew depressed at the diminishing role of progressive liberalism: "to be a liberal in the sense of believing that reason can light the path to a livable world is increasingly impossible," he lamented, but "to be anything else is to commit suicide."[14]

Prichard's own political fortunes were not diminished by Ardery's defeat. Prichard was often invited to speak at numerous civic organizations in central Kentucky in 1946. He was especially asked to discuss his ideas regarding Kentucky's need for a new constitution to replace the one that had been adopted in 1891. Among many problems in the current constitution, Prichard stated that the "basic flaw" was the limitation on the state legislature, which could meet only biannually for sixty days. He hoped that the voters would approve a constitutional convention at the 1947 general election. On one memorable occasion in late 1946, Prichard debated the subject at the University of Kentucky. Prichard's opponent was another Paris native, attorney Cassius Clay. The debate organizers matched Prichard and Clay each with a university student for the event. Prichard's student partner for the debate was Edward T. Breathitt Jr., who became governor seventeen years later. The ironies implicit in this small event are simply remarkable—for Ed Prichard faced a man who would soon play a highly visible role in his downfall. Likewise, he was teamed with a young man who would later play an equally significant role in his renewal.[15]

Prichard's national position within the party was on display for the hometown folks in May shortly before the Kentucky Derby. When a touring party including Margaret Truman, as well as Fred Vinson, Lyndon Johnson, Paul Porter, and their spouses, visited central Kentucky for the race, they made a special point of lunching the Friday preceding the Derby at the Prichard home in Paris. Prichard accompanied his guests to Churchill Downs the next day for the race, where they all sat in the choicest of box seats.[16]

On the personal front, Prichard remained lonely. Then one day in the spring of 1946, he went to lunch in Lexington with Robert Houlihan, another newly hired associate in his office. As they walked down Main Street, they encountered a twenty-seven-year-old woman, Lucy Marshall Elliott. A descendant of a wealthy and well-known family in nearby Woodford County, she was the daughter of J. Nathan Elliott, a prominent lawyer in his own right. He had been born in Missouri and had come to Kentucky when his father became president of a college in southern Kentucky. Nathan graduated from Transylvania College in Lexington and had taught school for a year in Independence, Missouri, where he lived near Harry Truman. He received his law degree from Illinois Wesleyan and began practicing law in Lexington in 1900. He had married Mary Louise Powell of Versailles, a descendant of Capt. Tom Marshall, whose brother was Chief Justice John Marshall. After their marriage, Nathan Elliott was appointed by U.S. District Judge H. Church Ford to be a bankruptcy referee. Nathan and Mary had three children, with Lucy born in 1919.[17]

Lucy graduated from the University of Kentucky in 1940, worked in Washington in the New Zealand diplomatic office, and had recently returned to the Bluegrass State. She was young and beautiful, with full lips, dark hair, and handsome eyes with arching eyebrows. Lucy recognized Houlihan, whose wife she had known at college, and he introduced her to Prichard. For the remainder of the day, Prichard "pumped" Houlihan for all the information he could on Lucy. Houlihan arranged another meeting for the two at the Keeneland racetrack. There, in the Kentucky spring at one of its most celebrated rituals, the beginning of racing season, Prichard fell in love. According to Houlihan, Prichard "just fell head over heels" for Lucy. A star-crossed relationship had begun.[18]

Lucy Elliott, a well-connected woman of the Bluegrass, was not to be so easily bowled over by the charming young attorney. Houlihan noticed that although "Prich was just wild about her," Lucy "seemed rather aloof." In fact, he recalled that during their courtship, Lucy kept Prichard in the dark as to her own romantic intentions—"God, she dangled him," Houlihan said. "She was interested in him . . . but she really made him dance."[19]

Despite all that he had accomplished professionally, the simple fact of the matter was that Ed Prichard was a lonely man, and in some ways had been all his life. Although he was the center of attention in virtually every social setting he encountered and possessed enormous charm, his intimidating intellect and ever-widening girth made him an awkward bachelor. He had grown used to living in rarefied households such as Hockley and sharing homes with Phil Graham and Isaiah Berlin. The two women who had garnered his affections in Washington, Katharine Graham and Evangeline Bell, displayed his rather lofty tastes. Away from Washington, Prichard grew bored with the women he met at parties and other social functions.

For Lucy, on the other hand, the selection of a husband suitable for her social standing made Prichard seem an unlikely choice. The son of a Paris beer distributor and state politician did not seem, at first, to fit the bill for an Elliott. But Ed Prichard certainly had endearing qualities that made him attractive to Lucy. She later stated that "a strong part of his attraction for me" was his "Kentucky-ness." She reveled in how "he and my father loved ticking off the names of remote places in the state and recollecting speeches of candidates."[20] And if money was a concern, Prichard was quickly making sure that it would not stand in his way.

The Prichard and Ardery firm, according to Houlihan, was "making plenty of money" in their first year of business. Besides several good retainers Prichard had obtained for the firm, he was also hired to represent several large corporate clients through the auspices of Tommy Corcoran. In one typical conversation, Prichard casually mentioned a railroad company that he hoped to represent. Corcoran glibly told the young attorney that if he wanted the job, "I'll get it for you." Corcoran also acted as a go-between in a fee dispute Prichard had with Stewart Hopps, the head of International Utilities in New York. Prichard and Hopps disagreed over a suitable fee for legal services Prichard had provided. Prichard told Hopps that he had inquired of several attorneys concerning what he should charge: "Their consensus was that $50,000 would be a fair fee. Of course," Prichard added, "I thought this excessive." Instead, Prichard placed his fee at $16,500 for writing several briefs. In the middle of the dispute, Corcoran told Hopps, "I'm being very honest with you, he's going to be the legal king of that state of Kentucky." Hopps replied, "Well, I want to tell you he's able." "Within five years," Corcoran said, "he's going to run the show." In addition to his legal work, Prichard became a partner in his father's beer distributorship, as well as a vice president of a Lexington radio station, WKLX. He told Corcoran later that his yearly income was "about $30,000"—a handsome sum for the 1940s.[21]

Prichard's Washington connections gained added weight in June 1946 when President Truman nominated Fred Vinson to fill the vacancy created by the death of Chief Justice Harlan Fiske Stone. After Vinson's confirmation, Prichard could now count three of his former bosses—Frankfurter, Jackson, and Vinson—on the U.S. Supreme Court, along with another Kentuckian and father of a classmate of Prichard's at Harvard, Stanley Reed. Prichard wrote Vinson that "I am sure you will be surfeited with a lot of gratuitous advice about how to conduct yourself and how to handle other members of the Court." Prichard added, "I have not found that you needed such advice. If I were to break my rule and offer any," he said, "it would be simply to act on the assumptions that matters in the past were not of your concern and that you considered all the Justices equal in integrity and devotion to duty." Although invited, Prichard was unable to attend Vinson's swearing-in ceremony because of attending a funeral for a family member of a Princeton classmate.[22]

Prichard's real notions about Vinson's new duties were revealed to Frankfurter. He advised Frankfurter that he would find the new chief justice "disappointing"—"essentially he is a man of good common sense, right purposes, and quite often of superb moral courage," wrote Prichard. But "he is not a reflective mind and he is in no sense profound, except in his decency." Frankfurter was indeed quickly disappointed in Vinson, writing in his diary that "Prichard . . . said amusedly that the Chief Justice said to him 'everything is going smoothly. . . . I don't think there is a man on the Court who doesn't like me.'" Frankfurter wrote, "Prich told me with knowing amusement. Vinson is a very ingenuous creature and of course Prich is the opposite." Frankfurter stated that "Prich said 'poor Fred Vinson is certainly foolin' himself by his idea as to what is smoothness.'" The justice concluded that "the nice man is going to have an awakening sooner than he thinks."[23]

In October 1946, Prichard was named the election officer for his precinct in Paris for the upcoming general election. Such activity reveals that he had his eyes on the local political scene as much as he did on the national one. The crucial race the next month pitted Democratic primary winner John Y. Brown against Republican John Sherman Cooper. Riding a wave of Republican resurgence around the country, where voters were asked "Had enough?" of Truman-style liberalism, Cooper defeated Brown. In Bourbon County, Brown won almost 60 percent of the vote, and in Prichard's Paris precinct, he won 146 votes to 93.[24]

Throughout their courtship in 1946, Ed made it clear that he wanted to marry Lucy Elliott. At this juncture, Lucy saw Ed Prichard in a dazzling world—heading a thriving law office, where he would be found speaking by phone with the newly appointed chief justice of the Supreme Court or with numerous other Washington notables; hosting the president's daughter at his home; and being casually mentioned as a future governor or senator. Prichard was quickly becoming one of the state's leading attorneys, and it seemed the future held nothing but higher rewards for one so bright and talented. Lucy agreed to his proposal in November 1946, and the wedding date was set for February of the new year.

The week of Lucy and Ed's wedding was a lavish affair. Parties were held throughout Lexington and at the Elliott home in Versailles. Numerous Washington friends attended the wedding, including Ben Cohen, Phil and Katharine Graham, and Edmund Gullion. Vinson and Frankfurter, of course, were too consumed with court business to attend but sent congratulatory telegrams and letters. Vinson wrote a poignant note to Prichard saying, "I feel toward you in this great adventure precisely like I know I will feel when Fred or Jim [Vinson's sons] break similar news to me in the future." Vinson concluded by telling Prichard, "I love you a lot."[25]

The wedding of Lucy Elliott and Edward F. Prichard Jr. occurred at Christ Church Episcopal in Lexington on February 15, 1947. Phil Graham served as Prichard's best man, and his wedding party represented the spectrum of Prichard's young life—his lifelong friend and law partner, Phil Ardery; two Hockley alumni, Ed Gullion and John Ferguson; Lucy's brother James Nathan Elliott Jr.; the man who had introduced Prichard to Lucy, Bob Houlihan; and one old friend from Paris, William "Billy" Baldwin. Lucy was especially happy the Grahams came to Kentucky, which "made everything perfect for Prich and me." The next day's newspaper was filled with detailed descriptions of Lucy's wedding gown and the eminent wedding party. The couple spent their wedding night at a posh hotel in Cincinnati and they announced that they planned to make their home in Paris.[26]

Despite his well-announced homecoming and his impressive first months at work, not everyone was enamored with the return of the New Deal "boy wonder" to Bourbon County. Prichard's name was often mentioned as a possible candidate for Congress, but some within the Democratic party in Kentucky were not disposed to give the Paris native the nomination just yet. The progressive wing of the state party—led by Rep. Earle Clements, Louisville's Wilson Wyatt, and *Courier-Journal* publisher Barry Bingham Sr.—found Prichard promising. But the more conservative old-guard wing led by former governor and senator A.B. "Happy" Chandler simply found Prichard an arrogant know-it-all who needed to pay his dues. A confidant of Clements stated that Prichard had "succeeded in making as big an ass out of himself in as short a time as possible since his return to Kentucky." The main problem with Prichard, according to the disgruntled observer, was that "he left as a boy and all he has learned has come from books." The same observer spoke with numerous Democratic Party leaders, "all of them from widely separated places," and found that Prichard could be "of no help except with the national headquarters—but who could tell Prichard that?"[27]

While local Democrats may not have been impressed, Prichard's reputation among party regulars soared. Worried that the Republican gains in 1946 would carry on to the 1948 presidential election, old New Dealers looked in vain for a "leader whose magic touch might bring them together." Feeling certain that leader was not Harry S. Truman, members of the progressive wing of the party were mentioned as the potential standard bearer for the mantle of FDR. A national magazine proclaimed that Henry Wallace, Fiorello

LaGuardia, Chester Bowles, and Ed Prichard were the leading contenders, but suggestively added, "None of these has a political following."[28]

The New Dealers' dissatisfaction with Truman produced an organizing drive that culminated in the founding meeting of the Americans for Democratic Action. In this gathering, a litany of old New Dealers met to form their own organization, which was adamantly prolabor and civil rights but also laced with a virulent anticommunism. Among those in attendance were Hubert Humphrey, Reinhold Niebuhr, Franklin D. Roosevelt Jr., Arthur M. Schlesinger Jr., and Ed Prichard. Kentucky's prominence in the initial ADA was reflected in the naming of Wilson Wyatt, Truman's housing expediter and former Louisville mayor, as the organization's first chairman. Prichard kept a low profile in these meetings, perhaps because, like many Democratic party faithful, he was judging just how far he could go in forcing the party leftward before sacrificing his own political fortunes, which were still firmly rooted with the party. Robert Nathan put it more succinctly: Prichard "liked to maneuver rather than to operate." By the fall of 1947 Prichard's inactivity within the ADA was a cause for some concern. Joe Rauh implored Wyatt to "tell Prich to do some work."[29]

Back home, Prichard faced enough political minefields of his own with the Kentucky gubernatorial campaign of 1947. A leading contender for the Governor's Mansion in 1947 was Rep. Earle Chester Clements of Morganfield in western Kentucky. Clements, a big, burly man who had played football at the University of Kentucky, had mastered the art of courthouse politics—an art that Prichard appreciated—in Union County, where he had held a succession of county offices, including county clerk and sheriff. Historian James Klotter has noted that Clements's "chief strength was not his presence, certainly not his oratory," but rather his "organization skills." He was an instrumental part of Tom Rhea's political machine, managing Rhea's unsuccessful 1935 gubernatorial campaign. Upon Rhea's death in 1938, Clements took control of the Rhea organization, a powerful faction in the state party hierarchy. He became a state legislator and was elected to the U.S. House of Representatives in 1944 and 1946. In Congress, he supported Social Security, antilynch and poll tax legislation, and voted against the Taft-Hartley act. His popularity in western Kentucky, as well as his dominance of the Rhea faction, was demonstrated in clear terms in 1946. In a national election that brought both houses of Congress under Republican rule, Clements survived despite his perceived liberal voting record. This combination of grassroots realpolitik and a shrewd political intellect with a progressive national vision attracted Prichard to Clements. Within a short time, Prichard became one of Clements's most vocal supporters.[30]

Clements's principal opponent for the party's nomination in 1947 was newspaper publisher Harry Lee Waterfield, another western Kentucky native. Waterfield lacked Clements's statewide organization but was a better stump campaigner. One of the most pressing issues of the 1947 primary campaign directly involved Prichard and worked toward dismantling the firm of Prichard and Ardery.

The issue of rural electric cooperatives became a focal point of the primary election. Since Kentucky remained in 1947 mostly an impoverished rural state, numerous people in western Kentucky would have been without electricity had it not been for the Tennessee Valley Authority (TVA). The state's rural electric cooperatives wanted to build upon TVA's service but were bitterly fought by the state's larger power companies, particularly the influential Kentucky Utilities Company.

Waterfield sought to capitalize on the explosive issue of public versus private power sources, and he saw a wonderful opportunity in a series of votes by Clements in the 1942 and 1944 Kentucky General Assembly. Clements had supported a bill sponsored by Republican Ray B. Moss, which would have allowed private utility firms to build power plants in areas served by TVA. The politically powerful Kentucky Utilities Company backed the measure, which its opponents, such as Waterfield, saw as harmful to public power. Clements's support of the Moss bill enabled Waterfield, in the words of political scientist Marc Landy, "to portray himself as a populist who would defend the public against the private interests." Waterfield painted Clements as a tool of Kentucky Utilities and as one who would work to kill TVA. For his part, Clements spent most of his time building up his party organization at the county level, receiving a large share of his support from the county courthouse rings throughout the state. Realizing, however, how unpopular his vote on the Moss bill had become, Clements quickly shifted course in Congress, voting repeatedly in support of TVA.[31]

Prichard was one of the few reform-oriented figures in the state who early in the race backed Clements. He had discussed Clements's possibility of running for governor the previous year as the two sat in Prichard's driveway in Paris, and Prichard had committed himself on the spot to Clements's candidacy. As Prichard had demonstrated in Washington, he had the certain knack of cultivating relationships with older politicians that were politically beneficial to his growing ambitions. Prichard was especially attracted to the type of earthy politician who resembled his father and the men he had known at the Bourbon County courthouse as a boy. Clements fit the bill, a tenacious bull of a man who, like Big Ed, thought nothing of grabbing a critical journalist by the lapels and throwing him against a wall. Prichard certainly saw Clements as a tough, country-shrewd politico who could be very helpful in serving

Prichard's own needs. But one prominent Democrat who opposed Clements was none other than Phil Ardery. Ardery said that on this issue he and Prichard hoped they "could agree to disagree" and thereby keep the firm intact. But quickly, in Ardery's words, "it became apparent that any such effort must fail if each of us was to give wholehearted and honest support to the candidate of his choice. So we split up."[32]

But there was more to the breakup of the firm than a difference of opinion over the governor's race. Ardery also stated that representatives of the Rural Electrification Administration (REA) in Kentucky, whom the firm represented, were distrustful of Prichard's relationship with Clements. According to Ardery, the REA representatives told him they would no longer do business with Prichard, whereupon Ardery went to his partner and told him they would have to disband. "The real thing that precipitated the split up was the factor that my rural electric people said we don't want Prich," Ardery revealed. On the other hand, Prichard expressed to friends a dissatisfaction with the relatively small amount of business Ardery was bringing to the firm.[33] In reflection, it seems only a matter of time before the already tenuous relationship between the two would break. The tension that existed during high school, Harvard, and during the 1946 campaign remained. The split finally occurred, with the two lawyers parting on rather friendly terms. Prichard remained in Lexington and kept Al Funk Jr. as his new partner, while Ardery kept his practice in Frankfort. Despite their breakup, the paths of Phil Ardery and Ed Prichard soon crossed again.

Prichard's work in Clements's campaign was the most significant work he had done for any major candidate to this point in his life. He not only advised Clements on strategy and wrote speeches and campaign material, he also appeared in various public assemblies in Clements's behalf. During a crucial stretch in July, Prichard made campaign speeches for Clements in such small locales as Owenton, Greenup, and Calhoun, Kentucky. At the latter setting, Prichard stood next to the candidate and declared, "As a constant supporter of public power and cheap electricity, I am confident that the cause of REA and TVA will be served by the election of Earle Clements as governor." Such public pronouncements, Clements knew, would help shore up his support among the state's old New Dealers. Privately, Prichard had told Clements he should adopt the public posture that his earlier votes on the Moss bill were "prompted by sincere conviction." Any attempts to "gloss over" the vote, Prichard said, should be avoided because "the opposition will not let us gloss it over." Prichard added that Clements could "legitimately say that your mind is always open to new arguments and that if the opponents to the Moss bill could convince you that they were right and you had been wrong, you were not precluded by any commitment to anyone from changing your mind." In campaign material Prichard wrote, voters were told they could be confident that with Earle Clements as governor, no attempt would be undertaken "to revive the deceased Moss bill, in whole or in part."[34]

Clements's ability to deflect the nettlesome utility issue—through Prichard's considerable help—was successful enough to give him a 33,000-vote majority over Waterfield in the primary election. After the victory, Prichard wrote Clements, "I am sure you realize that my services, for what they are worth, are at your disposal in the fall campaign." Prichard's services were, indeed, used by Clements's campaign organization. In October, Prichard went to Washington to discuss possible funding from the Democratic National Committee. After meeting with DNC officials Matt Connelly and Gael Sullivan, however, Prichard was disappointed to learn that the DNC did not know if it could fund Clements's campaign until after the new DNC chairman took office, which was not until after the November election.[35]

Prichard's skills in speech writing were also employed by the Clements campaign. In one speech he wrote for the candidate, the Prichard style shone through:

> The Republican nominee for Governor is a somewhat pathetic case. I do not envy him his task. Republicans in Kentucky have not had an easy life for the past twelve months. Amidst the confused alarms of selfish leadership engaged in a bitter struggle for power, their allegiances have shifted and turned with every new gust of political wind. . . . When the present administration, of which this candidate was a part, supported a potential rival in the Republican primary, he condemned it with words of bitter resentment. When this rival candidate, under the humiliating dictation of a ruthless and cynical political boss, withdrew from the race, the present Republican nominee once more heaped Hosanna's of praise on the administration.

Prichard added that "if more time were available" for preparing the speech, "I believe it could be given a bit more fighting quality."[36]

Clements won the Governor's Mansion by handily defeating Republican Eldon S. Dummit by 100,000 votes in the November general election. Days afterward, the governor-elect wrote to "my dear 'Prich'" thanking him for his committed devotion to the campaign. Obviously, Prichard had some considerable chits to call in with Clements, and the young attorney took full advantage of the situation to suggest various names for crucial appointments, particularly to the highly important position of highway commissioner. Having been back in Kentucky for only two years, Prichard had already basked in the glow of playing a kingmaker of sorts to the next governor—few individuals in the election had played a more crucial role in Clements's campaign and were more personally devoted to the Morganfield politician than the young

Ed Prichard.[37] In Earle Clements, Prichard had also found more than just a friend in a high place. The two developed one of the more poignant political friendships in the state. Some thoughtful observers naturally wondered if the new governor would return the favor by helping Ed Prichard into the Governor's Mansion himself in 1951. The crafty new governor was not ready to reveal his intentions just yet. Years later, the usually tight-lipped Clements revealed to Prichard that he had been convinced, just as Joe Rauh and other Washingtonians had been, "that it was just a question of time until you were going to be Governor of our state and that would have eventually led to being President of the United States."[38]

The governor's race had occupied a significant amount of Prichard's time in 1947, but he had other things to keep him busy. His law practice, which would now be known as Prichard and Funk, was doing well. Ed and Lucy bought a farm along Clintonville Road in Paris, where they set up their first home. Prichard, who had purchased the land with his brother, Henry, had borrowed $30,000 from a Paris bank to finance the deal, which was added to a previous mortgage he had taken out in 1943 for $15,000 on forty-three acres of land. On the Clintonville site, Ed and Lucy began furnishing their first home. Besides the considerable sum he now owed, Prichard also found Lucy's decorating tastes involved rather expensive furnishings. While Prichard enjoyed a relatively lucrative law practice, he was also spending a good deal of his income on the Clintonville Road farm and told some in the county that he had to work extra hard just to keep up with Lucy's spending habits.[39] The world of the young couple brightened that fall when they learned that Lucy was expecting their first child.

In addition to his law practice and political chores, Prichard found time to engage in other ventures. His considerable political experience was sought by Transylvania College in Lexington, where he agreed to teach a political science course as a visiting assistant professor in the spring semester of 1948. The fact that both J. Nathan and Milton Elliott were on the college's Board of Curators may have played a part in Prichard's academic appointment.[40]

Young Ed Prichard was becoming the toast of the town. Where, exactly, Prichard would now turn was a question on a lot of people's minds. One such interested individual was James Loeb, the executive secretary of the Americans for Democratic Action. Loeb dined with Prichard in early December 1947, and the next day he said how pleased he had been "to find out what the hell everybody has been talking about ever since I have been in Washington with regard to this myth called Prich." Loeb continued, "Now I understand." Loeb's agenda for the dinner included more than satisfying his curiosity about the "myth" of Ed Prichard. He had also come to offer Prichard the post of executive director of the ADA. Loeb explained he was "in search of a boss" and stated that the ADA needed a powerful leader who could "effectively represent the organization and its ideas to the public." Loeb concluded: "I am convinced that you are the guy and I can't think of anyone else," then added, "nor can anyone else think of anyone else."

Loeb was disappointed, however, at Prichard's refusal. What the two discussed that night over dinner provides the clearest window into what Prichard was considering in December 1947. Loeb spelled out the dilemma facing Prichard:

> It seems to me that the problem is whether the district and the state in which you have your political base are sufficiently liberal to make political success possible on an all-out New Deal program. Assuming that [Virgil] Chapman runs for the Senate, you probably can get the Congressional seat; but I assume that being one of 435 members of Congress is not your lifetime ambition. To be a powerful member of Congress takes 15 to 20 years. If you can come to Congress, you should, by reasons of your talents and ability, become the leader of the liberal bloc. The question is: can you be such an outright liberal and continue to be returned to Congress from a conservative district without a real fight every two years? Or would you have the problem that Jerry Voorhis had? One might cite the case of Senator Barkley to answer the question. But it seems to me that that is a different case. . . .
>
> In terms of the future, both your future and the future of the country, the ADA has much to offer. When we get to that depression everyone is talking about . . . there will have to be a tough-minded, realistic, constructive, non-Communist, fighting center of gravity. I see no reason why that center should not be the ADA. . . . I think your direction would pretty well make that certain.[41]

From his conversation with Loeb, it is evident that Prichard had already committed himself to running for the congressional seat that would be vacated if Paris native Virgil Chapman ran for the U.S. Senate. With his role in the Clements campaign, Prichard saw no reason to leave the comfortable environs of the Kentucky Democratic party to head an organization that was observed with considerable skepticism by party regulars. Having provided so much support for the party's chief in Governor Clements, Prichard, no doubt, earnestly counted on Clements's endorsement in any potential races. Prichard subsequently declined Loeb's offer, and his name no longer appeared on the ADA's national board.

Prichard made his plans official the next week. After Virgil Chapman announced he was indeed running for John Sherman Cooper's Senate seat, Prichard proclaimed that he intended to run for Chapman's vacated sixth district congressional seat. Prichard said he would visit the seventeen counties in the district "to line up support from political leaders." What Prichard needed to duplicate in the Sixth District was the web of political relationships he had cultivated in Washington. Writer James D. Squires observed that in order to understand southern courthouse politics, all one needed to know was "that politics was a matter of personal friendships."[42] In other words, in order to win the party nomination, Prichard needed the support of the county organizations and their courthouse rings.

In making his intentions public, Prichard crossed a crucial threshold in his life. Up to this point, he had never declared himself a candidate for any major political office. He had run for minor jobs within select clubs in college, where he felt certain of victory, losing only once in the Lincoln's Inn election at Harvard. The heady world he had occupied in Washington led him to believe all the things that close friends and national magazines had predicted—that it was only a matter of time before he would win major office. Buoyed by his marriage and, finally, a reprieve from the loneliness he had long endured, Ed Prichard's confidence soared in early 1948, and he readied himself for his climb to power.

But to those county politicians throughout the district, Ed Prichard was certainly a different figure from Virgil Chapman. In the words of journalist Mark Ethridge, Chapman was "a most rabid conservative" who opposed the party's recent stands on civil rights and labor. Prichard, on the other hand, made no bones about his political views, particularly on the matter of race relations. Prichard was firmly committed to civil rights and was so bold as to tell a Charleston, South Carolina, civic club that the days of the all-white election in the South were over. Such statements, coupled with his New Deal orientation and his public support for a state income tax, made him a dubious candidate, at best, to the courthouse crowd. The *Lexington Leader* understood that Prichard's New Deal credentials made him a "liability rather than an asset" to many local Democrats. Prichard's problems concerning his personal income taxes were also a considerable "embarrassment" to the party. Additionally, Prichard's well-known arrogance and his tendency for unkind stories concerning his political adversaries had circulated throughout the Sixth District. In locales where politics is ultimately personal, Prichard attracted little initial attention and support. Cumulatively, he simply could not raise support for a congressional race, and his candidacy was dead in the water before it began. The realization of his unpopularity hit Prichard hard, and he never even formally filed for the race. Democratic party regulars, perhaps at Clements's prompting, put their support behind the governor's campaign manager Tom Underwood, a longtime party regular and, according to Ethridge, "next to Barkley, probably the best after dinner speaker in the state."[43]

If Prichard had been expecting Clements's endorsement, it was not forthcoming. In the county courthouses and barbershops throughout the district, the "New Deal Wonder Boy" had received his comeuppance by the county politicos he had come to know so well as a child. The "Prichard for Congress" campaign petered out quickly. Happy Chandler's *Woodford Sun* later described the situation as one where "the Democratic powers-that-be in the Sixth District turned their heads upon the 'wonder boy.'" As Loeb had told him just a few weeks earlier, Prichard's return to Washington as a congressman would be no easy task. For the man who had seen everything come so easily so quickly, his failed candidacy was a major disappointment. Those who assumed Prichard would obtain high elective office ignored one of the demons that haunted him. Had he been driven to obtain power, as, say, Lyndon Johnson was, Prichard would not have let a preliminary rejection by some party functionaries keep him from running. But his fragile self-confidence could not withstand public rejection, and thus he quickly avoided the race altogether. He later claimed he had no "specific ambition to hold a particular office,"[44] further revealing his sensitivity to the debacle of his failed congressional bid. Just as Tom Underwood was being rewarded for a lifetime contribution of hard work to the party, if Ed Prichard was to be similarly rewarded, he would have to spend yet more time currying favors with the courthouse gangs of central Kentucky.

Before Prichard could resign himself to matters on the homefront, the national election of 1948 impinged. Like many other New Dealers, Prichard looked upon the party's nomination of Harry Truman with some foreboding. But when Franklin Roosevelt Jr. endorsed the possibility of drafting Dwight Eisenhower as the Democratic nominee, Prichard's worries only intensified. The move by other members of the ADA to enlist the affable general struck Prichard as a "crusade which is headed we know not where and run by we know not whom." Eisenhower's popularity was indeed strong, but it seemed foolhardy to support him, claimed Prichard, if Eisenhower did not reveal his true political philosophies. Prichard thought the selection of a military officer presented some problems in itself—"already," Prichard claimed, "the foreign policy of our nation is being distorted, compromised, and supercharged with hysteria by the forces of militarism and big business." Prichard hoped Justice William O. Douglas would announce his presidential candidacy. Douglas's "courage, liberalism, political shrewdness and capacity for leadership are assets of the first magnitude." If Douglas did not run, Prichard lamented, New Dealers had no choice but to support Truman. In that case, Prichard told Roosevelt, "We shall do it in a kind of trance in which neither we nor the people whom we are trying to rally will believe that anything is taking place other than a dumb show."[45]

In July, Prichard attended the raucous Democratic National Convention in Philadelphia. Although as general counsel to the DNC Prichard had access to the convention and its meetings, he gained further credentials when he was selected by the state party as a delegate-at-large. A crucial moment for the party and Prichard came during a debate over the proposed civil rights plank. Earlier in the year, Prichard had attended an ADA meeting that centered on the touchy issue of civil rights. The prospects for a Democratic victory in 1948 then seemed dim, and Prichard agreed with Jim Loeb that "we ought to go down fighting." The strategy adopted was to pursue a strong civil rights plank in Philadelphia.[46]

The Truman administration had proposed a civil rights plank similar in tone to the 1944 platform that had offered African Americans vague generalities. Southerners were anxious to emasculate any civil rights platform but were opposed by a sizable contingent led by Minnesota's Hubert Humphrey. Humphrey wanted the platform to adopt the findings of the 1946 presidential commission on civil rights, including four essential elements: outlawing lynching, creating a federal commission to curb employment discrimination, ensuring the right to vote, and opening military service to all regardless of race. A battle ensued in the platform committee that had lasting repercussions for the party's future.

The struggle within the committee centered around the administration's support of the 1944 statement on civil rights and the plank suggested by Humphrey and endorsed by the ADA and fifty other Democratic notables. Although Prichard was not an official member of the 108-member committee, as general counsel he participated in the meeting itself. When one Ohio delegate blandly claimed that "what was good for Franklin D. Roosevelt is good enough for me," Prichard roared back, "What *was* good for Franklin D. Roosevelt isn't good enough for Franklin D. Roosevelt." The split committee's fight went all the way to the floor, where Humphrey's amendment was adopted, causing South Carolina's Strom Thurmond and a number of other southern delegates to leave the convention hall. The southerners quickly formed their own party, popularly called the "Dixiecrats," with Thurmond heading its presidential ticket. One of the Kentuckians avidly supporting Thurmond was Happy Chandler.[47]

Prichard endorsed what many at the time considered to be a suicidal platform for the party. Not only had the Dixiecrats left a gaping hole in the party through their anger at the party's liberalism, but former Vice President Henry Wallace also bolted the party in protest of Truman's conservatism. Losing the southern white vote was almost assured with the Humphrey platform. But Prichard and other members of the party felt that a party that could not ensure civil rights for all was not worthy of support in the first place. The struggle that had started in that platform committee in Philadelphia foretold a larger division in the party and the country.

The high point of the convention came when Kentucky's senior senator,

Alben Barkley, gave a rousing speech that electrified the Philadelphia contingent. In fact, a movement was undertaken, supported by Prichard and Wilson Wyatt, to place Barkley's name in nomination for the vice presidency. Wyatt and Prichard went on national television to discuss themes such as party unity and Barkley's prospects.[48] With Barkley's eventual nomination, as well as the stand on civil rights, Prichard took great satisfaction at the outcome of the 1948 convention. His star continued to rise within national party circles. The DNC named Prichard to an advisory campaign committee of "sixteen prominent young leaders" of the party to help organize the vote for Truman. Joining Prichard on the select list were Margaret Truman, Edmund "Pat" Brown of California, and Lyndon Johnson.[49]

Prichard's enthusiasm was tempered, however, by the very real possibility that Truman and the Democrats might be in store for the same outcome that had faced the party in the 1946 election. Truman's chances for reelection looked dismal after the convention, and Republican Thomas Dewey confidently awaited the election in order to take advantage of the three-way split in the Democratic party, as well as the country's seeming turn to the right two years earlier. Prichard nevertheless fought hard for his party and gave several speeches for the Truman campaign throughout the country. In mid-October, he spoke at a Truman rally at his alma mater in Princeton. Back home, Paris's Virgil Chapman faced an uphill struggle to win his party's primary as well as John Sherman Cooper's Senate seat. Besides their usual involvement in the campaign, in July both Prichard and his father were selected as precinct officers—Prichard in his new precinct in Clintonville #3 and his father in Paris #4. Lucy Prichard was selected as the "ladies officer" for her husband's precinct.[50]

Chapman's rival for the Democratic nomination was, again, John Y. Brown of Lexington. Bourbon Countians wanted to support their favorite son, whose local campaign committee was headed by Billy Baldwin and Ed Prichard Sr. Chapman headquarters in Louisville asked Baldwin and Prichard "to aid in rounding up every possible Democratic vote." Chapman won the primary election, certainly helped along by his 2,012 to 148 vote margin in Bourbon County. For the general election, the *Paris Kentuckian-Citizen* predicted that "the Democrats in Bourbon County undoubtedly will give Paris' Virgil Chapman one of the greatest margins any Democrat has ever achieved." On the eve of the election, the paper's columnist wrote that "Bourbon Countians will rally to the voting places Tuesday, that is, every single Democratic voter, and help Virgil in the most important race of his career."[51]

Early on the morning of election day, Tuesday, November 2, 1948, a Republican precinct officer carried to the polls a ballot box he obtained at the county courthouse. When he heard a rattling sound at the bottom of the box, he asked Bourbon County Deputy Sheriff John Neal to see what was at the bottom of the box that was supposedly empty. The deputy used a penknife to extract the source of the noise, a ballot that had already been scratched in favor of the Democratic slate. Further extractions revealed that seventeen ballots were lying at the bottom of the box, all but one marked Democratic. The fraudulent ballots were brought to Sheriff J.M. Leer, who placed them in the county vault. The box in question was Clintonville #3, whose precinct officer was listed as Edward F. Prichard Jr.[52]

When Sheriff Leer went out to the Clintonville precinct to check the ballot book, the ballots in question were missing. Reports of missing ballots from six other precincts were soon verified. County Republicans were furious to discover the fraud, and local Democrats implied that it was a Republican setup. A statement released by the Bourbon County Democratic Committee, led by Frank Kiser, Dan Peed, William Blanton, and Billy Baldwin, declared, "We hope that whoever is guilty of this despicable trick will be detected and prosecuted."[53]

The outcome of the national election, of course, is best remembered by Harry Truman delightfully displaying a premature newspaper headline of his impending defeat. Despite enormous odds, Truman scored one of the great political upsets in the history of American presidential elections. Dewey's own overconfidence was extended to the Kentucky senate race, where he wired fellow Republican John Sherman Cooper shortly after 10:00 P.M. on election night, saying, "Am overjoyed at your reelection. Heartiest congratulations and best wishes, Thomas E. Dewey." When the votes were finally tabulated, Chapman defeated Cooper by 21,000 votes.[54]

In Bourbon County, the victories of Truman and Chapman were overshadowed by the continuing discovery of more forged ballots. The laborious task of weeding out the fraudulent ballots took almost a week. By Friday, a total of 254 forged ballots had been discovered, all but one marked for the Democrat Virgil Chapman. When he read of the vote fraud in Kentucky, Washington columnist Joseph Alsop recalled that his friend Ed Prichard lived in the county in question. Alsop sent Prichard a jocular telegram pointing out the coincidence and added, "I assume you stuffed the one vote for John Sherman Cooper."[55] Local Republicans and ministers were not so amused and demanded a full investigation by local and federal authorities. What few observers knew at the time was that the subsequent events surrounding the probe of the Bourbon County vote fraud would become the defining moment of Ed Prichard's life.

Part II
Star Falling

This was not a thing in our county in which only thugs and other totally disreputable people indulged. It was done by the most respectable people in the community, people who were leaders in the church. I don't know if it was the American way. But it was their way in Bourbon County.

—Edward F. Prichard Jr., 1982

8 "Press Vigorously and Thoroughly"

ON May 4, 1949, sealed indictments in the Bourbon County vote fraud investigation were opened in U.S. Federal Court in Lexington, Kentucky. The indictments implicated only two individuals—Edward F. Prichard Jr. and his law partner, Al Funk Jr. They were charged with conspiracy to violate the civil rights of Bourbon County voters by purposely defrauding them of a fair election. Friends and colleagues of the former New Deal "wonder boy" were shocked—some expressed profound regret, others thought, or at least hoped, he was innocent. Yet the most prevailing reaction seemed one of anger and dismay, and certain questions naturally arose: Why would someone with so promising a future throw it all away for 254 votes in a statewide election? Were others involved? Would the case go to trial? Finally, was it possible that Ed Prichard could be convicted and go to prison?

The complex and sometimes strange series of steps that led the grand jury to return the indictments against Prichard and Funk focuses on local politics and relationships, on national power, and even on J. Edgar Hoover and the role of the FBI. An examination into the interior dynamics of the Bourbon County election of 1948 also reveals some of the hidden corners of American politics. As Robert Caro has written, "Understanding political power in a democracy requires understanding elections."[1] A proper understanding of elections involves far more than simply studying platforms, speeches, or polling data. The scandal surrounding the 1948 election allows us a glimpse into a more cynical world where elections were blatantly manipulated with contemptuous impunity.

For days following the discovery of the fraudulent ballots, people in Paris and Bourbon County reacted in predictable fashion. County Republicans, at whose expense the ballots were forged, proclaimed their outrage. Others who shared their anger saw such electioneering as an example of corruption that needed to be weeded out of the Bourbon County political culture. The Republican *Paris Daily Enterprise* editorialized that "it was an outrageous and dastardly act" and stated that "there is no greater menace to society than to 'stuff' a ballot box." The paper's editors called for Circuit Judge William B.

Ardery to call for a grand jury investigation when he opened court the following Monday. County Democrats, on the other hand, were nonplussed. The Democratic *Kentuckian-Citizen* issued no such editorials but did carry a full-page petition that called for a federal investigation in order that Bourbon County's "good name remain unsullied." The petition was signed by numerous local officials, including Cassius Clay and Billy Baldwin. As county attorney, Baldwin had called for state aid by requesting a fingerprint expert from the state police to examine the ballots in question. But the latent feeling among county Democrats was best summed up by a *Kentuckian-Citizen* editor who felt that the whole matter was exaggerated, since the "stuffing of ballot boxes is no new thing in Paris."[2]

In local elections where ballot "irregularities" were suspected, the investigation was conducted—often fruitlessly—by local or state authorities. But since the vote tampering in Bourbon County involved a U.S. Senate seat, federal authorities could possibly become involved. Local Republicans—in full knowledge that unless the FBI was called in the investigation would probably wither—demanded federal intervention early on. Several days after the election, requests for a federal investigation were made to U.S. Attorney General Tom Clark by a number of Bourbon Countians, including County Judge George Batterton, Baptist minister J. Bill Jones, and Harry Horton, the chairman of the Bourbon County Republican party. Another request was made by Sen. John Sherman Cooper, who would soon be leaving his Senate seat to make way for the newly elected Virgil Chapman. Cooper was already something of a Kentucky statesman who seemed to transcend such petty maneuverings, yet in 1929 Cooper himself had been accused by a Republican challenger of having bought votes to win election as a county judge.[3]

The FBI was reluctant to investigate the case, however. The day following the election, FBI director J. Edgar Hoover wrote Assistant Attorney General Alexander M. Campbell that the bureau had received information regarding vote fraud in Bourbon County and that the FBI had been asked to provide a special agent to assist in the investigation. Hoover had denied the request, dismissively saying that "an agent could not be present," and further told Campbell simply that "no investigation is contemplated in this matter unless requested by you."[4] Campbell was busy at this same time investigating another of Frankfurter's former students, Alger Hiss.

The FBI's aversion to investigating the vote fraud in Bourbon County was understandable. In other recent cases involving similar charges, the reaction by the bureau and the Justice Department had not been energetic. Only two years earlier, an election scandal and its aftermath had stained the glossy image of Hoover's august agency. The Justice Department and the FBI came under severe criticism by some Republican senators for an investigation into charges of vote fraud during a 1946 primary election in Kansas City. The department's handling of the case brought implications that the investigation was emasculated in order to avoid shedding further light into the political machine that had, after all, elected Harry Truman to the Senate. The department had also been requested to investigate another election in 1948. When Prichard's friend Lyndon Johnson won a Democratic primary election in a Senate race in Texas amid widespread vote fraud, Johnson's challenger, former governor Coke Stevenson, asked for a federal investigation. Attorney general and fellow Texan Tom Clark agreed to look into the charges, but the FBI, in the words of one analysis, pursued the case with "a notable lack of investigative and prosecutorial vigor." One study concluded that Clark "delayed doing anything by turning the matter over to subordinates, who simply waited on events." Another Johnson biographer stated that "the best that could be said of the FBI's performance in the case was that the investigation was muffed. At worst, it could be concluded that the FBI refused to look for evidence."[5]

The untidy truth was that widespread vote fraud was America's dirty little secret, and thorough investigations promised to expose the methods whereby some of America's most powerful and popular political figures had reached office and maintained power. If the FBI was willing to overlook overwhelming amounts of vote buying, illegal ballots, and blatant ballot stuffing involving tens of thousands of votes in Texas and Missouri, it is evident why the Justice Department and the FBI were not anxious to investigate charges of stuffing a mere 254 ballots in a single Kentucky county. Underlying it all was the notion, best expressed by James D. Squires, that in the 1940s "cheating in elections was like cheating on your wife. Not everybody did it, but those who did viewed it as perfectly okay as long as you didn't get caught."[6]

Whereas the FBI had treated Clark's requests on the Kansas City and Texas cases with a response bordering on nonchalance, the same could not be said by mid-November. The bureau suddenly changed course and aggressively pursued leads within a week of the election. The investigation, in fact, abruptly caught the personal attention of J. Edgar Hoover for reasons that had little to do with law enforcement or the sanctity of elections. After Hoover had sent the memo to Campbell in which he deferred any activity, a teletype came across the director's desk on November 9 that changed the FBI's entire reaction. The teletype was sent to Hoover by the Louisville FBI field office, informing him that U.S. Attorney Claude Stephens had received a request from Attorney General Clark authorizing a preliminary investigation. The field office, however, again hoped to pass off the task, saying, "No investigation is being made by this office until specific instructions are received from the bureau."

The most significant element in the teletype, however, had nothing to do with investigative procedures. Within the teletype was a reference to a possible subject named "Pritchard" who, the FBI wrote, "is probably identical with individual by same name who was prominent in political affairs in Washington, D.C." Upon the entrance of Ed Prichard as a likely suspect in the case, the investigation suddenly changed course. On November 11, in commenting on a memo concerning the case, Hoover wrote in the margin his clear instructions to field agents for handling the investigation: "Press vigorously and thoroughly."[7] After this moment early in the case, Hoover took special interest in the investigation of the man he had first encountered as an assistant to the attorney general in 1941 and had wiretapped in 1945. The FBI director made sure throughout the course of the inquiry that his desire to press the case was strictly adhered to.

What the FBI knew within days of the election centered around Ed Prichard. In a "personal and confidential" memo sent to Attorney General Clark on November 17, Hoover outlined what the FBI had uncovered: "Information has been obtained from a source identified as anonymous to the effect that Edward F. Prichard, Jr., . . . obtained unused ballots from the Office of the County Clerk of Court during the week preceding the election and that Prichard's law partner, A.E. Funk, Jr., . . . forged the names on these ballots. Information from this source also indicated that County Attorney William T. Baldwin . . . thereafter placed these fraudulent ballots in the boxes." Hoover sought to head off any attempts to derail the investigation: "This same source further indicated that Mr. Prichard has discussed his predicament with Kentucky State officials and with prominent individuals, including you."[8]

In the ensuing months, FBI agents scoured Bourbon County, Frankfort, and Lexington, interviewing scores of people and collecting evidence. Handwriting and fingerprint experts were brought into the case as well. But the most damaging piece of evidence against Prichard came not from the FBI but from Prichard himself.

On the night of Sunday, November 7, 1948, Phil Ardery decided to go to bed early at his home in Frankfort. The phone rang, and Prichard was on the line asking if he could meet with Ardery that evening. "I had not heard Prich's voice in many months," said Ardery, "but somehow the call did not surprise me." Ardery got dressed and answered the door in less than an hour. Prichard told his former law partner, "I'm in a heap of trouble and I need some advice." In his grand jury testimony several weeks later, Ardery clearly recalled that Prichard had said he was in need of "legal advice." Ardery invited Prichard inside and, according to Ardery, Prichard admitted that "my fingerprints are all over those ballots in Bourbon County." What happened next is somewhat unclear. Years later, Ardery claimed that Prichard asked if Judge Ardery might talk to him, and Phil acted as a go-between. In his grand jury testimony, however, Phil Ardery was not sure who suggested talking with his father. Judge

Ardery was scheduled to charge a grand jury in the vote fraud case the next morning in district court. At any rate, Phil phoned his father and arranged to drive Prichard out to the judge's home in Paris.[9]

During the forty-five-minute drive from Frankfort to Paris, Prichard spelled out to his old classmate and partner what had occurred the preceding weekend. Describing what the FBI would soon know, Prichard explained that he and Funk "had gotten the county attorney William Baldwin . . . to open the vault where the ballots were kept." Prichard related that they took the ballots back to Prichard's Lexington law office, where they were marked, and then returned the ballots to the Paris courthouse, where they were placed in various boxes. Ardery suggested that his father would tell Prichard to admit his crime to the people of Bourbon County and beg forgiveness. Not surprisingly, Ardery admitted, "I did not get much response."[10]

At around 9:45 P.M., Phil's car pulled into the driveway of Rocclicgan, Judge Ardery's home on the Lexington Pike in Paris. The discussion that took place at Rocclicgan became the most fateful conversation of Prichard's life. He and Judge Ardery went into the living room and talked for approximately forty-five minutes. Phil Ardery stated in 1994 that he heard no part of the conversation between his father and Prichard, but admitted in his grand jury testimony in 1949 that he had sat in on a small part of their talk. It can be assumed that Prichard related to the judge the same details he had told Phil. Judge Ardery told Prichard he had indeed "written a charge to be read to the grand jury the following morning directing the grand jury to look into the vote fraud." What Prichard was doing in Judge Ardery's living room that night, spelling out the details of the crime he had committed to the judge calling a grand jury to investigate the very same crime, led many to conclude that he was flagrantly hoping to coopt the judge. Phil Ardery, for one, assumed that Prichard was there in hope of getting his father to cancel his charge.[11] Perhaps an even more looming question concerned what Judge Ardery was doing talking to Prichard about the case in the first place.

On the return drive to Frankfort, Prichard, according to Ardery, said the judge had suggested "that he make an appearance at a mass meeting to be held at the Bourbon County courthouse the following week." Phil claimed that with Prichard's charm, simply admitting his guilt would be sufficient to end the situation. Just how the Arderys assumed that admitting such a serious crime in front of his political enemies would end the situation is unclear. When they arrived at Phil's home late in the evening, Prichard naturally ignored this advice, got in his car, and drove home. The bizarre trip to see his boyhood friends Phil and William Ardery was over. More than any other single event in the entire investigation, this trip had placed the noose around Ed Prichard's neck.[12]

Who may have been the anonymous source that phoned the FBI indicating Prichard's complicity in the crime? The FBI records on the case do not shed light on this matter. Speculation has risen that perhaps either William or Phil Ardery was the source, since they had the full details just five days after the election. Phil Ardery later suggested that county Republicans had been tipped off beforehand and therefore might be the source. Other rumors pointed to Julia Ardery, the judge's wife, who was also at Rocclicgan on the fateful night of November 7.[13] In any event, within two weeks of the election, the outline of the case was clear to investigators. Their task remained collecting sufficient evidence to obtain an indictment.

The meeting at the courthouse to which Judge Ardery alluded became another crucial ingredient in the election fraud saga. Quite simply, a small number of energized people in Bourbon County would not allow the matter to go away. On Monday, November 8, as Judge Ardery read his instructions to the grand jury, the Bourbon County Ministerial Association met in special session and condemned the voting scandal. The ministers called for a federal investigation and asked that "as ministers of the churches of Bourbon County, we urge our citizens to join us in an insistent demand for regular and systematic purging of voting lists . . . and that voting machines be purchased." To solidify their protest, the association called for a "mass meeting" to be held November 10 at the courthouse. An estimated 275 people attended the meeting and elected Cassius Clay to head a "citizens committee" to make certain that the investigation proceeded without interference. Clay stated he wanted "a complete investigation, not to fasten guilt only on some wretch, but also to involve the person whose wishes the wretch was carrying out." Clay used his role as chairman of the citizen's committee as a crusade to rid the county of fraudulent elections. By early December, the Citizens Committee demanded that the Justice Department appoint a special attorney in the case.[14]

Cassius Clay thus became an essential element in the vote scandal probe. Clay came from one of the most prominent families in Bourbon County, and indeed central Kentucky. After graduating from Yale Law School in 1921, he had practiced law in New York City and in 1934 became general counsel to the railroad division of the Reconstruction Finance Corporation. After unsuccessfully seeking a federal judgeship, he had returned to Paris in 1944. Clay became known after the war primarily for his opposition to a new state constitution. He was active in the local Red Cross and was a vice president of the Kentucky Historical Society. He admittedly was not well known outside his home county but apparently had political ambitions of his own. Those ambitions were shared by his wife, Miriam Berle, whose brother, Adolf Berle, was one of the original brain trusters in FDR's administration. According to the FBI, Clay became heavily involved in the Citizens Committee primarily "because his wife is politically ambitious for Clay."[15]

What Clay and the Ministerial Association did not know, of course, was that the FBI was aggressively pursuing the case. Early on, however, the case did not look very strong from their standpoint. A preliminary report on handwriting samples on the ballots in question yielded no conclusive evidence. As the FBI sought new leads and additional evidence, Cassius Clay and another member of the Citizens Committee, Dodge Whipple, went to Washington on December 16, 1948, to see J. Edgar Hoover and demand that the case not be "whitewashed." Hoover was out of town for their visit, but his aide, Louis B. Nichols, met with Clay and Whipple and expressed the bureau's appreciation for their interest in the case.[16]

On the streets of Paris, rumors abounded as to what might occur and who might be involved. Those rumors intensified after Walter Winchell's national radio broadcast on November 21, when he said there "will be some red faces" after the FBI investigation in the Bourbon County vote fraud is completed, including "one individual who was formerly in Washington, D.C." In a small town such as Paris, it was not hard to find oneself in uncomfortable situations. One day, as Big Ed "ranted" in a Paris barbershop about Cassius Clay, he did not know that one of the shop's patrons was Clay's frightened son, who "shrank into the barber's chair and prayed he wouldn't be recognized." Weeks later, Republican J.M. Alverson, owner of the *Daily Enterprise,* was threatened by an unnamed "Bourbon politician" on the streets of Paris as the two argued over the impending vote fraud investigation. When Alverson responded that he would not quit publishing stories concerning the scandal, the "politician" allegedly raised his cane and threatened Alverson, who replied, "I don't want to hit an old man."[17]

The FBI's inability to find substantial evidence in the case against Prichard, Funk, and Baldwin proved frustrating to all interested observers. On his final day in the U.S. Senate, John Sherman Cooper stated that he had received reports from "substantial citizens" that the FBI might "minimize" its investigation. The *Lexington Leader* editorialized that it was too early to tell if such was the case, but stated that the crime had been perpetrated so clumsily as to suggest that "the persons responsible felt safe from any possibility of detection."[18]

One of the FBI field agents assigned to the case was Joseph Mooney of nearby Cynthiana. Agent Mooney had a different perspective on the investigation than others involved in the case. Considering the chief suspects—a popular local politician, the son of the Kentucky attorney general, and a former White House official with contacts at the highest levels in Washington and Frankfort—Mooney wondered if he'd "still be working" afterward because, as he well knew, "there's dynamite in this thing." Along with fellow agent John Core, Mooney interviewed numerous key witnesses, including a woman whose Paris apartment faced the courthouse. She told Mooney she had seen several men in and out of the courthouse on the weekend before the election, and that one was particularly noticeable because he carried a cane, a habit that Prichard had acquired in Washington. When Core and Mooney interviewed Prichard, Mooney got the impression that the young attorney was "arrogant and overbearing." Prichard claimed innocence, then asked the agents why they had come to him. After all, Prichard said, everybody knew that votes had been stolen for more than forty years in Bourbon County. Core responded, "The trouble is, Prich, you got caught."[19]

But finding the evidence to support this claim proved a difficult chore for investigators. As the inquiry continued into February 1949, Cassius Clay, for one, was getting increasingly frustrated. He often went to express his indignation to John Ed Pearce and Barry Bingham at the *Louisville Courier-Journal.* Like so many other elements surrounding the story, Clay felt the paper had not been adamant about getting to the truth in the ballot-box episode. Pearce recalled that Clay's "eyes would flash and his voice would tremble, and there's no doubt he was on a crusade."[20]

After some confusion over the release of the FBI's findings, Clay stated that the federal district attorney's office in Lexington was guilty of "incompetence or worse" in its handling of the case. He repeated the Citizens Committee's earlier request for a special prosecutor to handle the matter. The situation became even more complicated for the FBI when U.S. Attorney Claude Stephens filed a $50,000 libel suit against Clay for his charges of incompetence. In mid-February, Clay wrote Attorney General Clark, complaining that the investigation had not been completed. By early March, Hoover was irritated when he read that agents had not been able to gather enough evidence against the three suspects "to warrant indictments." Hoover wrote on the memo, "This isn't clear. I thought we had the statement of————that Pritchard [*sic*] admitted it." Whose name Hoover wrote in the margin as providing such a statement is unknown. The bureau's frustration increased with an FBI internal report that concluded "that both subjects Baldwin and Prichard have been eliminated by handwriting comparison as being the signer of any of the fraudulent ballots."[21]

When the *Louisville Courier-Journal* wrote a biting editorial on the FBI investigation, the agency placed a copy of the editorial in its file, indicating that the FBI was becoming increasingly sensitive to criticism of its proceeding investigation. After failing to issue a report on its findings, the *Courier-Journal* concluded that a "political whitewash" was under way. Barry Bingham's paper thundered, "The people of this State are not going to permit indefinite suppression of the findings of the Bourbon County vote fraud." The editors then mockingly made reference to Kansas City: "The Bourbon County vote fraud is fast assuming the proportions of a national scandal, and the Truman administration should not be burdened with another Kansas City."[22]

The *Paris Kentuckian-Citizen* took a somewhat different editorial stand. The Democratic newspaper stated on March 11 that following the November election "some of the good people, who seem to have condoned in the past by their inactivity what they must consider lesser violations of elections such as buying and selling of votes, have risen in sudden wrath." The newspaper took the strange leap that "consistent buying and selling of votes is an even worse offense than is the occasional stuffing of ballot boxes."[23]

The case took another turn in late March 1949 when further FBI tests concluded that Al Funk Jr. had signed at least 224 of the 254 fraudulent ballots. With a summary report in hand, U.S. Attorney Stephens sent the case on to a federal grand jury in Lexington. (W.B. Ardery's grand jury was temporarily halted when federal authorities impounded the ballot boxes and other pieces of evidence.) But before the FBI could feel confident of the report it presented to Stephens, another embarrassment occurred. When *Lexington Leader* photographer Ralph Looney came to Stephens's office on March 30, he asked the attorney to pose for a photograph. Stephens quickly grabbed from his desk an FBI memo on the investigation and struck an official pose reading the document. Stephens did not realize, however, that he had compromised the investigation by allowing himself to be photographed reading the files. A simple enlargement of the photograph allowed Looney and reporter Henry Hornsby to see clearly a November memo that read: "Through source identified as anonymous, it was reported that Prichard pulled the ballots from books; A.E. Funk, Jr., signed ballots, and Baldwin placed same in ballot boxes." The newspaper agreed not to divulge any of the pertinent information, but did print the photo with a caption that merely read: "District Attorney Studies Bourbon Vote Fraud Report." Upon learning of Stephens's gaffe, an angry Hoover wrote to Attorney General Clark that "it seems particularly unfortunate that this newspaper was allowed to include the Bureau's report in its photograph," adding, "It is felt that you may wish to call Mr. Stephens' attention to the impropriety of such action." When Stephens was informed of what had occurred, he was, in the words of the FBI, "flabbergasted."

Hornsby then went to question Prichard about the impending investigation with the information obtained from the photograph in hand. Prichard proclaimed his innocence to Hornsby, and, according to the reporter, Prichard called "on God as witness for innocence." He promised to answer all of Hornsby's questions if the *Leader* promised not to take photographs of him being escorted into the courthouse for arraignment. The newspaper did not mention names, but did relate that it had learned from "an unimpeachable source" that two prominent Bourbon County politicians and a Lexingtonian were under investigation.[24]

On April 7, Special Assistant Attorney General George Gallagher, who had arrived from Washington to assist in the case, informed agents Mooney and Core that he had received an anonymous telephone call that morning. The caller told Gallagher that Judge William B. Ardery "was in position to give valuable information in this case." Although the FBI's records indicate that the judge had previously been interviewed at least twice by February 4, this was the first time Mooney and Core had spoken with him. The two agents went to Rocclicgan, where Judge Ardery met them at the door, saying "Gentlemen, I've been expecting you." Mooney observed that the judge was upset, and Ardery proceeded to tell the agents about the conversation he had had with Prichard the night of November 7. Judge Ardery gave the FBI such damaging testimony, Mooney said, because the judge felt that Prichard had trapped him and that if the trial went to district court Ardery would be forced to recuse himself. To do so, Mooney said, was damaging to the judge's character and "hurt his feelings very much." Yet when asked if he would testify before the grand jury, the judge said he would claim privilege, therefore asking the court to allow him not to divulge the contents of his testimony.[25]

The drama in the vote fraud shifted on March 30, 1949, to the federal courthouse building in Lexington, where the grand jury was called by Judge H. Church Ford, who, ironically, had once held Judge Ardery's district judgeship. On the first day, members of the Bourbon County election commission testified, as did county clerk Ed Drane Paton. By April 2, interested observers noticed that the only election officer in the county who had not been subpoenaed to appear before the grand jury was Ed Prichard Jr. As the testimony progressed, observers were further surprised on April 8, when it was learned that Judge William B. Ardery was subpoenaed to appear before the grand jury. Less than a week later, Phil Ardery was also subpoenaed.[26]

On the afternoon of April 15, Phil Ardery appeared before Judge Ford in the federal courthouse. He had earlier refused to answer a question posed by the grand jury concerning the conversation he had had with Prichard. He asked that his claim of lawyer-client privilege be reviewed by the judge. Ardery claimed that "the statement made to me by this person was 'May I come to you for legal advice?'" Upon hearing that, Judge Ford ruled that Ardery's conversation with Prichard on the night of November 7 was indeed confidential. "Mr. Ardery," Judge Ford admonished, "I think under the facts that are stated here, I think it is your duty . . . to decline any statement that he made to you."[27]

But Phil Ardery did not heed Judge Ford's words as he left the courtroom. Outside, he saw an FBI agent and took him aside. According to the FBI, Ardery had become "angrier and angrier since he was approached concerning this matter." Phil told the agent he felt "he had been approached as an attorney probably with the hope that he would make known the contact and risk going ahead and testifying," whereupon if a guilty plea was returned, Prichard could then get an appeal based on a reversible error. An angry Phil Ardery felt that he had been used by Prichard and that the Ardery family was now implicated in the vote fraud. The FBI then stated that Phil was "equally willing as his father . . . to give additional information."[28]

In front of the grand jury, however, Judge Ardery was not quite as forthcoming as he had been with the FBI. The judge asked the court to rule as well on the matter of his claim of privilege. Judge Ford was hesitant to rule on the matter just yet. "I will have to have Judge Ardery tell me his opinion on this," Judge Ford said. The legal question involved was not quite as clear-cut as Phil's. Judge Ford had to rule on a delicate legal question: Can a sitting judge be afforded the same lawyer-client privilege as a practicing attorney? Thinking out loud, Judge Ford admitted that Judge Ardery was "not a practicing attorney. I don't know whether he could be placed in the position of attorney and client or not." Ford told the grand jury he would rule on Judge Ardery's privilege claim later.[29]

On April 15 the grand jury took less than two hours of deliberations to return two sealed indictments in the case. For the next several weeks, anxious reporters and observers were naturally curious to know who was named in the indictment, and they wondered why the indictments were sealed in the first place. J. Edgar Hoover, for one, when told that the indictments were sealed until Prichard returned from a business trip to Europe, responded, "It is shocking the way special consideration is given this thing. Just why was a sealed indictment returned?" Although he had a law degree, Hoover apparently knew little about judicial procedure. Judge Ford had ruled that according to rules of criminal procedure, an indictment may be kept sealed until the defendant is in custody.[30]

Cassius Clay's response to the news that the grand jury had returned indictments was that it "reassures one's faith in the fundamental soundness of our democratic system of government." The *Kentuckian-Citizen* responded that "rumors—ugly, vile, and unfounded, have been afloat," and stated that "it will feel no exultation in the sense of rejoicing at the plight in which some friend may find himself because of a wrongful but, probably, impetuous act."[31]

Meanwhile, FBI agents went to see Phil Ardery again on April 26 in his Frankfort office. He told the agents that Prichard had confessed the crime to him and had also told him that Funk and Baldwin were involved. Ardery hesitated to tell the agents the details of all he knew—after this encounter, agents reported that Phil said "he personally knew nothing else concerning the case." Phil informed the agents that he "has been on bad terms with Prichard since they broke up their partnership" and that "it would be personally embarrassing and politically embarrassing to him to voluntarily testify."[32]

As the sealed indictments awaited Prichard's return from Europe, he proceeded to enjoy himself as if he had not a care in the world. When he visited friends in France, they were oblivious to his pending problems. Susan Mary Patten wrote to Joseph Alsop that Prichard spent Easter with her and "was the greatest addition in my life in years," but added that he was "deliciously malicious and clearly still mad for Mrs. B." While Prichard longed for Evangeline, Lucy was home waiting to give birth. She too corresponded with Alsop, asking him to visit "our progeny" in the summer. "I can't believe there is only six weeks more of this uncomfortable state," she wrote.[33]

Prichard arrived back home in late April after inspecting French oil wells belonging to D.D. Stewart, president of the Kentucky Railway System. He certainly knew by now that he was about to be named in the indictments that were, as of May 1, still sealed. Prichard consulted with at least two different lawyers about his predicament. On April 28, the FBI learned that Paul Porter of Washington, acting as Prichard's attorney, persuaded the Justice Department to allow Prichard to surrender himself in the indictment. Four days later, however, the FBI was told by a U.S. attorney that Prichard had secured John Y. Brown as his attorney.[34]

The official opening of the indictments was delayed even longer until Judge Ford returned to Lexington from other court duties. Finally, on May 4, the court was convened and the indictments against Prichard and Funk were opened. If found guilty, they faced a maximum $5,000 fine and ten years' imprisonment. Noticeably absent in the indictment was the name of Billy Baldwin. FBI agent Mooney admitted that Baldwin was "awfully well liked" and that local people on the grand jury might not be disposed to indict such a popular figure. Phil Ardery wrote that "a member of the grand jury was later heard to say that Baldwin was quite popular . . . and for that reason was not indicted." One well-placed Bourbon Countian acknowledged that if Baldwin had been about to be indicted, "there would have been some on the jury looking out for him." All Baldwin ever commented was that "if it had been anybody else but Prich, it wouldn't have amounted to a hill of beans."[35]

The grand jury charged that Prichard and Funk, "and others not herein indicted, whose names are to the Grand Jurors unknown, did steal and purloin" the Bourbon County election books from the county clerk's office, forge the names of election officers, and then mark the ballots. Whereupon, "by themselves or in connivance with others whose names are to the Grand Jurors unknown," they stuffed the ballot boxes.[36]

Both Prichard and Funk pleaded not guilty and asked Judge Ford for an early trial. They were represented in court by a team of local lawyers, including Leslie Morris, Henry Duncan, and Victor Bradley. They were each released on a $5,000 bond signed by Lexington businessman Bruce Isaacs. The law partners quickly issued a statement that read: "We are completely innocent of the charge made against us of any participation in the election frauds committed in Bourbon County last November. Because of our innocence, we are requesting a speedy trial. The trial will reveal how destitute of fact or evidence is the charge against us. We ask our friends to have faith in us and the public to await the outcome of the trial at which we await vindication with complete confidence." The trial was set to begin on July 5, 1949.[37]

Word of the indictments spread throughout Kentucky and Washington within hours. That night, a friend of the Prichard family went to visit Ed Sr. and Allene at their home in Paris. There the friend found Allene "just crushed." While Big Ed vented his pain by "talking things out," Allene "just kept it inside." The trauma had an intense impact on Allene, who "went into a shell" following news of her older son's indictment.[38]

When told of the indictment in Washington, Vice President Alben Barkley simply muttered, "No comment." Sen. Virgil Chapman said he was "surprised" to learn of Prichard's involvement. What Chapman then did confirmed that some of Cassius Clay's fears of "whitewashing" were not completely unfounded. Chapman soon thereafter tried to influence Attorney General Clark to drop the case. Clark told journalist Drew Pearson that Chapman came to see him about Prichard's indictment "unshaven and half-drunk" and told Clark that "no harm had been done" and proceeded to spell out the details by which Prichard and Funk had secured the ballots. Chapman had evidently known the details by which the deed had been performed for some time. Clark warned Chapman that anything said about the case might be used in court, but Chapman "proceeded to talk anyway." Clark told Pearson that he had received pressure not to drop the case from Cassius Clay and John Sherman Cooper, and that "since he was accused of not prosecuting regarding the Kansas City frauds, he decided to prosecute in Kentucky."[39]

The news of the indictment had immediate financial impact on the Prichard and Funk firm. Two months earlier, Al Funk had been mentioned as a possible candidate for an appointment as city manager of Lexington. His chances of that position, following news of the indictment, were effectively ended. Lexington mayor Tom G. Mooney also said he hoped the partners would resign from representing the city in an upcoming annexation case. Although they were innocent until proven guilty, the mayor added that the indictment of Prichard and Funk placed the city in "an embarrassing position." While many other clients may have shared similar views, one client remained steadfast in retaining the firm—Big Ed's beer distributorship in Paris.[40]

For Ed Prichard, there was yet another task remaining—to go home and tell Lucy that he was going to stand trial for the vote fraud conspiracy. "I had no inkling anything was amiss," Lucy later said. "My parents, friends, apparently knew all about it and were wondering 'Does she know?'" Lucy felt that those close to her had not told her because of her imminent labor. Also, perhaps, they assumed it was her husband's duty to inform his wife of the impending trial. The timing of her husband's announcement was a devastating blow to Lucy. On May 14, ten days after the indictment was returned against her husband, she gave birth to a son whom they named Edward Allen Prichard. "The room was overflowing with flowers from friends," Lucy recalled. "I suppose they wanted to show they were sympathetic." But she added that those same friends "were furious at Prich, shocked, horrified."[41]

One individual who was informed of the new arrival and perhaps saw an opportunity to lift Prichard's sunken spirits was Chief Justice Vinson. Upon learning from Prichard that "another Edward arrived," Vinson wrote a poignant letter addressed to the newborn. It read:

Dear Prich:
    Your daddy informed Mrs. Vinson and me by wire that you had arrived and were doing fine. We are very happy about it, and know that you will be a real addition in the family of man.
    You are very fortunate in many respects. Your choice of a Father and Mother indicates to me that you are a wise little guy. . . . I remember the first time I met your Dad. He was some ten years older than you are. It was the opening of Barkley's campaign for the Senate in 1926. . . . He is a fine friend of your Dad's.
    It won't take you long, son, to ascertain that your Dad is a remarkable person—a man of great heart, soul, and ability—in fact, he is a most unusual individual. There will be times when you may not appreciate his greatness, particularly if he starts 'bossing you around,' but I do not know whether he will essay such a task. . . . The point of decision here is my affection and regard for your Daddy. We were associated together during the war years. He was a tower of strength in many a crisis. You have a difficult task in measuring up to that which your Father has been, is, and will be."[42]

Judge Ford complied with Prichard's and Funk's request for a speedy trial by setting the trial date for just two months from the indictment. In the interim, the defense team began the process of collecting evidence. Immediately after the indictment, defense attorneys requested that the court furnish them all photographic and photostatic copies of the ballots in question, as well as all handwriting samples. The FBI, however, refused to turn over such evidence and was backed by Hoover, who advised his agents to "watch carefully as there have been too many curves in this case." Judge Ford, however, sustained a defense motion to obtain copies of the ballots and handwriting specimens.[43]

Allene and Edward Fretwell "Big Ed" Prichard Sr. Courtesy Henry P. Prichard

Ed Prichard Jr. (right) with brother Henry, ca. 1921. Courtesy Henry P. Prichard

Above, the Bourbon County Courthouse in Paris, Kentucky, ca. 1930, where Prichard spent a good deal of his youth learning the art of local politics. It is also where the ballot books and boxes were kept the weekend before the 1948 election. Courtesy of Special Collections, University of Kentucky Library. *Below,* the Paris High School class of 1931. Prichard is on the first row (right) holding one of many scholastic trophies he earned that year. Phil Ardery is in the back row, third from left. Courtesy of Henry P. Prichard.

Prichard at age twenty *(above left)*, when he entered Harvard Law School. There he became a favorite of future Supreme Court justice Felix Frankfurter, who patiently listens to a Prichard oration *(above right)*. Although his enthusiasm for the study of law was never great, Prichard managed to make the staff of the prestigious *Harvard Law Review* in 1938 *(below)*. Prichard is in the back row, second from right. His roommate, future *Washington Post* publisher Phil Graham, is at center in the second row down. Harvard Law School Art Collection

Prichard served as Fred Vinson's chief assistant in Washington during the early 1940s. Vinson headed several major wartime agencies and was appointed Treasury Secretary in 1945. The next year he became Chief Justice. Courtesy of Special Collections, University of Kentucky Library

Prichard married Lucy Elliott in February 1947. Phil Graham served as his best man. Courtesy of *Lexington Herald-Leader.*

In early 1949, as rumors spread about the focus of the vote fraud inquiry, U.S. District Attorney Claude Stephens innocently posed for a Lexington newspaper. Reporters had the photo *(left)* enlarged, which showed that he was holding an FBI report with Prichard's name and other details of the case clearly legible, much to J. Edgar Hoover's anger. Courtesy of Special Collections, University of Kentucky Library

Judge William B. Ardery, with his son Phil outside the courtroom during Prichard's trial in July 1949. When the presiding judge ruled that Prichard's conversation with Judge Ardery was not privileged, Prichard's fate was sealed. Courtesy of *Lexington Herald-Leader*

Prichard with his law partner and co-defendant Al Funk Jr. during a recess in their trial. Although FBI experts testified that Funk signed many of the fraudulent ballots, he was acquitted. Courtesy of *Louisville Courier-Journal*

After his conviction, a smiling Ed Prichard emerges from the county jail on his way back to federal court to appeal his sentence. With him is Deputy Marshall R.A. "Buddy" Gayle. Behind them is Al Funk Jr. Courtesy of *Louisville Courier-Journal*

Above, on William F. Buckley's *Firing Line* in 1982, Prichard debates the legacy of the New Deal. Courtesy of Kentucky Educational Television. *Below,* Prichard with Katharine Graham at a 1979 dinner in his honor. Courtesy of *Louisville Courier-Journal*

Near the end of Prichard's life, diabetes and years of dialysis had taken their toll. Courtesy of Kentucky Educational Television

Former governor Bert Combs (right) brought Prichard into his law firm in 1983. Here they discuss a case in court. Courtesy of *Louisville Courier-Journal*

The prosecution, meanwhile, continued its work of collecting additional information.

On June 28, Phil Ardery was once again interviewed by the FBI. He told the agents that he had not been completely forthcoming in his previous interviews. He admitted that he had, in fact, heard portions of the conversation between Prichard and Judge Ardery, but not enough "to know what Prichard told him or what the Judge told Prichard." Ardery added that if his claim of lawyer-client privilege was not upheld, "he has long ago made up his mind to furnish every detail just as it happened" in court.[44] Why Ardery would voluntarily speak to the FBI about the case on three different occasions and in the process violate his lawyer-client privilege is yet another mysterious thread in the web that soon engulfed Ed Prichard.

The FBI was aware of what had transpired during Prichard's trip to see Judge Ardery, and in this way what Phil Ardery told the FBI did not necessarily seal Prichard's fate. But that is not the crucial point. Ardery's openness in discussing with the FBI what he knew to be privileged information disclosed the latent hostility that he now held for his former classmate and partner. Prichard clearly saw his relationship with Phil as one of lawyer and client. Ardery himself told the FBI that Prichard had asked him on November 7, "May I come to you for legal counsel?" Ardery later claimed, "Maybe I was slipshod in my thinking. But I just felt that there were ways I could be made to testify and that if I just testified falsely I would be incriminating myself." Of course, this was after Judge Ford had decided Ardery's testimony was privileged. In clear terms, Phil was protected from having to disclose any of his conversation with Prichard to a jury or the FBI. Ardery later admitted that his drive to cooperate with the FBI was motivated primarily by emotional, rather than legal, concerns: "I really was pissed off at Prich," Ardery said, when he realized the degree to which the Arderys were now involved in the sordid affair and the manner in which Prichard had tried to coopt his father. When asked if he should have spoken with the FBI at all, Ardery stated candidly, "Well, maybe I shouldn't. I can't defend everything I've ever done."[45]

As the trial approached, the case against Prichard and Funk seemed strongest against "Little Al." Although his father was the attorney general of Kentucky, the younger Funk seemed somewhat out of place involved in such seedy activities. Funk's personality was not the stuff of county election politics. He was rather quiet and reserved and much better known for driving new Cadillacs and wearing impeccable suits and two-toned shoes than for his political ambitions. "He's a very mysterious figure," commented his nephew, "even within the family."[46] FBI handwriting experts found significant evidence that a large number of the fraudulent ballots had been signed by Funk. Fingerprint analyses were not as conclusive. Besides witnesses who may have seen Prichard around the courthouse on the weekend in question, no physical evidence existed that connected Prichard to the ballots. Other questions then arose: Since the indictment charged the pair with conspiracy, could only one be convicted? Also, since the fraudulent ballots had had no impact on the outcome of the election, could it be reasoned that the conspiracy had violated any voter's civil rights? Would Judge Ardery's conversation with Prichard be ruled inadmissable? Would either Funk or Prichard take the stand? The prosecution thus faced an uphill struggle in the already difficult matter of proving conspiracy of vote fraud. On the eve of the trial, if anyone had proper reason to worry, it was Al Funk Jr. Prichard's lifelong ability to circumvent trouble, it seemed, might once again save the day.

9 Playing for Keeps

FOR Ed Prichard, who had walked the corridors of Harvard Law School and the Supreme Court and had affiliated with some of the most prominent lawyers in Washington, the selection of the attorneys to defend him against the indictment was a difficult issue. At first Prichard sought help from Washington. Prichard and Billy Baldwin, in fact, traveled to Washington shortly after the election and spoke with Frankfurter's first clerk and Prichard's close friend, Joseph Rauh Jr. When asked about the dynamics of the case, Rauh advised Prichard "to keep your goddamned mouth shut, will you?" not knowing that Prichard would soon speak with Judge Ardery. Prichard had also consulted with Paul Porter, a fellow Kentuckian who soon became one of Washington's most influential attorneys. Porter arranged for Prichard to turn himself in upon the unsealing of the indictment. But in the end, Rauh and Porter advised Prichard to retain only local attorneys for the case.[1] The image of Washington lawyers coming to Kentucky to defend the political insider with powerful connections was not the image Prichard wanted to present to a local jury. The team Prichard selected to defend himself and Funk comprised Victor Bradley of Georgetown, Kentucky, Henry Duncan of Lexington, and Leslie Morris of Frankfort, who had all been at court for the indictment. Also included was Marion S. Rider, a cagey Frankfort attorney and friend of the Prichard family.

Heading the prosecution was U.S. Attorney Claude Stephens, who was aided by an assistant district attorney, Kit Elswick, and the head of the Election Crimes Division of the Justice Department, George Gallagher. The prosecution's case rested primarily on handwriting analyses that tied Funk to the ballots, and the possible testimony of the Arderys, which would directly implicate Prichard. While expecting the court to rule that the testimony of both Arderys was privileged, the defense worked to punch holes in the prosecution's case.

Although they were not officially working as Prichard's attorneys, Porter, Rauh, and Phil Graham did their part to help an old friend. To counter FBI handwriting experts, the threesome searched for an expert of their own. Rauh suggested Ardway Hilton, whom he called the "greatest living expert" on handwriting. Wishing to keep the purpose of their meeting a secret, Rauh, Porter, and Graham each took separate planes to New York to meet with Hilton at a hotel. Much to his agony and, later, amusement, Rauh arrived in the hotel lobby to discover that the bulletin board listed prominently the room number for "Philip Graham meeting with Ardway Hilton." In the meeting, the four men looked over some copies of the ballot books and examples of Prichard's handwriting, all the while telling Hilton, "You know, he's got an awful lot of friends. You don't have to worry about money." Despite such assurances, Hilton refused to lend his help to the defense because he was not positive that the samples were not Prichard's. Rauh candidly recalled that he was disappointed with Hilton's refusal on grounds of principle—"We had hoped he was going to prove a big crook." The trio eventually managed to secure the services of another expert in Chicago, who agreed to testify that the handwriting on the selected ballots was definitely not that of Edward F. Prichard Jr.—in exchange for $4,000.[2]

On the night of July 4, 1949, only hours before the trial began, Prichard drove to Cincinnati to see his former roommate, Isaiah Berlin. Berlin was nervous throughout his flight into Cincinnati, not sure of what to say to Prichard concerning his impending trial. When he got off the plane, Berlin immediately went over and greeted his old roommate by saying, "I'm sure you're guilty—guilty as hell." Berlin recalled he needed to break the ice with his customary humor in order "to get it off my chest." Berlin was saddened, however, when Prichard said nothing in return. The two then had dinner, where Berlin noticed that Prichard was "very nervous, very upset," all the while refusing to admit any guilt. The British philosopher left, refusing to believe that Prichard was, indeed, guilty.[3]

The eagerly anticipated trial of Ed Prichard Jr. and Al Funk Jr. began on Tuesday, July 5, 1949. The trial coincided with another courtroom drama that involved another of Felix Frankfurter's former students, Alger Hiss. The sweltering heat of the Kentucky summer would be ever present throughout the course of the trial in the poorly ventilated courtroom in the Federal Building in Lexington. Prichard arrived for the trial's opening day sporting a dark suit, bow tie, broad-brimmed hat, and a confident grin, which he displayed to photographers and reporters outside the courtroom. Prichard was outdone, at least in fashion terms, by the more dapper Al Funk Jr., who arrived wearing a finely tailored suit and two-tone shoes. The younger Funk was accompanied by his father, the attorney general of Kentucky.

Most of the trial's first day was devoted to selecting a jury. After deciding on eleven men and one woman, Stephens delivered the opening statement for the prosecution late that afternoon. He spelled out the specifics of the Bourbon County courthouse, such as who possessed keys to the vault and where the ballot books were kept before the election. Stephens said that "a Mr. Baldwin" had an agreement with County Clerk Grace Haskins "that the key would be kept in a certain place, a rather secret place, and that it would be available to him at all times." Stephens added that the ballot boxes were stored in the hall of the courthouse, and the flaps covering the holes on the tops of the boxes were left open. Sometime during the weekend preceding the election, Stephens contended, someone got inside the vault, took more than 250 ballots out of the books, marked them, and placed them in various boxes in the corridor, where they were discovered on election morning. As he discussed Prichard's role in carrying the books to Lexington, observers noted that Prichard's "lips tightened," while Funk "appeared unmoved."[4]

Stephens then brought up the issue of the FBI investigation, particularly concerning handwriting. The FBI, according to Stephens, "is able to make a definite conclusion and will state to you that A.E. Funk Jr., signed his name to a large number of practically all of these forged ballots." Stephens concluded by asserting that Funk was not alone in his crime—he had had considerable help from Prichard. Upon closing, Victor Bradley, representing the defendants, surprisingly reserved his opening statement, and the jury was excused for the remainder of the day.[5]

The prosecution began presenting witnesses on the trial's second day, July 6. Stephens called a number of Bourbon County election officers, as well as County Clerk Haskins and Bourbon County Sheriff Leer. The sheriff testified that after the fraudulent ballots were discovered, he encountered Prichard and Billy Baldwin on their way to the Clintonville precinct. To the packed courtroom audience, the first day of testimony was uneventful, except for the room's noticeable discomfort. The heat inside the courtroom was measured at over ninety degrees.[6]

On the third day, Stephens presented some of the damaging testimony against Funk. Walter G. Blackburn, a document examiner in the FBI laboratory in Washington, testified that some of the signatures on the fraudulent ballots conclusively "were written by A.E. Funk, Jr." While Funk himself had refused requests for samples of his handwriting, examples had been obtained from some of his student papers written at the University of Kentucky Law School. After carefully analyzing certain selected ballots and Funk's handwriting, Blackburn's testimony was the most compelling to date.[7]

On the trial's fourth day, Friday, July 8, the evidence against Prichard was finally introduced. The prosecution dropped a bombshell when it called to the stand both Philip and Judge Ardery. The defense, of course, raised an objection concerning the lawyer-client privilege with both witnesses. Judge Ford remained hesitant to rule on the objection just yet. With the jury out of the room, Judge Ardery took the stand. With an angular nose, brooding eyes, and a sharp crewcut of gray hair, he presented, in the words of one journalist, "a stern, Roman, profile." Four years earlier, doctors had removed a malignant tumor in Judge Ardery's throat, as well as his larynx. Determined not to employ artificial aids to speak, Ardery mastered a technique whereby he learned to expel air against his esophagus with such force that it created a slight, mumbling sound. With great effort, he could then fashion those sounds into words. In the courtroom that day, listeners strained to hear the judge over the noise of the electric fans.[8]

The judge testified that Prichard and his son came to see him on the night of November 7 and that Prichard told him, "Judge, I am in deep trouble and I want your advice." The defense objected to any further testimony on grounds of privilege. Leslie Morris, on cross-examination, asked, "You understood from that that it was legal advice" Prichard was seeking. Judge Ardery replied, "I thought I could give it to him, and if anything transpired later, I would not sit in the case." Judge Ford decided to postpone his decision regarding the judge's testimony until the following Monday. The same process occurred when Phil Ardery was called to the stand. He stated the basic outlines of the events of November 7 but did not give any details until Judge Ford's ruling on lawyer-client privilege.[9]

In order to guide Judge Ford in his critical ruling, Prichard was allowed to take the stand, out of the presence of the jury, and testify as to the nature of the conversations he had had with the Arderys. Prichard said he went to see Phil Ardery that November night because "I sought legal advice from him." Upon Phil's suggestion, Prichard said, they drove to Paris to see the judge. Why see the judge? Prichard said, "We felt the need of further legal advice . . . after consulting with Mr. Philip Ardery, I decided that I wanted to seek that legal advice from Judge Ardery." On the issue of whether he went to see Judge Ardery "in good faith," Prichard replied, "I believe that while there might be some question as to the right of Judge Ardery to represent me, at least in Circuit Court in any matter, I believed after studying the law to the best of my ability that he did have a right to give me legal advice as an attorney." Prichard then supported Judge Ardery's claim that his first words upon seeing the judge were, "Judge, I am in trouble, and I need some legal advice." On cross-examination, Prichard related that when he returned from Europe and was awaiting indictment, he saw Phil Ardery in Frankfort, whereupon Phil "asked that I release him from any further service." By this time, of course, Prichard did not know that Phil had already divulged details of his conversations with Prichard to the FBI. When asked why he sought legal advice from Judge Ardery, Prichard responded, "Ever since I have known him, and that is since my childhood, I have believed that I could get sound competent legal advice from Judge Ardery." If such advice conflicted with his duties as a judge, Prichard added, "Judge Ardery would be disqualified in the event of any subsequent trial, because of his having given me legal advice."[10]

Before the court recessed for the weekend, the prosecution called to the stand Kentucky State Police Commissioner Guthrie Crowe, who offered more compelling testimony. Just a few days after the election, Crowe testified, Prichard came to see him in Frankfort and the two discussed the developing events in Bourbon County. Prichard stated to Crowe that he thought the boxes had been stuffed by Republicans. Prichard inquired if the state police were investigating the case. Then he took out a piece of paper, or, as described by Crowe, a "ballot" paper. Prichard asked the commissioner if such paper could retain fingerprints. Crowe said the paper would retain "only an oily print," and he and Prichard then went to lunch. By late afternoon, Judge Ford dismissed the jurors until Monday morning. On Saturday, July 9, Judge Ford said he would hear additional arguments concerning the privilege matter in his chambers.[11]

The Louisville field office kept J. Edgar Hoover abreast of all developments in the trial. Following the session on July 8, the FBI director was informed that a ruling was upcoming on the admissibility of the judge's testimony. Hoover was also told that Stephens was "undecided as to whether he intended to discuss previous allegations with the judge." Stephens had brought up the subject of admitting other evidence that indicated Prichard had participated in ballot-box stuffing in 1943 and 1946, on which Ford had also not yet ruled.[12]

On July 9, journalist Drew Pearson wrote about the developments in the Prichard trial and then defended his once-reliable source. "If 'Prich,' in a fantastic flight of political melodrama, did stuff a ballot box," Pearson wrote, "the public should know about it and act accordingly. However the public should also know that there were some qualities on the other side of the ledger." During his days at OES, Pearson added, "it's frequently the ghost writers and the administrative assistant who have to do a lot of the dirty work and who get the brickbats with none of the credit. 'Prich' was in that category." Privately, Pearson mused that the evidence against Prichard was "flimsy."[13]

Before going to court on what would be one of the singular days of his life, Prichard drafted a letter to Thomas Corcoran, who had written inquiring about Prichard's legal fees and his overall financial situation.

Dear Tom:

Your letter has arrived and touches me deeply. The trial is now in progress. Going well except for one matter as to which the Judge rules this morning on a confidential communication to Phil Ardery and his father.

Frankly, you are the first person in offering help who has mentioned money, and it is a critical factor— temporarily but not permanently. I have been making about $30,000 a year but due to expenses of the trial am short of cash and have a note due at the bank as well as an income tax payment. If you have a rich client

who would take a flier on a retainer for a troubled young lawyer, it would be a
life-saver. But do not feel that I want or am asking you to delve into the Corcoran
personal exchequer.

"This thing has hit me between the eyes," Prichard confided, and promised to tell Corcoran the entire story once the trial concluded.[14]

The heat, as well as the sheer drama of the trial, was palpable as Prichard
walked into the courtroom on Monday morning, July 11. Before allowing the
jury into the room, Judge Ford told a packed courtroom that he was to rule
on the crucial motions regarding the privilege claims of Phil and William
Ardery. Concerning the admissibility of Prichard's conversation with Phil
Ardery, Judge Ford quickly ruled that the conversation between them was
clearly "under circumstances which show that the relationship of attorney and
client subsisted between them." Phil's claim of privilege was therefore upheld.

Whether Judge Ardery would have to testify was a more complex legal
matter. Ford stated that the rule of secrecy and privilege "should not be extended beyond the purpose it is designed to serve. . . . That purpose," Judge
Ford found, "is to preserve inviolate the confidence which is essential between
an attorney and his client." Then Prichard heard the crushing weight of Judge
Ford's next words: "I am of the opinion that one who seeks the advice of the
Judge of the Court in which his case is to be tried, when it is apparent to him
the giving of such advice by the Judge would disqualify him from sitting in
the case, is not entitled to the privilege accorded by the law to confidential
communications between an attorney and his client. To allow the privilege
under such circumstances," Judge Ford declared, "would invite frustration of
the administration of the courts." The conversation between Prichard and
Judge Ardery, then, was not privileged and could be introduced as evidence.
Ford also found that the mentioning of other defendants by Prichard to Judge
Ardery constituted hearsay. Ardery's testimony, Ford said, "is only competent
against Mr. Prichard."[15]

Judge Ardery's chair was brought over next to the jury box so that he could
be clearly heard. Judge Ford then stepped down from the bench and assumed
a seat in the witness box. Once the jury and the judge were seated, Stephens
began asking Ardery about the events of the night of November 7. Over repeated objections by the defense, Ardery told the jury that on that fateful night,
he and Ed Prichard had talked in his living room, while Phil "sat silently" for
part of that conversation. Then the damning testimony came:

MR. STEPHENS: Now, Judge, will you please tell the jury, and in detail, as near as
you can now remember, the conversation which you had with E.F. Prichard, Jr.,
there on that occasion.

JUDGE ARDERY: Mr. Prichard told me that he and two other young men prepared the ballots here in issue and put them in the ballot boxes before the election began. I remember two details. He gave no details as to the time and place of this happening. . . . He said one of the young men wrote the names of the election officers on the ballots and that he stamped the ballot that scratched Senator Chapman. Mr. Prichard was greatly disturbed, both mentally and emotionally. His mind was not on the past. It was on the future, at what it might hold for him. He asked me if I had a suggestion which would help him. I had none at that time.

Throughout his testimony, reporters noticed that Prichard "sat with his eyes closed," and that "he gripped the arms of his chair, alternately tilting his head to one side and resting his chin on his chest." Out of the presence of the jury, Ardery related that he had encountered Prichard the next Wednesday, November 10, when "I suggested to him that he go to his pastor and talk over the matter he had told me of. He didn't seem inclined to receive that suggestion favorably," Ardery concluded. The defense declined to cross-examine the witness, and the judge stepped down.[16]

The defense team had a difficult decision to make regarding whether it would attack Judge Ardery's credibility in cross-examination. In strategy sessions, Marion Rider angrily wanted to "go after" Judge Ardery but realized the risk the defense would take in harshly questioning one of the most esteemed members of the Kentucky bar and one of the most respected citizens in central Kentucky. Rider wanted to question the judge as to why he allowed Prichard to even discuss the case with him, and in the process imply that the venerable judge had violated numerous ethical principles in the process. But to question the character of a district judge, the defense team reasoned, was a strategy that could too easily backfire. All that attorney Joe Rauh could later say about Judge Ardery was—"Son of a Bitch! Ardery turned him in."[17]

The FBI, while delighted with Judge Ardery's appearance on the stand, was worried that there might be some tampering of the jury by the defense. Stephens and Judge Ford had been advised that such a possibility existed, but Judge Ford "desired no investigation in view of the possibility that trial of instant matter might be prejudiced." Hoover, for one, wrote "certainly in future cases of such importance we should be sure to investigate jury ourselves and not leave it to some other governmental agency. This was a grievous slip on our part."[18]

The remainder of the day went somewhat better for Prichard. A prosecution attempt to introduce evidence that Prichard had stuffed ballots in 1943 and had attempted to do so in 1946 until an election officer refused to allow him to remove a ballot book from the precinct, was ruled inadmissible by Judge

Ford. Following the ruling, Stephens rested the prosecution's case. When the court adjourned for the day, Stephens told a reporter that he might try to bring a case against a third defendant in the vote fraud case but had not yet decided to do so.[19]

The first person to take the stand for the defense on the morning of July 12 was Al Funk Jr., who categorically denied he was involved in any way with the vote fraud. When asked his whereabouts on the night of Saturday, October 29, Funk said he was home with his wife baking a chocolate cake. Throughout his testimony and Stephens's cross-examination, Funk remained cool and calm, saying he had no knowledge of the vote fraud and had signed none of the fraudulent ballots. Funk's wife, Nancy, then took the stand to corroborate her husband's story about the weekend in question.[20]

The next defense witness was the Chicago handwriting expert, R.B. Salmon, who had been obtained by Rauh and Phil Graham. Salmon, who said he had been a handwriting analyst for thirty-five years, sought to counteract the testimony previously given by the FBI's Walter Blackburn. Salmon concluded after examining the ballots that Funk had not signed any of them, that the ballots were signed by a "careless" writer, and that Funk's handwriting was "careful and meticulous." During the lengthy testimony on handwriting, reporters noticed that Prichard "yawned, gazed at the ceiling, frowned, took drinks of water from a glass on the defense table," and on one occasion even left the defense table to talk with a state senator who was sitting behind him. The stifling heat of the courtroom was noticeably affecting some of the jurors, who were caught napping during some of Salmon's testimony. By the end of the day, the question surrounding the courtroom concerned whether Prichard would take the stand in his own defense, as Funk had done.[21]

The defense decided against placing Prichard on the witness stand. Instead, on the morning of July 13 Rider called upon numerous character witnesses. A star-studded lineup of witnesses took the stand to sing Prichard's praises, including Gov. Earle Clements and University of Kentucky president Herman L. Donovan. Lucy Prichard was also summoned to testify as to her husband's activities on the weekend preceding the election. Her husband, according to reporters, "beamed at her" as she tersely answered questions. She was not cross-examined.[22]

After calling several other witnesses who claimed Prichard was busy at home over the weekend, the defense closed its case. Victor Bradley then made a closing statement that the *Courier-Journal* described as "masterful." "I am so firmly convinced, I am so firmly persuaded in my own mind that the evidence in this case has fallen so short of the proof of the conspiracy between these two young men here," Bradley said, "that it oughtn't take you all of five minutes to go out there and return a verdict of not guilty."

Bradley then sought to place doubt as to the case against both defendants. Concerning Funk, Bradley stated that the FBI evidence was nothing more than the "opinion of one individual." That opinion, in Bradley's estimation, "is insufficient to convict a citizen . . . be he high, be he low, be he the FBI." If the jury doubted the handwriting evidence, which Bradley said, "I wouldn't give a dime for," then the jury, Bradley argued, could not find a conspiracy charge against Funk and Prichard.

When he turned to Prichard, Bradley stated that "there is not one syllable of evidence" to suggest Prichard was near the courthouse on the weekend before the election, and he regarded Judge Ardery's testimony as merely "uncorroborated." In the end, Bradley told the jury not "to guess people out of their liberty and their lives."[23]

Then Claude Stephens rose to face the jury. The prosecution knew that the handwriting evidence was crucial, at least in convicting Funk. Stephens recalled his earlier career:

> I used to try cases back up in the mountains of Kentucky . . . but it seems that nearly all the time most everybody was against me, and I didn't have any help. I didn't have anybody to go out and make investigations and talk to witnesses . . . and they organized what is known in this country as the Federal Bureau of Investigation. I don't know what you think about it, but in all of my experience of 16 long years here . . . I have never found occasion nor had the occasion to upbraid an FBI agent for doing anything, only to commend them for righteous and honest things.

In giving what some observers noted was one of his finest moments in court, Stephens brought up the issue of Judge Ardery:

> Poor Judge Ardery! Sick, looking from the back to the beginning of his life, to the future when within a few years, no doubt, he will step from this mundane sphere to his heavenly home; and with those things in mind he told you that this man came to him, all excited, with a weight upon him, deeply troubled, on the day before the Grand Jury was to meet and before he found out whether or not finger prints could be obtained from the ballots.

In closing, Stephens gave the court an oratorical flourish that may have secretly appealed even to the former Princeton debater.

> I say to you that you ought not only to consider this case for the defendants and consider their plight, but you ought to consider the plight of these other people back here in the country that are staying about their homes attending to their duties there. They haven't got time to take much interest in politics. All they can do is to go and vote and have their sons and daughters go and vote themselves on election day. They

can't be there and watch these fellows try to steal the ballots and drop them in the boxes. Those are the kind of people I am pleading for in this case—the good, honest citizens who live back in the backwoods and out in the Bluegrass, who want to see the rights of the Government upheld, who want to see a man convicted of crime when he is found guilty, when he is proven guilty.[24]

When Stephens finished his summation, Judge Ford began the task of instructing the jury. There were several complex issues that the jury needed to know. First, Judge Ford spelled out the legal definition of "conspiracy," which he said "means an agreement or an understanding of two or more persons to unite their efforts." Ford also said that "to constitute a conspiracy it is not necessary that they all be present when each of the acts was done." Ford added that a defendant's refusal to testify is not an admission of guilt, and finished by adding that Judge Ardery's testimony could be used only in considering Prichard's guilt, not Funk's. With that, the jury left the courtroom to begin deliberating the case against Ed Prichard and Al Funk.[25]

It took only three and a half hours for the jury to reach a verdict. As the jury reentered, Funk sat expressionless, while Prichard, according to one observer, "leaned forward with his elbows resting on the table, his hands tightly clasped, his moon face glistening with sweat." Judge Ford asked the jury foreman if a verdict had been reached. When the foreman nodded, the slips of paper were handed to the court clerk, who pronounced: "This is case no. 7688, United States of America versus Alvarado Erwin Funk, Jr. We the jury agree and find the defendant Alvarado Erwin Funk, Jr., not guilty." At that, Funk's father, the Kentucky attorney general, hugged his son and then wept "violently" in court. Funk's wife, Nancy, let out an audible squeal and struggled through attorneys and spectators to reach her beaming husband. Then, the clerk continued. "In the case of United States versus Edward Fretwell Prichard, Jr., we the jury agree and find the defendant, Edward Fretwell Prichard Jr., guilty. Signed, C.M. Brooking, foreman of the jury." The muted celebration in the courtroom suddenly changed after those words, and the crowd "sat in awed silence" as Ford thanked the jury, dismissed Funk, and then called Prichard forward.[26]

Judge Ford asked Prichard if he wished to make any statements before sentencing. With his hands still tightly clasped, and in a strained voice, Prichard simply said, "I have no statement to make at this time, Your Honor." Observers now noticed that Judge Ford himself was "obviously nervous," and his hands trembled as he passed sentence: "It is the sentence of the court that you are to be committed to the custody of the Attorney General for imprisonment of two years." Upon hearing the sentence, observers noticed tears well up in the eyes of "Little Al" Funk.[27]

Prichard's attorneys tried to get Judge Ford to release their client pending an appeal but were denied. Prichard then went with his attorneys to a nearby witness room. On his way out of the courtroom, he put his hand on Funk's shoulder. As soon as he reached the privacy of the witness room, Prichard laid his head on a table and sobbed. As reporters saw this emotional demonstration, the doors to the witness room were quickly closed. A U.S. marshal ordered that no photographs be taken as Prichard came from the witness room. Within a few minutes, a more composed Prichard emerged and was escorted across the street in a light rain to spend his first night in jail.[28]

Lucy was not in the courtroom when the verdict was delivered. Her friend and Prichard's associate, Bob Houlihan, agreed to drive to Paris to tell her. When he approached the house, Lucy was working in the garden. As he prepared to tell her the verdict, she told him that the expression on his face was all she needed to know. Realizing all that had happened, Houlihan said, Lucy was simply "devastated."[29]

Outside the courtroom, a beaming Funk gushed, "It just couldn't have been any other way. I knew they wouldn't convict me." Jurors, meanwhile, privately shared their deliberations with journalists. One juror stated that in their opening deliberation, they took a voice vote on whether a conspiracy existed. They agreed, unanimously, that there had been such an arrangement. Then a written poll was taken separately on Funk and Prichard. The juror said the poll was "lopsided" on one and "about even" on the other, not disclosing who was which. Another juror disclosed that two ballots were necessary before Prichard was convicted. The jurors agreed that Judge Ardery's testimony was "damning," and one juror admitted that since Prichard did not testify to deny the conversation, they had no choice but "to accept it as true." Another juror admitted that despite Judge Ford's charge to the contrary, Prichard's failure to testify was "a factor" in the verdict, but also said that had Prichard testified, the jury would not necessarily have believed him over Judge Ardery. Based almost entirely on Ardery's testimony, the jury reached its guilty verdict against Prichard at around 3:00 P.M. As to Funk, the jury deliberated for less than half an hour before reaching its decision. The FBI's handwriting evidence, it turns out, was not conclusive to the jurors. Several found that their own comparisons of the handwriting samples contradicted the findings of the FBI's expert. One of Prichard's attorneys later revealed that Prichard's case before the jury was not helped by the contradictory image of a nattily attired and calm Funk accompanied by his beautiful wife, as compared with the image of Prichard, all alone, sweating profusely throughout the trial.[30]

Prichard's conviction became major news. The story was a front-page item in the *Washington Post*, and *the New York Times* headline read "Prichard Is Guilty of Election Fraud." The major Kentucky dailies made the story their leads, while the *Paris Kentuckian-Citizen,* which had not reported news concerning the indictment nor the trial itself, produced a headline that simply said, "Prichard Gets Two Years." The *Louisville Courier-Journal* soon issued an editorial that greatly disturbed Prichard. The paper's owner, Barry Bingham, was a close friend of Prichard's, as was editor Mark Ethridge. Bingham and Ethridge, along with reporter John Ed Pearce, drafted an editorial stating that Prichard "was convicted of an incredibly cynical and stupid act. The fact that the forged ballots made no difference in the election results of Democratic Bourbon County is beside the point. If anything, it deepens the offense, suggesting a feeling that ballots are only paper to be manipulated to show how closely a precinct may be controlled." The editorial concluded that "it is a great pity that a man so endowed with exceptional qualities should have been lacking in the essential element of integrity concerning the ballot, the very basis of democratic government." After reading the editorial, an outraged Prichard refused to speak with Barry or Mary Bingham for many years to come. An angry Joe Rauh asked Bingham's attorney, Wilson Wyatt, "why you and your newspaper have been so hard-hearted about Prich?"[31]

After spending what jailor Austin Price described as a "very good and restful" night in the Fayette County jail, Prichard appeared the next day, July 15, for further hearings. His attorneys filed an appeal with Judge Ford stating that Prichard requested a new trial on grounds that the court had erred in admitting Judge Ardery's testimony, as well as several other tangential items. Ford released Prichard from custody on a $5,000 bond pending appeal.

Prichard would have to live with several vital decisions he had made during the trial. In addition to the defense team's decision not to cross-examine Ardery or to put Prichard himself on the stand, Prichard's decision to hire a team of local lawyers seemed the first thing he was going to rectify. To head the appeal, Prichard hired Hugh Cox, a former Rhodes Scholar who had been Thurman Arnold's assistant in the Antitrust Division of the Justice Department in the early 1940s and had later worked in the U.S. solicitor general's office. In 1951 Cox joined the powerful Washington firm of Covington and Burling, termed by one writer as "Washington's premiere law firm." Cox also involved Joe Rauh in preparing the appeal brief. Rauh held Cox in high esteem for his legal skills, calling Cox "a crackerjack" lawyer. Prichard also relied more heavily on Thomas Corcoran's personal and legal advice.[32]

The FBI, meanwhile, was not finished with its involvement in the Prichard case. As long as appeals were pending, J. Edgar Hoover was kept informed of all developments. Hoover was diligent in his attempts to put Prichard behind bars and to keep him from pulling any last-minute strings to save himself from prison. On one occasion, he wrote a memo to Assistant Attorney General Alexander M. Campbell stating that "some of the people in Bourbon County feel that Prichard will never actually serve any time even though he was convicted. The reported basis for this feeling," Hoover wrote, "is that Prichard has too much political influence to actually serve time in jail." Within the FBI, a certain satisfaction in having convicted Prichard transcended any disappointment over the not-guilty verdict returned on Funk or the inability to secure even an indictment against Billy Baldwin. The fact that the lengthy fieldwork and laboratory work conducted by the agency had failed to persuade the jury to convict Funk did not seem to bother the FBI at all. In the FBI's eyes, neither Al Funk Jr. nor Billy Baldwin nor a righteous desire to clean up Bourbon County elections really mattered. The investigation had been grounded primarily in politics and ideology, with its primary aim to destroy the career of a member of the New Deal wing of the Democratic party who had been a target of Hoover's predatory eye since 1941. In other recent election fraud investigations of rampant vote buying and ballot-box stuffing, the FBI had often looked the other way when it concerned the president's former jurisdiction or the election of a conservative Texan and close friend of Hoover's, Lyndon Johnson. Only after Prichard's name was mentioned in the affair did Hoover direct the bureau to press the case to the fullest extent. In its internal memos following the conviction, the FBI acknowledged that the cooperation of both Philip and William Ardery in the investigation was crucial to winning the case. They had been, in the words of Louisville Special Agent in Charge Fred Hallford, "sufficiently honest and substantial to take a stand without fear of any type of pressure or reprisal."[33]

But for Judge Ardery, the consequences of testifying against Prichard were soon felt. A *Courier-Journal* writer, Allan Trout, noted that in Frankfort the sentiment was strong that the judge "had signed his political death warrant." The talk around the capital was that Franklin County would be removed from Ardery's jurisdiction as punishment. Removing the county containing the state capital and all of its attendant judicial business would leave Judge Ardery with considerably less political clout. Trout wrote that Ardery's actions constituted an "unpardonable sin," and that within Kentucky politics "it is the unwritten code of politicians that any man beholden to politics is honor-bound to remain 'one of the boys.'" Rhetoric concerning high principles was fine, Trout argued, but the unwritten rules "insist upon unswerving loyalty when the time comes to play for keeps."[34]

From the moment Prichard was indicted for the vote fraud, a series of questions has continued to surround the case: Was he guilty? If so, why did he do it? Why would someone blessed with so much ability and brilliance throw it all away for a mere 254 votes in a statewide election? If he was not guilty, was he set up?

The answer to the first question was provided by Prichard himself. Although he privately implied his guilt to selected friends soon after the trial, he did not publicly affirm or deny his participation in the vote fraud until 1976. Then, in an interview with John Ed Pearce, Prichard candidly proclaimed, "I did it. It was wrong, and I know it was wrong."[35] Prichard never commented on the parts played by Funk or Baldwin.

The question of why he did it is not so easy to answer. From the very beginning, a rumor spread throughout Bourbon County that the real reason Prichard stuffed the boxes was an election bet. FBI agent Mooney knew of the bet rumor but could never find solid evidence to support the contention. Phil Ardery, for one, wrote that he, too, felt that an election bet was behind Prichard's actions. Although Prichard did not tell either Phil or William Ardery that a bet was involved, Phil Ardery highlighted the rumor in his account of the episode. As the story goes, a Lexington bookmaker named Ed Curd had taken a bet from either Prichard or his father for $20,000 on what the Democratic majority would be in the Bourbon County election. Wishing to improve his chances, the younger Prichard conspired to enlarge the majority vote by stuffing the boxes before the election.[36]

In his interview with Pearce in 1976, Prichard denied such allegations. In fact, he never publicly said why he committed his crime except to generalize that "it was sort of a moral blind spot." Toward the end of his life Prichard said, "I was raised in a county where monkeying with elections was second nature; my father did it, my great-grandfather did it. I was raised to believe that was just second nature. There I was on the one hand with all those great moral and intellectual principles, believing I ought to stand for the good, the true and the beautiful; and on the other hand thinking it's perfectly all right to stuff a ballot box. Now that's an absolute dichotomy, but that's the kind of dichotomy I got into, and it's absolutely unforgiveable."[37]

These candid admissions came at a point in Prichard's life when he could discuss such matters with complete honesty. For more than twenty years, however, he groped for a public posture that evaded the matter. In private he told friends and associates varying stories concerning the scandal. To Joe Rauh and Isaiah Berlin, Prichard shared a unique version of what had really occurred. The primary culprit, he said, was actually Billy Baldwin, who came to Prichard and told him that unless he helped with the ballot books, then, in Berlin's words, "you're not one of us." Prichard at first refused, but Baldwin informed him that Al Funk Jr. had already signed over two hundred. To Rauh, it was explained that "they'd done it as sort of a dare for Prich to be a real guy like the rest of them." In this way, Prichard went along as an unwilling accomplice in order to further his own political prospects with the local courthouse crowd. After all, Prichard had been rebuffed as a congressional candidate months before, and in helping Baldwin he was demonstrating that he had not lost touch with the locals after being in Washington for six years. To Berlin, the entire episode was completely out of character. Prichard was, in Berlin's estimation, "by temperament anything but a cheat, a forger and a crook." But Berlin knew little of the political dynamics implicit in Bourbon County elections. Prichard later amusedly referred to stuffing a ballot box in Bourbon County as similar to "losing your virginity."[38]

To some friends, the notion of Prichard's guilt seemed unthinkable. To others, such as Lyndon and Lady Bird Johnson, it was not so much a matter of his guilt as it was the virtual irrelevance of the act itself. Lady Bird stated that she and her husband "felt what Prich was accused of—and finally in-dicted—was a political prank—an act of bad judgment—and not a crime." Joseph Alsop concurred that Prichard's act was "very trivial" and was motivated by a need "to show that he was one of the Kentucky boys." Overall, Alsop observed, "there was a strong smell of a malicious county courthouse conspiracy about the whole thing."[39]

Yet with a young law associate, Prichard revealed a different story. Days before the election, he told Joseph Terry he had been at a party where he had boasted on the margin of victory in Bourbon County and a bet was indeed made. Feeling anxious as the election approached, Prichard wanted to make sure that the margin was guaranteed and conspired with Billy Baldwin to stuff the boxes. In all versions, the one constant ingredient was that Al Funk Jr. had been a minor player in the episode.[40]

It seems in retrospect that the story Prichard related to Rauh and Berlin was grounded in the respect and love he had for these protégés, and therefore Prichard cast himself in the best possible light—as a victim of a cynical po-litical system that forced him to participate in corruption in order to survive politically. There were elements of truth in this version, but it failed to acknowl-edge some underlying components. After all, Prichard had grown up sur-rounded by election fraud and saw nothing morally disturbing in what was considered common practice. His father's complicity in vote fraud in past elec-tions obviously added to his childhood acceptance of such acts as part of the political process. Election fraud seemed as commonplace as taking a drink during Prohibition, and, as Prichard related, it was akin to earning one's "man-hood." It therefore seems inconsistent for Baldwin to have to talk a reluctant Prichard into participating.

The election bet story is also not without some interesting angles—Ed Curd lived on a 340-acre farm on the Paris Pike and operated one of the country's largest gambling houses out of the Mayfair Bar in Lexington. One of Curd's "runners" in his bookmaking operation was supposedly Prichard's uncle, Thomas. During World War II, Curd's operation handled more than $500,000 in college football bets on an average weekend. Curd was known to cover bets not only on sporting events but on elections as well. And not all of Curd's associates were local gamblers. During the Kefauver crime investigations of the early 1950s, New York mafia boss Frank Costello testified that he had done business with Curd in 1950. Curd was best known as the sinister figure who corrupted several University of Kentucky basketball players during a gambling scandal in 1951. His activities became so notorious that the state filed suit asking that he be barred from gambling in Lexington because he corrupted "the morals of the community." Curd was indicted by the IRS in 1953 for tax evasion, whereupon he fled to Canada and, ultimately, Las Vegas. The bet scheme also helps explain why Prichard was intent on stuffing a mere 250 votes in a statewide election involving more than 138,000 votes.[41]

But an examination of the election scandal should not get bogged down in deciphering the precise reason that animated Ed Prichard in this specific race. Whether he did it to prove he was "one of the boys" to Billy Baldwin or to win an election bet is not the point. As Prichard acknowledged, stuffing ballot boxes was a family and a county tradition as far back as anyone could remember. No one had ever been indicted before for stuffing boxes in Bourbon County, and the thought of getting caught probably never entered Prichard's mind. When considered in this light, the question of why he was willing to risk it all for just over 250 votes misses the mark entirely. In the mind of Ed Prichard on the weekend preceding the 1948 election, what would it hurt to help one of Paris's own on election day, especially considering that the number of votes involved was inconsequential? Casual observers may wish to label the act as a childish "prank," comparing the stuffing of a ballot box to a fraternity joke, but the Bourbon County election fraud was anything but a mindless act on Prichard's part. Whether for financial or political gain, Prichard saw his role in the affair as entirely self-serving. And as he had displayed when he smuggled Frankfurter's opinion out of the Supreme Court building eight years before, an end-justifies-the-means mentality was an established part of Ed Prichard's moral makeup by the late 1940s.

In light of what transpired at the trial, it is something of a judicial oddity that Prichard was convicted at all. Considering the prosecution's inability to convince the jury of Funk's guilt, even supported by the best efforts of the FBI and the personal involvement of J. Edgar Hoover, it seems altogether reasonable to conclude that one could participate in a rather modest amount of traditional "electioneering" in 1948 and face no grand juries or other penalties. As the glaring example of Lyndon Johnson affords, one more often than not benefited from such a crime.

Is it conceivable that Prichard was framed? Phil Graham, for one, assumed Prichard had been set up by the FBI. John Kenneth Galbraith concluded that

Prichard had been singled out because of his political persuasion.[42] Did local political forces seek revenge on Big Ed or his arrogant son by setting up the younger Prichard? This, too, seems unlikely. While there were certainly numerous people of both parties in Bourbon County who talked with the FBI and were delighted with Prichard's conviction, the lack of convincing evidence on hand against Prichard dispels this notion. At the very least, conspirators could have had Prichard sign some of the ballots or obtain other damaging evidence. The topic of a conspiracy against Ed Prichard skates on thin evidentiary ice in light of his own role in his downfall.

Public anger toward Prichard, however, mounted in the days after the trial. In a letter to the editor of the *Courier-Journal,* a writer named "Citizen" stated, "Prichard and his co-defendants were not on trial by themselves. Into the courtroom and taking their seats alongside these boys went long lines of men and women. Silently and invisibly they took their places in the defendant's seats facing the judge they never had to face in person." The letter continued: "Every man who ever sold his vote, bought votes or furnished money for both, stuffed ballot boxes or contributed in any way to corrupt elections sat with these boys. . . . Have we taken our country for granted? Is there any one of voting age anywhere in our great land who hasn't heard of fraud in elections? We try to teach our children courtesy, politeness, civility . . . but do we teach them early and late the love of law, the sacredness of the vote?"[43]

To those who felt Prichard's only real source of guilt was his progressive politics, the figure of Ed Prichard during the trial takes on dramatic proportions reminiscent of Greek tragedy. They perceived a brilliant youth shot down at his zenith by a youthful indiscretion and betrayed by inferiors who surrounded him. If there was any tragedy in Prichard's plight, at least in the classical sense, it was not in his essential innocence but in his attempt to hide his guilt. One of the recurring themes of Greek tragedy is the role the tragic hero plays in his own downfall. The hero's attempt to extricate himself from danger only serves to contribute to his destruction. In this way, Prichard's trip to see Phil and William Ardery days after the election was a vital part of the tragic saga that soon befell him. In its final ironic twist, considering the fate of both Billy Baldwin and Al Funk, Ed Prichard could have gotten away with it all had he simply refrained from going to see Judge Ardery on the night of November 7, 1948. In retrospect, his Machiavellian plot to coopt Judge Ardery was the single determining action that ultimately sealed his fate.

The trial of Ed Prichard lasted a little over one week. The jury's deliberations took less than four hours. Yet the events of those ten days in July 1949 became the defining moments of Prichard's life. In the span of less than a year, his lofty world had been turned upside down and now seemed destroyed. Just a year earlier, he was an oft-mentioned candidate for Congress or governor;

had been offered the position of executive director of the ADA; had been a partner in a thriving law practice; had served as the general counsel of the Democratic National Committee; and had become a valued and trusted adviser to the new Kentucky governor. By mid-July 1949, he was a convicted felon with only the thin hope of an appeal to save him from jail.

10 Ashland

In the fall of 1949, Ed Prichard lived on borrowed time. His attorneys continued to piece together his appeal, while his personal and financial affairs came unglued. Prichard lived under the cloud of knowing that if his appeal failed, a two-year prison sentence loomed. Additionally, his hefty legal fees mounted, and in time financial pressures consumed him as intensely as his fears of a long jail stay.

Prichard's conviction on July 14 placed his entire legal career in jeopardy. Many clients took their business elsewhere, while others looked for ways out of retainers they had signed with Prichard. A week following the trial, Prichard told the City of Lexington that he was willing to rescind his contract with the city and forgo $2,500 in possible fees. Mayor Tom Mooney quickly announced that Prichard's resignation was accepted.[1]

Prichard shared his growing financial woes with Thomas Corcoran. In August 1949, he wrote about the general shape of the appeal and its expenses:

Dear Tom:
. . . The situation here is still bad. We just had an estimate from the printer of $3,000 for printing the record. This is on top of $2,200 for the typewritten transcript and $4,000 for a handwriting expert. I have not yet received a bill from my lawyers, so do not know about that. There were other expenses, such as $1,500 for photographing ballots and handwriting exhibits, etc.

I managed to get hold of enough from my father to pay my income taxes and an overdraft at the bank which arose during the trial. We are now trying to collect a few fees and complete some pending business, but those matters are always problematical. You can imagine that my practice is at a virtual standstill—at best until the appeal is finally acted on. Even pending matters cannot be pressed, since I hate to appear in court under present circumstances. Indeed, Judge Swinford, who presides over the Federal Court at Covington, where I had some cases set for trial in September, took it upon himself to write my clients and instruct them to obtain other counsel.

There is a note overdue at the bank, on which I have been paying about $500 and renewing it from time to time. The bank is calling the note—which is $3,500. There is another note for $1,500 which is due today. . . . Could you give me some immediate word as to the lay of the land. If there is no possibility of immediate relief, then I must try elsewhere. . . .

As a postscript, Prichard reiterated his growing anxiety—"If you could let me know *something,* whether good or bad, I should be immensely grateful."[2]

The "lay of the land," as Corcoran soon discovered, was not good. Corcoran had sought the help of one of Washington's most prominent attorneys, Edward Burling, of the powerhouse firm Covington and Burling. Upon receiving Corcoran's note for help in the Prichard appeal, Burling fired back: "I can't see any reason in the world why I should be asked to aid Prich's appeal." Claiming that he had not the money to help anyway, Burling added, "I see no reason to help Prich out of capital. He was reported to have said he was making a huge income."[3]

When Corcoran told Prichard of Burling's response, Prichard replied with gracious disappointment. "I understand perfectly," Prichard said, "and hope you will make no further approaches" to Burling. On the whole, Prichard thought, "I think it is better if I just worry along with my problems (financial ones, I mean) and do the best I can here." Several weeks later, Prichard wrote Corcoran to tell him that he had made it through yet another financial emergency. This time, "Phil Graham and John Ferguson sent out a call to a few old friends and pulled me through." One friend who provided a substantial amount was Bob Hannegan. But, Prichard acknowledged, "I am still in plenty of financial difficulty." Prichard had to pay half of the attorney fees charged to him and Funk plus a $600 insurance premium he owed on December 1, 1949. "I am still plenty in the soup." Prichard then asked "if there is any way you could find quickly about $2,000 or $2,500. . . . I am deeply discouraged, and need cheering up more than money."[4]

It is a reflection of the severe straits in which Prichard found himself that he was more depressed in late 1949 with his looming financial difficulties than with an imminent visit to prison. Obviously, the appeal process would be even more expensive and did not guarantee that he would not eventually go to jail.

Prichard's appeal, written primarily by Hugh Cox and Joseph Rauh in Washington, rested on three major points. First, it argued that Prichard could not be convicted for a conspiracy since Funk had been acquitted. In essence, Cox and Rauh asserted, Prichard had to be conspiring with himself if the conviction was upheld. Second, since the number of fraudulent ballots involved had no bearing on the election's outcome, the crime itself was therefore minimized. Finally, the appeal contended that Judge Ardery's testimony was privileged and therefore inadmissible. The defense filed the appeal in the U.S. Circuit Court of Appeals in Cincinnati on February 10, 1950. Prichard was well pleased with the work of Cox and Rauh, telling Phil Graham that his attorneys provided "the finest legal effort which money could not buy."[5]

As the appeal process was under way, Gov. Earle Clements made a sudden trip to Washington. Shortly after his return, Jesse K. Lewis, who had worked for the Bourbon County Citizens' Committee and was a former assistant Kentucky attorney general, accused the governor of making the trip in order to secure a presidential pardon for Prichard in case the appeal failed. Clements angrily denied the allegation, and Prichard himself said, "Mr. Lewis sat at the Government's table during the recent trial . . . and had ample opportunity to make Governor Clements testify under oath as to the truth or falsity of the statements he now makes." Prichard called Lewis's allegations simply "a lie."[6]

For months after the trial, Prichard tried to balance his mounting financial woes and his struggling law practice with the appeal itself. His firm, Prichard and Funk, disbanded when Al Funk Jr. decided to move to Middlesboro, Kentucky, where he served as resident attorney for the American Association, an English land company that owned vast eastern Kentucky coalfields. Before Funk's departure, however, he was indicted in Fayette Circuit Court for vote buying in the 1949 September city elections. Funk's second indictment in less than a year on election fraud charges never went to trial. In December a circuit judge ruled that the indictment was invalid since the statutes regarding vote buying pertained only to party primaries and general elections— not city elections. A relieved Funk claimed the indictment was "obviously an attempt to embarrass me for political reasons." Funk never spoke about his legal troubles, and family members were advised never to bring up the sensitive subject when he visited. Prichard meanwhile kept to himself. J. Edgar Hoover was informed by local agents that Prichard "is scarcely ever seen anywhere . . . and his law office shows no sign of life."[7]

Prichard's Washington friends responded to his worsening financial troubles in a remarkable way. Beginning in January 1950, Phil Graham launched an effort to raise money for Prichard. Graham acted as an unofficial treasurer, soliciting checks from the likes of former Attorney General Francis Biddle, Eugene Meyer, Isaiah Berlin, and Drew Pearson. Graham then sent Prichard a check with the combined funds from nearly twenty contributors. In just over two months, he raised $6,200 for his former Harvard roommate and best man. Prichard responded warmly to Graham's effort, humorously noting to Phil, "Your genius as a financier is equal, if not superior, to that of your father-in-law." The money was a heartfelt expression of kindness by a coterie of Washington attorneys and politicos for an old and cherished friend. Prichard also told Graham that of all the checks he had received, "I noted one which touched me more than the others, one signed by you and attributed to no other donor." In thanking Graham, Prichard was placed in an awkward position: "I am enough of a cad to accept it, and enough of a gentleman to say you should not have done it."[8]

The efforts by Washingtonians to raise money for Prichard did not stop there. The network of friends who sought contributions was a poignant testimonial to the esteem in which some of Washington's luminaries held Ed Prichard. One was James Rowe, who wrote an impassioned letter to Frank Pace, the secretary of the Army. "I remember telling you, when I ran into you at the Chicago Airport about a year ago," Rowe wrote, "that I could fully understood you might have a problem about retaining Prich because of the complications of your company and your industry with the Government." Then Rowe cut to the chase: "You do need to raise some hard cash for Prich. I agreed to get six friends to put up $500 apiece. . . . I got all five and we all agreed that Frank Pace ought to be the sixth." Rowe added that the money would "undoubtedly never be repaid." Then he added a personal note:

> Now, a word about Prich. I know that all of us, in one way or another, have all had to do something. Sometimes I think that people like myself and Tom Corcoran, who were as close to Prich as were the rest of you, have done a great deal more than some of his close friends. . . . I do know he has caused us all problems . . . practically all of us have gotten irritated at him at one time or another.
>
> The fact is there is not a silver lining and I really think he is on the way up at last. His old friend Earle Clements . . . told us recently that there is no sense in talking about psychological rehabilitation with Prich until he is economically rehabilitated. . . . Therefore, Brother Frank, please rally once more to the flag. . . . I know that there are unconscionable drags of this nature on all of us which other people don't really understand. But this is an old, old friend who has very good stuff in him and who has brought brilliance and gaiety to all of us.

Rowe ended by saying "none of us can afford it but none of us can afford not to."[9]

Perhaps underneath the rush to write checks on Prichard's behalf was the certain sense of guilt that seemed to emanate from many of Prichard's friends and acquaintances. Much like the "enabler" who provides an atmosphere for an alcoholic friend to go on drinking, some of Prichard's closest friends seemed to nourish those habits of irresponsibility that eventually destroyed him. As Mary Bingham remembered, "You couldn't help spoiling him." When Prichard was careless with money, a legal brief, or a political secret, friends treated it all with casual delight, always willing to step in to save Prichard from trouble rather than let him face the consequences of his actions. To them, that was simply the price one paid to know Prichard, and they, too, could then add to the considerable repertoire of "Prich stories." Such enabling did not, sadly enough, end with Prichard's conviction.[10]

Prichard's own troubles spread to his father, who weeks following the trial ran in a primary for reelection to his statehouse seat. He was opposed by J. T. Snapp, who accused the elder Prichard of being an arrogant, "self-appointed czar of Bourbon County." Without mentioning anything concerning his son, Snapp accused Big Ed of tinkering with voting lists, resorting to insults and intimidation, and using "the tactics of a dictator." In the August 1949 primary, Prichard lost the election and never again ran for elective office. Billy Baldwin, meanwhile, won his race for county attorney by a comfortable margin.[11]

On April 4, 1950, Rowe's worst suspicions about Prichard's future were confirmed. The Court of Appeals unanimously upheld his conviction. In an eight-page opinion, the court turned down Prichard's contentions point by point. On whether the conviction should be thrown out because the number of votes involved was not enough to affect the outcome of the election, the court said bluntly "the argument has no merit." The judges elaborated that "the deposit of forged ballots in the ballot boxes, no matter how small or great their number, dilutes the influence of honest votes in an election, and whether in greater or less degree is immaterial." Concerning whether one person can be convicted in a conspiracy case, the court held that "it is the rule that all parties to a conspiracy need not be named in the indictment" and that Prichard's conviction was proper "if it is shown by substantial evidence that the parties unknown at the time the indictment was returned committed overt acts therein alleged. Such evidence," the court concluded, "there was."

The weight of the court's ruling dealt with the delicate matter of Judge Ardery's testimony. The Appeals Court found that "by all standards of ethical conduct which govern the conduct of a judge it was morally, if not legally, impossible for Judge Ardery to enter into an attorney-client relationship with one whose conduct was to be investigated by a grand jury already called and," the court added, "this Prichard knew or must have known." The court then admonished Judge Ardery. By all modern standards of judicial ethics, the court maintained, "the judge was not only disqualified from sitting on Prichard's case, but doubtless was also disqualified from organizing and instructing the grand jury."[12]

With the bad news from the Circuit Appeals Court, Prichard and his lawyers decided to take their case to the U.S. Supreme Court, thus facing another delicate hurdle. Since Prichard had worked with Justices Frankfurter and Jackson and Chief Justice Vinson, the question of who would sit on the case was immediately raised. Court rules do not require justices to disqualify themselves automatically. Instead, justices are allowed to determine whether they will sit on a case by their own discretion. But before that question could be settled, Prichard had to wonder whether the Court would even grant a hearing on the case. As the summer of 1950 approached, his chances for avoiding prison seemed rather slim.[13]

As the appeal was being prepared for submission to the high court, Chief Justice Vinson was asked by a reporter about Prichard's appeal. Vinson refused to make any comment on the specifics of the case, but added, "I have no question as to what my position will be if and when the case is presented." Meanwhile, Vinson received several anonymous letters about Prichard's appeal. One said, "It is widely talked that you sit as Chief Justice . . . and through the medium of your man 'Friday' E.F. Prichard, Jr., you meddle in Kentucky politics and it is the opinion of many that you will fish him out of this mess and he will not be punished.—We shall see."[14]

But these were not the only letters received by the chief justice. A Lexington businessman wrote Vinson that "you people in Washington took a young, fat Kentucky boy and turned his head." As a friend of Vinson, the writer urged the Kentucky judge to intervene with the president in order to obtain a pardon for the young Prichard. A pardon would enable justice to "be best served, the ballot protected and a brilliant young man rescued to give of his talent to Kentucky and his country."[15]

To those who felt Prichard might maneuver his way out of serving his sentence, news leaks of a proposed presidential pardon added more fuel to the fire. When Bourbon County sheriff Reuben Arnsparger signed a pardon petition circulating in Paris in early June 1950, he claimed that the petition was written by Billy Baldwin. In denying the claim, Baldwin said that Arnsparger was mistaken and had signed an earlier letter circulated by Baldwin, of which he refused to divulge the contents. "If I was going to circulate a petition," Baldwin said, "I believe I would wait for a more propitious time," referring to the fact that Prichard had not started serving his sentence. Paul Brannon, the publisher of the *Paris Kentuckian-Citizen,* admitted the following day that more than twenty letters had been sent to President Truman requesting a pardon for Prichard. Brannon also stated that one of the letters had been prepared by Baldwin. No petition, Brannon added, was being circulated in the county, although "there have been many inquiries from people who said they want to sign one."[16]

On June 5, 1950, Prichard's defense reached the end of the appeal process. On the final day of court business before its summer recess, the U.S. Supreme Court issued its ruling on Prichard's case. Not surprisingly, Chief Justice Vinson and Justices Stanley Reed (a Kentuckian), Felix Frankfurter, and Tom Clark (who had been attorney general during the trial before his appointment to the high court) disqualified themselves. Surprisingly, Justice Robert H. Jackson, the man for whom Prichard had worked in the early 1940s, did not recuse himself. Whenever fewer than six justices rule on a case, the Court applies a provision whereby the lower court ruling is simply allowed to stand. Since a quorum could not be reached, and because the "majority of the qualified justices are of the opinion that the case cannot be heard and determined at the next term of court," Hugo Black wrote, the Appeals Court ruling was upheld. Prichard's only remaining hope was to appeal the sentence back to Judge H. Church Ford. His attorneys requested a hearing to consider reducing his sentence, perhaps to probation. That hearing was set for mid-July.[17]

With the news of the Supreme Court's ruling, the once-quiet effort to win Prichard a presidential pardon shifted into high gear. A massive petition drive circulated in Bourbon County, and its sponsors hoped to obtain 3,000 signatures. The movement was organized by Prichard's father and Paul Brannon. Although they did not mind the release of the names on the petition, J. Nathan Elliott, Prichard's brother-in-law, asked that the names remain secret. The petition admitted that vote fraud was a long tradition within Bourbon County politics, and that therefore Prichard's guilt "is shared by all those who permitted these conditions to commence long before he was born and to continue over these many years." Among those whose signatures were on a petition obtained by the *Courier-Journal* were Mrs. Virgil Chapman and old Bourbon County political boss Will McClintock. Another signer of the petition was the Rev. J.W. Clotfelder, pastor of the First Presbyterian Church. Clotfelder had been a friend of the Prichard family and was the only member of the Ministerial Association who signed the petition. The county's ministers met on June 17 to oppose the pardon drive. Claiming that the act of a pardon demanded "full confession and genuine repentance," which had not been forthcoming from Prichard, the ministers asked that the sentence be meted out. The real question, in the minds of the Ministerial Association, was a moral one: "public and individual honesty and integrity are at stake." Prichard himself wrote to President Truman requesting a pardon, even though Prichard had referred to the president in a letter to Joseph Alsop as "a small man who sometimes apprehends big ideas but never really appreciates big men." The only word from Washington concerning the matter was that the request was "under review."[18]

On the morning of July 14, 1950, precisely one year after his original conviction, Ed Prichard stood once more before Judge H. Church Ford in a federal courtroom in Lexington. Prichard's motion was argued by Leslie Morris, who noted that probation could provide offenders a chance for rehabilitation. But Morris was reluctant to place guilt upon his client, who, after all, "for the first time in the history of our judicial system . . . was deprived of his liberty without an opportunity to have determined by the highest court of the land the very substantial questions of law upon which his liberty depended." Morris concluded, "Is the record—the promise of a young lifetime—to be blotted out by this offense?" Morris spelled out that Prichard "has been chastened and humiliated far beyond the lot of the most hardened criminal. . . . If the ordeal through which he has gone will not reform him," Morris said, "nothing will reform him." U.S. Attorney Claude Stephens then rose and told Judge Ford he was not pleased to recommend the two-year prison sentence, but that the nature of the crime warranted the sentence. Throughout the hearing, Prichard sat with his hands tightly clasped on the table and his head bowed.

Judge Ford then stated he was aware that there were cases where probation was called for, such as a young man "motivated by carelessness" or "an ignorant man who is unacquainted with the law." Judge Ford did not find such conditions in Prichard's case. After all, Ford said, Prichard was an educated man with considerable experience in law and politics. "It would be a perversion," Ford concluded, "an abuse of the law of probation," to issue it to "persons who so deliberately violate the law of the country. I can do nothing else without abusing this great principle upon which probation rests." With that, Judge Ford denied the motion and placed Prichard in the custody of U.S. Marshal Charles Dudley.

As he was led out of the courtroom, Prichard told a friend, "I suppose they'll quarantine me and I'll be deloused." When he saw some reporters outside the courtroom, he asked that since they had "made a living off of me for the last time, how about some cigars?" In another remark that perhaps revealed some of his inner feelings, Prichard smiled at reporters and said, "They'll take away all of my utensils to keep me from killing myself." Prichard was then driven the hundred miles or so to the Federal Correctional Institution in Ashland, Kentucky, where he was handed over to the warden that afternoon.[19]

Within days of beginning his sentence, prisoner Prichard released a candid personal statement, the first since his trial. "I cannot at this time refrain," Prichard wrote, "from expressing the abiding gratitude which I feel for the literally thousands of friends . . . who have stood by me so loyally through all my troubles." He continued:

> Fully conscious of my own unworthiness and deeply penitent for any wrongs I may have done, I can only say that I hope that in the future the confidence and faith of these friends will not prove to have been misplaced.
>
> Especially do I wish to thank those who have made zealous efforts to secure presidential clemency for me. While it is apparent that at this time no pardon will be granted me, there is always hope for the future. . . .
>
> One word more, and I am finished. I go in good heart and spirits, with no malice in my heart, deeply regretting all the mistakes I have made, eagerly looking forward to the time when I can return to my family, fervently hoping that in the future my life and conduct may justify the faith of my friends.[20]

Prichard's state of mind as he entered prison was revealing. There was no bitterness, no brash pronouncements (as he had exhibited after his temporary suspension from Princeton), and no attempts to avoid responsibility for his actions. Upon his jail term, Prichard's delicate psyche was confronted with the sobering reality that the two things he had always feared the most had now come true. Under quarantine in Ashland, Prichard found himself utterly alone as well as publicly humiliated and rejected. As the letter suggested, the foremost thing on Prichard's mind was not rebuilding his tarnished career. Rather, he was concerned primarily in winning back the respect and admiration of his friends and loved ones. That would prove the most daunting challenge of his life.

Shortly after entering prison, the matter of Prichard's law practice arose. Under Kentucky law, a disbarred attorney cannot apply for reinstatement for at least five years after the commission of a crime. In order to save his license, Prichard submitted his resignation from the Kentucky bar in August 1950. Under this condition, upon his release from jail he could apply for immediate reinstatement, which would be heard by the Kentucky Court of Appeals.[21]

While in Ashland, Prichard was allowed to write only three letters per week, and his correspondents were limited to seven. One of the first letters he drafted, written only two days after he entered Ashland, was to Paul Porter. The letter revealed a resilient prisoner whose morale was high and whose mind was focused on the clemency process. Prichard's legal suggestions displayed the breadth of his mind's grasp of the legal details at hand. Writing from his cell, he commented that even if a pardon were not forthcoming, he felt certain commutation could be obtained "since that was done in the two Harlan County cases (Poer and Saylor) in which Ford imposed two-year sentences." Prichard also told Porter that if he could not receive immediate action from the Kentucky bar on reinstatement, he had offers from "national magazines" for writing some articles. On a personal note, Prichard learned that Lucy's parents had moved in with her to help with the baby.[22]

In another letter to Phil Graham, Prichard wrote about some of the specifics of prison life. The prison itself, Prichard reflected, was "as good as one could hope for: mild in its discipline and a comfortable enough stopping place." After serving a short time in quarantine, he began teaching classes to other inmates. He taught three classes per day, and although the material was on a fifth-grade level, Prichard was pleased to perform these duties simply because they made the days pass faster. Phil Graham, meanwhile, wrote to Lucy on a "private matter that is certainly none of my business." He hoped to make the best of the immediate tragedy—"Can our boy possibly take advantage of this enforced rest to do something about his weight?" Lucy replied that she did not want to raise the weight issue and preferred instead to leave it to her husband.[23]

In his prison letters, Prichard wrote often about Lucy's courage, her "self-control and cheerful comfort." His parents, on the other hand, "indulged too much in self-pity." Perhaps it was nothing more than the frustration of a son who knew he had broken his parents' hearts and could not bear to see the disappointment in their faces. Prichard added that he had "no time" for such emotions from his parents, or from anyone else for that matter. The last thing he could deal with at this crucial time was viewing himself through his parents' eyes. Lastly, Prichard confessed he also had no time for "plotting against those who have treated me badly (tho' I hate them badly)."[24]

Although his sentence was for two years, Prichard was eligible for parole in mid-March of 1951. Unless a pardon or executive clemency was forthcoming, he would remain behind bars for at least eight months. This certainly wore hard on him. Although his early letters to Porter and Graham displayed strong morale, the ensuing months of imprisonment took their toll. A remarkably introspective letter to Paul Porter in early December 1950 casts a revealing light on Prichard's thoughts as he wrote from his prison cell. Porter was having no luck in winning clemency for his client. Prichard wrote that he wished Porter would tell him if this was the case. "The small, gnawing uncertainty which comes from lack of complete knowledge is worse than the killing of hope— and I never had much of that," Prichard wrote. His despondency reached further: "The disadvantages of 16 months on parole are grave: travel is restricted . . . one's affairs are under constant supervision; and, most important, it would be extremely embarrassing to ask the Court of Appeals for readmission while I am still serving a sentence."

"It now becomes me to try and think straight about the future," Prichard wrote. Before considering the future, however, he reviewed his past and provided a poignant assessment of his shattered world:

> I do not mean in just the ordinary sense but in the sense of facing up to the moral and temperament inadequacies which have led to my situation. Bad luck, jealousies and all the rest of it have played their part, but I should not have been thus vulnerable to the slings and arrows of outrageous fortune had I not yielded— not once but constantly, and not just in this sort of thing but in many others— to those devilishly reckless and irresponsible impulses which are the old Adam in me. It is the misfortune of the too-much indulged child, maturing unevenly and never quite subduing the vestiges of infancy and adolescence. It's too long a story to bore you with, but I think I understand it better than I ever have before. And I hope that, under the discipline of adversity and humiliation, I may acquire enough iron to break the shackles of self-indulgence.
>
> After all, there is a certain justice and a certain wisdom in it all. Since a very early period in life I have been favored and indulged beyond all reason or justice by fortune and friends: and I had grown to a too great degree dependent on that indulgence. Fortune has failed me but not my friends. But it is not a purposeless disaster such as so many seem to be. I am like a boy who has gone through college but never learned the multiplication table and must go back and painfully acquire what would have been much easier when he was eight years old but is

still necessary. At any rate, I hope I am not too habituated to my weakness to learn what I need.

Lucy and Allen are the real victims of this debacle, for I may in the end be its beneficiary. It is my hope that I can find some field of activity which will enable them to avoid too great a deprivation beyond the acute suffering that they have already undergone. So far as the ambitions I may formerly have held, they are gone. My longing is for quietness and peace of mind—with, I hope, a modicum of prosperity and leisure for reflection. But I should be satisfied with a guarantee that my name would never again appear in a newspaper.

You and my other friends have placed me a heavy burden to justify your confidence and kindness by taking to heart the lessons to be learned from a grievous failure to measure up to what I know were sound standards of judgment and conduct.[25]

Despite his predicament, Prichard could often resort to his sense of humor to relieve some of the pain and humiliation. When inquiring of friends as to what they would like for Christmas, Prichard amusedly asked, "How would you like a striped suit?"[26] But such instances betrayed a somber and increasingly depressed man who watched as his life crumbled about him.

Another of the many ironies that suffused Prichard's life was that his fate was held in the hands of the man he had once described as a Charlie McCarthy and who, in turn, had read with incredulity Prichard's phone conversations. The matter of Prichard's pardon requests had been evaluated by the Office of the Pardon Attorney within the Justice Department. For six months this office had considered the case before recommending to the attorney general on December 20, 1950, that Prichard's sentence be reduced to time served. Attorney General and Democratic National Committee Chairman J. Howard McGrath approved the recommendation the same day, citing that although the views of the trial judge were not obtained, "I feel that the interests of justice will not be ill served by terminating his sentence at this time." On the following day, December 21, McGrath had an "off the record" meeting with the president in the Oval Office. What was discussed, of course, is unknown. But on the president's desk lay the recommendation to commute the sentence of Edward F. Prichard Jr. to time served.[27]

Prichard's inability to obtain a presidential pardon had some profound repercussions. A commutation implied no forgiveness, and there were still matters related to restoring Prichard's full civil rights and law license. To win those items, Prichard had to have the state government and the state bar review his case. In the interim, it seemed the best Prichard could hope for was commutation.

The extent to which Prichard's friends—including Vinson, Frankfurter, and Alben Barkley—lobbied the president on his behalf is unknown. Chief

Justice Vinson may have spoken with the president about Prichard's case. Frankfurter's influence with the president was nominal, and Barkley was not among those closest to Prichard. The only written evidence of intercession by Prichard's friends is a letter written to Truman by Earle Clements on December 19. Clements listed some factors that called for executive clemency, including that other conspirators were not convicted and that the Supreme Court did not hear his case. Clements wrote, "Compassionate reasons are cited. Visitors at the Ashland institution report that Mr. Prichard is showing the effects of his confinement and that an early release would lessen the prospect of physical or mental deterioration. The plight of his wife and infant son are also cited."[28]

Whether Clements's letter helped persuade Truman is unknown. What can be discerned is that by this time Truman no longer held any animosity toward Prichard. Even though the wiretaps may have revealed some statements that hurt the new president in 1945, a more seasoned chief executive in late 1950 saw Prichard certainly in nonthreatening terms. Besides, the Missouri native valued political loyalty, and Prichard's work on behalf of the Democratic party as general counsel in 1947 and to the Truman-Barkley ticket in 1948 was not forgotten. On December 21, 1950, Truman accepted the Justice Department's recommendation and signed the warrant commuting Prichard's sentence to time served.[29]

Word of Truman's action reached Ashland the next day. Warden R.O. Culver received the news from the director of federal prisons and released Prichard from custody at 8:00 P.M. When reporters called Culver to inquire about the rumor that Prichard was released, Culver simply replied, "He's gone. I had instructions from my superiors to release him." When those reporters went to the Prichard home in Paris, the elder Prichard told them that his son was inside with his family and "does not care to talk at the present. . . . My son only wishes at the present to wish his many friends a Merry Christmas. He wants to be left alone. He only wants to rest now and enjoy his family." The White House had no comment on the matter.[30]

While he made no public statements, Harry Truman received some varied responses to his commutation order. One of the first letters to arrive at the White House was from Lucy Prichard. "I want to tell you what you must already know," she wrote, "of the great rejoicing and happiness you have brought to a lot of people this Christmas; the release from the suffering always attendant on such a situation, not to just one but the many affected by it." Foremost in her mind was that her husband "can see our child in his first response to Christmas." Truman replied to Lucy: "I am very happy that you were made happy by the procedure which we followed with regard to Ed."[31]

But not all the letters received by the president lavished such praise for his commutation. One telegram stated, "Congratulations for your reprieve of Edward F. Prichard, Jr. A typical example of your political pusillanimity. Why not reprieve 300 pounds of American boys from Korea?" An enraged Louisvillian wrote, "This is another of the flagrant and frequent examples of your administration sanctioning the felonious activities of its members. Those responsible for his release," the telegram read, "are greater law violators than he."[32]

Prichard himself did not respond directly to the president for several weeks. Shortly after his return home, he suffered some cuts and bruises in an automobile accident outside Paris. He was a passenger in a car that was driven by none other than Billy Baldwin. Although Baldwin had emerged from the voting scandal unscathed, that did not harm his friendship with Prichard. After spending several days in bed recuperating from what he described as "painful but not serious injuries," Prichard wrote to Harry Truman, expressing "my deep and lasting gratitude for your compassionate action in restoring my liberty and letting me come back to my family." Prichard described the president's actions as providing "moral bail," and concluded, "I hope and pray that in the months ahead I may make of my life, with God's help, something which will make you glad that you gave me a helping hand."[33]

In his letter to the president, Prichard returned to a theme he had repeated since his imprisonment—a hope that he could somehow redeem himself to all those who had helped him and Lucy in this period of personal crisis. After celebrating his early return home from prison, the sobering reality of what lay ahead consumed him. Prichard knew that the challenges facing him were daunting—not just personal challenges, but an array of imposing professional, financial, and legal hurdles remained. To add to his despair, any hope for a renewed role in politics had, of course, been significantly damaged from the moment of his conviction. Prichard had spent a total of 160 days in prison, but he understood fully that his trial by fire was just beginning.

11 New Trials

PRICHARD'S early release from prison temporarily buoyed his spirits over the holiday season of 1950. But as winter set in the cumulative impact of all that had happened in the preceding two years weighed heavily on his shaken spirit. Considering all his looming professional, financial, and personal difficulties, the world Ed Prichard faced in early 1951 seemed empty and, at times, hopeless.

Shortly after the new year, Prichard was invited to a dinner in Washington for Justice Frankfurter's former clerks. He was in no mood for such a public gathering just yet, particularly if he had to confront his old mentor. Since Prichard was confined to his bed for several days following his auto accident, he used the excuse of his infirmity to decline the invitation. He nonetheless wrote to another clerk that he planned to attend the next annual dinner "unless presented by some rampaging grand jury." He also wanted all in attendance to know "the high regard in which Mr. Justice Frankfurter and his juristic views are held by the criminal classes."[1]

One of Prichard's options was to leave Kentucky. Resettling in, say, Washington or even New York might allow him to escape the stares and insults he inevitably faced back home. But leaving home was simply not an option that Lucy would seriously consider. Central Kentucky was her home, and she wanted to remain near her family's farm in Woodford County.

There was another critical roadblock facing Prichard—he had no license to practice law. Until the state bar reissued his license, Prichard could only offer his legal knowledge to other practicing attorneys. Just weeks after his release from Ashland, Prichard was naively optimistic of his imminent return to law practice. When former Texas congressman Maury Maverick sought to hire Prichard as a lobbyist on a gas pipeline matter, Prichard declined the offer since "it will require my presence in Washington for too large a fraction of the time." Prichard told Phil Graham that he could not afford to be away from Kentucky for a long period, since he anticipated readmission to the bar "in April or July, probably the latter, as decorum would indicate that my application should lie over from one meeting to the next." Meanwhile, Paul Porter contacted a New York liquor company about hiring Prichard to write a history of the liquor controls initiated during World War II. Prichard received a delayed and polite response to this proposal that said hopes for work were not "particularly encouraging," but blandly encouraged him to come to New York at some point and said the company's general counsel "would do what he could to find out what there was available with other companies in this area."[2]

Prichard was not aware of the extent to which some of his friends went to secure him a way of earning a living. A most unusual request came to Averell Harriman from a "begging" Joseph Alsop. After providing Harriman a history of Prichard's troubles, Alsop said Prichard "is beyond question the very best mind among the younger American progressives." Alsop suggested that what was needed was a new magazine that was "real" and "practical" that could speak for these progressives. "What do you think," Alsop asked, "of financing a sort of Fabian branch of the ADA, in which Ed could find his niche" editing such a publication? Harriman decided not to invest funds in such an enterprise.[3]

Prichard told a former Harvard classmate that he was optimistic of resuming a normal law practice in Kentucky. "It will take me four to six months to do this and meanwhile I hope to find some work for other lawyers." The life Prichard intended, as he informed Phil Graham, was rather fanciful—"what I really long for is to engage in law practice of the most litigious, non-social and technical sort; bury myself in books and briefs; and forget about politics, Washington and all the rest except as a cynical observer." One wonders if Prichard or Graham took this proclamation seriously. Prichard's exposure to the practice of law had never been steeped in "non-social" or "technical" matters. This notion of engaging himself fully in practicing law while ignoring politics was little more than an effort to convince himself that he could enjoy a life that excluded his true passion. In retrospect, a philosophical Prichard wrote, "Greatness," if there was such a quality in him, was a menace without "goodness"—"by which I mean the balancing force of humility and responsibility. Perhaps a little less greatness and a little more goodness would have served me better," wrote Prichard. "Of course we all regret bad breaks, but in my case 'the fault, dear Brutus, is not in our stars, but in ourselves that we are underlings.'"[4]

As he had done in the past, "Tommy the Cork" Corcoran came to Prichard's aid during this personal crisis. Corcoran gave Prichard several appellate briefs to research and write in 1951, paying him $2,500 for this work from August to December 1951. Prichard admitted he was "flat broke" and told Corcoran, "You have been more than generous in my time of trouble and I shall never forget your kindness." By year's end, Corcoran informed Ben Cohen that "I took as good care of Prich as I could this year—in memory of you."[5]

One option that never crossed Prichard's mind was to rebuild his nascent political career. While the stigma surrounding his prison sentence was a profound liability, it had not stopped other politicians in similar circumstances from seeking, and sometimes winning, elective office. The truth of the matter was that while Prichard gave lip service to elective office, as seen in his ill-fated 1948 campaign for Congress, he had not the ambition and drive for power that motivated the likes of Happy Chandler. He later admitted that "it never was a matter of great sadness to me that I never held an elective office."[6] Prichard had once basked in his Ivy League and New Deal "boy wonder" reputation and in being the intellectual and social life of the party. The aura of being the best and the brightest disappeared following the humiliation of the prison sentence. That lofty position, Prichard understood, was gone, perhaps for good.

Prichard's growing economic woes and the anxiety that accompanied them were increased in 1951 when Lucy became pregnant again. Still unable to practice law, Prichard needed to find other means to earn income until his license was restored. Offers continued to come in from well-placed friends. Former Connecticut senator William Benton offered Prichard a job with the *Encyclopedia Britannica,* which Prichard declined. Edward Weeks, editor of the *Atlantic,* also sent some book reviews Prichard's way. In a pattern that soon emerged, Weeks found Prichard an unreliable reviewer. He missed his deadlines, and in Lucy's understated words, "got very erratic."[7]

Meanwhile, things did not go well for Prichard the entrepreneur. An indication of his failing financial condition and loss of political entrée came in late 1951. Prichard sought to obtain permission from the FCC to buy part of a Lexington radio station in which his father had interests. The FCC rejected Prichard's request because, as the agency claimed, the application was "not in proper form." All that remained for Prichard to do was to work at odd jobs on his father's farm.[8]

Prichard's relationship with his father grew more distant every day. He confided to Phil Graham that "I have no responsibility over the family farm unless something goes wrong" and that his father's "chief delight is to call up when I am deep in something of my own and tell me to 'jump in your car' and deliver some inconsequential message to one of the tenants who has already been in bed for an hour." This underscored a troubling pattern that would repeat itself over the next decades—the depressed and alienated Prichard too "deep in something of my own" to attend to the nominal duties of meeting his responsibilities and making a living. Prichard revealed that his "bitterness" toward his father and Allene derived from the fact "that they fail to appreciate Lucy, and deep inside are jealous of her gay, proud defiance of the blows which fate and I have dealt her." Prichard proudly described Lucy as "a perfect wonder of steadfastness, humor and forgiveness."[9]

In political circles, Prichard confronted a painful new set of realities. Ever since he had campaigned for Happy Chandler at the age of sixteen, Prichard was accustomed to appearing on the campaign stump with various Democratic candidates. With his prison sentence behind him, such appearances were no longer possible. An example of the new political rules by which Prichard now operated came in November 1951. When Vice President Alben Barkley visited Kentucky to campaign for Democratic candidates in the statewide election, the Republican candidate for governor, Eugene Siler, issued an attack that would become all too common for Ed Prichard, even in the distant future. Siler criticized the fact that Prichard was seen accompanying the vice president on a campaign stop. Prichard refused to comment on the situation, while a Democratic party official summarily denied Prichard's involvement.[10] Even having Prichard appear in a campaign became a liability, and Democratic candidates were forced to adopt the public posture of denial. No other circumstance could inflict as much damage on Prichard's fragile psyche and self-confidence. Having always feared public rejection and having stayed safely behind others, Prichard was no longer welcomed, even behind the scenes, by image-conscious politicians. He understood that the new dynamics of his situation extended beyond the borders of his home state. When he asked Arthur Schlesinger if Averell Harriman could use him in his campaign for New York governor, Prichard knew it would have to be "in a secret and confidential capacity."[11]

During this period of despondency, a different Ed Prichard began to emerge. The once brash and arrogant nature that had assumed great things were in store became suddenly humbled. Journalist John Ed Pearce noted that prison "leavened and seasoned" Ed Prichard, "and when he came out, he was humble in some ways . . . at least he could see himself with some objectivity." Yet despite all that had happened, Prichard became neither defensive nor bitter. Instead, to his friends Prichard seemed quite introspective and brutally honest with himself. He wrote to Felix Frankfurter: "This may sound absurdly vain, but I do not mean it to be when I say that I do so wish that nature had endowed me more stingily in some respects (physically, yes, but that's not what I mean) and given me instead a better balancing mechanism." The letter continued:

> It has taken me so very, very long to grow up; I never really started until about ten years ago, and just when it was beginning to be noticeable the whole business caught up with me.
>
> Let's not fool ourselves, either: it is a mess. That I have survived it at all is due to the goodness of friends and above all to Lucy's unbelievable courage and humor. But, at best, things can never be the same. This is not altogether bad, for perhaps radical moral surgery was indicated. Sometimes, though, I wonder if there can be anything left for me in the fields of activity where my first interests lie.
>
> The great urge one feels is for privacy—not only for one's self but for family

and other innocents whose burden has already been more than heavy. There is the ever- present dread that no matter what one does, someone like Siler will point the finger and shout "Stop, thief." And how can one expect the mildly interested spectator to stop and ask, "Is it true this time?"

This doesn't disturb me as much as it might, save for the fact that it almost violates some law of nature for me to lead a private life. It's not merely a matter of inclination on my part, far from it in fact: often the best privacy comes when I seek it most. It is something chemical in the way I affect others—even the knowledge that I exist seems to create some stir or urge.

Don't think I don't know what a rotten deal it has all been for you and Mrs. F. To know that those you have loved and on whom you have showered your hopes and goodness are foolish, reckless and unworthy is no trivial matter. And however comfortable it may be—or even effective for purposes of presidential clemency—to call a moral lapse a prank, it's nonsense to talk that way about grownups or those who if they aren't grown up ought to be in some place for retarded boys.

Despite all this down-at-the-mouth talk I'm really quite disgustingly happy—partly, and large partly, because you and Mrs. F. still love me. I hope you may yet find it has not been a worthless exercise.[12]

Such poignant statements displayed the tight bonds that existed between Frankfurter and his onetime clerk. It also revealed that Prichard's remorse over his crime—contrary to the notions of the Bourbon County Ministerial Association—was profound. What may seem on the surface flagrant self-pity was, in reality, a deeply honest appraisal of his life. Finally, there was an implicit desire to redeem himself in the eyes of a man he admired and loved as he did few others. This need for redemption became a consuming drive in Prichard's life.

But before he could consider how to pick up the pieces of a broken life, Lucy gave birth to a second son on December 16, 1951. Christened James Nathan, the child would be known as Nathan, after Lucy's father. Now with two young mouths to feed and dim prospects for the future, Prichard grew even more despondent as the new year 1952 approached.

Part of Prichard's anxieties rested on his uncertain legal state. Truman's clemency orders had only reduced his sentence. Until his full civil rights were restored, Prichard could not seek reinstatement to the state bar. To grant those rights, he turned to the newly elected Democratic governor of Kentucky, Lawrence Wetherby. Wetherby had served as lieutenant governor to Earle Clements and had succeeded to the governorship in 1950 when Clements was elected to the U.S. Senate. Wetherby was elected in his own right in November 1951—an election, incidentally, in which some had earlier assumed Prichard would himself be running for the governor's mansion.

The new administration in Frankfort needed to handle the matter of restoring Prichard's civil rights with some delicacy. After all, it did not wish the attendant publicity of aiding a convicted felon who was perceived to have political connections. But there was also the knowledge that Prichard had, in a very real way, been broken through the process. Wetherby was a close ally of Clements and knew firsthand the esteem in which the powerful former governor, and now U.S. senator, held Prichard. On April 28, 1952, Wetherby signed Prichard's restoration papers, which not only provided him with his full civil rights but also enabled him to apply for reinstatement to the state bar. There was no official announcement from the governor's office, however, and the press did not know of the action for almost two months. When later queried about the matter, Wetherby said the action was merely "routine" and had been recommended by the parole board. Accompanying Prichard's file were letters of support from Bourbon County officials such as County Clerk Ed Drane Paton and Sheriff Reuben Arnsparger.[13]

The door was now opened for Prichard to apply to the Kentucky Court of Appeals for reinstatement to the state bar. But that process involved months of waiting. In the interim, at least, some measures of his past associations were not forgotten. During the 1952 presidential race, the Americans for Democratic Action, which had once offered Prichard the position of its executive director, now came to him in a different capacity. The ADA supported the candidacy of Illinois's Adlai Stevenson, but questions remained concerning the possible candidacy of incumbent Harry Truman. When Truman declined to join the race, a new possible contender for the Democratic party's nomination was Chief Justice Fred Vinson, who was a personal favorite of Truman's. James Loeb and other members of the ADA staff came to Prichard and asked if he would be willing to go to Judge Vinson and inquire as to his possible candidacy. Prichard went to Washington and met with his former boss and discussed the weighty issue of running for the presidency. Vinson disclosed to Prichard that he would have run for president had he been earlier named secretary of state but now thought it best to decline. Foremost on Vinson's mind was that he did not wish the post of chief justice to be seen as a stepping stone to the White House. Vinson told Prichard that he had agreed to endorse Stevenson when he saw Truman. Later, when he visited with Truman at Key West, Vinson officially declined to run for the presidency, and afterward Truman placed his support behind Stevenson.[14]

Prichard's awkward new political role, as evidenced in his visit to Vinson, was one he had no choice but to accept. While his numerous contacts and his own political acumen were still highly prized by the ADA and the Democratic party, Prichard could not politically function in public, as demonstrated by the episode in the Kentucky campaign with Barkley. Instead, any influence he exercised would necessarily be from behind the visible layer of power. This condition was not new—after all, since arriving in Washington more than a decade before, he had operated in the shadows of others and felt comfortable in this role. But there was a considerable difference for Prichard in Washington in the 1940s and in Kentucky in 1952. While he did not have the responsibility attendant on an executive appointment, Prichard nonetheless thrived on the recognition he received from the inner circle of knowledgeable Washingtonians. As things stood in 1952, he was a political Lord Jim whose nominal presence even on a campaign stump was a matter of shame. The question remained: Could Ed Prichard find a niche from which he could function politically, and would he be satisfied with his invisibility?

In July 1952, Prichard formally applied for readmission to the Kentucky Bar Association. In his application, he said he had been earning a living over the past year and a half by assisting "my father in farming in Bourbon County and occasionally I have done research work for lawyers and journalists in Washington." Accompanying the application were affidavits from Victor Bradley, Prichard's attorney, and County Judge J. Monroe Leer of Bourbon County testifying to Prichard's good character. Also included was a letter from the Rev. J. Perry Cox of the St. Peter's Protestant Episcopal Church in Paris, who said that if Prichard should be returned to his law practice, he would be "a credit to the bar."[15]

When the Board of Bar Commissioners met to consider Prichard's request in July, a stumbling block arose. Instead of immediately restoring Prichard to his practice, the board instead opted to conduct a "character investigation." The investigation, one board member acknowledged, was the first the board had ever ordered. If the results of the inquiry were positive, the board said, Prichard would be eligible for reinstatement in October. If the board declined to reinstate Prichard, it was learned, he could not reapply for three years. For the time being, then, Prichard's ability to earn a living as an attorney seemed in some peril.[16]

Prichard's greatest love—politics—continued on without him and the young politico starved for the arena. He attended the 1952 Democratic National Convention, but not, of course, in any official capacity. On one memorable occasion during the convention, he continued to dazzle the old New Deal warriors with his indomitable wit. As he sat in a hotel lobby with James Wechsler and Arthur Schlesinger Jr., Truman's appointment secretary, Matt Connelly, walked by. Like Prichard, Connelly had recently been released from jail. As Connelly strode by, Prichard reflected that he might try to organize the "ex-cons" of the party. Wechsler, who had once been a communist, said that he would try to organize the "ex-coms" of the party. Without missing a beat, Prichard then asked, "Which of us will get Alger Hiss?"[17]

As hard as he might wish never to see his name again in the newspaper,

Prichard could not escape headlines on two occasions in late 1952 and early 1953. During a House subcommittee hearing in September 1952, former Assistant Attorney General T. Lamar Caudle disclosed that Prichard had once tried to obstruct a Justice Department investigation. Caudle testified that in the late 1940s, several individuals privately told him to drop charges involving illegal whiskey originally bought from a Kentucky distillery. When Caudle discovered the whiskey had been illegally sold, he claimed that Prichard, as general counsel of the DNC, had tried to persuade the department not to send the case on to a grand jury. Caudle's claims, as consistent as they sounded with the pre-1948 Prichard, were never investigated.[18]

With Dwight Eisenhower's election in November 1952 coinciding with Republican control of Congress, Prichard faced the prospect of living in a national political environment that was far different from his cherished New Deal. A Republican had not sat in the Oval Office since Prichard was a freshman at Princeton, and the smiling general seemed intent on backing away from most of the New Deal's orientations. Prichard lamented to Joseph Alsop that he feared the "junta of businessmen which seems to be taking charge of the government," who were "inclined to think of politics and politicians as an interloping and alien force." Personally, Prichard also had to acknowledge that with the new regime, there would be few friendly faces welcoming him into their offices as he had grown accustomed to since the 1930s.[19] But before the new president was inaugurated, Prichard was again embroiled in a controversial matter coming from what critics considered an impetuous Harry Truman.

On January 16, 1953, just four days before he left Washington, Harry Truman pardoned Ed Prichard. The pardon was not immediately made public, and Truman never disclosed his reasons for issuing it. Weeks later, Eisenhower's attorney general, Herbert Brownell, discovered that Truman had pardoned Prichard without even a recommendation by the pardon attorney. Brownell was further angered to learn that Truman had pardoned six other individuals on the same day, including the former Democratic governor of Louisiana who had been convicted for mail fraud—all without conferring with the pardon attorney. With Eisenhower's approval, Brownell announced that the new administration would publicize all future pardon recipients. Brownell later characterized Prichard's pardon as a "scandal" and another example of the overall "mess in Washington."[20]

When he received word of his pardon, a grateful Ed Prichard wrote to the former president in words that were similar to those he had written following his commutation. "I pray you will never have reason to regret the consideration which you extended to me." Prichard added he did not wish to appear "meeching and self-serving," but that their mutual friend, Chief Justice Vinson, could testify as to the sincerity of Prichard's feelings. "I feel a double sense of responsibility to you," Prichard wrote the former president, "because, in helping me, you had to rely upon the word of others whom you know and trusted rather than upon any personal knowledge of my character." After returning to Independence, Truman responded to Prichard by writing, "I think the right procedure was followed in your case." Commenting on an April 1944 letter Prichard enclosed in his correspondence that predicted that the Missouri senator would be the vice presidential nominee, Truman replied, "I haven't read a letter with as much interest as I did yours. . . . You were an excellent prophet."[21]

No evidence exists indicating exactly who had persuaded Truman to grant the pardon, although Prichard's letter implied that Vinson had played a significant role. In any case, the pardon allowed Prichard to close the door on any remaining legal hurdles that originated from his conviction. The task of his license renewal with the state bar was still pending. But if Prichard assumed that the pardon allowed him to close the door on his looming financial problems, he was sadly mistaken. His financial troubles were compounded. Not only did he owe fees to his attorneys for his trial and appeal, but he also became embroiled at this time with a difficulty that would haunt him the rest of his life—taxes.

The IRS audited Prichard's father in 1953 and, in time, the inquiry included his son. When Edward Ruby of the IRS arrived unannounced at the People's Deposit Bank in Paris and requested the bank records of both Prichards, Big Ed appeared with his accountant. Records as far back as 1944, the elder Prichard claimed, were beyond the statute of limitations unless fraud could be proven. On Big Ed's request, the bank refused to release the records. The skirmish between the bank and the IRS went to federal court where, ironically enough, Judge H. Church Ford heard the case. In June 1953, Judge Ford ruled that the bank had to turn over its records of Edward Prichard Sr., Allene, Edward Jr., and Lucy Prichard. Because Big Ed and his son shared part ownership in several business ventures, especially in Big Ed's farm, both were liable for any back taxes. Soon, Big Ed and his son's past financial affairs came under IRS examination, and the younger Prichard's personal money problems grew deeper and deeper.[22]

Prichard related his growing problems to Frankfurter. "I am in a state of great discouragement these days," Prichard wrote in March 1953, "greater than at the depths of what Lucy calls 'the late unpleasantness.'" Prichard expressed his fear of ever building up a respectable law practice. "You and I know the fickleness of clients, and indeed one cannot blame them for standing off under circumstances of this kind." Prichard told the justice that in order to survive, "I shall be dependent largely on work which other lawyers bring me." The anxiety and the fear were palpable in his tone to Frankfurter. "When I think of my prospects, I just break into a sweat of anxiety and have to mouth to someone."[23]

When Prichard's prospects seemed bleakest, he always turned to his old Washington friends. "I am really in quite a bad situation," Prichard wrote Phil Graham. "I have had less work this year than in either 1951 or 1952, and find myself for the first time since getting out of the clink slipping deeper into debt all the time." Prichard added that working on his father's farm "is perfect hell." He begged Corcoran to find "any possible project on which you could use me at this time," and added that his only income prospects were from the farm, "but anticipate no returns until sale of tobacco next winter." If there were any financial ventures that could help, Prichard reminded Graham, "Don't forget, my tongue is hanging out." The pressure on Prichard to find alternative sources of income was only increased in August 1953 when Lucy gave birth to their third child, another son, named Louis Lanier Prichard. "We are still living— and creatively or at least procreatively," Prichard claimed.[24]

Amid the tumult of 1953, Prichard declined an invitation to attend the fifteen-year reunion of Harvard Law's Class of 1938. Earlier when he missed the reception for Frankfurter's former law clerks, he assured the justice that he was greatly appreciated by the "criminal classes." On this occasion Prichard was more reflective, telling Frankfurter that "it seems only a few months ago" when the two learned in Cambridge of Frankfurter's nomination to the Supreme Court. "You and I rode about Boston . . . while I pouted because you were leaving me there for a few months, to watch Jim Landis' dandruff fall as gently as the last leaf." Having to face his mentor and former classmates was still too much for Prichard to bear.[25] The relationship between Prichard and Frankfurter was never the same as it had been in the halcyon days of Cambridge and Washington. Prichard's relationship with another former boss, Fred Vinson, unfortunately never had sufficient time to recover. The chief justice died in September 1953.

Prichard's bleak financial horizon brightened somewhat on March 31, 1954, when the Kentucky State Bar Association finally reinstated his license to practice law. It had been more than three and a half years since he had resigned from the bar, and nearly two years since he had reapplied for readmission. The state bar noted that Prichard's conduct since leaving prison had been proper and that there "is nothing against him." Although Prichard could now legally hang out his shingle once again, the question remained as to what kind of practice he could build from the ashes of his previous accomplishments.[26]

The good news of the reinstatement was short-lived. As he informed Corcoran, "Not a single one of my creditors has failed to read the announcement in the papers. Apparently," he added, "they all believe that this mere act of the Commissioners has put money in my pocket." As Prichard summarized his condition, "I find myself a briefless barrister, hounded by creditors, with nothing except prospects to hold them off, and damned few of them." In his usual candid way, he described the looming prospects that he faced:

> My opinion is that the next eight to twelve months will tell the tale. That is to say, if I can open an office—a modest one—make a modest living and keep my creditors from suing me for a year, I believe that I can take hold and keep going on my own steam. It will take me many years to get where I was before I was struck down; perhaps I shall never get there. . . . My great enemy is debt. Up until 1953 I did not owe any more than when I was sent away in 1950. No more, no less. But my earnings in 1953 were practically nothing. In addition, I tried to take on some farming and lost heavily at that. . . . So, I find myself many thousands worse off than I was a year ago. I have lived entirely on borrowed money, and mortgaged everything I have, which isn't much.

Prichard revealed that his family lived on Lucy's savings, which came to only $291. "I couldn't borrow another hundred to save my life without panhandling personal friends, which for me is the gutter and I would take a Goering cocktail before I did that." Prichard compared his new situation to that of a strange dog: "For a year or so everyone will sniff at me . . . waiting to see what will happen. If I survive, they will begin to drift back, slowly." The young lawyer then dipped at a well he had been to before. "Thomas," Prichard implored of Corcoran, "you are the only miracle man I know. I stand or fall by what happens in the next year. Can you, anywhere, find someone who will hire or retain me to work under your supervision?"[27]

In a similar letter to Frankfurter informing the justice of his readmission to the bar, Prichard related that his prospects seemed dim, and that in order to build a substantial office he would require an income of at least $450 a month. Characteristically, he also included a small synopsis of political developments in Kentucky, informing Frankfurter that "needless to say, I shall vote the straight ticket from Senator to Constable."[28]

Prichard's struggles in rebuilding his practice, his finances, and his reputation required him to look deeper into the recesses of his mind and spirit for strength. By the mid-1950s, he began reading Reinhold Niebuhr. Niebuhr, incidentally, had become interested in Prichard as well. When told of Prichard's rise and fall by mutual friend Isaiah Berlin, Niebuhr expressed a fascination with the young Kentuckian. Berlin managed to introduce the two, and Prichard attended several of Niebuhr's sermons whenever their respective paths crossed.[29]

But Prichard's religious reflections were not the product of some prison-bed conversion. Although raised a Methodist, he had decided to convert to the Episcopal Church out of respect for Lucy. Throughout his youth, Prichard was by no means a religious individual. His brother remembers that the political animal enjoyed the visiting preachers and revivals that came through Paris only for their oratory, and not for some religious purpose. In a 1954 passage to Frankfurter, Prichard revealed the frustration he felt in considering the notions of a deity. He was not persuaded by the religious ideas of his friend Isaiah Berlin. In Prichard's estimation, Berlin's espousal that he did not necessarily believe in God but did believe in a "kind of private poetry to it all" was nothing more than "asking the best of two incompatible worlds." To Prichard, the question of God's existence was rather bleak—"either it's true or it isn't; I have never been able to see the basis for the sort of intermediate waffling which treats it as a matter of taste, sort of like a modern painting." He suggested that if Frankfurter "were in a migratory mood," he might consider coming "on over with R.N. and me, and don't waste your time with a church where the name of Christ is mentioned only when the sexton stubs his toe."[30]

But Prichard had little time to debate theology—his mounting debts and sputtering law practice consumed him. Although he had told Corcoran just months before that he would not call upon friends for financial help, he resorted to doing so in the summer of 1954. Realizing that he had tapped Corcoran too many times, Prichard instead called upon another old New Deal warrior, Ben Cohen. Prichard's plea began starkly: "Dear Ben, I am in terrible trouble, and I hope you will not think less of me for asking your help. Please believe me," Prichard implored, "when I say I would not ask it if I were not desperate." Before getting his law office off the ground, Prichard said he was confronted with yet another old debt of $500. "If I do not meet it immediately," Prichard said, "the consequences will be grave—not criminal or scandalous, but ruinous to my feeble prospects." In asking for the $500, Prichard felt compelled to share with Cohen a sense of his financial problems. For the first six months of 1954, Prichard said, he had earned $2,250, which included a fee he had received from Jane Ickes for his help in editing the diaries of her late husband, Harold Ickes. In exchange for help in producing what Prichard called a "dishonest presentation," Prichard charged Ickes "a large fee." He commented, "This did not comfort my conscience but numbed it satisfactorily." Since he claimed debts of $850, Prichard told Cohen he was living on $1,400. When the bank called a loan for $2,000, Prichard said, he had to allow his father to pay it. "I simply cannot ask for more help from him," he wrote. "He has already helped me beyond his means." The trouble, as Prichard related, had more to do than with a son's embarrassment. His father had diabetes, "is financially entangled, and to boot engaged in a controversy with Treasury agents about taxes for past years which involves considerable possibility of financial damage." The good news for the struggling lawyer was that he had the promise of a retainer from the State Highway Department concerning condemnation proceedings, as well as some other possible cases. In requesting the money, Prichard claimed he could repay Cohen in ninety days and implored his old boss to not let anyone know of the matter. "I am more sensitive than ever about such matters," Prichard added. Within a week, Cohen sent the beleaguered Prichard a check for $500.[31]

Prichard's reference to his father's diabetes disclosed another matter that soon plagued him as harshly as his other problems. Diabetes had been prevalent in the Prichard family—not only did his father have the condition, but also his uncle, Thomas. Since childhood, Prichard had battled obesity, and a lifetime of being overweight vastly increased his own chances of acquiring diabetes. And, in fact, at some point in the early 1950s, he was told by his doctors that he had the condition. Perhaps this is what Prichard referred to when he informed Ben Cohen in June 1954 that "the doctor scared me and I am now dieting seriously. I hope to lose about 75 pounds and keep them lost." More was at stake with the diabetic condition, Prichard knew, than vanity, and losing weight was central to maintaining his health—"pray for my fortitude, for I really must do this for the sake of Lucy and the children."[32]

If Prichard could not control his weight and alleviate the strain on his system caused by his diabetes, he faced some daunting health risks. Not only would his life expectancy be significantly diminished, but also a list of possible complications loomed—among them, kidney failure, impotency, and blindness. The latter affliction had already affected his father, who had lost the sight in one eye due to his diabetes. Prichard's chances of avoiding such maladies if he did not change his lifestyle, and especially his eating habits, were not good. He had tried to lose weight on numerous occasions in the past, all of them futile. His lifelong inability to control his weight now took on a more serious light with the diagnosis of diabetes.[33]

Prichard's diabetes differed, somewhat, from that of his father, who had to take daily injections of insulin. Prichard's diabetic condition was of a type that afflicts many people. Called noninsulin-dependent diabetes, this variety of the disease requires no insulin injections, but does require a close monitoring of diet and exercise.[34] In addition to these two requirements, which had never been important to Prichard, he was also told to stop smoking his beloved cigars and control his blood pressure. Prichard's new strict regimen, which he obviously knew the importance of following, tested his own self-discipline in new and sobering ways.

As Prichard struggled to confront his new physical condition, his financial problems only increased. After seeking the help of Ben Cohen, he returned once again to Tommy the Cork in late 1954. "You are, I am sure, tired of Macedonian cries from me," Prichard wrote, "but this is the first in a long time, and I believe the last." Prichard spelled out an all-too-familiar theme—"I believe that if I can hold out for about six months, I shall be over the hump." He added that Paul Porter had helped with some legal referrals, but even his payment from Porter could not meet his overdrawn bank account. Prichard pled for help: "Is there any way you could possibly help me at this time? If you could put me on the rolls for a retainer, or monthly stipend, for just three or four months." The desperation was evident in Prichard's request that Corcoran not write but call immediately "and tell me the lay of the land."[35]

Within another six months, Prichard's tone was even more depressed. "I tread water down here," he began yet another pleading letter to Corcoran, "fighting what seems to me so often a losing battle," one he now concluded he might never win. "I guess I won't ever get on my feet," he lamented after discussing his law career since reinstatement.[36] Four and a half years after his release from Ashland, Ed Prichard's world was a never-ending cycle of dashed hopes, mounting debts, and constant anxiety. The simple truth was that the once-brash clerk to Justice Frankfurter, the man who possessed one of the country's most impressive legal minds, could not pay his bills as a small-town lawyer.

Making the adjustment all the more difficult for Ed Prichard was the fact that he never really enjoyed the daily practice of law. His interest in going to Harvard Law School, after all, sprang from political motivations, and when he launched his practice in 1945 he was more attuned to casually writing briefs and representing prestigious and wealthy clients. The rarefied atmosphere of daily conferring with the Corcorans and Porters on lucrative legal matters, while conversing with the chief justice of the U.S. Supreme Court or a precinct chairman in an eastern Kentucky county on political matters, was now gone. To survive, Prichard had to master the rudimentary skills of a lawyer who could not expect hefty retainers. Hard, consistent work, as Prichard well knew, was not one of his strengths. In time, his friends, who wanted so badly to help him, recognized this as well. Paul Porter and Joe Rauh continued to send briefs and other legal papers to him, usually paid in advance, only to see Prichard never do the assigned work. In his own cases, Prichard often simply did not appear for meetings with prospective clients. Nathan Elliott, who was a bankruptcy referee, also gave his beleaguered son-in-law several cases, but in numerous instances Prichard mismanaged the client's money to the point where Elliott and Big Ed had to rescue him.[37]

Prichard spelled out his growing problems to Phil Graham in early 1955. Although he had regained his law license, he admitted that an "agonizingly slow dribble of business" came his way. For 1953, Prichard said he had gone $6,500 in debt, "for in that year I had no income whatever." Lucy and the three sons had survived mainly on gifts from the Elliotts and Big Ed and Allene. Beginning in 1949, Prichard said he had received a staggering $19,000 from his parents and, in a phrase he had repeated so often over the past four years, he simply could no longer ask them for further help. Once again, short of cash, Prichard pleaded with Graham for an additional $1,100. Prichard ended, "Please do not chide me or judge me harshly for asking you. . . . It is humiliating to be in this position."[38]

The land that Prichard owned along the Clintonville Pike in Bourbon County and where he and Lucy had lived for seven years, was one place where the financially strapped couple could look for help. Unable to meet their mortgages totaling $45,000 on several plots of Bourbon County land, Prichard sold part of it to famed local horseman A.B. Hancock Sr. The notation in the courthouse books documenting the sale underscored how Prichard wanted further news of his insolvency kept under wraps: "Please, do not publish." The house Ed and Lucy had shared was put up for lease. The young couple with three children did not go homeless, however. In May 1955, Nathan Elliott gave each of his three children, including Lucy, equal shares of his estate in Woodford County. Lucy received a plot totaling 138 acres, which included the elegant Elliott family home, Heartland. In two years, Ed and Lucy moved into their new home, a large brick house with expansive, high-ceiling rooms, surrounded by a grove of tall trees. A Princeton classmate visited Prichard during the move and observed that as Lucy "worked like a beaver unpacking and settling things," Prichard spent the day "yawning and reading."[39]

Despite his political liabilities, Prichard returned to Washington as many times as he could throughout the 1950s. Besides reminiscing about the New Deal, however, there was very little real work for him to do in Washington. Friends knew that to help Prichard by giving him anything less than cash would fail. Prichard was simply too unreliable to be presented with briefs or any other legal work. His time in Washington was usually relegated to visiting old friends Phil and Katharine Graham, Tom Corcoran, Ben Cohen, and Isaiah Berlin, and lunching with new acquaintances such as Robert F. Kennedy. Back home, Prichard could not help but pay close attention to the governor's race as it shaped up in 1955. Running for his second term was A.B. "Happy" Chandler, who now lived only a couple of miles from Prichard in Versailles. Chandler had spent eight years vilifying the Clements/Wetherby terms. After serving as baseball commissioner, he had returned home ready to defeat the more liberal Clements wing of the Democratic party and reclaim the governor's mansion. One of Chandler's leading campaign aides in 1955 was Julia Ardery, Judge Ardery's wife.[40]

The man who emerged as the heir apparent to the Clements wing of the party in the 1955 primary was a dark horse candidate from the eastern Kentucky coalfields named Bert Combs. Prichard had first met Combs when the young mountaineer was a commonwealth's attorney in Floyd County. Combs was a quiet, soft-spoken former Appeals Court judge whose accent may have led some to dismiss him as a backcountry bumpkin. But Combs had graduated second in his class at the University of Kentucky Law School and proved to be one of the shrewdest minds in Kentucky politics over the next thirty-five years. Combs was the man tapped to head the Clements wing in the 1955 primary against the more charismatic Chandler. As one account aptly described the race: "Clements didn't care who was governor of Kentucky as long as he could run the state, while Chandler didn't care who ran Kentucky as long as he could be governor."[41]

One day in the spring of 1955, Prichard wrote Combs asking him if the campaign could use his services in any way. Although he knew little of Combs, Prichard had remained a devoted supporter of Clements, and perceived Happy Chandler as a power-hungry conservative demagogue. What went unstated was that Prichard longed to be, once again, involved in the heat of a gubernatorial race. Combs obviously knew of Prichard's past, and also knew that if word leaked that the former ballot-box stuffer was involved in his campaign, Chandler would use it with deadly force. But Combs went ahead and told Prichard to join the campaign staff at Louisville's Seelbach Hotel, the traditional locale for Democratic campaigns. Prichard arrived at the hotel in short order and began work with research, speech writing, and discussing strategy.[42]

Prichard faced an unenviable situation within the Combs camp in 1955. He desperately wanted to be back "in the arena," giving his diverse talents to help elect the next governor. But in order to do so, he must remain invisible, an unpaid and unacknowledged stowaway whose recent past could, at any moment, become a political liability to Bert Combs. Having been in the political shadows throughout most of his political life, Prichard was not especially troubled with this aspect of the campaign. But the constant fear, as he had told Frankfurter, of being discovered and told "Stop, thief" weighed heavily on his mind, just as it had during Barkley's visit.

It did not take long for the moment Prichard had feared to arise. When Combs appeared on a television interview show, he was asked: Is Ed Prichard working in your behalf in campaign headquarters? Combs did not hesitate and answered that Prichard was, indeed, working in his campaign. Combs added that Prichard had made a terrible mistake in the past but that he had paid the price. Combs then proclaimed without apology that he was glad to have Ed Prichard in his camp. Combs's pronouncement effectively took the fire out of any verbal assaults that might emerge from the Chandler campaign. When Combs went back to the Seelbach that night, a grateful Prichard was waiting for him and thanked him for the public acknowledgment. As Combs walked away, he could see tears welling up in Prichard's eyes. Such private encounters are sometimes the raw stuff of lifelong political relationships. By this one act of public recognition, Combs earned the devoted loyalty of Ed Prichard.[43]

Various demonstrations of political courage on Combs's part—such as his expressed willingness to raise taxes in order to upgrade Kentucky's schools—nonetheless played into Chandler's demagogic tactics. Chandler accused Combs of being one of "the tax-crazy, spend-crazy, and waste-crazy dictators" and called Prichard a "jailbird" who was heavily ensconced in Combs's camp. The reserved Combs had run head-on into one of the most effective campaigners in the state's history, and the eastern Kentucky judge was clearly outmatched by the more experienced Chandler. On primary day Chandler won by 18,000 votes, a much smaller margin than expected.[44]

With Chandler's election in November 1955 to his second term as governor, Prichard no longer had a friendly face in the governor's mansion. What had once been an open entrée into the corridors of state and federal power now seemed a closed door. But it had not all been for naught. Prichard's support of Bert Combs's candidacy and Combs's subsequent public acknowledgment of Prichard had opened the possibility that Prichard might one day be able to participate in Kentucky politics in some significant way. While Combs went back to eastern Kentucky on the heels of his defeat in the primary, Prichard did not know that Combs would return to the political stage in four years and that the relationship the two had struck in the 1955 campaign would bear fruit for the next quarter century. In the midst of what seemed a devastating defeat and bleak chances for the future Prichard had unknowingly built the foundation of his political and financial renewal in his unswerving loyalty to Bert Combs. For a change, fate was silently smiling on Ed Prichard.

12 "Wandering in the Wilderness"

THE last years of the 1950s were some of the darkest of Ed Prichard's life. Unable to build a profitable law practice, his personal financial prospects dimmed. Additionally, the IRS continued its lengthy investigation into whether Prichard and his father owed back taxes. These financial troubles were not the only ones Prichard endured. Emotionally, his fragile self-confidence had been destroyed by the stigma of the ballot-box episode. All of these tensions subsequently took a terrible toll on his personal life. With no political outlets to channel his intellect, nothing, it seemed, could pull Prichard out of his depression.

"My problem was not reorganizing myself in some political activity," Prichard later admitted. "My problem was using that [political work] to some degree as a refuge from facing the problem of working harder to make a living."[1] Despite his legal training, the simple fact was that Ed Prichard could not operate a successful small law office. Writing wills, researching deeds, and settling divorces were not the barrister's chores that Prichard found inspiring. He had never taken a great interest in the study of the law while at Harvard. Instead, he seemed to enjoy only participating in the great constitutional issues (as he had with Frankfurter at the Supreme Court) or with highly lucrative legal work that did not involve enormous amounts of time (as he had done with Thomas Corcoran). Coupled with the fact that he had always seen law as a means to a political end and not simply as a way of making a living, Prichard's fall from political grace in 1950 only added to his misery within the bar.

The toll that Prichard's personal struggles took on his relationship with Lucy was severe. Like so many other "political wives" of the era, Lucy had to accept the subordination of her own ambitions and desires to those of her husband. Yet Lucy Prichard suffered the worst of both worlds—she remained a political spouse through it all, yet could not even reap the financial or social benefits attendant on such duties. Instead, she was left to feel the quiet humiliation of the stares she inevitably received in public. In addition, their strong personalities clashed repeatedly. Increasingly, Prichard spent little time with Lucy and became an absentee father to his three sons. While Lucy devoted her life to raising her children and keeping the Woodford County farm, her husband lapsed into his own inner world, which had little room for her, the family, or even the obligations of providing a modicum of income. Lucy was left to anguish and uttered words that countless other political wives have no doubt harbored: "I used to pray that something would happen to get him out of politics. Just pray."[2]

With his mounting personal problems, Prichard grew increasingly depressed. Having always been rather exaggerated in his personal appearance and demeanor, when he hit rock bottom in the late 1950s, Prichard's flights from reality took on their own bizarre routines. Without any notice, he would simply disappear for days. Unable to come to grips with his failing practice and with Lucy's growing impatience with the mounting bills, Prichard resorted to what his close friends labeled "submerging," which was Prichard's way of escaping the increasing pressure of his broken world. Often this meant going to Louisville, where he would check into a local hotel and read mounds of books and articles he obtained at the library for days at a time. In one typical instance, he asked a friend if he could borrow his car in order to take some laundry to the dry cleaners. The friend obliged, but Prichard did not return with the car for almost a week.[3] For those who knew and worked with him from 1955 to the early 1960s, "submerging" was one aspect of Prichard's complex persona that one simply had to acknowledge.

Adding significantly to Prichard's depression were the tax problems that had dogged him since his return to Kentucky. It was not simply a matter of his attempting to cheat on his taxes and getting caught. For many years, Prichard had had joint responsibility with his father for their business interests. He had never been able to manage his personal finances. Bert Combs added one more issue—during these years Prichard purposely overreported his income to the IRS in order to persuade Lucy that things were not as bleak as they seemed. Such childish machinations, in Combs's opinion, revealed Prichard's hope that if he could only buy more time, something might work itself out.[4]

Had Prichard's political fortunes been different, it is likely that in the late 1950s he would have been in Washington, perhaps working in some way for Sen. Earle Clements. By this time, Clements had emerged as Majority Leader Lyndon Johnson's chief lieutenant in the Senate and actually served as acting leader during Johnson's convalescence from a heart attack in 1955. Clements did not lose contact with Prichard, and the two often visited when Prichard came to Washington. When Clements threw a party for LBJ over the holidays in 1959, Prichard attended, much to the satisfaction of the future president. "I'm grateful to you for coming," Johnson wrote Prichard, imploring him to "let me hear from you." But Clements understood just how emotionally vulnerable Prichard was during this time, and that attempts to help him were futile. He knew, as so many of his friends knew, that Prichard was not in proper shape to stand on his own feet.[5]

A possibility that Prichard's political fortunes might turn arose during the 1959 Kentucky gubernatorial campaign. Although he could not succeed himself, Happy Chandler's presence in the primary campaign that year was palpable. Chandler's hand-picked candidate was his lieutenant governor, Harry Lee Waterfield. Opposing Waterfield for the primary was Wilson Wyatt, the former Louisville mayor and federal housing expediter under Truman. Wyatt had an extensive political background and was supported by Barry Bingham's *Louisville Courier-Journal*. He had run Adlai Stevenson's 1952 presidential campaign and had served as chairman of the Americans for Democratic Action. Wyatt seemed certain to win the Clements wing's support until Bert Combs decided to enter the race. In mid-1959, Waterfield, with Chandler's backing, was ready to take on his two opponents, who seemed certain to split the liberal vote and provide the winning margin for Waterfield.

For Ed Prichard, there was never any doubt as to whose candidacy he would support in 1959. Despite Wyatt's impressive résumé and solid liberal credentials, Prichard refused to leave the camp of the man who had proudly claimed Prichard's presence in his campaign four years before. When Combs opened his campaign headquarters in Louisville, Ed Prichard once again moved in to occupy a key role in shaping Combs's strategy. For the remainder of the race, Prichard lived in a room at the elegant Seelbach Hotel, immortalized as the "Muhlbach" by F. Scott Fitzgerald in *The Great Gatsby*. The campaign paid for his room and expenses, but he received no salary except for an occasional stipend. All the while, Lucy remained at home, tending to her three sons and wondering when her husband would return.

Combs's hopes gained a new life when Wyatt withdrew from the governor's race and became a candidate for lieutenant governor, in the process giving his full support to Combs and merging their campaigns into one. Since Earle Clements blamed Chandler for his defeat in his reelection bid to the U.S. Senate in 1956, he chafed at the chance for revenge and took over the Combs charge. (Instead of supporting his fellow Democrat Clements in 1956, Chandler had bolted and thrown his support behind Republican Thruston Morton. In another Eisenhower avalanche, Clements lost his seat, which he added to a long list of grievances he had with Chandler.) Subsequently, the Combs campaign took on a new light as the primary election approached, driven by the combined political skills of Earle Clements and Ed Prichard.[6]

Considering what both Chandler and Combs had on the line in 1959, the vitriol accompanying the campaign was not surprising. In late April, Chandler announced he would openly campaign for Waterfield. Since Chandler raised a good deal of money for Waterfield, primarily through deductions taken from state employees, Waterfield had little choice but to watch as his boss grabbed the headlines. Chandler started in his usual way by ridiculing Combs and Wyatt. He referred to Combs derisively as the "Little Judge" and described Wyatt as "Ankle Blankets," a reference to the spats worn by well-to-do urban gentlemen. Chandler went on to describe the team of Combs-Wyatt as nothing more than the tool of the Clements and Wetherby machine, which he derisively described as "Clementine and Wetherbine."

What Chandler did not count on in 1959, however, was a very different campaign by Combs. With the direction of Clements and Prichard behind the scenes, Combs roared back, hitting Chandler with his own dose of ridicule. Chandler had imposed a 2 percent assessment on state payroll checks and deposited the funds in a Cuban bank, and was embarrassed when Fidel Castro's revolution toppled the pro-U.S. regime and nationalized all Cuban banks. The Combs campaign, as suggested by Prichard, hit back with a portrait of a pathetic Chandler crying on a Florida beach, screaming at the water, "Castro! Castro! Send back my two percent!"[7]

As is the case in many American elections, the most crucial element in the 1959 campaign came down to taxes. Complicating matters was a referendum put on the ballot by the 1958 legislature that called for a veterans' bonus financed by a sales tax. Chandler claimed that Combs and Wyatt were ready to impose new and expensive taxes on the people of Kentucky. Numerous members of the campaign staff within the Seelbach wanted Combs to oppose new taxes and avoid a repeat of the 1955 defeat at the hands of Chandler on the very same issue. But what if the voters approved the referendum in November? Veterans groups eagerly awaited Combs's response. The campaign staff agonized over how to approach the problematic question of the bonus versus taxes. Combs decided to take a direct route—he announced he was not going to make a decision until he saw how the voters responded in November on the referendum. He said he had heard other governors swear they would never raise taxes, only to renege once they got into office. Flat out, Combs proclaimed he would not lie to the people. Prichard later said "it was the best statement made during the campaign." On election day, the voters rewarded Combs's candor and feistiness with a 33,000-vote plurality over Waterfield. Chandler somehow interpreted the loss as "overwhelming approval of what we have given the people."[8]

Despite the fact that Combs seemed certain to win the Governor's Mansion in the November general election, Prichard was not overconfident. Combs's opponent was a colorless Republican named John Robsion, who had been an undistinguished member of Kentucky's congressional delegation. While he may have been an underdog, Robsion came out fighting. He claimed Combs would impose severe taxes and made the seemingly bizarre charge that

Earle Clements would become highway commissioner if Combs was elected. In July a worried Prichard wrote to Clements that "there is no leadership or direction in the campaign," and that Combs had taken on a "lackadaisical attitude." Prichard then urged the party to organize more independents and Republicans, since a light vote was expected and "the greater proportionate influence the bolter exercises."

Then Prichard broached a new subject. Talk was rampant within the campaign of Clements becoming highway commissioner. The appearance of a former governor and U.S. senator taking on such a post reeked of a payoff. In no other appointed post could one exercise more political and patronage control in Kentucky than in the Highway Department. Prichard added, "I am telling you all this in the strictest confidence because . . . you know who owns me." Such a self-deprecating remark led Prichard to the matter of money. He mentioned that besides his expenses, he had received only $300 from the campaign. Prichard estimated that his family's monthly expenses were approximately $500. He pleaded with Clements to find other sources of money. He then wrote in a painful, anguished note:

> I am greatly discouraged in many ways. Some days I feel hopeful and on others absolutely hopeless. You are the finest friend I have ever had, and I shall never forget the many times you have sustained, aided and supported me. I only wish that I had the fibre and strength of character to justify your confidence and affection. It is doubtful to me whether, in view of circumstances, I can ever do well in practice in Lexington. What I need very badly is a connection of some kind, not necessarily a partnership but some fairly close and constant connection with a firm of other lawyer or lawyers who can help me build back my confidence and stability by keeping me under surveillance and control, guiding me into habits of self-discipline and constant work, building up my morale in times of neurotic pressure. Under such circumstances, I believe I could once more turn my talents to good use but it is very hard to face the difficulties of my situation sitting alone in an office from day to day.[9]

During the last months of the campaign, there were flashes of the old Prichard—turning out strategy and research memos and calling numerous party officials in disparate counties, urging their support. But there were also moments when the depression set in and the call would go out within the Seelbach to "find Prich." More often than not, he would be found alone in a nearby hotel room amid books and magazines. The Combs campaign had no choice but to accept such dark periods as part of the package. Combs later described these uncertain and dark years of Ed Prichard's life as "wandering in the wilderness."

A telling moment in the campaign came on October 23, when Harry

Truman came to Kentucky on Combs's behalf. Governor Chandler refused to welcome Truman to the state, telling the former president in an angry letter that "Combs is the biggest liar I ever met." Robsion sought to use Chandler's statement as evidence that the state would be torn asunder if Combs should be elected. But such last-minute bravado from Chandler could not turn around what had been a masterful campaign by the eastern Kentucky judge. On election day, Combs won the governor's office by a crushing 180,000 votes.[10] Once again, as with Chandler in 1935 and Clements in 1947, Prichard had a friend in the governor's chair, one who was well aware of the sacrifices Prichard had endured on behalf of his election.

Shortly after the election, Combs verified the worst fears of Robsion and many Democrats when he made the stunning announcement that Clements had accepted his offer to become highway commissioner. Chandlerites cried of a payoff, while other observers, including Barry Bingham of the *Courier-Journal,* flatly opposed the appointment. Others wondered who would be the "real governor" if Clements controlled so much of the state's patronage. Another prevailing rumor was that Clements was going to be Lyndon Johnson's point man for the Texan's possible run for the presidency the following year. Whatever the purpose of Combs's decision, by the spring of 1960 Earle Clements was once again a vital player in Frankfort politics. Accompanying Clements was an old friend who had fallen on hard times and who, for the first time, had his own unique role to play in Frankfort.

In Combs's first months in office, one action taken by the new governor may have originated in the fateful conversation between Prichard and Judge Ardery some eleven years earlier. On March 27, 1960, Combs signed a bill removing Frankfort and Franklin County from Judge William Ardery's jurisdiction, otherwise known as the "Ardery ripper bill." Franklin County was the single most important county within Judge Ardery's district, and it consequently made him perhaps the most powerful district judge in the state. Soon after Prichard's conviction, local politicos discussed the possibility of punishing Ardery by removing Franklin County from his district. The actual task of doing so took more than a decade, but the legislature finally passed the necessary legislation and Combs quickly signed it. Supporters of the bill offered the nominal explanation that Franklin County needed to be separated into its own separate jurisdiction. But it was not lost on some that it may also have been a payback for Judge Ardery's testimony against Prichard in 1949.[11]

Earle Clements repaid Prichard's years of steadfast loyalty by giving him a semiofficial position within the highway commissioner's office. Prichard was not a full-time employee and had no official title or job description, but at least he was provided a desk. In time, that vacant desk became littered with papers and memos. Prichard's uncertain role in the department presented some awkward moments. The business manager of the Highway Department, C. Leslie Dawson, naturally assumed that Prichard was on the payroll. When Dawson assigned Prichard a state car to drive from Versailles to Frankfort, he was called in to face an angry Earle Clements. Under no circumstances, Clements ordered, was Prichard to be given a state car or to be put on the payroll. In order to provide Prichard some means of transportation but to avoid the appearance of state-sanctioned activity, Dawson was forced to lend Prichard his own personal car on numerous occasions.[12]

During Combs's campaign in 1959 he had promised to rid the state government of Chandler's appointments, whom he referred to as "drones." Upon assuming his duties as highway commissioner, Clements was well prepared to implement this directive. One day Prichard walked into the commissioner's office and found Clements going over a list of highway employees. Clements marked beside several names the letter "D." Prichard inquired as to what the letter signified. "Drones," Clements answered, and proceeded with his task. When Clements gave that insignia to a particular name, Prichard interrupted. "Earle, that man's not a drone," Prichard said, telling Clements the individual in question worked hard and did not deserve what Clements intended. "Very well," Clements replied, "let the 'D' stand for 'Departed.'"[13] In such ways, the powerful leverage of patronage was sustained within the new administration by one of its more shrewd practitioners.

While lending his photographic memory concerning advice on patronage of highway crews and other department matters, Prichard also aided Clements in his role as Lyndon Johnson's point man within the Combs administration. In the Democratic primaries in 1960, Sen. John F. Kennedy had emerged as the party's front-runner, while the Senate majority leader waited in the wings. The all-important West Virginia primary would either swing the nomination for Kennedy or throw open the race and allow Johnson to come in at the last minute and win the nomination on the convention floor. Clements often discussed the campaign by telephone with John Connally, one of Johnson's closest aides. Money flowed through Clements's office in Frankfort to Hubert Humphrey's campaign in West Virginia in an effort to arrest the Kennedy tide.[14]

But Kennedy prevailed in West Virginia, and Johnson's last-minute entrance into the race could not stop the momentum when the Democrats met in Los Angeles in the summer of 1960. As a reward for Prichard's service to the campaign, Bert Combs named him as an at-large delegate to the convention, the first time Prichard had been an official delegate since 1948. It must have been bittersweet for the once-wunderkind of the party to see old comrades such as Phil Graham, Thomas Corcoran, and Lyndon Johnson playing such crucial roles within the party. Graham, in fact, was a longtime friend of both Kennedy and Johnson. As an indication of Prichard's declining status among his old friends as well as his fallen self-confidence, Prichard remained on the periphery as Graham and Corcoran engineered the selection of the Texan to the second spot on the 1960 Democratic ticket. As LBJ accepted the vice presidential nomination, Prichard must have recalled those days, almost twenty years before, when he had befriended the little-known congressman from the Texas hill country. Three years later in Dallas, Johnson would assume the office that some in Washington had once speculated would be Prichard's.[15]

Before Prichard could digest what had occurred that summer, his personal financial problems again impeded. This time, the IRS concluded that Prichard's father owed delinquent taxes going back to the mid-1940s. The total amount assessed against Ed Sr. and his company was a whopping $465,477. Several months later, the IRS placed a lien against the younger Prichard for $29,476, which the IRS claimed was owed in taxes from 1953 to 1959, the years of Prichard's "wandering in the wilderness."[16]

While the IRS was through investigating Big Ed, it was not finished leveling new penalties against his son. On November 8, 1960, the very day the Kennedy-Johnson ticket squeaked to victory, the tax agency placed further liens on the younger Prichard's property totaling a staggering sum of $701,739.19.[17] The IRS derived this amount from Prichard's own back taxes and his financial responsibility as part owner of the E.F. Prichard Company. The Prichard family home, Heartland, was solely in Lucy's name and therefore could not be seized by IRS auditors. But if Prichard's looming financial prospects seemed dim in late 1960, the tax liens placed against him represented a seemingly insurmountable obstacle.

The overwhelming financial news sent Prichard into a deeper depression and renewed instances of submerging. The tension it created with Lucy became greater as well. When IRS auditors seized Lucy's car when she left it in downtown Frankfort, that seemed to be the final straw. Lucy was indignant that "these IRS people just came and jerked my car from under me." An irate Lucy came home to inform her husband to leave and not return home until he could get his financial affairs—and his life—in proper order. Whereupon the marriage of Ed and Lucy Prichard entered a long period in which the two lived apart—Lucy at Heartland and her husband in a series of small apartments in downtown Frankfort. Adding to Lucy's anger was the certain notion that Prichard had kept her unaware of his problems for many years. "I had no idea he was having tax troubles," Lucy later remarked.[18]

During this period, as his depression deepened, Prichard's weight problem increased. He simply ignored his doctor's orders to regulate his diet and quit smoking cigars. Instead, he indulged in both with the type of reckless disregard for the consequences that had marked some of his past political judg-ments. By 1960, Prichard's weight ballooned to over 300 pounds, he chain-smoked cigars, and he remained in terrible physical condition.

As his personal life disintegrated, Prichard's political life also underwent further trauma. When reports emerged that the state had leased a number of trucks from a Louisville auto dealer named Thurston Cooke—who had also been finance chair of the Combs-Wyatt campaign—suspicion fell on Earle Clements for overseeing the tainted lease, and Combs refused to come to Clements's rescue. Clements, in turn, refused to acknowledge any wrongdo-ing. When Combs canceled the deal, a proud and defiant Clements felt that the governor had smeared his integrity. Perhaps underlying Clements's anger was his loyalty to Prichard. Combs later said that "the real reason Earle got into the deal was because of Prich." Combs was certain that "Cooke had put Prich on a retainer as counsel for the company, no doubt at Earle's request." As everyone knew, Combs acknowledged, "Prich was still having his troubles and needed the money. That was the biggest reason Earle didn't want to hurt Cooke."[19] Within months, an angry Clements left Combs's administration, leaving an already vulnerable Prichard split between two men to whom he owed so much.

While his tenure within the highway commissioner's office was rather brief, Prichard remained a close confidant of the governor. Combs recognized Prichard's unique gifts and gave him the nickname "Philosopher." Combs began to consult with him on a variety of matters as part of an informal "kitchen cabinet" that usually met in the first floor of the Governor's Man-sion, which stood adjacent to the Capitol. In Combs's words, Prichard could be "a very valuable man to advise a Governor provided you understand going in that you have to sift these proposals and run them through a sieve." Combs was no simpleton bedazzled by the brilliance of Prichard's intellect and politi-cal experience. Instead, the wily, tight-lipped "silver fox," as Prichard called him, listened to Prichard formulate strategy but knew he could not, at least in the early going, be relied upon to advocate administration policy in the leg-islature, for example.[20]

Combs also understood that, considering Prichard's dire financial straits, he had to be watched closely. For example, a bill circulated in the state legis-lature in 1963 authorizing the 3M Company to manufacture reflective license plates for the state. One day Prichard casually asked Combs his opinion of the proposed legislation, and Combs replied he had not made up his mind whether to give the company the contract if it came to his desk. Combs soon discov-ered that Prichard was acting as a lobbyist for the company and stood to make a sizable fee if the bill was signed into law. When Combs vetoed the bill, an angry Prichard came to see him, and the two debated the merits of awarding one company a lucrative contract at a time when, in Combs's estimation, the state needed other areas funded.[21]

If Combs knew that Prichard might be willing to persuade him to sign bills solely as a lobbyist with his own personal financial well-being taking precedence over his role as an adviser, he also knew of Prichard's other compulsion—leaking news items to the press. Just as he had relished the role of providing journalists with inside information while in the White House, Prichard lost little time in doing the same in the Combs administration. After discovering that constant leaks were coming from Prichard, Combs began to edit what Prichard knew about impending legislation and other administration items. But he did so in a shrewd way that allowed Prichard to maintain his dignity and avoid the embarrassment of a gubernatorial snub. Combs did not confront Prichard in an attempt to threaten or humiliate him. Instead, he played into Prichard's humorous notions about the governor. On questions originating from Prichard on sensitive issues, Combs often responded by shaking his head as if he had not made up his mind and said, "Let's play that one by ear." Prichard later assumed that this hesitancy was just part of Combs's governing style. In fact, the legend of Combs's "let's play that one by ear" grew into one of Prichard's favorite stories. He pictured the pearly gates where one day the righteous and the unrighteous were being separated. The Lord called upon Bert Combs to help him with the decision of judging someone's assignment to a heavenly bliss or a fiery furnace. "Lord," Prichard would mock Combs's twang at this point, "mind if we play this one by ear?" The story was related in the context that Combs could not easily make up his mind and often deferred difficult decisions. What went unnoticed was that few others ever heard Combs make the statement. The governor resorted to this device in Prichard's presence in order not to divulge any information he did not wish to see in the next day's newspapers.[22]

Despite his propensity for talking with news reporters, Prichard remained an invaluable political resource for Combs. He could overwhelm and dazzle people by predicting, with stunning accuracy, local races in all 120 Kentucky counties. Given any problem within any county, "the philosopher" could be quickly brought in to analyze who should be consulted in a given precinct and who should be avoided. Prichard knew the history of so many politicians and their families in the state that he became a walking encyclopedia on—in political terminology—"where the bodies are buried." He also represented a democratic impulse that Combs found energizing. Lastly, Prichard was a vociferous opponent of Happy Chandler, which made him particularly welcome in the Combs camp.

But Combs also knew to keep Prichard at arm's length. While he was invited for occasional Sunday brunches at the mansion to discuss politics and strategy, Prichard was not a permanent fixture in the governor's office. A staff member recalls seldom seeing him in the office—usually only in cases where a complicated bill needed writing. On those occasions, Combs simply ordered his aides to get "the philosopher" in to write the technical language of a bill. Concurrently, Prichard was not an unabashed supporter of every item that Combs passed. The two differed, for example, on the matter of a state sales tax, which Combs advocated. Prichard considered this to be a regressive tax, while Combs felt it was the only way to raise sufficient revenue for education and other underfunded services.[23]

Throughout the Combs administration, Prichard remained nothing more than an unpaid adviser, and his law practice continued to fail. His tiny Frankfort law office brought in little income, and his heart was simply not in the task of building a sizable and sustainable practice. But his New Deal reputation, even considering his questionable legal commitments, still made him a lawyer to whom one went with matters that were central to Prichard's core beliefs. One area, for example, was civil rights. Prichard represented some African American students arrested for participating in sit-in demonstrations in Frankfort in 1962. To help in the case, he enlisted the counsel of his old friend Joe Rauh. Along with advice concerning how to proceed in court, Rauh also wrote that he had received a forty-seven-dollar check from Prichard to the Mayflower Hotel in Washington to cover a past-due bill. Rauh assured Prichard that "your credit rating is restored." The Mayflower soon received the check back, due to insufficient funds.[24]

A respite came with yet another campaign. Prichard took up residence again in the Seelbach Hotel in mid-1962, working on the campaign of Lt. Gov. Wilson Wyatt for the U.S. Senate. Although Wyatt and Prichard had known each other since the 1940s, their relationship was not exceptionally close. After all, Prichard had backed Combs early in the 1959 primary, and Wyatt felt "skeptical" of Prichard's involvement in his Senate campaign. Wyatt's defeat that November by Republican Thruston Morton effectively ended his elected political career and indicated that voters might be ready to bolt from the Combs wing for more conservative candidates.[25]

But considering all that Combs had done to help rehabilitate Prichard's declining fortunes, there was still the looming physical and political presence of Earle Clements. Prichard found himself caught in the middle of a political war between the present governor and the former senator. The emerging discord between Clements and Combs not only threatened to undermine the progressive wing of the state party and throw future elections to the Chandlerites, it also threatened the already vulnerable political fortunes of Ed Prichard.

By late 1962, one of the questions that burdened Combs and the party was who would win the 1963 Democratic primary for governor. In three years, Combs had established himself as one of the most progressive chief executives in the South. He had instituted a sales tax in order to provide more financial resources for the state's beleaguered school system; had instituted a merit system for state employees; had started an extensive road-building program in eastern Kentucky; had initiated building a series of community colleges; and had enhanced the state parks. The matter of raising any taxes, of course, bothered Happy Chandler no end, and the former governor and baseball commissioner contemplated yet another run for the Governor's Mansion. Chandler, in fact, had earlier set up an office outside the State Capitol building with a sign emblazoned "ABC in '63!"

Since Wyatt did not wish to make another run for the governor's office, a field of candidates emerged seeking the administration's backing for the May 1963 primary. One candidate was a young western Kentuckian, Edward "Ned" Breathitt, who had directed Combs's Public Service Commission. Breathitt had served in the state legislature before working in the Combs campaign in 1959. With no higher experience than heading the Public Service Commission to his credit, Breathitt was a long shot, at best, to win the governor's backing. Realizing he had to cultivate Combs's key advisers, Breathitt came to see Prichard in early 1963.

After pleasantries were exchanged and the purpose of the visit was announced, Prichard asked his first question of the young man who wanted to be governor: "How do you feel about the black folks?" The question took Breathitt aback. After all, civil rights was a delicate issue that most advisers wanted deeply to avoid, particularly in an election year. Prichard began to probe Breathitt concerning his own feelings about race in general. The question, in retrospect, was not inconsistent with Prichard's own political makeup. He had been one of the members supporting the minority, pro–civil rights plank at the 1948 Democratic convention. With the emerging civil rights movement that was sweeping through the South, Prichard wanted to make certain he was not placing his support behind a latent George Wallace or Orval Faubus. Lastly, his first line of questioning revealed that Prichard sensed how significant the matter of civil rights was about to become in state and national politics.

After Breathitt assured Prichard that he held no racist notions and would stand firmly behind advancing civil rights, Prichard probed other areas. One was the particularly delicate Kentucky issue of strip mining. With vast deposits of coal in both eastern and western Kentucky, the coal industry had long been one of the most powerful voices in Kentucky's economy and politics. The industry had also been the primary target of environmental reformers, who witnessed the devastating effects strip mining had on the state's landscape.

When Breathitt responded that he, too, hated strip mining, Prichard asked about education—would Breathitt defend a sales tax to support education against Happy Chandler? Since Kentucky had passed a law allowing eighteen-year-olds to vote, Prichard said it was crucial to get the young vote mobilized, and a strong support in defense of education could do that. When the meeting was over, Prichard made no commitment, and Breathitt left knowing that the extensive probing was done to see "whether he thought I was strong enough to be Governor."[26]

Whether Prichard advocated Breathitt's candidacy to Governor Combs is unknown, although it seems unlikely that Combs would be easily swayed by his advisers in any case. Nevertheless, perhaps wishing to anoint a fresh face who had no extensive record that Chandler could use to his advantage, Combs threw his support behind Breathitt's candidacy on May 2. But when Combs flew to Washington to visit with Earle Clements in an attempt to persuade him to support Breathitt, he received an icy reception. The likelihood that the breach between the two would not be repaired worried the governor. But even worse was the chance that Clements would do the unthinkable and back Chandler in the primary. When the unlikely scenario became reality and the two Democrats whose names had identified the opposing strands of the party were suddenly merged, Prichard found himself in desperate straits. Would he side with his longtime friend Clements or with Combs, who had been the first to proudly claim Prichard after Ashland back in 1955? Prichard interpreted the split between Combs and Clements as one that originated in Clements's "very considerable ego." Since his defeat for the U.S. Senate in 1956, Prichard noted that Clements "never quite saw things as realistically in politics as he had before."[27]

Upon careful inspection, there was really little for Prichard to decide in 1963. He was closer in ideology to Combs and Breathitt than he was to Clements, and no amount of loyalty to Clements could put him in the Chandler camp. Prichard threw himself completely behind Breathitt's campaign, precipitating a bitter break between himself and Clements—a friendship that was almost twenty years old. The break caused Prichard considerable grief. When dining with some reporters in Frankfort, he was brought to tears when the matter of his parting with Clements arose.[28] The ego of Earle Clements, which had been ruffled by Combs, had now consumed even his relationship with Prichard. The break also threatened Breathitt's candidacy and the legacy of reform that Combs had begun and Prichard supported.

Naturally, Combs hit the campaign trail in Breathitt's behalf. As one of the rare governors from the mountains, Combs was especially crucial to Breathitt in eastern Kentucky. Chandler counted on a great deal of support from the traditionally more conservative mountaineers, and Breathitt sought to use the popular governor to offset a Chandler base of support. Meanwhile, Prichard became once again a resident of the Seelbach Hotel and worked feverishly in Breathitt's headquarters. He wrote a number of highly inflammatory campaign speeches that were edited by campaign manager Foster Ockerman to tone down their controversial content. But it was Breathitt's decision to use Prichard himself in a campaign appearance in Hindman, Kentucky, that proved one of the most courageous acts of the entire campaign.

When the campaign team of Bert Combs and Ed Prichard pulled into the quiet mountain town of Hindman on May 24, 1963, they were met with a steady rain that threatened to diminish the crowd that came to hear them. Standing on the back of a pickup truck, the soft-spoken governor told the crowd how essential it was for the mountaineers to elect Ned Breathitt over Happy Chandler. Then he introduced Ed Prichard, who was biting at the bit to talk before his first public gathering in a decade and a half, as well as to speak on behalf of a candidate he strongly supported. Most of all, it was a platform that finally allowed Prichard to go after Happy Chandler. The former governor had hired men to pose in prison uniforms at rallies in an obvious slur upon Prichard, so Hindman presented him with the chance to say what he had kept inside for so many years, and it provided the old campaigner and Princeton debater a chance to display his rare oratorical talents. If anyone felt that the Hindman crowd would not find much of interest in the former Ivy Leaguer, a recording of Prichard's speech in Hindman dispels such myths. Copies of that tape, in the words of a Washington journalist, are still circulated around Kentucky and Washington "with the same sort of devotion that some hold for rare Lenny Bruce recordings."[29]

Without, of course, prepared notes or a written speech, Prichard spoke extemporaneously and in no time was in a groove that had the crowd in the palm of his hands. Combining the rhythms of a country revivalist with a memory that knew the sordid record of Chandler's history, Prichard blasted away at the moral integrity of his opponent:

> He says he's gonna build some country roads. Well, all right, I'll tell you how he built country roads during the last time he was governor. He took $869,000 out of the rural road fund and gave it in contracts to his son-in-law, Jimmy Jack Lewis. And 40 percent of it was for designing roads that were never built. Now that's what he did with your rural road money. You've heard about paying a farmer not to grow tobacco, not to grow corn, but this is the first time in history that they ever paid an engineer not to build a road [laughter, applause].
>
> Now if you want to fill the sack for Jimmy Jack, if you want to pay $17,000 for a road grader that only cost $11,000 today, if you want to take rural road money to build a four-lane, concrete road from Versailles to Frankfort—cause

that's where he got the money to build that road from his home to his golf course, nine million dollars . . . that highway from Versailles to Frankfort, that money they used to Fill the sack for Jimmy Jack.

The phrase "fill the sack for Jimmy Jack" became part of the folklore that surrounded the 1963 campaign. Such phrases usually came from the mouth of Chandler, but in Hindman Prichard used one of Chandler's most potent weapons with devastating effect—ridicule.

If that was not enough, Prichard continued—all the while raising the level of laughter and applause among the three hundred or so who where there. "You know, you and I were taught in Sunday School and church at the end of the Lord's prayer to say: 'And thine be the kingdom and the power and the glory.' But for thirty years, Happy Chandler has been saying 'And MIIIINE be the kingdom . . .'" [laughter, more applause].

Then Prichard attacked Chandler's patriotism and integrity in a personal way:

> He lives by the side of a swimming pool that was given to him by a war contractor when he was a member of the United States Senate, on the military affairs committee that had jurisdiction over war contracts. That swimming pool used up the steel and the concrete and the metal that was needed for our war effort! Three days after Pearl Harbor he resigned his commission in the United States Army and spent the war floating around on top of that swimming pool. And I say a man who accepts that kind of a gift ain't fit to be Governor of Kentucky! [heavy applause and shouts].

Typically, Prichard ended with a story that delighted the crowd. "If you don't vote for Ned Breathitt, you're gonna be like the calf I heard a feller talking about the other day. Boy comes up to his daddy and says, 'Pappy, the calf stopped running after the cow and now he's running after the bull.' The old man didn't seem to be very excited. Little boy says, 'Daddy, you don't understand. The calf has stopped running after the cow and now he's running after the bull.' The old man says, 'That's alright. He'll learn the difference when suppertime comes!'"[30]

The speech displayed many of the political talents of Ed Prichard. He adjusted his language to fit the audience, with such flourishes as "ain't fit to be Governor." He identified with the endemic concerns of the mountain crowd, constantly reminding them of previous Chandler promises that could have done a lot for them by building a road or fixing a school in Knott County. Prichard peppered the speech with biblical injunctions, humorous stories, biting satire, and inspiring rhetoric that made coming out in the rain well worth the trouble. It was a style of campaign oratory that once so enraptured the young boy in Paris but was already seeming out of place in a political culture coming increasingly under the deadening influence of television.

To those who watched the campaign closely, the transformation of Ed Prichard was under way. Foster Ockerman, Breathitt's campaign manager, attributed Prichard's visible role in the campaign as something that "helped to get him back his confidence." Ockerman sensed what few others knew. The trauma of the preceding fourteen years had nearly destroyed Prichard's once-ebullient confidence. Lucy later touched on this theme of her husband's life, suggesting to Barry and Mary Bingham that they had also contributed "to Prich's confidence in himself." Restoring that confidence remained a painful and laborious process.[31]

No one in Kentucky—not even Happy Chandler—had a larger reservoir of "dirty tricks" to employ in a campaign than Ed Prichard. Late in the 1963 primary race, Prichard humiliated the Chandler staff with a stunt that earned Chandler's permanent ire. The Breathitt campaign produced a film called *The Chandler Years,* which was a biting satirical look at Chandler's term in the governor's office from 1955 to 1959. The film appeared to be a complimentary campaign documentary but featured such scenes as a little girl eating an ice-cream cone when a hand suddenly jerks it away. The scene implied that Chandler had advocated a sales tax that had inadvertently raised the tax on ice-cream cones. Staff members posing as reporters even went to Chandler's home and told Mrs. Chandler they were filming a documentary and were looking for old photographs of her husband. After they left, Chandler wrote, "Mama realized they had picked out only the most unflattering." But even then, Chandler did not realize what was afoot. Prichard organized the Breathitt campaign staff to call pro-Chandler supporters in the counties and inform them to get out their supporters to watch the film on television. In some places, the Chandler campaign even bought ads in local newspapers informing the local citizenry of the upcoming documentary! When the documentary aired, the Chandler campaign was caught completely off guard and more than eighty county organizations were hoodwinked into getting their campaign workers to watch it. An angry and humiliated Chandler likened the tactics of the Breathitt campaign to those of Hitler and Mussolini and added, "This is the vilest and filthiest campaign the opposition has ever conducted." He even threatened a lawsuit for the incident, and the film was never aired again. Throughout it all, Prichard delighted in having done Happy one better in the subtle art of campaign trickery.[32]

Chandler's hatred for Prichard raged throughout the 1963 campaign. Never one to forget an unkind remark, Chandler had been the subject of Prichard's biting wit earlier in the Combs administration. When the former governor called Prichard a jailbird, Prichard responded that he had indeed served time in a federal prison. "I have associated with murderers, robbers, rapists, and forgers, criminals of all kinds," Prichard recalled, "and let me say, my friends, that every one of them was the moral superior of A.B. Happy Chandler."[33]

Partly owing to a strong showing in the mountains, Ned Breathitt shocked political observers in the late May primary by defeating Chandler by more than 60,000 votes. A typically ungracious Chandler later wrote, "I think I won the race . . . we think it was stolen. . . . Breathitt didn't have any more chance to be governor than my grandson."[34] The victory had several repercussions for the renaissance of Ed Prichard. First, it guaranteed that for at least four more years, the Chandler wing of the party would be on the outside looking in at the Combs-Breathitt forces. Second, the usually sour relationship between Prichard and Chandler erupted into a bitter feud that never subsided. Last, Prichard's support for the underdog Ned Breathitt and his ardent work, both behind the scenes and in the light, had earned the devoted loyalty of the man who was a November election away from being governor. Almost thirteen years after leaving Ashland, Ed Prichard had recovered his political voice. His years of wandering in the wilderness, it seemed, were almost over.

Part III
Star Reborn

The process of overcoming infirmities is the process of staying alive.
                                              —Edward F. Prichard Jr., 1979

13 Back in the Arena

IN the summer of 1963, between the Democratic primary and the November general election, the Breathitt campaign geared for the fall race against Republican Louie Nunn, who had headed Richard Nixon's presidential campaign in Kentucky three years earlier. The Combs administration, in its last months in power, was expected to do the usual things sitting governors can do to help their anointed candidates win—award road contracts in key counties, extend patronage to loyal campaigners, and refrain from any controversial measures that might cost votes. But during the summer of Birmingham and the March on Washington, the issue of civil rights could not be ignored, and the Kentucky gubernatorial race of 1963 became embroiled in the matter of public accommodations and civil rights. For Ed Prichard the issue was a heartfelt one that made clear that he was not just another cynical courthouse politico with his eyes always centered on future elections.

As a nominal border state, Kentucky had long seemed devoid of the racial climate that poisoned the Deep South. Throughout the early 1960s, Kentucky escaped many of the civil rights protests that engulfed the South, and casual observers might have been led to believe that race was not a divisive issue in the Commonwealth. But underlying the calm facade was the reality of a caste system every bit as destructive as that of Mississippi or Alabama. African Americans in Kentucky faced most, if not all, of the discrimination and blatant racism that affected those in the Deep South.[1] By the summer of 1963, despite the desires of its political leaders, Kentucky found itself in the middle of the civil rights movement.

In early 1963, when Louisville mayor William Cowger signed an ordinance forbidding racial discrimination in public accommodations, the attention focused on Frankfort and Governor Combs's reaction—would he sign a similar order? Combs had failed to include civil rights in special legislative sessions called in 1963, and state civil rights leaders began pressuring the governor to implement a strong civil rights agenda. When the governor visited the White House that summer, President Kennedy repeated his request to Combs that all southern governors issue such proclamations. Combs sampled the legislature but found little support for a public accommodations bill. Displaying a brand of political courage that was rare in 1963, Combs acted anyway. Despite the danger it afforded the Breathitt campaign, he signed an executive order on June 26 that outlawed discrimination in any state-regulated establishment because "the denial of equal opportunity . . . is unfair, unjust and inconsistent with the public policy of the Commonwealth." Although the order affected only a small number of businesses, Combs's act became one of the central issues of the 1963 campaign.[2]

The reaction by Bourbons in both parties was swift—Happy Chandler called the order an "illegal act"; a Democratic state senator said the order would cause 100,000 Chandler supporters to support Nunn in the November election; and Nunn himself raised the loudest cries, calling Combs's order "a dictatorial edict" that had been ordered by Bobby Kennedy. Nunn went on television to exploit the issue to the fullest. Surrounded by the American and Kentucky flags, the constitutions of the United States and the Commonwealth of Kentucky, and the Holy Bible, Nunn declared that his first order of business after his inauguration would be to rescind Combs's order.[3]

Chandlerites backed Nunn for other reasons as well as the civil rights issue. Ben Chandler wrote in his father's Versailles newspaper that "'Little Ned' Breathitt, tutored by 'Big Ed' Prichard waged the filthiest campaign in all of Kentucky's history" against Chandler in the primary. With Breathitt's election, the newspaper warned, the next step would be for Combs to run again, "and by that time, Kentucky will be ready for Ed Prichard to serve as Governor, in fact, rather than by proxy." Republican radio ads portrayed Breathitt as a "stooge" for President Kennedy and even deceptively quoted the president as saying "We are going to have a mix . . . this will be true racially," implying that Kennedy was advocating miscegenation. The ads finished with: "Breathitt supports this Kennedy policy. Vote against it. Vote Nunn."[4]

While members of Breathitt's staff wanted to put as much distance between the order and their candidate as possible, Prichard urged Breathitt to stand strong on the order and make no apologies for opening up public accommodations without regard to race. Breathitt recalled that Prichard was adamantly opposed to any statement that would weaken the order and, in Breathitt's words, "was there to keep me from fiddling around on the edges" of the issue of civil rights. But to soothe his worried staff and to stop the vote bleeding, Breathitt promised that if elected, he too, would rescind the order. Breathitt then vowed he would replace the order with a stronger bill that he would introduce in the General Assembly. Prichard essentially agreed with Breathitt's statement, since executive orders could easily be rescinded by future governors.[5]

With the introduction of the race card into the election, usual party lines were broken in ways that came to typify southern politics in the 1960s. As Chandlerites bolted to Nunn, some Republicans, including John Sherman

Cooper and Louisville County Judge Marlow Cook, decried Nunn's reaction. The issue certainly did a lot for Nunn's campaign, and on election day the Breathitt camp held its collective breath. When the votes were finally counted, Breathitt received 50.7 percent of the total vote, winning the governor's office with a razor-thin 13,000-vote margin. The size of Breathitt's victory in a heavily Democratic state over a little-known opponent said something about how divisive the race issue was in a border state like Kentucky, and threatened to undermine any mandate the young governor-elect hoped to bring to the office.[6]

Breathitt's victory, regardless of its margin, gave Ed Prichard his greatest entrée yet into the executive mansion. Whereas Bert Combs had held Prichard at arm's length, Ned Breathitt embraced Prichard's political ideology and depended on his advice and counsel to a degree no other governor—neither Clements nor Combs—ever had. Ever since he was a young college student at the University of Kentucky, the new governor had admired Prichard's intellect and political insight. During the days ahead, Ed Prichard emerged as the governor's chief adviser on a host of delicate and significant issues.

Although his own political life seemed to be turning around, on the personal front, Prichard's life remained in turmoil. He stayed separated from Lucy and had taken to living in a variety of small apartments in Frankfort. His weight continued to rise, exceeding 300 pounds. His tax problems dogged him constantly, and his law practice was virtually nonexistent. On top of this, a series of personal tragedies soon touched Prichard.

The first occurred on August 4, 1963, when at breakfast with Breathitt campaign staff member Don Mills, Prichard opened the morning's newspaper. Tears came to his eyes when he read that Philip Graham had killed himself the previous day. Prichard had seen little of Graham since leaving Washington, but their shared early histories tied them together in ways that eclipsed the distance that separated them. Each had taken Washington by storm with his brilliance and charm. Both became accustomed to superlatives about their futures—Joseph Alsop once described Phil Graham as "probably the most successful man of all his contemporaries"; Joe Rauh characterized Graham and Prichard as the two most likely men in Washington to one day be president of the United States. Each, in the end, shared similar fates. While Prichard went to jail, Graham emerged as one of the country's leading newspaper publishers with the *Washington Post* and was a close friend to both John F. Kennedy and Lyndon Johnson. But in the late 1950s, Graham began to suffer from manic depression. In between furious episodes of activity, such as his behind-the-scenes maneuvering on behalf of LBJ at the 1960 Democratic National Convention, Graham underwent sustained periods of depression. His doctors advised against medication, and Graham's condition worsened over the years.

In the summer of 1963, he entered a mental hospital but managed to convince doctors by early August that he was better, and was released, whereupon he went to his vacation home with Katharine. Hours later, he shot himself. "If he had lived," the *New York Times* commented, "Philip Graham could have made a notable contribution to his country." Perhaps adding to Prichard's anguish was that he had to learn of his best man's death in the newspapers. At Graham's funeral, which was attended by President Kennedy, Joe Rauh recalled Prichard looking "like the wrath of God." Thus began a series of personal tragedies that over the next decade exacted a heavy toll on Prichard.[7]

As the January 1964 session of the General Assembly approached, the new young governor had a full plate. As promised, he offered a public accommodations bill to replace Combs's executive order. Not surprisingly, the bill met with stiff opposition in the legislature. In fact, throughout his first General Assembly, the young governor was outmaneuvered on numerous matters, including civil rights and strip mine control. As both bills stalled, Breathitt was accused by even his supporters of being strong on rhetoric but weak on action. The inaction over the civil rights bill brought a major demonstration to the quiet streets of Frankfort. On March 5, more than ten thousand people, led by Martin Luther King Jr., Ralph Abernathy, and Jackie Robinson, marched to the Capitol in protest of the bill's failure in the General Assembly. Marching in the procession as well was Ed Prichard, who had to join the throng midway through its course because his 300-pound frame could not endure the entire distance. King and other movement leaders later met with Breathitt to seek support of even stronger measures than the administration was pushing. Conservative members of the legislature, such as Republican House Whip Harold DeMarcus, refused to budge, saying, "Their marches and demonstrations are pointless . . . if things keep going this way, we're going to have to pass laws protecting the white man."[8]

Republicans and wary Democrats won the day, and the legislative session came to an unsuccessful conclusion for Breathitt in March 1964. His staff rehuddled, in full knowledge that the odds were now stacked against them. Since a Kentucky governor could not succeed himself, Breathitt's first General Assembly was the one in which he was seemingly the most powerful. Considering that future sessions would find legislators hoping to curry favor with those considering potential runs for the governor's office, and considering his small margin of victory the previous election, Breathitt's administration was in deep trouble following the 1964 General Assembly.

In May 1964 a second personal tragedy befell Ed Prichard—the death of his father. Big Ed had been in poor health for several years, his body racked with diabetes. Big Ed had suddenly fallen unconscious while riding in a car in Paris. He was taken to the county hospital, where he soon died. His relationship with his son had grown strained following the ballot-box scandal. By the 1960s, the younger Prichard sometimes recoiled at a ringing telephone in anticipation of hearing his father's angry lectures. The pain the younger Prichard had caused his father left wounds that never fully healed. The elder Prichard was buried in the Prichard plot in the Paris cemetery, alongside the Fretwells. Ironically, Big Ed's friend and driver on the day he died was William Collier, a Bourbon County election commissioner.[9]

While Prichard knew the new governor well, he knew the new president perhaps even better. Lyndon Johnson's ascension to the presidency had special meaning for Prichard. The two shared similar backgrounds—both had fallen in love with politics at an early age, watching their fathers at the local courthouses and statehouses while dreaming of their own political future. Both knew the cynical world of local politics, and each had tasted an intoxicating brand of power in Washington during the New Deal. Their profoundly different paths following 1945 must have played on Prichard's mind as he watched LBJ's run for his own term in the White House in 1964. Prichard, of course, fully supported Johnson's campaign but played no significant role in it.

At the Democratic National Convention that summer, Breathitt appointed Prichard as an at-large delegate, Prichard's third time as a delegate. At this convention, the role of a delegate was a relatively ceremonial one, as the Atlantic City convention came to be known as "Lyndon's convention." The presidential staff selected various bright lights of the party to present seconding speeches for Johnson's nomination, and the Kentucky governor was one chosen for the task. It was a heady time for such a national appearance, and Breathitt wanted the speech to be right. Prichard, naturally, wrote it, and Breathitt gave the final draft to Douglass Cater, one of Johnson's staffers, for approval. Cater read the speech with Prichard and Breathitt in attendance and recognized immediately that this was no ordinary speech. Cater asked Prichard, "Is this yours?" Breathitt replied proudly, "Word for word, Doug." "It will probably be the best thing at the whole convention," Cater said. Prichard was not willing just to let his words do the job. He made Breathitt practice the speech before TelePrompTers the night before. Breathitt remembered that Prichard "wanted his governor to do it right."[10]

Breathitt appeared before the convention on August 26, 1964. As the convention went about its usual business during seconding speeches, Breathitt began reading Prichard's words:

> "The World's great age begins anew." So wrote the poet Virgil two thousand years ago, as he foreshadowed an era of Roman greatness.
>   We are a party of perpetual renewal, a party which has not only seen great visions but made those visions into growing, breathing realities and brought them

into the lives of ordinary people. The history of this nation records that the great ages of America have been the ages of Democratic leadership—or of Republican leadership like that of Lincoln and Theodore Roosevelt, which carried the ideal of our party into the ranks of the opposition.

Four years ago young America heard the voice of a young leader, a leader of unique quality who sounded the trumpet call for another great age of national renewal. He asked us to get America moving again. We joined him and moved from strength to strength, from the idea to the reality, from the vision to the accomplishment.

As he spoke, Breathitt noticed that "the convention became quiet and they listened." What drew the crowd's attention to Breathitt were his words, written by Prichard, that transcended the rambling, often shrill rhetoric of convention speeches. Many in the convention were captivated by the poetic and powerful prose:

> To strength and prosperity we have joined compassion. Ours is the vision and ours the growing reality of a great society in which the accidents of race and color, parentage and poverty, location and geography, will not be allowed to dim the light of human hope and to cripple the possibilities of human growth. . . .
>
> Mr. Valiant-for-Truth in *Pilgrim's Progress* said, "My sword I leave to him who can wield it." The mighty arm of Lyndon Johnson has carried the flashing blade of John Kennedy, signaling to an anxious world that the forces of freedom, of compassion, of decency and progress cannot be conquered even by death itself. . . .
>
> There are some Americans in this year of 1964 who scorn our ideal of perpetual renewal, for a ceaseless quest for the Great Society. For the vision of Lincoln, of Franklin Roosevelt, of Truman, of Kennedy, of Johnson, they would substitute a vision which finds its inspiration not in the better angels of our nature, but in the dark and hopeless corners of the human heart. Theirs is a vision of injustice as a condition decreed by fate; a vision of poverty as man's inevitable lot; a vision of atomic war as just another routine problem.

In closing, Breathitt spoke of Johnson's relationship with poverty and war: "Lyndon Johnson—as a young man—has known poverty at first hand, has known economic collapse at first hand, and he has known war at first hand. These are the enemies of youth, indeed the enemies of all mankind, and in the battle against these enemies the young people of this nation will enlist for the duration with Lyndon B. Johnson as their commander-in-chief."[11]

As the convention roared its approval at Breathitt's inspiring prose, somewhere in the convention hall that night Ed Prichard shared the moment as well. Standing in the shadows, his words, which had animated "his governor" and spoken in behalf of his friend Lyndon Johnson, reached down somewhere in the hearts of the thousands listening in the hall and brought a poetic beauty to the quest for the Great Society. All the luminary hallmarks of Prichard's past culminated in Breathitt's Atlantic City speech. The speech was the quintessence of Prichard's political ideology and skills, employing both classical references and inspiring recollections of past Democrats. An implicit understanding that politics could be used to uplift the downtrodden was the trademark of Prichard's politics, and it provided the core reason for his passionate pursuit of politics since his boyhood.

Lyndon Johnson had kept distant contact with Prichard while in Washington, and the two had never lost sight of one another during the ensuing twenty years. After Ashland, when Johnson saw the lone figure of Prichard at a funeral, one of his aides advised Johnson not to go over and be seen with the ex-convict. Johnson later told Ned Breathitt how he had reacted to this advice: "I'd rather have my pecker cut off than to deny Ed Prichard." Johnson added that when the two were younger and were ambitious politicians in Washington, Prichard saw to it that Johnson had access to the White House. When he was president, Johnson told Breathitt's aide Robert Bell to take a cigar to his old friend.[12]

But as Johnson rose to the very highest echelons in American politics, he did not keep close contact with Prichard. During the 1964 campaign, a jubilant and noticeably proud Ed Prichard went to Louisville to see the president at a boisterous campaign stop. Little stood in Johnson's way of an overwhelming mandate by the people for his own presidency. But in late October, Prichard felt compelled to write to Lady Bird Johnson to praise her husband's handling of the revelation that a longtime aide, Walter Jenkins, had been caught soliciting sex from an undercover policeman. Prichard wrote that he "felt very close to you and the President during the tense, recent days—on account of the Jenkins matter." Prichard added, "I think I know something of the pressures and strains that come under such circumstances," and that the courageous way LBJ supported Jenkins demonstrated what Prichard called "Christian concern," or "that heroism which Hemingway once defined as 'grace under pressure.'"[13]

Events such as the Atlantic City convention displayed the heights Prichard was capable of reaching. His life in Frankfort at times displayed the depths to which he could also plunge. Throughout the 1960s, Prichard lived with roommates such as Don Mills, Breathitt's press secretary, and young lawyers Marvin Coles and Jim Hudson in a series of efficiency apartments in downtown Frankfort. His roommates remember these years with fondness, as well as some sadness. As an example of Prichard's increasing problem with his weight, Coles and Hudson recall one evening when they broiled some steaks in the oven. Early the next morning, Hudson heard a noise in the kitchen and went to investigate. He found Prichard on all fours, eating white bread from a packaged loaf after dipping it into the grease pan left over from the previous night.[14] For an overweight diabetic, such binges were examples of sheer self-destruction.

Approaching his fifties, Prichard found himself as lonely in the 1960s as he had been as a teenager. Lucy remained estranged, and he saw his sons intermittently. When Ed and Lucy spoke, roommates remember, "she reminded him at all times about how he had messed up and how they were not living in the style that they should." One roommate sadly remembers that Prichard was, at bottom, a "very lonely man."[15]

The saving grace in Prichard's life in such a vulnerable period was Governor Breathitt, who saw Prichard as a crucial adviser and was proud to be associated with a figure who was beginning to take on legendary proportions, at least in some circles. One such circle was the coterie of men around Lyndon Johnson. On the night before Johnson's inauguration in January 1965, Breathitt and Prichard attended a series of parties and ceremonies in Washington, one arranged by Paul Porter and Prichard to honor the Kentucky governor. When Breathitt arrived, he was stunned to find that people such as Thomas Corcoran, James Rowe, and Thurman Arnold were in attendance, along with Johnson aides Jack Valenti and Bill Moyers. Both groups represented the continuum between the Roosevelt and Johnson presidencies. Breathitt was "bedazzled until I realized they came to see Prich, not me." In a short time, Prichard drifted over to a big overstuffed chair, lit a cigar, and started telling stories. The crowd in this glittering assembly gathered around him, and some sat on the floor, entertained, stimulated, and inspired by Ed Prichard. "These young Johnson people," recalled Breathitt, said, "'My gosh, this is the most incredible guy I've ever met.'" In this "spellbinding" performance, Breathitt was impressed with "the power of his personality, and his intellect, his total recall, over the people who in three administrations had led the free world."[16]

But just as Combs had done throughout his administration, Breathitt at first kept Prichard around the governor's office as an unpaid advisor, with little or no public recognition. That soon changed. Breathitt appointed Prichard to his first public post in almost two decades, as a member of the Democratic state central committee. But Breathitt had more in store for Prichard. The matter of revising Kentucky's constitution, which had first brought the two together in 1947, remained in the foreground of both men's minds. As governor, Breathitt wanted a constitutional convention to revise what he considered to be an outdated and inefficient document. Shortly after his inauguration, Breathitt succeeded in getting the General Assembly to approve a Constitutional Revision Assembly. The assembly was organized to adopt a model constitution and put it before the electorate of Kentucky in the way of a referendum. Breathitt, on Prichard's advice, made Earle Clements the chair of the convention and appointed fifty diverse Kentuckians to serve in the assembly, including Happy Chandler, Bert Combs, and Louie Nunn. As a reward for his work in the campaign, and as an acknowledgment of Prichard's long-standing advocacy of constitutional reform, Breathitt also decided to appoint Prichard to the select assembly.

Before Prichard could concern himself with public recognition or the task of writing a new state charter, however, the matter of Clements's chairmanship became an overriding issue. The two had not spoken since Prichard sided with Combs against Clements in the 1963 campaign. At the opening session of the assembly, Prichard wanted to meet with Clements to iron out their differences, but Clements snubbed him. Prichard then wrote him a personal and poignant letter. If Clements wished, Prichard said he would resign from the assembly. "Continuous attendance and arduous work in a body where I must almost daily be exposed to the emotional strain of bad relations with you will be very hard for me," wrote Prichard.

> I doubt whether it would do any good to explain to you why I chose to support Breathitt rather than Chandler. Whatever my reasons (some of them were selfish and some were disinterested), you would remain convinced, and justly convinced, that I had not done right by you. All I ask you to believe is that never a day has gone by since that time that I have not felt regret and sorrow because, for the first time in our friendship, I was not able to be with you.
>
> Certainly I hope that we may maintain genuinely cordial personal relations— and you know just as well as I do the difference between correct relations and cordial relations. Prichard, as well as Smith, knows coolness when he feels it.
>
> Apart from any other reasons, you have a sufficient basis for your feelings from the fact that I did not go with you in the primary campaign. I do not for a moment minimize the seriousness of that offense, especially in view of the fact that I had led you to believe that I would stay with you. When a change of circumstances made a contrary course necessary, I should have talked with you: my only excuse is that if I had talked with you, I could never have taken a course contrary to yours.
>
> Senator, I ask nothing from you but a chance to earn your confidence and friendship—perhaps it will be, as Browning once wrote, "never glad confident morning again"— but neither need it be the black midnight of resentment and rejection.[17]

The letter expressed, in the way only Prichard could, the deep pain he felt for the broken relationship. He knew what he owed Clements, not just in politics and clemency, but also in friendship. The fact that Prichard was willing to leave his post on the assembly (his first public activity in nearly two decades) displayed his heartfelt loyalty to Earle Clements. The letter also exposed the apparent reason for Clements's coolness—Prichard had promised

Clements he would side with him and had then recanted without personally telling him. Few things angered the Morganfield politician more than that.

But the imposing Clements also had a special fondness for Prichard and on occasion revealed a tender side toward him often ignored by other observers. One such occasion was in his reply to Prichard's letter. Clements wrote, "If I were to express one wish with reference to the Assembly membership and my relationship to it, it would be this—I would be tremendously gratified if my contribution would have a modest relationship to that made by you." With this, the strained relationship between Prichard and Clements was eased. The two men reconciled and remained close friends to the very end.[18]

The prospects facing Clements, Prichard, and the revision assembly were daunting. The effort to revise Kentucky's 1891 constitution had a long and tortuous past. In 1931, in a statewide referendum considering a new constitution, supporters of revision received a scant 22 percent of the vote. In 1947, the question was again put before the voters—this time the figures supporting revision increased to 43 percent. In 1949, a Constitutional Review Commission was created, that suggested sweeping changes in the state's charter. The commission's first suggestion was to change a clause stating that only two amendments could be offered before the voters in a general election. That effort too failed. In 1960, a referendum that allowed offering up to twelve amendments at a time was also defeated, but by only a slim margin. By 1964, when the General Assembly approved a fifty-delegate convention that would submit a new constitution to the voters, advocates of reform felt confident of finally winning.[19]

The assembly was divided into select committees, and Prichard was chosen to serve in the Local Government and Revision Process Committees. He was even chosen to chair a subcommittee on finance within the Local Government Committee.[20] Although he nominally operated a law office on Ann Street in Frankfort, he threw himself wholeheartedly into the constitutional revision process. Prichard understandably enjoyed the chance to be in the arena of public affairs once more, and to lend his considerable experience to the task of writing a new constitution. Whatever it cost him personally or professionally, Ed Prichard was determined he would play a leading role in redesigning the state's basic charter.

The long series of personal losses, however, continued. After the deaths of his father and Phil Graham, Prichard lost another beloved figure who had been one of the singular influences on his life. Felix Frankfurter died in February 1965 at the age of 82, three years after suffering a debilitating stroke. Since serving as a surrogate son and law clerk to the justice more than two decades earlier, Prichard and Frankfurter had seen little of each other. In a span of fewer than three years, Prichard had lost three of the central figures in his

life—Phil Graham, his father, and Frankfurter—and his personal life continued to disintegrate.

While the committees on the constitution met intermittently throughout 1964 and 1965, Prichard was also concerned with other matters. One of
the failures of the 1964 legislature was a strip mine control bill sponsored by
the administration. Stopping the raping of the eastern and western Kentucky
countryside by coal operators became one of Prichard's most pressing concerns.
An example of the human abuses of strip mining came shortly before Thanksgiving Day 1965. It also gave the Breathitt administration an opening to pursue
more vigorous strip mine regulations.

When powerful coal operator William Sturgill ordered his bulldozers to
begin strip-mining some property in an eastern Kentucky area known as Clear
Creek in Knott County, a longtime resident named Ollie Combs refused to
allow the heavy equipment onto her land. She sat in front of a bulldozer for
more than an hour before sheriff's deputies forcefully carried her off to jail. A
photographer from the *Courier-Journal* recorded the dramatic event, but he
was arrested alongside Combs. The photographer managed somehow to
smuggle his film of the affair back to Louisville, where the newspaper ran the
provocative photograph of Combs being dragged from her own property on
Thanksgiving. The courageous woman's story of defying a powerful coal mag-
nate in protection of her property captured the public's attention.[21]

Sturgill's strong-arm tactics came at a propitious time for the Breathitt
administration. Following a successful election just weeks before in which
numerous pro-Breathitt candidates were elected to the statehouse, the governor and his staff were ready to push for stringent anti–strip mine laws that
would protect property owners. The coverage of Combs's arrest provided a
compelling example to the general public of what was involved.

In the governor's office, Prichard came up with an inspired public relations plan. He dubbed the imprisoned woman "the Widow Combs" and advised Breathitt to capitalize on the public outrage. The governor publicly called
upon Sturgill and all strip miners to cease their operations until the legality
of the coal operator's rights to mine on private property was tested in the courts.
The governor proclaimed: "I want the Widow Combs and all other Kentuckians whose houses are threatened with destruction to know that I am on their
side." When the General Assembly opened a few weeks later, Breathitt capi-
talized on the publicity generated by the "Widow Combs" affair to push for a
strip mine bill.[22]

The bill regulated the types and methods of strip mining. But the heart
of the matter, as everyone knew, was the legal foundation of the entire process, a questionable document known as the broad-form deed. The original
broad-form deeds had been signed by coal operators and landowners in the

late 1800s. While allowing property owners to maintain ownership of the surface, such deeds also allowed miners to excavate the coal underneath the surface. This posed little real problem until the advent of large excavation machines that literally dug up the surface to expose the seam of coal. The process, termed strip mining, seemed to invalidate the intent of the original deeds. After landowners found themselves helpless to stop the stripping of their land, numerous suits were filed. But Kentucky courts consistently recognized the right of the companies to mine the land in question without any regard to the landowners' wishes. One of the most noted practitioners of strip mining in eastern Kentucky was the American Association Company, a British corporation that owned vast amounts of coal deposits near Middlesboro. Its American manager, ironically enough, was Al Funk Jr.[23]

Serious discussion occurred within the administration about whether to include the outlawing of the broad-form deed within the bill itself. Few matters in eastern Kentucky generated such emotional debate, and few issues could draw forth the wrath of one of the state's most financially and politically powerful entities—the coal industry. Prichard advised the governor that his strip mine bill would never pass if a broad-form deed clause was included. He urged instead that a separate bill on the deed be written, to which the governor agreed. Nevertheless, the strip mine bill faced an uphill struggle in the committee. After a parade of coal company executives spoke, the Widow Combs herself testified before the committee of her recent encounters. Thanks to the powerful testimony of many landowners and an outraged public, the bill passed and was signed into law by Governor Breathitt. The broad-form deed bill, however, went nowhere.[24]

The next item on Breathitt's agenda was a civil rights bill. The governor introduced another bill early in 1966 that guaranteed access to all public accommodations without regard to race, and a provision was included prohibiting job discrimination. In all, the Kentucky bill was broader than the federal civil rights bill passed in 1964. The bill cleared committee and reached the floor in January 1966. The only African American in the General Assembly, Jesse Warders of Louisville, rose before a packed and silent House. "I rise to speak on the issue of civil rights," Warders said. "It is altogether wrong that I should have to do so. It is not wrong that I do so, but wrong that I have to do so. It is wrong in modern America . . . that men should still have to rise to see that all men are treated equally." Warders then reached the climax of his poignant and impressive speech: "It is wrong but nevertheless true, that in 1966 Negroes are turned away from places of public accommodations in Kentucky because of the color of their skin. It is wrong, but true, that in our state qualified Negroes are denied equal access to job opportunities. It is wrong, but true, that each year Kentucky loses the cream of the crop in terms of Negro college graduates who . . . are unable to find meaningful work." Warders's speech was followed by a roll-call vote, which passed the bill 76 to 12. Warders later told a journalist that his poignant speech on that crucial night was written by Ed Prichard.[25]

A week later, the state Senate followed suit, passing the bill with only one no vote, and on January 26, 1966, Breathitt signed the bill at the base of Lincoln's statue in the Kentucky Capitol rotunda, claiming the legislation was "a promissory note long overdue." Breathitt was flanked by state legislators, members of his administration, and civil rights leaders. Breathitt later gazed at a photograph of the historic signing—one of the first state civil rights bills in the South—and wished he had put Prichard directly behind him as a symbol of how he had held the governor's "feet to the fire."[26]

In addition to civil rights and strip mine legislation, Prichard was always a vocal advocate for increased funding for education. Breathitt appointed him to a commission to form a state Council on Higher Education. In deciding whom to appoint to the council, Breathitt admitted that he considered other factors: "I had a guilt feeling about what time he had devoted to me and not to his family." Realizing that the only thing he could give back to Prichard was recognition, Breathitt appointed Ed Prichard to the council shortly after its formation. But Breathitt did not make the appointment solely out of "guilt" or as a personal favor. The governor also knew Prichard possessed certain abilities that made him ideal for the post. "We had to have someone who could see what the state needed," Breathitt said, "where it should be, and what the budget could stand, someone intellectually strong enough to stand up to the college presidents." In retrospect, Breathitt concluded, "Prich proved to be that man." Prichard's appointment was one of the seminal moments in the history of educational reform in Kentucky.[27]

The greater part of Prichard's time in 1966, however, was devoted to his role in rewriting Kentucky's constitution. He felt strongly that the state's ruling charter, written in 1891 by an assembly anxious to put clamps on governmental power, was now an anachronism. In his committee assignments and in the revision assembly itself, he threw himself into the once-in-a-lifetime fight to overhaul the outmoded document. It quickly became a mostly futile and frustrating cause.

The assembly allowed Prichard a challenging intellectual task. He had long been a serious student of both the U.S. and the Kentucky constitution, and he had gained a unique education in the study of constitutional law at Harvard and through his work for Frankfurter at the Supreme Court. Although he paid little serious attention to the more mundane practice of law, Prichard had spent many evenings in various Frankfort apartments reading advance sheets of federal court decisions. He told his law partners that the federal courts were the cutting edge of constitutional law, whereas the Supreme Court usually heard appeals. In a sense, then, Prichard's days with Phil Graham and Felix Frankfurter in Cambridge and Washington, arguing the great constitutional issues of the day, had never left him. He had always remained attentive to state and federal constitutional matters.[28]

In ways that he perhaps did not fully understand at the time, Prichard advanced one clause of the revised document that had special meaning. In discussions about a proposed Bill of Rights, Prichard advocated a section in the new charter that prohibited any type of electronic surveillance. Prichard knew that FBI transcripts of his telephone conversations in Washington existed, and he was especially sensitive to this issue. All electronic surveillance, according to Prichard, was "perfectly abominable." The assembly decided, nevertheless, not to include the provision in the Bill of Rights section of the new charter.[29]

During debates, Prichard resorted to an oratory that sometimes transcended the ordinary. During one exchange concerning the Kentucky Department of Education, he argued that the school bureaucracy had become too powerful and thundered with righteous anger that it had become "imperium in imperio." To journalist Bill Greider, such phrases were part of what made Prichard such a singular figure. "He took what was a fairly mundane and crass political issue and raised it to Churchillian oratory." But Greider was with him not long afterward when the other side to Prichard's past was again opened. While the two were having a drink in a Frankfort restaurant, a stranger approached, stopped, and yelled, "I know you. You're the guy that went to prison." The restaurant grew quiet, and Prichard sat still, hoping the boorish patron would soon leave. It was an all-too-frequent reminder of a past that always haunted him.[30]

During committee meetings, it was apparent that Prichard was the intellectual force of the assembly. He was knowledgeable of the history of Kentucky's previous constitutions, familiar with numerous other state constitutions, and was even aware of proposed changes under consideration in other states. Part of what frustrated Prichard about the current constitution was that so many local and state offices were elective rather than appointive. Prichard was successful in getting the assembly to adopt a measure calling for offices such as the superintendent of public instruction to be positions appointed by the governor.[31]

Prichard's efforts in revising Kentucky's constitution provide a unique glimpse into his paradoxical notions of governing. While committed to such democratic causes as civil rights, the labor movement, and economic equality, he also held a certain distrust of the raw stuff of democracy. In centralizing power in an executive, Prichard remained true to his career, which had always been in either the executive or the judicial branch. He was more comfortable advising Supreme Court justices, appointed wartime executives, and one-term governors who had little need to worry about popular consent, than in putting himself or his policies in the public arena where they could be rejected by an uncooperative legislature or a fickle electorate. This deeply embedded view saw "the people" as somewhat tangential to the democratic process and as sometimes needing to be manipulated for their own good. Such notions, which had animated the precinct officer in 1948, had not completely evaporated over the years.

Even during some detailed committee debate, there were flashes of the unique personality that endeared Prichard to some and infuriated others. During a discussion on the composition of the General Assembly, Prichard relied on his storehouse of Bourbon County stories to drive home the point that the state legislature was unduly looked down upon by the public. He recalled that when he was six years old, he had gone to church one day when the prayer was offered by a local minister. "He prayed for the missionaries and he prayed for the bigots and he prayed for the heathens and then he prayed for the President and prayed for the Congress and he prayed for the Supreme Court," Prichard said, "and he prayed for the Governor and then he began in an inspired tone, 'Oh, Lord, bless the Legislature, if possible.'"[32]

As the assembly hammered out its new charter, Prichard was at the forefront, urging members to adopt measures that would significantly change the state's governmental structure. But, again, the time necessary to do this work took a great deal from his private life. He continued to have imposing IRS debts and little income. The financial pressure even made him consider some work that seemed to present another moral dilemma. In June 1966, he received some correspondence between Rodgers Badgett, the owner of a western Kentucky strip mine, and James F. Gordon, a federal judge in Louisville. Gordon had been asked by Badgett who would make an effective lobbyist for Badgett in Frankfort, considering the "political problems of the strip operators." Gordon replied that Ed Prichard possessed the "best legal mind" in Kentucky and had represented "special groups in matters of this type" before. Prichard badly needed the money involved in lobbying for strip miners but was well aware of how this work would be perceived, considering that he had been one of the principal architects of the anti–strip mine legislation earlier in the year. When he confided in Earle Clements about Gordon's "exceedingly kind and generous efforts," he asked Clements to keep the information in the "strictest confidence."[33] He did not want the Breathitt administration alerted that he now represented the strip mining industry. While the attorney Prichard could rationalize taking the retainer, the politician Prichard had a much harder time justifying accepting Badgett's offer.

While Prichard's willingness to accept money from an industry he apparently despised remained confidential, his leadership in the assembly allowed opponents of the revision effort to exploit his all-too-public past. In the eyes of some Kentuckians, Ed Prichard's advocacy of a new constitution was reason enough to oppose the effort. "I have studied Prichard's record and qualifications rather carefully," said one editorialist, "and I cannot see that he is any better qualified as an expert on state constitutions than I am." Another disgruntled letter written to Lt. Gov. Harry Lee Waterfield likened Prichard to the "Jews" and other socialists who wanted to eliminate all forms of local government. In such a likelihood, the man "running the show probably won't be from Kentucky, and his name will end in a 'ski.'"[34]

The extent to which Prichard was vulnerable can be seen in letters sent to W.C. Flannery, the county judge of Rowan County. Flannery, who was staunchly opposed to the revision assembly, received a letter one day from a friend, Ken Toomey, who wrote Flannery that he was good friends with Prichard's uncle, Tom. In Toomey's words, Tom "hates Ed Prichard's guts as no one else!" If supplied with "a few dollars to help supplement his inadequate and meager pension," Toomey was certain Tom Prichard could tell a "tremendous story that will kill Ed Prichard and the revised constitution." Whatever information was obtained from Uncle Tom was gladly received by Flannery, who sent a packet on Prichard to other county judges. Flannery wrote the judges that Prichard was "well educated in how to deprive the people the right to elect and a exclent [sic] character to repisent [sic] our future generations. . . . I have the full record which I have obtained if you need it. No wonder he is not satisfyed [sic] with our present day courts."[35]

The assembly finished its work in the summer of 1966, and the revised constitution was submitted to the voters for the November ballot. More than two-thirds of the new charter incorporated sections of the existing one. The major alterations were lengthened terms for members of the General Assembly; an annual session of the legislature; gubernatorial succession; a unified court system headed by a Supreme Court; and a general reordering of local government. The last item was one of the most controversial. In fact, the new charter sought to decrease the power of local "courthouse crowds" that Prichard had known so well since he was a child.[36]

Prichard not only took a leading role in drafting the new constitution but also became one of the revised charter's principal spokesmen as the referendum date approached. Not surprisingly, one of the leading opponents of the revised constitution was a member of the constitutional assembly itself—Happy Chandler. Chandler offered bland excuses as to his sudden change of heart. One of his primary reasons for opposing the new constitution was that he had been placed on the Bill of Rights committee, "notwithstanding the fact that his greatest asset would have been to the Executive Branch since he had been twice Governor," a Chandler aide wrote.[37]

The opposition to the new constitution was well organized and well financed. Two organizations that sought to defeat the referendum were the "Save Your Local Government Committee" and the Kentucky Sheriffs Association. In a mailing sent throughout the state, these two groups included the following direct quote from Prichard:

> MR. PRICHARD: Now as to the coroner. I don't believe anybody really believes that you are going to upgrade the office of coroner by leaving it an elective office. And—I don't know—maybe in some places the people are jealous and alert and aware and dying to elect coroners but most towns I have been in they regard it as a great bore and causes perennial contests between body snatchers. . . . The sheriff is a tax collector and why should the tax collector be an elective officer?[38]

Such biting remarks, made in the heat of assembly debate, were not well taken by the thousands of local officials, who saw such comments as outright attacks on the very basis of their power.

Other organizations bespoke other fears of the proposed change. Marion Vance of Glasgow, vice president of Kentucky Heritage, Inc., wrote that the new constitution would abolish the present "Democratic system and establish the marxist system." It had become standard procedure by this time, particularly in the South, for conservatives to equate any progressive cause ultimately with communism. Vance's newsletter condemned the abolition of numerous elective county and state offices as evidence of "how the Marxists in control of the re-writing of the Kentucky Constitution would trick the innocent people . . . and centralize authority." Vance even objected to the clause outlawing wiretapping, since it was obviously written "so the U.S. Security agents cannot have surveillance over the Communists' operations headquarters in Kentucky!"[39]

In television debates, personal appearances, and newspaper coverage, Prichard became the leading voice supporting the new charter. At an appearance at Murray State University, he was not afraid to make grand pronouncements. On whether he wanted a more powerful governor or legislature, Prichard responded he would rather see a powerful governor than an all-powerful legislature "dominated by a group or clique of lobbyists representing special interests. . . . If I had to choose, I would take executive supremacy anytime over lobby supremacy." Prichard neglected to mention his own attempts at lobbying the legislature. In an entertaining speech peppered with stories and booming oratory, an out-of-breath Prichard ended by stating that his greatest fear was not losing the referendum but that the public's apathy would cause the referendum to go down to defeat by special interests.[40]

As the day of the referendum approached, Prichard continued his role as the convention's leading spokesman. The *Courier-Journal* ran a full-page discussion between Prichard and Joseph Leary, an attorney opposed to the referendum. Leary took issue with Prichard that the new document was a "conservative, careful document" and that those who opposed the charter "are fighting against a progressive constitution" and "have axes to grind and selfish interests to serve." Leary repeated the claims that the new document would centralize power, destroy local government, and erode personal freedom.[41]

Prichard's visibility, however, worried a number of pro-revision supporters. C. Gibson Downing, in fact, wrote to Governor Breathitt that "unfortunately, as a practical matter, the continued . . . appearances of Mr. Prichard as a leading advocate of the proposed revisions . . . continue to damage rather than help the effort." Downing hoped the governor could get Earle Clements to "impress on Mr. Prichard the damage which most of us feel he is doing" and will "secure his agreement to cease making public statements, cease appearing in public debates and cease making television appearances."[42]

Prichard's visibility did indeed subside, but it made little difference. By claiming that the new document would raise taxes and "destroy local government," the forces against it gained the upper hand. On election day the new constitution suffered a blistering defeat, losing in all 120 counties. The final vote tally was 140,210 for revision and 510,099 against, the revisionists receiving a scant 21 percent of the vote. It proved a humiliating and devastating defeat for Prichard and for constitutional reformers.[43]

The loss sent Prichard into another spiral of depression. But at least the past two years had seen his very visible return to the political arena, and he had had some major triumphs—the civil rights bill among them. Additionally, he reveled in the fact that one of his old protégés was in the White House, sponsoring a series of Great Society programs that promised to accentuate the New Deal legacy of FDR. Breathitt's appointment of Prichard to several committees and boards had also done a great deal to return Prichard to some political prominence. Of all the new tasks Prichard undertook, including the revision assembly, none would eventually prove as significant as his appointment to the Kentucky Council on Higher Education. Prichard's days as an education reformer were born in the midst of his failure to revise the state constitution. But it would be years before the fruit of his education efforts would be seen. For the time being, his newfound political rehabilitation only partially offset his continuing personal and financial problems.

14 "Picking up the Pieces"

NED Breathitt's final months as governor in 1967 marked yet another crucial point in Ed Prichard's redemptive odyssey. For eight years, he had been a close confidant of two successive Democratic governors who, in turn, had provided him entrée back into the political world of Kentucky. But the gubernatorial election of 1967 would drastically change Prichard's personal, political, and financial prospects. If a Republican won the governor's office, he would have to concentrate on earning a living and have to face his daunting IRS debt without any governmental distractions. Throughout it all, Prichard lived with the certain memory that he had failed in such attempts in the 1950s.

In his broken personal life, Prichard continued as a semibachelor, sharing efficiency apartments with other attorneys in Frankfort. Observers noted that the relationship between Prichard and Lucy by this time had grown increasingly distant and cold. Friends, in fact, wondered aloud what kept Lucy from filing for divorce. She certainly had ample reason to be angry. Over the past two decades, her husband had proved an abject failure at providing the family a livable income. His periods of submerging and working for months within various political campaigns for no money may have helped Prichard's own sense of worth, but they proved of little value to his wife and three children. Lucy kept the marriage intact but was not willing to welcome her husband back home until he got back on his financial and personal feet. But Prichard's financial problems only mounted. His IRS liens continued, and as of January 1, 1967, he still owed more than $700,000 in back taxes. Since the first liens placed on him in 1960, he had been able to discharge only $54,533.88 of his accumulated debt over the following seven years.[1] Now he had to bear other financial considerations—his oldest son, Allen, was preparing to enter college in the fall of 1967 at the University of North Carolina at Chapel Hill, and Nathan and Louis were just a few years away from college themselves.

On the political scene, the 1967 gubernatorial election approached and the Democratic primary field was wide open. In the tumultuous political milieu of that year, the legacy of the Breathitt administration proved a liability among conservative and wary voters. As expected, Happy Chandler announced that he was going to run for a third term, and Highway Commissioner Henry

Ward and Lt. Gov. Harry Lee Waterfield also entered the race. Among the Breathitt loyalists, no one emerged to carry the mantle of the Combs-Breathitt years to their satisfaction. Rumors ran rampant that Combs himself might enter the fray, but instead he deferred to take a federal judgeship. Eventually, Breathitt and Combs endorsed the colorless Ward, who won the May primary rather easily over an increasingly bitter and inefficacious Chandler. The Republicans, meanwhile, once again chose Louie Nunn of Glasgow, the man whom Breathitt had narrowly defeated four years earlier.

For Prichard, the candidacy of Henry Ward offered little to him or the party. Ward had a sterling reputation as an effective administrator of the state parks and highways but was a rather bland campaigner who excited few in his defense of the Combs-Breathitt years. Louie Nunn, on the other hand, had the experience of 1963 behind him and offered the Republicans their first real opportunity to win the governorship in six elections. Nunn seized on the tumultuous events gripping the country in 1967 to promise a "law and order" response to civil rights advocates and war protestors in Kentucky. Ward was clearly out of his league responding to such emotionally charged issues. Neither Ward nor the Democratic candidate for lieutenant governor, Wendell Ford, promised to enlarge or sustain the momentum created by the eight years of leadership of which Prichard had been such a crucial part. Indeed, the Democratic ticket seemed to suggest a step backward, and accordingly Prichard looked upon the 1967 general election with considerable trepidation.

It was during late July 1967 that Prichard and attorney Marvin Coles were walking in downtown Frankfort and overheard the news that Judge William B. Ardery had died in Paris. Since the Prichard trial, Judge Ardery's reputation in central Kentucky had grown to considerable proportions. In the 1950s, the city of Paris officially renamed the street adjacent to the county courthouse "Ardery Place," and in 1954 the state bar association designated Ardery the outstanding circuit judge in the state. He was widely mourned as an honest and fair judge, and as one of the state's leading citizens. Ed Prichard, on the other hand, had different feelings. He felt that Judge Ardery had betrayed him in 1949. When he drove past the Ardery house outside Paris once, Prichard caustically mentioned to a passenger, "A famous conversation occurred there, and I've regretted it ever since." In the ensuing years, Prichard's animosity toward both Judge and Phil Ardery had not lessened. Upon hearing of Judge Ardery's death, he remarked to Coles, "I can't say that I disapprove."[2]

Prichard's active involvement in the Ward campaign was certainly not to the extent he had earlier played in the campaigns of Combs, Wyatt, and Breathitt. He was brought into the headquarters late in the fall campaign, but he exercised only a limited role in Ward's faltering candidacy. Compounding Ward's difficulties was the fact that the state's Democrats were again split. As he had often done in the past, Happy Chandler endorsed the Republicans. Some loyal Democrats simply could not become very enthusiastic about a Ward administration, and it showed. On election day, Democrats throughout the state suffered their first major gubernatorial loss since 1943 as Nunn defeated Ward by nearly thirty thousand votes. Wendell Ford won the lieutenant governor's race, and in the process became the titular head of the state Democratic party.[3]

In retrospect, Louie Nunn's victory in 1967 could not have occurred at a better time for Ed Prichard. The loss meant that he would be forced to return to the private practice of law—he could no longer use the excuse of state politics to occupy large portions of his time. Almost thirty years after receiving his law degree, Ed Prichard was finally ready to apply his considerable legal talents to the daily task of making a living as an attorney. Ironically, Louie Nunn's administration subsequently brought a great deal of business to Frankfort attorneys who knew both law and politics. In a strange twist of fate, as it turned out, Nunn may have unintentionally done as much to aid Prichard in his personal renaissance as did either Bert Combs or Ned Breathitt.

A month following the election, Prichard underwent back surgery at the Cleveland Clinic. The convalescence had one beneficial effect—it caused him to lose weight. Prichard claimed he had lost more than seventy pounds, and that he had not weighed under two hundred pounds since he was fifteen. He confided to Earle Clements that at the root of his back problem "was a deep emotional depression resulting from the defeat of the New Constitution at the 1966 election." In his first major public role since Ashland, his work in redoing the Kentucky constitution had placed his self-confidence in a highly vulnerable position. Prichard interpreted the staggering defeat of the assembly's work by the voters as a personal rejection that sent him into another round of depression.[4]

Close friends noticed that Prichard had displayed symptoms of clinical depression over the years, and the late 1960s were certainly very dark years. He had lost Phil Graham, Felix Frankfurter, and his father in the span of a little over two years, and he had to cope with his own mortality as his diabetes worsened. With his ubiquitous indebtedness and new loneliness came yet another personal tragedy—his son Louie was diagnosed during this period with cancer. Doctors were able to treat Louie's condition successfully, but his illness was a constant worry for both his parents.[5] The aggregate worries of personal, financial, and political losses took their toll on Prichard's health. It is no wonder, as he said to Clements, that he was depressed and his health was failing. How he would manage, no one knew for sure.

As governors do who come into office on the heels of a long-entrenched incumbency, Nunn sought to exert the enormous patronage that came from the governor's office, since Democrats had for decades secured the wealth of state jobs all the way down to the county level. Nunn could, of course, fire all Democratic executive appointments and replace them with individuals loyal to him and the Republican party. But replacing a range of state employees—workers on road crews, for example—proved much more difficult. The Combs administration had passed the state's first widespread merit system, whereby a number of state employees could not be fired for merely political reasons, as had been the case since time immemorial in Kentucky. Prichard found the implementation of the merit system to be one of the most significant accomplishments of the Combs years. The greatest change, according to Prichard, came in the fact that state employees could no longer be threatened with dismissal if they did not vote a particular way.[6]

Governor Nunn, however, felt differently. When the Highway Department fired nearly twenty county road workers in early 1968, it appeared that the new governor was flagrantly ignoring the merit system law. After more workers were fired, the disgruntled former employees hired Prichard to sue the state government for back wages. Despite his unimpressive legal career to this point, the workers knew that no one was more familiar with the merit law than Prichard. Over the next several years, he and his young law associates labored over the case as it made its way through several layers of state courts. At stake was whether the merit system could legally withstand gubernatorial assault, as well as eventually millions of dollars owed to the former employees, which promised a lucrative payoff for the attorneys involved. Another more personal question that worried those who knew Prichard was whether he would accept the full responsibility of the case and see it through or submerge himself in hotel rooms while the case languished.

A series of young lawyers, virtually all of them recent graduates of the University of Kentucky Law School, came to work in the Prichard law office in the late 1960s. Prichard's fledgling practice moved to a cramped, unassuming perch on the second floor of an old building on Main Street in Frankfort. Attorneys such as Jim Hudson, Marvin Coles, Joseph Terry, Phillip Shepherd, and William Graham worked with Prichard, and as a sign of the enormous respect in which they held their boss, they often referred to themselves as Prichard's "clerks."

The law office began to take on a whole new light to Ed Prichard, who became emotionally and intellectually involved in his law practice, determined this time to make a successful living. Roommates recall him parking his girth in the bathtub, his weight displacing water all over the floor, and spending hours in a tub of hot water, smoking a cigar and reading the briefs of appellate court decisions and other law books. His memory, they well knew, digested each case with exact precision. Prichard's office consequently needed few law books, one clerk recalled, because Prichard remembered thousands of cases in such detail that he simply did not need them.[7]

Also typically, some of Prichard's well-connected friends wanted to help him obtain legal work. The same process had been attempted in the aftermath of Ashland, but Prichard simply had not been ready in the 1950s to devote himself to such mundane legal chores. This time, he enthusiastically accepted the assignments. Ned Breathitt, for example, went to Washington after leaving Frankfort and worked for the Southern Railroad. From this post, he secured a sizable retainer for Prichard that endured for many years. Prichard also began representing a large Kentucky insurance company, whose president paid Prichard with a considerable amount of company stock.[8]

During 1968, the events engulfing Lyndon Johnson were not lost on Prichard. "I do not believe there is anyone in Kentucky who has known him and been on fairly close terms with him over a longer period of time than I," he claimed. As the specter of Vietnam consumed LBJ's presidency, Prichard refused to support insurgent elements within the Democratic party designed to "Dump Johnson" from the party's nomination. Instead, he remained loyal to his New Deal protégé: "It greatly angers me to see some of my old friends adopting a double standard aimed at blaming all our adversities on President Johnson while apologizing for and glossing over the steps taken by his predecessors which made our present involvement almost inevitable." Prichard claimed that the criticism launched at Johnson was essentially "dirty pool."[9]

After LBJ announced he would not run for reelection in March 1968, the president told Ned Breathitt one day in an aside that he would like to see Prichard. "Naturally, I was greatly pleased," Prichard remarked, "and was touched at the President's concern for me." Breathitt was told by Johnson to call his White House staff and arrange an appropriate time to bring Prichard to the Oval Office. By the time this was arranged, Robert F. Kennedy's assassination gripped the White House, and Johnson and his staff were confronted with more pressing matters. Breathitt consequently never tried to arrange the meeting after the Kennedy funeral. "I have nudged him once or twice," Prichard said of Breathitt, but relented. "I know the President is extremely busy and I cannot imagine that he would appreciate being dogged and deviled about a matter of this sort," Prichard wrote Clements. Prichard nonetheless hoped Clements could use his influence with LBJ to arrange a meeting, but Clements, too, failed, and a disappointed Prichard missed an opportunity to sit with Johnson in the Oval Office. What Prichard wanted so badly to discuss with the president is unknown, but it seems likely it had to do with more than reminiscing and telling stories. In August, when Prichard learned that Breathitt had arranged for a possible state dinner with Prichard in attendance, he remained disappointed. A state dinner, he wrote, "is nice but I don't think it will butter any potatoes." Prichard implied to Clements that he hoped a presidential meeting might develop into some legal opportunities that "might have proved beneficial to me." Just as he had done before Ashland, Prichard, it seems, was once again seeking to use his Washington connections—this time no less than the president of the United States—to secure lucrative legal work.[10]

Prichard later told Earle Clements of his views concerning the historical legacy of LBJ: "I believe that President Johnson will, in due time, receive a just and deserved appreciation from the historians and the American people." Prichard was well aware that Vietnam was a singular tragedy that would affect LBJ's legacy, but he saw another side—Johnson's "leadership in the fields of civil liberties, social legislation and other progressive causes brought about an enduring change in our society, mostly for the better." Despite the president's increasing unpopularity, Prichard refused to speak harshly about him: "He was always my friend and champion . . . he stood by me with great steadness[sic], in periods of adversity, echoing the words of the old hymn that we used to sing: 'I shall not fear to own his cause or blush to speak his name.'"[11]

Prichard's weight loss in early 1968 belied the fact that years of obesity coupled with his diabetes had seriously damaged his health. By early summer, he complained that he still had little energy and did not "feel especially well." The news worsened when he learned the cause of his increasing vision problems. Doctors discovered that his right eye had glaucoma and feared that he would lose sight in that eye. Because of the devastating impact diabetes can have on the tiny blood vessels in the eye, the disease is often directly related to such eye problems. Doctors advise diabetic patients to follow a controlled diet, maintain a normal weight, exercise, and not smoke, yet Prichard had broken all of these rules in the years following his original diagnosis. By the late 1960s, his health had become as great a burden on his morale as his tax problems had earlier been. "I am plugging along the best I can under the circumstances," he lamented to Clements.[12]

What is extraordinary about this period in Prichard's life is his newfound resiliency. As his health declined, he no longer fell into spells of submerging his problems beneath a pile of books and magazines in a Louisville hotel room. Instead, he directed his energies toward work, and no one around him noticed any self-pity or depression. Indeed, as he battled the glaucoma and his general fatigue, Prichard hustled as he had in 1946 for lucrative clients, and, not surprisingly, he turned to the figure of "Tommy the Cork" Corcoran for help. By this time, Corcoran was a partner in the powerful firm of Corcoran, Foley, Youngman, and Rowe, one of best-connected firms in Washington. James Rowe was another of Prichard's longtime associates, and Robert Amory Jr., who had attended law school with Prichard, also worked in the firm.

Corcoran once again came to Prichard's aid by sending him the case of a northern Kentucky shopping center that needed representation over a dispute with the state highway department. The case was significant to Prichard because, in words revealing the strain a decade of IRS problems had caused. "If the fee is substantial, it can help me materially in getting the government off my back."[13]

While Prichard continued to seek new clients, he could not ignore presidential politics in the 1968 election. He lamented with Joe Rauh over "the bloody and pitiful Chicago convention" and predicted "there is no way on earth Nixon can be defeated this fall." Calling the upcoming election the "worst slaughter of the innocent . . . in more than a quarter of a century," Prichard told Rauh he had not become more conservative as the years had progressed. With Johnson now out of the way, Prichard confided that had he been a delegate to the convention, he would have supported antiwar candidate George McGovern. "See how impractical I have become?" asked Prichard. But always the loyal Democrat, he campaigned when he could for Hubert Humphrey, including making several speeches and offering "a financial contribution which was not very large but more than I could afford, and gave whatever advice and assistance was sought" to the Humphrey campaign. In November, election returns brought the worst possible news. With the election of Richard Nixon, with Kentucky's two Senate seats held by Republicans, and with Louie Nunn in the governor's office, Prichard said sadly, "Here we are where we are and all I know to do is pick up the pieces and start from here."[14]

Picking up the pieces was a metaphor Prichard could have used to describe more than just the Democratic party's position in 1969—it also described a process that had been under way in his own personal and professional life for almost twenty years. Ironically, although he had dismissed legal work for unpaid political assignments for so many years, his law practice now gave Prichard the day-to-day respite from his increasing personal problems. Financially, new liens came from the IRS in the late 1960s, totaling more than $775,000 in back taxes. Despite the fact Prichard had made little income during those years "in the wilderness," his past partnership with his father's varied businesses and those associated tax problems, coupled with his own inability to manage his finances, had made his mounting tax bill overwhelming. Even a figure from Prichard's past was confronted with charges of financial impropriety on Prichard's part. Phil Ardery, who was now practicing law in Louisville, claimed that a client of Prichard's came to him seeking to sue Prichard. In Ardery's recollection, Prichard had not remitted the client $5,000 owed in a divorce settlement. Although Ardery refused to bring suit and the state bar took no formal action against Prichard, law partners and roommates admitted that Prichard was not above "floating" checks from clients from time to time—that is, using money intended for a client to pay his own bills, hoping in time to recover other fees that then could be used to compensate the client.[15]

Despite his nagging financial problems, Prichard's legal career gained wings as he approached his fifty-fifth birthday. By 1970, eager clients began to drift Prichard's way. Owing to his past associations and his obviously brilliant mind, a number of individuals and corporations sought his advice and counsel, convinced now that his history of irresponsibility was behind him. But there were still hurdles for the relatively unknown barrister. An illustrative example occurred shortly before Johnson left office. An Italian mining firm needed Prichard's help in settling a problem with the Justice Department, so Prichard and Marvin Coles went to Cincinnati to meet with some department officials. By this time, Prichard had allowed his hair to grow over his ears, and his usual unkempt suits seemed sloppier than ever. Additionally, his bad eye was puffy and discharged fluid. When he arrived at the government office in Cincinnati, a receptionist took one look at the strange figure before her and told him to sit down and his immigration case would be heard. Over Prichard's objections, the receptionist refused to budge. Outraged and humiliated, Prichard ordered Coles to drive him back to Frankfort at once. Upon their return, Coles watched as Prichard asked his secretary to call the attorney general's office in Washington, so he could speak directly with Ramsey Clark. Within a few minutes, Prichard was on the phone, telling Clark of the treatment he had received in Cincinnati. The next day, Coles observed, Justice Department officials came to confer with Prichard in *his* office. "I think those Italians are still mining down there to this day," laughed Coles.[16]

For the first time, Prichard applied in the courtroom the experience he had first acquired by watching lawyers argue their cases in the Bourbon County courthouse in the early 1920s. When he entered a courtroom, opposing lawyers were often stunned to see the shuffling figure come and sit at a table barren of any books or notepads. Some lawyers may even have fallen into the trap, as Prichard's teachers and professors had, of assuming that the person before them, whose head was slumped and eyes tightly closed, was either sleeping or not paying close attention to the arguments at hand. Only when Prichard raised his head did his opponents learn of his photographic memory, his razor-sharp debating skills, and his eloquent and persuasive oratory. "After half a century of totally undisciplined life in which my law practice came after everything else," Prichard observed, "I've proven an old dog can learn new tricks." William Graham, echoing the words of many other lawyers, later said that from his experiences as a judge, had Prichard applied himself to the courtroom after law school instead to politics, he could have been one of the country's most formidable and richest trial attorneys.[17]

The bulk of Prichard's legal work in the early 1970s was devoted to the

cause of the fired state employees. He had successfully presented his case before Franklin Circuit Judge Henry Meigs, who ruled that the state personnel
board had violated the statutes relating to the merit system and ordered the
workers reinstated with back pay. The state then appealed the case to the Kentucky Court of Appeals in early 1970. Although only twenty-two workers were
involved in the suit itself, a favorable ruling by the Appeals Court promised
to bring a flood of back-pay requests from hundreds of other workers fired by
the Nunn administration.

On June 26, 1970, the Appeals Court handed down its ruling in favor of
Prichard's clients and in the process brought judicial sanction to the Kentucky
state merit system. The court ruled that "the discharges were motivated by
political reasons," and added, "it would be difficult for a reasonable man to
reach any other conclusion." The ruling awarded the fired workers more than
$220,000 in back pay. For Ed Prichard, who received 30 percent of the award,
it was the first big payday in more than two decades. More clients came
Prichard's way soon thereafter as more than 200 fired state workers hired him
in filing a class-action suit claiming similar circumstances.[18]

Young attorneys like Coles, Hudson, and William Graham were helpful
to Prichard in preparing the merit system case and seeing it through. Graham
had first encountered Prichard when a Frankfort theater showed a film containing nudity, and local ministers and politicians wanted to pass an ordinance
forbidding such films in their community. Prichard defended the first amendment in a town meeting that Graham attended, at which the young law student was immediately impressed by Prichard's eloquent and forceful oratory.
When Graham graduated from the University of Kentucky Law School, he
worked for Prichard for several years. He soon developed a pattern with his
boss whereby he would drive Prichard to the office. By 1971, glaucoma had
finally wrecked the sight in Prichard's right eye, and it was removed and replaced with a glass eye. Prichard continued to drive despite his impaired vision, but after he opened his car door into the path of an oncoming car that
tore the door off its hinges, Prichard allowed Graham and others to drive him
to his destination.[19]

What struck these young lawyers working with Ed Prichard on a daily basis
was his unflagging commitment to work. They had not known him in the years
after Ashland, when he would allow cases to slip by or not attend scheduled
meetings or court dates. What they saw, in Graham's words, was a special attorney who simply "had a gift for it." With his mind's vast storehouse, Prichard
was indispensable for researching a difficult case, and his celebrated oratorical skills were singular. Prichard knew instinctively "how to get up in front of
people and persuade them," commented Graham. As Frankfurter had
mentored him when he was a young man just out of law school, Prichard be-

came a mentor for a number of bright, young legal minds. Graham recalled a typical episode that continued his legal education: "I could spend all day researching some question for a brief and come in and discuss it with him and he could just tell me cases that I had overlooked."[20]

In a sense, Prichard's new devotion to the practice of law was a hurried attempt to make up for lost time. By the early 1970s, all three of his sons were in college, and mounting tuition bills only added to his financial burdens. All of the Prichards' sons grew up under Lucy's care as their father spent his "wandering in the wilderness" years. The tasks of childrearing were borne by Lucy, who did so with considerable success. All three enrolled in fine colleges and seemed set for successful careers of their own. After Allen graduated from the University of North Carolina in 1971, he began law school at Georgetown University. Nathan followed his father's course to Princeton. Louie, meanwhile, enrolled at Centre College, his grandfather's alma mater.

But lapses of the old Prichard sometimes occurred. As had been the case at Princeton and throughout his life, he simply did not bother to budget money. His early office finances were in utter disarray, and only after he hired a secretary to look after the bills did they begin to make sense. The IRS, meanwhile, would not go away. Agents often came to the law office on Main Street seeking Prichard in person to discuss his tax problems. When an agent arrived, Prichard often hid in the law library of his office, pathetically asking associates, "Is he gone yet?"[21] The day he would be free of all tax obligations, it seemed, remained far away.

Although law now consumed the lion's share of Prichard's time, politics was never out of the question. In 1971, he worked in a more limited way in Bert Combs's third bid for governor. The two old warhorses shared one last campaign, which ended in May when Combs lost the primary to Lt. Gov. Wendell Ford, whose more moderate form of Democratic politics meant that Prichard would have less influence with the new governor than he had had with either Combs or Breathitt.

Throughout the years following Nunn's election, Prichard also remained actively involved in the state Council on Higher Education, to which Breathitt had first appointed him in 1966. While some may have viewed the council as a ceremonial body, Prichard saw it as an opportunity to have an impact on a segment of Kentucky life that would have a lasting effect. The state's universities had long been the recipients of only limited state support, and the primary tie the people of Kentucky had for the University of Kentucky remained its athletic teams. The salaries of professors, institutional support, the physical plant, and the research productivity of the state's "flagship" university all remained well behind that of other comparable regional systems. Few issues struck such an impassioned response in Ed Prichard as educational reform.

What had started in Lee Kirkpatrick's schools in Paris in the 1920s remained with Prichard throughout his life—a determination to seek excellence in all modes of education as "a path to a better life," as he later put it. With the exception of a period when Louie Nunn failed to reappoint Prichard, he was an integral part of the council and helped make it a vital part of a statewide reform effort designed to overhaul the entire school system.

When Combs returned to law practice following the 1971 primary, he began to call on Prichard's legal advice as he had once called on his political advice. Combs joined a powerhouse Louisville law firm that held numerous corporate contracts, particularly with coal operators. On especially difficult cases, Combs relied upon the legal mind of Ed Prichard. When a mine explosion in Leslie County, Kentucky, killed thirty-eight miners in December 1970, the mine's owners, Charles and Stanley Finley, hired Combs to defend them. The Finleys were charged with various mine violations that could have resulted in lengthy prison sentences and stiff fines. Combs quickly sought the advice of Ed Prichard on this case. With the caseload provided by Breathitt and Combs, supplemented by the ongoing class-action suit against the state by the fired state workers, Prichard began to make a reliable and steadily increasing income for the first time in almost twenty-five years. More important, he finally displayed the professional and emotional responsibility and maturity his friends had hoped for in the 1940s.[22]

By the early 1970s, the bitterness that had racked Ed and Lucy's marriage subsided somewhat, and they were finally reconciled. Lucy knew that her husband needed considerable help now with his worsening vision problems, and his financial recovery displayed that he had somewhat changed his colors. After living for almost a decade in small apartments in Frankfort, Prichard moved back to Woodford County to live at Heartland. The years of estrangement, however, could not hide Lucy's resentment toward her husband at the pain she felt he had caused her and their sons. Her latent anger with Prichard never completely subsided. "Lucy has a temper," Prichard admitted, "and she is a dominant person." Old frustrations did not disappear. Prichard's inability to control his weight irritated Lucy, who once commented that she only wished he looked at her with the same loving desire he displayed when opening a refrigerator. While the marriage was never again close, there was no doubt in anyone's mind that Prichard was dedicated to his sons. He was visibly proud of their educational attainments and never once hesitated to give "the boys" any available money. Although he earned enough to write three separate tuition checks each semester, the IRS still loomed.[23]

There remained instances in which Prichard's once-luminary position within national politics shone through. In 1973, shortly after the death of Lyndon Johnson, Lady Bird Johnson invited Ed and Lucy to the LBJ Ranch in Texas. Before attending a function in New Orleans with Breathitt for the Southern Railroad, the Prichards flew to Austin, where they were driven to the Johnson ranch and spent the night with the former first lady. Lady Bird later fondly recalled that during the Prichards' visit, the three "had many sweet-sad reminiscences."[24]

But just as his financial situation began to improve, Prichard's left eye began showing signs of deterioration. Reading became a more labored exercise, requiring more light and more concentration. To a man who loved reading as much as Prichard, this was perhaps the cruelest blow of all. Throughout his life, books had been a respite from loneliness, stress, and depression, and the gradual loss of sight in his remaining eye proved almost unbearable. By 1973, he began laser treatments at the University of Kentucky Medical Center for his left eye to remove scar tissue. When these treatments did not halt his increasing blindness, Katharine Graham interceded to get Prichard an appointment with a renowned eye specialist at Johns Hopkins. But after examining Prichard in Baltimore, doctors there could not provide him any relief. Prichard's failing eyesight was not a cause for self-pity, although he admitted that his eyesight was "chafing, irritating, and sometimes discouraging."[25] As he approached his sixtieth birthday he did not look like a sick man. His full head of dark hair remained, and his face was unwrinkled and youthful looking, although years of obesity had loosened his skin, and his chin sagged well beneath his collar.

But personal tragedies continued to dog Prichard and Lucy. Prichard's mother, Allene, developed Alzheimer's disease, and her once-vibrant mind became cloudy. As Allene's health continued to deteriorate in the 1970s, her condition worsened to the point that Prichard's brother Henry, who had become a successful songwriter and musician in Hollywood, returned to Kentucky to help care for his ailing mother. Henry later took Allene with him to California, where she lived in La Jolla, never to see her oldest son again.[26] Moreover, Lucy was diagnosed with cancer in the early 1970s. Surgery was able to halt the disease, and Lucy's cancer never reappeared. Over a course of several years, Prichard witnessed both his wife and his son overcome cancer. He was greatly relieved that Louie's health "continues to be fine, as does Lucy's."[27]

Prichard's own health, driven by his diabetes, on the other hand, continued to rack his body. One day as he was being driven to work by Bill Graham, Prichard noticed a strange sensation in his one good eye. He remarked to Graham that he could only see an orange glow, and Graham immediately took Prichard to an emergency room in Lexington, where doctors quickly diagnosed it as a retinal hemorrhage. Laser therapy was used to treat the bleeding and the damage, which significantly lessened Prichard's field of vision. In time, he could read only with the help of a magnifying glass and very intense light, but by the mid-1970s, even those items proved fruitless. For a man who was consumed with reading and knowledge, the curse of blindness was to test his mettle to a degree he had never before known.[28]

Yet Prichard managed to develop the strength to confront the multitude of problems he faced. One source of this resiliency resided in his new public persona, where he was regarded in Kentucky as a wise political sage whose brilliance and wit overshadowed any lingering memories of Ashland. His new reputation was on visible public display in September 1974. As part of its "Distinguished Kentuckian" series, Kentucky Educational Television selected Ed Prichard to be the subject of a televised reception in his honor. After Bert Combs introduced the guest of honor, journalist John Ed Pearce interviewed a delighted Prichard before a luminary audience, including the new governor, Julian Carroll, and a number of Prichard's closest friends and associates, such as Barry Bingham. Also noticeably present was Lucy, who began to accompany her husband to all his public meetings. As the night proceeded, Prichard displayed all the traits that endeared him to so many—telling stories that entertained the crowd and mimicking some in the audience with devastating accuracy. Prichard also demonstrated his dazzling range of knowledge, discussing civil rights, the world economy, the history of Catholicism, and the structural consequences of worldwide starvation, mixed as always with stories of Kentucky politicians. When Pearce recalled a story he had written about Combs more than a decade before, Prichard effortlessly recited the article verbatim back to its stunned author and an equally astonished audience.

The event demonstrated the new public perception of Ed Prichard twenty-five years after his trial. The one-time "jailbird" who had been a pariah in campaigns was suddenly viewed as a political sage in Kentucky, known for his wit, humor, humility, compassion, and brilliance. No longer a pathetic wreck who could not be trusted with responsibilities, Prichard had come through his personal crucible with a courageous resiliency that engendered authentic admiration and respect among even some of his enemies. F. Scott Fitzgerald remarked that there are no second acts in American lives. Ed Prichard was prepared to flout the rules once again.

15 Twilight Renaissance

BY the early 1970s Ed Prichard's once-battered reputation had taken on a new luster. The trial and imprisonment were a distant memory to a new generation of lawyers, politicians, and journalists, many of whom were now eager to bask in Prichard's reflected brilliance. Despite yet another round of challenging personal tragedies and dilemmas, Ed Prichard's resilience provided ample testimony that his personal renaissance in his declining years would continue.

Part of the new image of Ed Prichard had been created through a heightened interest in his life by reporters and journalists. In October 1973, Prichard's comeback was the subject of an article in the *Washington Monthly* by Frank Browning that sought to connect the contemporary problems of Watergate with someone who had survived his own brand of political scandal. Overall, the article was fairly complimentary, but there were some moments in the piece that irritated Prichard and, most of all, Lucy. Browning quoted Prichard as saying, "I'm not sure I want to see myself described in print. I think I might rather be just talked about as some kind of folk villain." When quoting Prichard as saying he valued loyalty above all else, Browning concluded that "Prichard seems tragically blind to the source of his mistake. . . . He has not wholly redeemed himself, has not completely transcended his experience and grown beyond it."[1]

Although Prichard was neither "offended nor embarrassed" by the Browning article, there was the matter of Lucy's reaction. Prichard noted that both Lucy and his oldest son, Allen, "felt the hurt far more than I did."[2] Allen was in law school at Georgetown when the article appeared and was embarrassed to have the story of the political prodigy who fell from grace repeated again in his new home city. Lucy had always been opposed to historical or journalistic accounts of her husband's downfall and felt that any such stories were unwarranted invasions of privacy.[3]

When the Browning article appeared, other journalists were considering more ambitious projects concerning Prichard. At a party in Versailles in 1974, John Ed Pearce of the *Louisville Courier-Journal* broached the subject to Lucy of doing a series of articles about Prichard. Pearce recalled that after several minutes, Lucy grew cold and implored Pearce not to bring up such painful subjects on the eve of Allen's wedding. For the time being, Pearce dropped the notion of bringing Prichard's story to the pages of the state's leading newspaper.[4]

An even more ambitious project was suggested by a former *Louisville Times* reporter, William Greider. A Cincinnati native, Greider had worked in Louisville during the mid-1960s before leaving for the *Washington Post*. Greider approached Prichard with the question: "Are you at all aroused by the idea of someone writing a book about you?" Stating he was "eager" to attempt the project but only with Prichard's cooperation, Greider said, "It is a great story, I think, and worthy of sensitive telling, perhaps even illuminating for some small corner of truth."[5]

Early on, Prichard was noticeably excited about the prospect of Greider doing his biography. "Though I am possessed of my full degree of vanity, I also have a portion of humility which to some degree makes me think that a book about me is bound to involve a certain degree of unwarranted pretention on my part," wrote Prichard. He agreed that the matter called for more serious reflection and discussion and hoped to confer with Greider on an upcoming trip to Washington.[6]

Prichard gave a great deal of consideration to the idea of a biography. He well knew the attendant embarrassment and pain that would necessarily come to his family, as well as the damage it might do to his newfound reputation. He decided to consult two friends who knew a great deal not only about him but also about the world of publishing—Katharine Graham and Barry Bingham. Prichard wrote that "my own sensitivity has been protected by scar tissue built up over the years but there is the real problem with Lucy and the boys." He raised the issue of the Browning article and disclosed that "Lucy was much put out with me" over his limited role in cooperating with Browning. Prichard admitted he had discussed Greider's letter with Lucy and that "her initial attitude is one of hostility." "If that hostility continues," Prichard wrote, "I should feel bound to respect her feelings, and to understand them. On the other hand, I suppose that there is a certain vanity—and perhaps a certain pride in the sheer fact of survival—which makes me want to take Mr. Grider [*sic*] up." In his honest and forthright manner, Prichard asked for advice from both Graham and Bingham on the matter of a potential book, yet he could not escape the "gnawing doubt in my mind as to whether there is enough significance in my life to justify a book."[7]

Katharine Graham responded that "the idea of a book about you is very appealing to me, although I can see it would have a whole lot of sensitive areas for you." She noted that Greider was "in many ways the biggest talent on the paper" and would be superbly qualified to undertake a Prichard biography. Barry Bingham was even more supportive, writing Prichard that "a properly written book about you would be a lasting treasure and a pride to such old friends as ourselves." Bingham seconded Katharine Graham's thoughts about Greider's abilities but added a caveat: "There would be a drive" by profit-seeking publishers, Bingham stated, "to focus attention on one incident in your life and its consequences." Considering what was at stake, Bingham acknowledged, "It would be a genuine loss to the public interest if such a book as Grider [sic] contemplates should not be written."[8]

The correspondence between Katharine Graham and Prichard belied the distance that had grown between them. In a poignant letter to Joe Rauh, Prichard wrote of the sadness he felt about Graham's growing "estrangement." When Allen Prichard, the oldest son, did not hear from Graham during his years in Washington, the elder Prichard admitted that "it has hurt my feelings." When Graham did not attend Allen's wedding, Prichard noted that when Graham's daughter was married, he and Lucy "went to great trouble and expense (during quite hard times for us) to attend all the festivities at Kay's request." Whenever visiting Washington, Prichard felt she acted as though it was "troublesome for her to make some effort to squeeze us in." What went unsaid was the implicit notion that some friends were still ashamed of Prichard's past. Noting Hemingway's remark about the rich being different from "the rest of us," there was no masking the pain Prichard felt.[9]

Katharine Graham, however, felt no such estrangement. She continued to have Prichard sent a complimentary *Post* daily as a token of her genuine affection. After Lyndon Johnson's death, Prichard wrote Graham that he was now the lone remaining individual to receive a free copy of her newspaper and told her, with characteristic humor, that the paper was "well worth the money" he paid for it.[10]

The matter of a book on Prichard, however, fell through. Greider's interest in the project declined after Prichard's less than enthusiastic reply. Additionally, Katharine Graham discussed with Greider the matter of opening up "all those wounds," whereupon Greider dropped the matter completely.[11] For the time being, Prichard's scar tissue remained untouched, and Lucy avoided one more attempt to write about her husband's life.

Perhaps what really disappointed Prichard in the failure of a book was that as he approached sixty his health was becoming an ever bigger concern. He compensated by sporting a salt-and-pepper mustache that he told Earle Clements was like Samson's hair in that it provided him his strength. But Prichard's strength was sagging. When he fell down a flight of stairs at his home in Versailles, the fall broke no bones but left him visibly shaken and depressed. As the retina in his remaining eye continued to hemorrhage, his doctors informed him that such bleeding was a byproduct of his chronic diabetes.[12]

But his mind, as ever, remained sharp, and Prichard continued to work, finding in his newfound legal success a welcome respite from increasing tragedy. He maintained his humble office on the second floor of an old building on Main Street in Frankfort, located next door to Belinda's Singer Sewing Center. One had to climb a narrow flight of stairs and walk past an out-of-order water fountain under a faded portrait of Robert E. Lee to find Prichard's unassuming law office. His own room was usually heavy with the odor of stale cigar smoke, even though the affection for expensive and fine cigars he had once shared with Eugene Meyer had abated somewhat—his choice was now mainly Dutch Masters. His desk was a slate top that Lucy had designed for him.[13]

In 1975, a case Prichard had worked on closely with Bert Combs finally came to a "successful" conclusion. Almost five years after the Finley mine explosion, Combs and Prichard's clients pleaded "no contest" to mine violation charges. Their plea arrangement with federal prosecutors therefore dropped sixteen other counts produced by the explosion. In all, the Finleys were fined a mere $122,500 with no jail time, and the presiding judge told Combs that the charges involved were misdemeanors, which was "the wisdom of Congress and not the court." Outside the courtroom, Combs told reporters that the fine was not a mere slap on the wrist for his millionaire clients, saying "the fellas will be digging coal for the rest of their lives to pay this off." The no-contest pleas were significant—with numerous suits against the Finleys brought by families of the dead miners still in the courts, a "guilty" plea would have been admissible in the civil case as evidence of the Finleys' negligence, whereas a no-contest plea saved the Finleys from potential damaging lawsuits. Once again, although he personally detested the coal industry, Prichard could not refuse to help Bert Combs, nor could he refuse the money involved in hefty legal fees.[14]

Despite his troubles with the IRS, Prichard refused to let his financial problems impede his helping his sons. He had neglected their financial needs and had been essentially an absentee father for so many years. With Allen finishing up law school at Georgetown University, Louie ready to graduate from Centre College, and Nathan at Princeton, Prichard found paying their tuition a significant burden. But education had always been a primary motivating factor in Prichard's life, and he would spare no expense to see his sons well educated. The fact that Allen had been hired to clerk for a U.S. district judge in Washington made it all the more worthwhile. In writing his last check to Georgetown, Prichard said he felt compelled to write on the check, "Free at last, free at last, thank Godalmighty, I'm free at last."[15]

By 1975 various journalists and scholars were mining Prichard's inexhaustible supply of political knowledge. While Greider's plan for a biography fell through, Prichard cooperated with Neal R. Peirce in supplying various ruminations about Kentucky politics for his book *The Border South States*. In the process, he bedazzled Peirce so much that he became a subject himself in the book. Peirce devoted three full pages to what he described as "The Sovereign Electorate and the Tragedy of Edward F. Pritchard [sic], Jr." While Peirce spent most of the section recounting Prichard's rise in Washington and his imprisonment, he could not ask Prichard the salient questions about his "tragedy." "I chose deliberately not to discuss the matter," wrote Peirce. "To think that Kentucky and the country were robbed of this man's services by 254 lousy faked ballots is still enough to make one weep."[16]

Prichard's most critical health crisis occurred shortly after his sixtieth birthday. One cold morning in the winter of 1975 as he walked to the office with Bill Graham, it soon became apparent that something was wrong. The three-block walk Prichard usually made without any effort became an exhausting ordeal. Halfway there, he had to stop and rest inside another law office. When he and Graham arrived at their own office, friends told Graham that unless he took Prichard to the hospital he might die. Graham asked Prichard if he wished to go to the hospital, and all Prichard could do was nod that he did. When doctors at the University of Kentucky Medical Center emergency room examined him, they found his body swollen and diagnosed kidney failure. Graham called Lucy, who rushed immediately to the hospital. To save his life, Prichard's doctors placed him on a dialysis machine. For the remainder of his life, doctors informed him, he would have to undergo kidney dialysis two to three times a week, with each session lasting four to six hours. The dual prospect of both blindness and rigorous sessions of dialysis three times a week loomed.[17]

Prichard's life expectancy significantly decreased after his kidneys failed, and he admitted to Ben Cohen that he was beginning to feel frequently old and tired.[18] More than ever before, the daily matters of making a living and providing for his family became paramount concerns. In 1976 a significant series of events revealed how Prichard's political ambitions had changed through the years. When Kentucky's court structure was overhauled in the mid-1970s, as Prichard had unsuccessfully advocated in the Constitutional Revision Assembly in 1966, Gov. Julian Carroll received a list of fourteen finalists for seats on the newly created Kentucky Court of Appeals. The list was compiled by a Judicial Nominating Commission and was then narrowed by the governor's cabinet secretary. Despite Prichard's uneasy relationship with the governor, he was among the finalists for the appellate court. It was, it seemed, a fitting recognition of Prichard's legal talents and judicial background, but it was also a political gamble. All judges appointed by the governor would have to stand for election to a full term in November 1977. Although few could be found who would say Prichard lacked the necessary qualifications to sit on the court, there was always the stigma of the past. In blunt terms, how could the governor appoint to the court an ex-convict with tax problems, and how could the aging Prichard withstand a demanding election?[19]

On August 16, 1976, Prichard called Governor Carroll and withdrew his name. He mentioned several legitimate factors in his decision—his debilitating kidney condition and his blindness made the long hours and endless reading of briefs and statutes that were requisite to being a judge virtually impossible. He also mentioned his primary need to make money—the judgeship paid only $37,000, which simply could not meet all of Prichard's sundry bills. Although these were powerful reasons, no doubt the certainty that the ballot-box episode would be brought up again also forced Prichard to decline. Running for office would require exposing his past, which Lucy opposed, and the possible public rejection at the polls was something Prichard would not risk. Unanswered questions remained about the ballot-box scandal. Perhaps that was a primary reason Prichard decided to meet with John Ed Pearce in the fall of 1976 for a lengthy interview about his life.

Pearce had put off doing the article for two years but now decided the time was ripe for a candid interview. He even tried to enlist the help of Lucy but had predictable problems. Repeated attempts to interview her were rejected until she finally agreed to meet Pearce for lunch in Lexington. Lucy had more on her mind than the disinclination to "open up old wounds." An angry Lucy told Pearce that all he wanted to do was write a "fluff" piece. She then told the astonished journalist, "You won't write what a black-hearted son-of-a-bitch he has been to me and all who loved him." Such statements should not have been surprising. For more than two decades Lucy had endured a waking nightmare—she had not only watched her husband go to jail, she had also watched the public assassination of his character. After Prichard's imprisonment, she hoped just to live a normal life. Instead, she saw Prichard time and again leave for months to join a campaign, work in a constitutional assembly, or simply leave without anyone knowing his whereabouts, all the while ignoring her, their three sons, and the family's finances.

When Prichard's financial and tax troubles mounted in the 1960s, Lucy had endured more than she could bear. The estrangement between Ed and Lucy had been a painful one, and the bitter memories lingered. Even after their separation ended, living with Prichard presented its share of challenges. His growing infirmities meant he was now dependent on her for a number of daily tasks—driving him, dressing him, and helping him with his food. While she maintained a supportive public posture, Lucy was still bitter. As the daughter of a leading central Kentucky family, she had perhaps expected to marry the next governor. Instead, life had been terribly unkind to Lucy Prichard. As friends remarked, Lucy was never the same after Ashland. In some ways, she remained a strong-willed, independent woman who endured more than her share of troubles. Yet in more subtle ways, she had been almost broken in the process.[20]

Pearce managed to obtain a recorded interview with Lucy, but the means by which he did undoubtedly angered Lucy. When he put a tape recorder on top of their table, Lucy demanded that he turn it off and not record their conversation. Pearce obligingly clicked the recorder to satisfy his guest. What Lucy was unaware of, however, was that the recorder had been off when he put it on the table. When he reached over, ostensibly to turn it off, he actually turned it on. Their entire conversation was recorded. When Pearce later listened to Lucy's disjointed recollections, he found he could make little coherent sense of what she said, but he did plan to use some of her more significant statements.[21]

When he went to interview Prichard at his house on Waitling Street in Frankfort, Pearce did not know what to expect. For more than twenty-six years, Prichard had made no public comments concerning the ballot-box episode. Realizing Lucy's adamant hostility to the subject, Prichard had not discussed it, even though his admittedly tough scar tissue was strong enough to undertake the problem. Perhaps because of his health, or of an inner peace he had obtained over the years, when Pearce came to his house in 1976, Prichard was ready to talk candidly about his life and "the episode."

Early in the interview, Pearce realized that Prichard was leading him to ask the crucial questions about the ballot boxes that Neal Peirce had not asked. At the right moment, Pearce asked, and Prichard did not hesitate. Did Prichard stuff the boxes? The answer was unequivocal. "I did it," Prichard told Pearce. "It was wrong, and I know it was wrong, and I think you may grant that I paid for it." As to why he stuffed the boxes, Prichard explained: "I just didn't appreciate the implication of what I was doing." He recounted stories of how his grandfather "had done people out of elections after the Civil War," and that Ed Sr. "I'm sure, engaged in it many times." In fact, he acknowledged that "it was as common in Bourbon County as chicken-fighting, and no more serious." Prichard admitted that the political culture of Bourbon County was not a proper excuse. Instead, he laid the blame entirely on himself. "It was sort of a moral blind spot," he admitted. "It is hard now to make one realize that it was regarded as little more than a local sport, something you wouldn't do anywhere else, but was expected at home."

Prichard denied that the scandal had anything to do with an election bet, leaving open the question of why he engaged in the illegal practice, except to say that it was a commonplace event. Prichard also denied ever considering running for governor but did say, "I had no definite plans. I'm not saying that at times I haven't wanted to hold office, but I've never felt any great frustration that I didn't." All Prichard wanted, he told Pearce, was "to be active."[22]

In late October, Pearce's articles on Prichard's life appeared in the *Louisville Courier-Journal Magazine,* a section of the Sunday paper. The first article bore the remarkable title "The Man Who Might Have Been President." It recalled Prichard's early rise and return to Kentucky after World War II. But it was the second week's installment, titled "Adversity and Atonement," that included Prichard's first public statement on the trial in twenty-seven years. The reaction among numerous people who knew Pearce was "Is this it?" Was the dark secret of Prichard's past nothing more than 254 ballots? In the post-Watergate era, such revelations drew little public indignation. Another typical reaction came from James Rowe, who had known Prichard since the New Deal era. Rowe told Barry Bingham that the articles were "excellent" but added that reading them "made me want to cry."[23]

Others, however, were not so understanding. One was Henry Hornsby, the reporter for the *Lexington Leader* who had covered the Prichard trial. Like many who respected and admired Prichard, Hornsby refused to believe that the New Deal wunderkind could have participated in the affair. In 1949, when Hornsby had discovered that Prichard was under investigation by the FBI after the photograph of U.S. Attorney Claude Stephens inadvertently revealed the information, Prichard disavowed his involvement to Hornsby. Prichard "denied the charge," wrote Hornsby, "calling on God as witness for innocence." At the time, Hornsby said, "I was younger and naive, and I believed him." In the ensuing years, Hornsby had continued to believe Prichard's statement made during the investigation, and he was now angered by the Pearce articles.[24]

The most severe reaction of all was Lucy's. She was furious at Pearce for the articles and never spoke to him again. Her anger may have originated in the fact that Pearce had deceived her into thinking her comments were not being recorded when she could obviously see they had been. Perhaps her anger was also produced by the "embarrassment" that rehashing the old story produced for her family. And, as she had told Pearce months before, the pieces were, indeed, written by an old friend who loved Prichard, hence the rather spectacular title about Prichard and the White House. Lucy never enjoyed such friends of Prichard's as Pearce, who she felt kept him away from her and the family.[25]

Pearce's articles implied that Lucy hated politics and her husband's involvement in all matters political. Prichard wrote Katharine Graham that "Lucy did not 'abhor' politics. She may have abhorred some of my involvements, immersions, and preoccupations," but she had always been a politically involved woman in her own right. Lucy had, after all, served as a precinct captain in Paris alongside her husband in the late 1940s and had always taken an active interest in state and local political affairs. Prichard noted that Lucy's perceived revulsion to politics may have had more to do with Pearce's "sexism" revealing itself. But Prichard also knew that while Lucy was not completely disinterested in politics, she had little use for the campaign dynamics that so captivated her husband. Once when asked why someone would run for elective office, Prichard tersely replied, "Well, my wife Lucy says it takes a good deal of ego-mania."[26]

On the whole, the Pearce articles were significant in the renaissance of Ed Prichard. Throughout the preceding ten years, as he had become a more visible public presence, the shadows of the trial and Ashland had hung over his political and personal life. The almost cathartic expression of his guilt removed the single-most damaging weapon his critics could wield, and he now seemed freed by the public confession. Even Phil Ardery, who was under the mistaken impression that Prichard had never admitted his guilt to anyone—and had in the process made his father appear a liar—was now ready to resume a speaking relationship with his old friend and rival.[27]

In the winter of 1977, the case of the state workers fired under Louie Nunn (who had been out of office for six years) finally ended. Franklin Circuit Judge Henry Meigs signed an order approving the settlement between 225 former employees and the state's attorneys, under which the state agreed to pay the workers $1.25 million in back pay. For Prichard and his firm, the $310,000 in legal fees was a welcome reward for the considerable work involved. The Nunn administration's blatant disregard for the merit system had resulted in the state owing almost $2 million in total to the workers in the round of lawsuits since 1967. But there was yet another hurdle before Prichard's payday could be realized. Gov. Julian Carroll refused to accept the settlement and asked the state attorney general to see if some way could be found to set the agreement aside. In addition to political conflicts within the judiciary and Carroll, it was also well known that the governor wanted to negate the settlement because of his increasing dislike of Ed Prichard. The two had had a tension-filled relationship for years. While Carroll was lieutenant governor in the early 1970s, Prichard made several caustic comments about Carroll's ambition. The two had tangled over appointments to the Council on Higher Education, but they had seemingly smoothed things over when Carroll considered the Appeals Court position in August 1976. Prichard expressed the dilemma in his usual candid way: "I think he [Carroll] is torn between advice by people in his administration that the case ought to be settled . . . and on the other hand by his intense desire not to see me benefit from any settlement."[28]

Despite Carroll's intransigence, the settlement was agreed to, and for the first time in his legal career, Prichard enjoyed a lucrative settlement of his own—a case he had argued and won without the benefit of Tommy Corcoran, Bert Combs, or Ned Breathitt. The fact that it came in defense of one of Bert Combs's reforms in the early 1960s and at the hands of a Republican governor made it all the sweeter. The fee also allowed the beleaguered Prichard to escape some of the mounting tax liens that had dogged him for two decades. After dividing the fee with his law partners, Prichard was able to pay off $14,458.18 in back taxes in 1974 alone. Since beginning to practice law after Nunn's victory in 1967, Prichard had paid off almost $31,000 of the liens facing him. The settlement also provided Prichard a chance to begin negotiating with the IRS some kind of settlement that would finally release him from a mountain of back taxes, interest, and penalties that still exceeded $700,000.[29]

But the welcome financial news was offset by the worsening health of Prichard's mother. In 1977 Allene died of Alzheimer's disease in California. She was brought back to Paris, where she was buried in the family plot in the Paris cemetery next to her husband. In her later years, Prichard did not see his ailing mother, leaving the task of taking care of her primarily to his brother Henry. The fact that he did not contact Allene was due, at least in his brother's estimation, to Prichard's shame over the pain he had caused his mother since 1949.[30]

During these trying personal periods, Prichard's attention was increasingly directed toward theological issues. Religion had never been a strong part of his life, except that he had reveled in stories told him in the Methodist Sunday school as a boy. When he married Lucy, Prichard became an Episcopalian to appease his new wife and her family, and he remained an Episcopalian to his death. He often said in jest that the Episcopal Church "never caught a live sinner, they just got them at the door of other churches." After he and Lucy moved to Woodford County from Paris, they both joined the St. John's Episcopal Church in Versailles. One of the more frequently attending members of St. John's parish was another Versailles resident, Happy Chandler, who had joined the church in 1928. Throughout the 1960s, Prichard rarely attended church services, as he spent most of his time living in Frankfort. By 1970, the church officially removed him from its rolls, declaring his membership "inactive." But as a sign of his increasing attention to religious matters, Prichard's membership was restored in 1974. He became devoted to St. John's for the remainder of his life.[31]

Yet it would be a misnomer to describe Ed Prichard as a religious convert. He had once described himself to Felix Frankfurter as a "believing unbeliever." Like so many other parts of his life, Prichard's spiritual notions were a paradox—he had little use for the staid, comfortable religion practiced by the American middle class, nor for the dogmatic variety undertaken by zealots. Yet somewhere in his mind rested an implicit Christian impulse.

Of all the personal losses that his physical "infirmities" brought, none was more distressing to Prichard than his inability to read. But as a testament to his newfound resiliency, Prichard decided to use his hours at the dialysis clinic to the best advantage. He usually went to dialysis three times a week—Tuesday, Thursday, and Saturday—at the University of Kentucky Medical Center in Lexington. He went early in the mornings for sessions that would often last four to five hours. During the laborious treatments, Prichard displayed his courage and his determination not to let his blindness sap his intellectual zeal. He also did not allow the painstaking treatments to lessen his sense of humor. One Saturday morning, Prichard was hurriedly asked by the president of the Young Democrats of Kentucky to help with a speech to be given that night. Prichard agreed to help and told the young man to come over to the hospital where the speech would be dictated while Prichard underwent dialysis. In the middle of the speech, Prichard characteristically remarked, "Well here I am. I used to write speeches for Franklin Roosevelt and now here I am, on a dialysis table, dictating a speech for the Kentucky Young Democrats."[32]

A ritual soon developed at the dialysis clinic whereby friends, associates, or others who wanted to get to know Prichard would sit and read to him. Some, like Bill Graham, Don Mills, Bob Sexton, and Louisville mayor Harvey Sloane, had known him for years and knew how much reading meant to him. Others, including University of Kentucky professor John Stephenson, had heard of the brilliant legend of Ed Prichard and wished to make themselves available to him. The material Prichard wanted read to him covered a wide range. A typical stack of reading material would be several newspapers—Louisville, Lexington, Washington, and New York; poetry; magazines such as the *Economist,* the *Manchester Guardian,* the *New Republic,* the *Nation,* and the *New York Review of Books;* correspondence; political monographs; classics; and some recent appellate court decisions. When his readings began, Prichard would sit with his eyes tightly closed, seeming at times to be asleep—just as he had at Paris High and Princeton. But Prichard was absorbing the material with his usual acuity and passion and remained well informed on diverse issues. Friends and colleagues admired his refusal to allow his blindness to rob him of obtaining knowledge. In ways that mirrored those days in his dorm rooms in college and in hotel rooms in his adult life, Prichard used the dialysis table to submerge into his most comfortable surroundings—great books and great ideas.

After the complicated machines cleansed his blood, Prichard had more energy than at any other time, and he often returned to the office and worked the remainder of the day. In any case, it was imperative that he be driven home before 5:00 P.M. so he could listen to National Public Radio's *All Things Considered.*

To those who had long known him, the ailing Ed Prichard was a far cry from the brash wunderkind of the 1940s or the pathetic wreck they had known in the 1950s. After seeing a sickly Prichard helped out of a New York cab in 1979, James A. Wechsler wrote, "I almost flinched." Both were attending a fundraiser for Louisville mayor Harvey Sloane, a candidate for governor in 1979, at the home of Arthur Schlesinger. After talking with Prichard for just a few moments, Wechsler concluded that his mind remained as brilliant as ever. Sloane recalled a remarkable conversation at this event between Prichard and Kentucky natives Col. Harland Sanders of Kentucky Fried Chicken fame and heavyweight boxing champion Muhammad Ali. Seeing Prichard there reminded Wechsler that he was not only "the brightest of the young men whom FDR attracted to Washington . . . he was also ultimately proved to be the bravest." But another old friend detected a certain sadness behind the courageous facade. Sir Isaiah Berlin, who had known Prichard in Washington as well as anyone, was also struck by his friend's mounting physical infirmities. Unlike Wechsler, Berlin concluded that Prichard was simply not "the same man" he had once known and that the tragedy of the late 1940s had ultimately rendered him "a broken man."[33]

Those who encountered Prichard for the first time in the 1970s had a far different reaction. Prichard's reputation soared among reporters and editors in Louisville and Lexington who knew few details of his past. They could always count on him to provide sound background or a usable quote on just about any political issue. Some charged that the *Lexington Herald* allowed Prichard some leeway in its editorials. Editor Don Mills, who had known Prichard since the Breathitt years, candidly admitted that Prichard simply wrote a number of editorials for the paper in the 1970s, a practice that ceased after Mills's superiors discovered the process. Prichard also amused reporters and editors by writing letters to the editor using a variety of pseudonyms. Just as he had done in the 1940s, Prichard loved to talk with reporters about breaking news and to use the press to ridicule an adversary.[34] Prichard's access to the press allowed him a greater latitude in some of his new political forays than was given others in the state.

Prichard's political and economic ideology did not remain tied to an anachronistic New Dealism. He had once been a devoted Keynesian, but the failure of the 1974-75 recession to halt staggering levels of inflation had convinced him that the old notions of Keynesian economics did not necessarily work. He further criticized economists who advocated that wage and price controls could combat inflation. Instead, Prichard turned to "radical" internal reforms as the proper solution, reforms that would usher in "workplace democracy, guild socialism, or worker co-determination." This "workplace democracy," in Prichard's estimation, could be coupled with other neighborhood self-help measures such as credit unions and food coops. What became a central theme in Prichard's final years was his newfound commitment to democratic forms at the local level. "I'm still not out in the open politically as far left as I feel," he admitted.[35]

To many of his old friends, the renaissance of Ed Prichard was a marvelous occurrence. To recognize his accomplishments, and perhaps to honor a man in failing health, John Ed Pearce organized a dinner for Prichard in Louisville in November 1979. Bingham and John Ed invited a veritable Who's Who of Washington and Kentucky politicos to the dinner. Among those invited who could not attend were Tom Wicker, Jay Rockefeller, and John Kenneth Galbraith. Numerous old friends from across the country did indeed attend, among them Katharine Graham, Evangeline Bruce, Joe Rauh, Arthur M. Schlesinger Jr., and Princeton classmate Ed Gullion. Dozens of Kentucky lawyers, politicians, and judges attended, including newly elected governor John Y. Brown Jr. and his wife, former Miss America Phyllis George.

The dinner in Louisville became a fitting tribute to the life of Ed Prichard. The *Courier-Journal* understated the case the following day when it said, "It's likely there has not been a dinner quite like it in Kentucky in recent years." Before dinner, guests lined up in front of Prichard's chair for a chance to shake his hand or kiss his cheek. Bert Combs emceed the ceremony, and following dinner a number of luminaries made their way to the microphone to sing Prichard's praises. Ed Gullion remarked, "You see some remarkable people in one's lifetime, and he is one of the most remarkable." Schlesinger delivered the evening's keynote to a man he termed "a hero of our time" and the "undisputed king" of the young New Dealers in Washington in the 1940s.

At the conclusion of the evening's events, Prichard was escorted to the podium for remarks of his own. He admitted he had gotten little sleep the night before his testimonial dinner in anxious anticipation. Noting that his health and eyesight were failing, Prichard proclaimed that "the process of overcoming infirmities is the process of staying alive." He then paid a humorous but poignant tribute to Lucy. Journalists had often asked him, Prichard said, if living in Washington during the war years had not been the most exciting time of his life. "I do not want to say, or have been perceived to have said," said Prichard tongue in cheek, "that anytime I haven't known Lucy is the most exciting time of my life." He added that Lucy was "not just a beautiful, loving, wonderful woman. She's tough as hell and won't let me get away with the foolishness and the fraud to which I am prone." The man who first stood to applaud Lucy, ironically enough, was John Ed Pearce.

Then Prichard turned to address his own life. It became one of the singularly revealing public moments of his life. He noted that among his weaknesses was a tendency to "spread myself too thin." Then he added that two competing strains had always battled for supremacy within him—a "strong egalitarian impulse" versus "a strong love of tradition." That specific "tension,"

Prichard remarked, "won't be resolved. Most paradoxes are not." Peppering his ad hoc speech with quotations from Niebuhr and Bourbon County politicians, Prichard said he was always reminded of an example provided him by Sir Isaiah Berlin on egalitarianism. If you have an apple and four children, each automatically receives an equal-sized piece. In other words, as Prichard explained to his guests, if you don't divide the wealth on an equal basis, you must explain yourself. The burden, then, was on those who advocated free markets to justify gross inequities. Such sentiments revealed how the socialist notions that had intrigued him at Princeton had not completely evaporated more than forty years later.[36]

The evening in his honor vividly represented the extent to which Ed Prichard's once-sullied reputation had come full circle. No longer a pathetic figure hidden in hotel rooms and campaign hideaways, he was now an acknowledged "hero" who brought inspiration to the rarefied crowd that had come to Louisville. What the contingent collectively remembered of the aging figure too weak to stand by himself was the robust "king" they considered perhaps *the* best and *the* brightest of the generation that had come to maturity during World War II. As with all occasions surrounding Prichard, there was also the implicit sadness in everyone there as they considered all that had been lost in 1948, when Prichard's "love of tradition" overcame his impulse for egalitarianism.

16 The Final Struggle

BY 1979, as the lavish dinner in Louisville gave evidence, Ed Prichard's personal and political reputation had enjoyed a remarkable recovery from the nadir of the 1950s. Despite his many infirmities, he had built a successful law practice on his own and had been transformed into one of the most respected political voices in Kentucky. Prichard had suddenly become a model of personal courage. Perhaps the most remarkable aspect of his later life is that he remained passionately committed to reforming his beloved home state, and that his singular achievement in this regard was still ahead of him.

For anyone wishing to devote time to a cause sure to bring about sweeping change and quick approval in Kentucky, the area of education reform would be the last place to start. The state had long lagged behind the rest of the nation in educational standards, teacher pay, and the reputation of its state-supported universities. Obtaining more tax funds, as always, presented a massive barrier to real reform. What was worse, Kentucky's school systems were intimately connected with the courthouse politics that Prichard knew so well. Patronage of school systems in a poor state like Kentucky was one political carrot a number of locally powerful people would not be willing to sacrifice in the name of reform. In his role as a member of the state Council on Higher Education, which examined the state's public colleges and universities, Prichard saw all of these forces at work.

In October 1979 the council formed a committee to "examine the trends and issues likely to affect Kentucky higher education in the future." Thirty people from across the state were appointed by the council to serve on a special commission to be called the Committee on Higher Education in Kentucky's Future. Prichard was selected to chair the committee, a duty into which he poured himself over the next two years. While most committees or task forces designed to study such amorphous problems have little impact other than to recommend politically safe suggestions, Prichard was determined at the outset that this committee would be different. Its final report would become one of Prichard's greatest legacies.

Prichard's political skills were called upon often in chairing the committee of diverse individuals, some of whom held very different political outlooks. Republican Wade Mountz had never met Prichard before the initial meeting but recalled that Prichard was "a real charmer." Prichard mentioned a number of Mountz's previous appointments and interests, much to Mountz's shock. Mountz's political inclinations presented no special problems for Prichard—he blithely remarked that Mountz was "of the other persuasion."[1] Humor aside, Prichard's skills were vitally necessary if the committee's recommendations were to have any significant impact on the state's moribund educational system.

Meeting in the Shakertown retreat south of Lexington, Prichard asked everyone on the committee to consider a basic question—"What is an educated person?" In this way, as member Pat Kafoglis remembered, "Prich inspired all of us. We were earnest souls and he provided the spark of genius." In asking such questions, Prichard was determined that training for careers was not necessarily the primary objective of a higher education. As he had understood in Paris, Princeton, Cambridge, and throughout his entire life, instilling a knowledge of language, history, economics, politics, and poetry was not an outmoded way of educating students in the 1980s. Such disciplines, in Prichard's estimation, provided the foundation for any educated person.[2]

The meetings held in the Shaker village also allowed some devoted friends to see Prichard in new ways. One such individual was John Stephenson, at the time a professor at the University of Kentucky. Stephenson was delighted to be matched with Prichard when roommates were selected for the event. One night, Stephenson and Prichard stayed up late talking about myriad subjects. Throughout it all, Stephenson hesitated to ask any questions about the sensitive topic of 1948. But as Stephenson recalled, such occasions sometimes produce moments where "you are maybe somewhat more likely to reveal yourself than in the cold light of day." As the two talked late into the night, Stephenson finally asked about the infamous episode and its impact on Prichard's life. Prichard became "as emotional as I ever heard him," Stephenson remembered. His voice rose, taking on, in Stephenson's phrase a "sort of ministerial tremor," and he thundered, "Oh, John, I would give anything, anything at all, if that had never happened." A philosophical Stephenson, not realizing the depth of Prichard's painful ordeal over the past thirty years, suggested that he was "grateful" for the events of 1948 if only for the sake of education reform. Had it not been for the ballot-box episode, he suggested, Prichard's life might have turned out very differently, thus making it highly unlikely that he would be at a retreat discussing educational reform in the early 1980s. Prichard "appreciated" such a kind remark, but no doubt pondered in his mind the roads not taken in his life.[3]

But Prichard had little time to waste on such reflections. In March 1980, Gov. John Y. Brown Jr. named Prichard to the Kentucky Board of Tax Appeals. Although he had not backed Brown in the 1979 primary, the young governor seemed intent on engaging his support. The tax appeals job provided a stipend of $22,000 a year and required only a nominal investment of time. Unlike the judgeship he had earlier declined, the Tax Appeals job was an appointed post and did not require Prichard to run for the office in a statewide election. Statutory regulations required that no individual could serve on two boards at the same time, and Prichard could always use the money provided by the governor's offer. While absorbed with the writing and preparation of the education committee's report, Prichard resigned from the Council on Higher Education. "My principal reason" for taking the job, said Prichard, "was my own security." He candidly admitted, "I am not a rich person and I thought this appointment might be of help to me in making provision for my own retirement, whenever that time comes." The irony of the fact that someone with a history of tax burdens himself would be appointed to such a post was lost on observers at the time. Although Prichard was no longer on the higher education council, he continued in his role as chair of the ad hoc committee studying Kentucky's higher education.[4]

But Prichard could not put his past completely behind him. A committee at the University of Kentucky decided to award Prichard an honorary doctorate at the May 1980 commencement. University president Otis Singletary noted that Prichard "presents a special case" and that Prichard's greatest contribution came from his role in "the policy-making decisions in Kentucky and the United States." The Board of Trustees was the final arbiter and had to approve all such nominations. One member of the board, however, was not about to see his beloved alma mater award Ed Prichard its highest honor. Happy Chandler voiced strong opposition to the nomination, saying that Prichard "hadn't done anything of service to the university." Prichard's nomination was also opposed by eastern Kentucky coal operator William Sturgill, the man who had precipitated the "Widow Combs" affair in the 1960s. Sturgill simply noted that awarding Prichard the degree was not "in the best interest of the university." Chandler and Sturgill were the only dissenting votes. In May, Prichard received his honorary degree from the state's leading university.[5]

Over the next year, Prichard remained devoted to the education committee. As in the past, such work was not compensated and came at the expense of his law practice. But just being back in the arena gave him a satisfaction no other area of his life could. And, as always, he remained committed to politics. In the summer of 1980, Prichard displayed some of his maverick tendencies when he lent his support to Massachusetts senator Edward Kennedy's attempt to wrest the party's nomination from incumbent president Jimmy Carter. Prichard remarked that Carter's renomination "would lead the Democratic party through a slaughterhouse to an open grave" (quoting *Courier-Journal* editor Henry Watterson's remark concerning Grover Cleveland). Prichard had planned to attend the 1980 Democratic convention as an at-large delegate but stayed home on doctor's orders. As Lucy remarked, "I guess it would have been his undoing." She told Ned Breathitt, "You know he couldn't have missed a minute when there was anything going on." When Carter won the party's nomination, however, Prichard was no Happy Chandler, and he staunchly supported Carter over the Republican nominee, Ronald Reagan. He wrote an impassioned letter to the *Courier-Journal* in October 1980, noting that "reflection since the Convention . . . compels us to support President Carter. We believe the time for bitterness is over."

> The problems of our economy are complex and troubling. Will our hope for sensible industrial and economic growth, more jobs and international stability be encouraged by an insane nuclear arms race? Will our schools be improved by dismantling the new Department of Education and by prescribing prayers for schoolchildren? Will the frustration of the industrial worker be reduced by Ronald Reagan's opposition to the minimum wage? Or by his derision of health and safety standards in the factory and shop? Or by his contempt for organized labor? Are the inequalities of blacks in America to be judged by a candidate whose opposition to the Civil Rights Act of 1964, which we would not presume to call racism, at minimum reflects basic insensitivity?[6]

As the letter underscored, Reagan's professed desire to end the New Deal disturbed Prichard, who remembered the economic collapse of the late 1920s and early 1930s, and understood that the former Cailfornia governor opposed matters dear to Prichard, such as extending civil rights and environmental protection. Reagan's victory in November 1980 spelled a certain death to the politics of the New Deal and ended a Democratic coalition that had lasted for almost five decades. Prichard also grew concerned about the increasing political clout of religious fundamentalists such as the Moral Majority to swing the vote for hard-line Republicans. People like Ed Prichard who celebrated the legacy of FDR's New Deal and seemed to have been imbued with certain "egalitarian impulses" were increasingly on the defensive by 1980. The political tide was turning, and for those on the left, the areas in which they could be effectively heard were narrowing.[7]

On the other hand, Prichard by this time had acquired a unique political voice. In February 1981, Gov. John Y. Brown Jr. approached Prichard about becoming head of the state Democratic party. Prichard seriously considered the post but told the governor that his blindness, his health, and his law practice were primary reasons why he might not take the position. Prichard acknowledged, however, that his "contacts with the regular disaffected Democrats" might help bring the party together with Brown, the millionaire Kentucky Fried Chicken king. In exchange for the job, Prichard demanded access to the governor on policy issues, much as he had enjoyed with Clements,

Combs, and Breathitt. Perhaps Prichard's conditions, or his own anxiety over leaving his law practice once again to assume political responsibilities, led him finally to decline the governor's offer. Instead, he remained as a vice chairman of the Democratic state central committee.[8]

Within weeks of asking Prichard to take the party's top post, John Y. Brown found out how independent Prichard could be. When Brown remarked that higher education was the state's "biggest crybaby" over proposed massive budget cuts, he discovered Prichard's fearlessness in publicly challenging a governor. Robert Sexton, who was working on the committee drafting the report on higher education, was exasperated that the governor would attack higher education, and he went to see Prichard at a dialysis table. Sexton read Prichard the governor's remarks and then hastily scribbled down Prichard's dictated response. As was customary, a first draft was all that was necessary. "If the Governor would examine the prospective plight of higher education in Kentucky under additional budget cuts," Prichard said, "even he might be moved to tears." Prichard discussed meetings with Brown in which the governor had responded that new taxes might be necessary to offset cuts to higher education. Now it seemed he had changed his mind. Prichard was particularly upset by Brown's use of the word "demagogue" to describe those who supported higher education. "I for one would be loath to hurl the epithet 'demagogue' back in the governor's face," said Prichard, "but I should suggest to him that a demagogue is one who changes his position from day to day on a sensitive issue." Brown claimed he was "a little surprised" at Prichard's response but offered nothing substantive to counter his claims. Within months, Brown slashed university budgets.[9]

The issue of raising money to improve Kentucky higher education always hung over the drafting of the education report. The more the committee wanted to list an amount that would adequately increase the quality of higher education, the more likely they were to encounter political opposition. The committee considered the sum of $91 million. Prichard concurred with the amount but added that "heaven is not gained at a single bound." If the committee asked for such a figure in one sitting of the General Assembly, Prichard knew their chances of success were nonexistent. Even more, Prichard was not a partisan in the fight for education reform. He understood how the structural dynamics of the budget cuts would hurt an increasingly impoverished citizenry: "Here we are with 31,000 people losing their medical cards," said Prichard. "Here we are with child care centers being closed, the mental health centers phased out. . . . I don't want us to get in such a competition with every group that feels the quality of public services is facing decline."

During the same committee meeting, Prichard argued that, like North Carolina, Kentucky needed to convince the state legislature that increased funding for higher education was "an investment, not a cost." How to do this, of course, was one of the key problems facing the committee, and the answer provided by Prichard revealed yet another part of his evolving political thinking: "The willingness of the legislature to consider favorably the needs of higher education will depend in large part on what the legislature thinks is the will and the deposition of the citizenry of the state." This, in essence, was not a political issue that could be won over with clever oratory or political machinations. To realize the type of groundswell that Prichard wanted required a democratic effort to enlist the citizens of the state in their cause. The report must speak not only to experts in higher education, Prichard reasoned, but also to parents and teachers in the local communities. This expressed attempt to create a democratic movement for education reform began within the committee in 1981. Three years later, it bore fruit.[10]

For a man who had closely advised three governors, the strange relationship between Prichard and Governor Brown was befuddling. Prichard once remarked that in John Y. Brown he had the "best of both worlds"—he could advise the governor on the one hand and, on the other, criticize his policies in public without retribution. In fact, as Prichard noticed, the harsher his remarks, the harder Brown attempted to soothe Prichard's anger. On one memorable occasion, Prichard derisively claimed that the last book the business-oriented governor had read was *Little Black Sambo.* "John Y. likes businessmen because he sees the world through his own experience," Prichard stated, adding that Brown's "experience is that by selling fried chicken he made himself a great man." As time went on, Prichard's comments about the governor became even more candid. In September 1981, he tangled with the governor in public over remarks concerning a proper education. Prichard stated that Brown simply did not "know the difference between a job and a career. If you look down the spectrum of the future, you will see that a career today encompasses, in many cases, as many as five or six different jobs." Prichard then added what he felt all students should know when entering the job market, a list reminiscent of the educational philosophy of Lee Kirkpatrick in Bourbon County. In order to be properly educated, Prichard said, "they have to know something about the economics of this country and the world. They have to know something about the age-old issues of philosophy and values and ethics that have plagued people for thousands of years."[11]

By the fall of 1981, the committee had finished its work and was ready to submit its report, called "In Pursuit of Excellence." Before doing so, the committee paid special homage to its chairman and agreed that the name of the board should be changed to the Prichard Committee on Higher Education in Kentucky's Future. In his preface, Prichard noted that the report concerned more than the need for increased funding for the state's universities, and he asked the General Assembly to adopt the committee's recommendation that a "Fund for Academic Excellence" be established to support scholarships and endowed chairs. The committee also discussed the paring down of programs, particularly at the professional and graduate level, which naturally provoked severe criticism from individuals involved with those programs.

The Prichard Committee report was a provocative and challenging document that sought to answer some of the basic questions Prichard had outlined at the original Shakertown meeting. What is an educated person? The report said, "The educated person should have the desire, curiosity, and ability to continue to learn independently and to stay informed. . . . The seeds of curiosity, sensitivity to the importance of knowledge, and tolerance for new or unusual ideas must be planted early in life and nurtured throughout. The capacity for independent thought in the face of conventional wisdom requires personal courage, the ability to form and establish personal values, and a personal philosophy."[12]

The report did not end Prichard's involvement in reforming education. It was, in retrospect, only the beginning. The Prichard Committee refused to disappear. When Governor Brown, in effect, summarily ignored the report, members of the committee felt slighted. "We were greatly disappointed," Prichard later said of Brown's obstinacy. Another member, Dot Ridings, said the committee was "mad as hell . . . and we decided to fight back." What Prichard and other members of the committee wanted was "a role for a group of citizens who are not beholden or responsible to any official body." Prichard and Bert Combs joined forces once again and went about the task of raising money to make the Prichard Committee independent and permanent.[13]

The release of the Prichard Committee report had the effect of introducing Ed Prichard anew to his home state. The memory of 1948 was increasingly dim, and a new appreciation of his many considerable talents helped shed on him a new and vibrant light. In some ways, Prichard was seen as a dynamic intellectual force in the state. For example, when a volume of the poetry of Kentucky writer James Still was published, Prichard was asked to provide a foreword. While lying on the dialysis table, he dictated a masterful introduction that contained not only an enlightened reading of Still's poetry but also perhaps some autobiographical messages. In discussing Still's work, Prichard wrote that he appreciated Still's understanding of "the humorous, the quirky, the ironic side of life." The environment of the eastern Kentucky mountains "has brought forth particular types of characters who exhibit a certain saltiness. They are individuals. They are not part of a mass; they are not just people in a lonely crowd. They have been seasoned in their separate places as well as in the shared identity of their community. [Still] sees everything that is wrong with them and yet he is still able to write about them with a deep understanding, a love, and perhaps even a forgiveness. This insight comes from his very keen appreciation of the moral ambiguities which affect all mankind."[14]

Prichard probably confronted some of those ambiguities himself in the fall of 1981 when he learned that Billy Baldwin had died in Paris. Prichard's and Baldwin's fates divided sharply after the grand jury in 1949 indicted Prichard but not his close Paris friend. While Prichard's life was nearly destroyed by the ballot-box episode, the affair had no apparent impact on Baldwin, who remained highly popular in Bourbon County. Besides holding various elective offices, Baldwin was the county Democratic chairman from 1942 until 1976. The local chamber of commerce elected him as its president, and he was on the board of a Paris bank. Baldwin never admitted his own complicity in the county's most infamous ballot scandal, but this never soured his close friendship with Prichard. When Baldwin was buried in the Paris cemetery, Ed Prichard was an honorary pallbearer.[15]

Throughout 1982, Bert Combs and Prichard solicited funds from some of the state's most prominent individuals and corporations to make the Prichard Committee a viable, independent institution. By early 1983, enough money had been secured to allow the members to announce the formation of the Prichard Committee for Academic Excellence. The board was increased to sixty members, and the expressed goal of the committee was to reform education at all levels, not just in the universities. With the creation of the permanent Prichard Committee, Ed Prichard's name became forever synonymous in Kentucky with education reform.[16]

Although his work with education and his law practice proceeded, Prichard's health continued to decline. His once rosy cheeks and smooth face appeared haggard and drawn from the rigorous dialysis treatments. He endured bouts of fatigue yet all the while refused to exhibit self-pity. Prichard went about his dialysis treatments with his customary good humor, allowing his "readers" to keep him informed on the great variety of matters that still engaged his mind. He kept his eyes closed mostly, in a tight, concentrating fashion. He knew that at times he proved an awkward figure, as when he ate in a restaurant and fumbled for his food with his fingers or needed help walking.

Despite the toll his health took on his energy, Prichard still remained an intellectual powerhouse, and nowhere was that more visibly on display than on national television in October 1982. To commemorate Franklin Roosevelt's hundredth birthday, William F. Buckley Jr.'s *Firing Line* show came to Lexington and Prichard was selected to defend the New Deal against Buckley in an hour-long exchange. It proved a memorable debate between the irrepressible Yale conservative and the still-dazzling Princeton "egalitarian."

The evening got off to a tension-filled start when Buckley noted in his introduction that "in 1949, Edward Prichard had his Watergate." When

Buckley mentioned the ballot-box episode, an audience member recalled that an icy chill came over Lucy's face that took most of the night to dissipate. Prichard sat, eyes closed, with a wry, unperturbed smile, listening to Buckley's pointed introduction. Here was a man who had spent twenty years running away from public exposure and the residue of the vote scandal. Having built up a considerable amount of "scar tissue," Prichard was not be to caught off guard or put on the defensive by the mere mention of his past troubles. He remained gracious, calm, and ever ready to exchange political and literary interpretations with Buckley.[17]

Buckley charged that FDR had been something akin to a king. Was not the purpose of the U.S. Constitution, Buckley inquired, "to guard against plebiscitary spasms?" Prichard brushed off the verbal bluster with characteristic humor. "Not all plebiscitary spasms are born free and equal," said Prichard, which delighted the 150 or so people sitting in the audience. Later, when Buckley interrupted Prichard's recounting of the 1932 Democratic platform, which had called for a balanced budget, and said "they were right," Prichard was not taken aback. "Oh, of course they were insane," said Prichard, dismissing Buckley as a professor would treat an overly eager freshman—"You can't balance the budget in a recession or a depression without pushing the economy over the brink."[18]

But Prichard was neither pompous nor arrogant. He openly admitted that he had supported FDR on the court-packing plan, and he disarmed his host by admitting that such support was improper: "I was totally wrong." Buckley's efforts to intimidate his guest through excessive verbal descriptions did not work with Prichard. When Buckley rattled a phrase concerning "the individual distribution of income," Prichard gently interrupted his host and inquired, "You mean, per capita income?" Taken aback, Buckley acquiesced.

The most revealing moment, for several reasons, came when Buckley, in connection with some of FDR's more blatant personal and political foibles, casually mentioned Lord Acton's phrase concerning absolute power. Prichard quickly reacted: "Acton had a third line in there . . . 'All power tends to corrupt, absolute power corrupts absolutely, great men are seldom good men,' and I think that is true, true, true." The autobiographical reflection was not lost on many in the audience. "I think that you find moral complexities, moral ambiguities, antimonies, in the greatest of political leaders," he said. Then Prichard uttered a statement he had been known to repeat often in his later years, and it certainly had an autobiographical ring: "All have sinned and come short of the glory of God and I don't deny it for a minute." When Prichard added that FDR had all the personal inconsistencies that Buckley described, Buckley leaned forward and said, "You make things very hard for me by agreeing with everything" but then arriving at a completely different conclusion.

With a satisfied grin, Prichard told Buckley that was precisely what he intended. The audience erupted in applause as the agile host appeared checkmated.

Still, Buckley refused to allow Prichard to gain the upper hand. When discussing what FDR had done for African Americans, Prichard provided a list of accomplishments, including giving blacks jobs through the WPA. The gift of a job, Buckley mentioned, "didn't enhance the daughters of King Lear with their father." If Buckley thought such veiled references could slide by Prichard, he was quickly corrected. At the mention of Lear, Prichard's face brightened, and he fired back, "That's right. But they weren't the daughters of a king. If they had been in the royal court they might have felt differently."

The only moment when Prichard seemed to lose his patience with Buckley came over Prichard's discussion of government assistance. To Buckley's charges that the federal government had no role in the economic affairs of the nation, Prichard countered by listing those acts that benefited business, such as the homestead act, high tariffs, and assistance to railroads. "Those were incentives," Buckley said, not bribes in exchange for a vote. Prichard seized on Buckley's comment and said, "That's it. One man's bribe is another man's incentives!"

By the end of the night, Prichard remained unscathed. After the taping, *Firing Line* producer Warren Steibel seemed shell-shocked. "Who is this guy?" he asked members of the crowd. Prichard's allies who watched the show were almost giddy from observing his masterful performance, perhaps recognizing that a national audience might finally understand what they had known for years.[19]

It was as if a new generation had suddenly found a brilliant and unabashedly liberal voice that had been hidden in the political dustbin for decades. One who had known this voice since the days at Hockley, Arthur M. Schlesinger Jr., recalled that "to the end, he remained a New Dealer." Underneath the memory, the raconteur, the humor, Schlesinger knew that Prichard "was a deeply serious and radical man, more radical than he publicly admitted." The core of this radicalism, Schlesinger said, was that "he cared in age even more fiercely than he had in youth about the powerless and the dispossessed and the humiliated."[20]

Prichard's past was on national display again in 1983 when *U.S. News and World Report* broke the story that Prichard had been the subject of a wiretap while in Washington in 1945. Prichard had been told by Fred Vinson that his phone had been tapped, but it was not until a Kentucky senator on the Senate Intelligence Committee informed him of the FBI's wiretapping that he understood its full dimensions. Prichard called the wiretapping "a damned outrage" but felt confident it had yielded little valuable information. "The worst thing that they could have picked up," Prichard said, "was some comment as to whether the administration was going the way I thought it should."

Prichard refused to believe Truman had authorized the tap and said J. Edgar Hoover was "a paranoid neurotic of the worst order." The fact that Hoover had him under surveillance only surprised Prichard because "he found me significant enough to tap."[21] Prichard's wiretap, the article concluded, was one of the first documented cases of a president using the FBI for purely political reasons.

By the early 1980s, Prichard's newfound prominence within the Kentucky bar was generally acknowledged. As he had done for thirty years, Bert Combs wanted to help his dear friend, and he saw a wonderful opportunity. After leaving politics in the 1970s, Combs had teamed up with Wilson Wyatt to form one of the state's largest and most lucrative law firms. Combs wanted to bring Prichard into the firm in recognition of his skills as an attorney, and he wanted to provide a way for Prichard to make a sizable salary and receive other benefits. Although he had some health benefits from his inglorious stint in the U.S. Army, Prichard still owed the bulk of the back taxes that the IRS had hounded him about since 1960, and he needed a secure salary. Joe Terry, one of Prichard's old "clerks" now at Combs's firm, helped Prichard negotiate, in Terry's term, "a good deal." On January 3, 1983, Prichard officially joined the Lexington office of the state's premiere law firm.[22]

The "good deal" Prichard negotiated involved a significant amount of money. A week after joining Combs's firm, another significant event in Prichard's life occurred. After having earlier reached a settlement with the IRS for an undisclosed amount, the tax agency officially discharged him from his remaining tax liens, totalling $792,767.57, bringing at long last an end to the tax troubles that had plagued him for over two decades. Without such imposing debt on their backs, Ed and Lucy took out a mortgage for $200,000 to buy from Lucy's sister 138 acres of land around their home in Woodford County. Considering what he was up against, the surmounting of his IRS debts was yet another private struggle from which Prichard emerged victorious. It was a silent victory of which only he and Lucy knew the full parameters.[23]

Another of the perks he received from his new firm was a car and driver, which were especially helpful for his dialysis treatments. Lucy, it was said, was also delighted that her husband now worked for a prestigious firm. Just how valuable Prichard was to the firm is unclear. He handled mainly administrative law but could not endure too much work, considering the amount of time he had to spend on the dialysis table.

The dialysis came to dominate even the simplest of plans for Prichard and Lucy. They often spent time in the autumn at the summer cottage of New Dealers James and Libby Rowe on Cape Cod, where they would often see the Binghams. Throughout the vacation, however, Prichard had to undergo dialysis. When the forty-fifth reunion of the Harvard Law Class of 1938 was held, Prichard had to arrange dialysis treatments in Cambridge before he could attend. Accompanying Prichard to Massachusetts was none other than Phil Ardery. To those who attended the reunion, Prichard's appearance was a solemn and heartfelt moment. Robert Amory Jr. described Prichard's impromptu remarks as "terribly impressive" and added that following Prichard's appearance, "there was not a dry eye in the room." The trip with Ardery showed just how far Prichard had come in making peace with his former partner.[24]

Throughout his long relationship with the more pragmatic Bert Combs, Prichard had usually assumed the role of ideologue, but the scenario was reversed when Combs approached Prichard and Bob Sexton with a case he was considering undertaking. A number of school districts in the poorer counties of Kentucky sought Combs's help in a lawsuit they were filing against the state education system. Since the Kentucky constitution required that all students receive a fair and equitable education, the fact that large urban areas surrounding cities such as Louisville and Lexington had considerably more funds to spend on schools than the poorer counties presented a problem. The poorer school districts felt that the existing school system in the state was unconstitutional. Combs came to Prichard to inquire of "the philosopher" if the case had any merit. Prichard considered that the chances of winning were slim and recommended that he not pursue the case. Combs, as he had always done with Prichard, went with his own instincts and decided to press ahead. While neither Combs nor Prichard knew it at the time, it was the beginning of one of the most significant cases in education reform in Kentucky, and American, history.[25]

Shortly after joining the new firm, Prichard's time was divided between his work with the Prichard Committee and politics. Another gubernatorial primary loomed, and Prichard threw his support again behind Louisville mayor Harvey Sloane. Sloane's chief opponent was Lt. Gov. Martha Layne Collins. Prichard considered her "a lightweight" and was not afraid to send some pointed barbs her way. Before unleashing some remarks that criticized Collins, he told reporters that it was similar to "the taming of the shrew." He also used the term "cowardly" to describe a Collins TV ad against Sloane. But Prichard's final attempt to get "another governor" failed when Sloane lost the primary to Collins in May 1983. Prichard held no grudges and threw his support to Collins in the general election. He attributed Sloane's defeat to his candidate's refusal to take a stand on right-to-work laws and on Sloane's antiabortion rhetoric. When asked by reporters following the primary if he would retract his statements about Collins, Prichard said she "wouldn't be the first shrew I've supported, nor the first coward."[26]

Prichard seemed to relish his role as chairman of the committee named for him. Robert Sexton recalled that Prichard was back in his element—"He

enjoyed being the center of attention from the press and the movers and shak-
ers." With its newfound independence, the Prichard Committee became the
state's leading advocate for educational reform and was often at odds with
Governor Brown. Hopes were raised when Collins was elected governor in
November 1983. As a former educator herself, Collins proposed some major
changes in the state's education system, but those hopes were dashed when the
General Assembly quickly defeated the new governor's reforms in the 1984
session. State legislators voted against Collins's tax package for education because they sensed no groundswell of support for such actions. The Prichard
committee regrouped and decided to launch a statewide town forum to allow
the state's lawmakers to see firsthand the democratic aspirations of the citizenry. But the task of organizing the town forums was immense. Nearly 150
communities across the state were to be linked via educational television. If
this enterprise failed to document widespread support for reform, the chances
for the ensuing years looked bleak. Prichard understood the seminal importance of the forums and told an early organizing meeting of more than four
hundred people that they were "the shock troops in the battle for educational
improvement." Personally, Prichard told the organizers that "as long as I draw
breath, I will give everything to this cause." Throughout the summer of 1984,
Prichard worked the phones and traveled throughout the state to help ensure
that the forums, scheduled for November, would work. Concurrently, his once-
damaged reputation continued to soar. A poignant honor came in June when
he was awarded an honorary doctorate from Centre College, his father's and
Fred Vinson's alma mater. In the fall, Berea College (of which John Stephenson
was now president) approved the granting of an honorary degree to Prichard,
to be awarded in the spring of 1985.[27]

What Prichard understood in the final year of his life was the very essence
of democracy itself. For years, he had implicitly scorned democracy while devoted to furthering the causes of the Democratic party. As a boy, he had learned
all the techniques of skirting the people's will by resorting to various fraudulent voting procedures. As a young man, he had acquired a certain understanding of liberalism that infused the upper echelons of the New Deal—that
exceptionally bright, talented, well-educated elites, the "best and the brightest," would make the best managers of a "democratic" society. After the harsh
lessons of his imprisonment in Ashland, he had continued to work behind the
scenes with various governors to effect changes in social and political policy.
But to obtain something as fundamental as educational reform, Prichard understood that his usual methods could not work. He could make phone calls
to his well-placed contacts, he could raise money, he could use Churchillian
oratory, but none of that would have any significant impact without a democratic movement pushing for reform from below.

In a call for the public to attend one of their local forums, Prichard wrote that people should ask a fundamental question: "What do you want your schools to do?" In his opinion, Prichard suggested that the "chief aim of the schools is to help our children become a part of the larger community and to nourish them with those intellectual disciplines which should be a vital part of our lives." If successful, schools should help internalize in each student "a kind of intellectual independence, the ability to think for themselves and make choices in their family lives, and choices in the community and in society at large." A certain democratic flavor came through in Prichard's last public statement: "My view is based on the faith that if people are equipped with these basic capacities they can crown their education by learning to think for themselves and speak for themselves."[28]

Other areas of political life still remained passionate areas of Prichard's world. In September 1984, he addressed one of the central problems of modern politics, calling for public financing of campaigns to lessen the damaging influence of well-financed special interests. Describing most television ads "blarney," Prichard also said he would "outlaw every political commercial on television that was shorter than 15 minutes." Having been raised in a political milieu that relished long, serious debates that pitted one candidate's wits against another's, Prichard was greatly worried by the modern age of TV politics. He had earlier noted, "What we need is a use of television that will serve to reveal more about the candidate, instead of doing what it's doing now, which is to conceal most of what's really true." In considering how Lincoln might have fared in modern American politics, Prichard commented, "They'd have made him shave his beard off, put on a double-knit suit, go to some skin doctor and have the mole removed from his face, take speaking lessons to sound like a soap salesman." His call for public financing, of course, went unheard by state and national office seekers.[29]

As the night of the town forums approached, Prichard's health declined rapidly. As he dined in Lexington with Lucy and his old associate William Graham (by now a district judge), Prichard's energy was visibly sapped. He could not even make it through dinner without resting his head on the table. He wanted desperately to give the address that would begin the televised forums, but he simply could not do it. He was suffering from a fever and low blood pressure, and his doctors told him to remain at home and rest. On November 15, the day of the forum, a very ill Ed Prichard was home in bed.[30]

That night, the town forums were nothing short of remarkable. Bert Combs replaced Prichard in delivering the statewide address on education and then turned it over to the parents and teachers sitting in gymnasiums and town halls throughout the state. More than 20,000 people attended the forums in 145 different communities throughout Kentucky, and thousands more watched on television. In response to Prichard's call, thousands of suggestions and comments came in to the committee. In general, citizens of Kentucky said they wanted quality programs that stressed a mastery of fundamentals such as reading, writing, science, and mathematics. They wanted students to receive more individual attention, teachers to receive higher pay, and less politics within county school systems. Finally, there was universal agreement that more money was necessary. The "groundswell" that the General Assembly had said only months before did not exist was in high visibility that November evening.[31]

Two days after the forums, Prichard's health worsened. He checked into the Veterans Administration hospital in Lexington, where it was announced that he had an "undisclosed illness" and was in serious condition. For several days, his doctors ran a series of tests to determine his ailment. He continued to run a high fever and had an abnormal white blood count. Doctors decided Prichard's symptoms indicated a problem with his gall bladder, so they informed him that they needed to conduct exploratory surgery.

At age sixty-nine, having undergone dialysis for several years, and perhaps sensing that his body could not withstand the surgery, Prichard signed his last will and testament on November 21, 1984. With William Graham as a witness, he made Lucy the executrix of his estate. It was a succinct document with three unusual stipulations. He bequeathed $500 each to three of "my faithful helpers" who had provided much of the day-to-day assistance he needed to get by. Prichard also gave his church, St. John's in Versailles, the sum of $5,000. The final part of his will was revealing as well: "I hereby release all oral history taped interviews or dialogues which belong to me to my wife." Of all the things Prichard knew Lucy held dear, the dearest was her protection of his tragic history. Prichard signed the will in a scrawl that was vaguely reminiscent of the once-confident signature. Hours later, he underwent a four-hour operation to remove his gall bladder, but following the surgery his condition deteriorated, and he was listed in critical condition.[32]

Over the next few hours, Prichard made a comeback. He was "alert and able to communicate" within two days of the surgery, according to hospital officials. The only visitors allowed to see him were immediate family members. By the next day, his condition was upgraded from critical to "serious." For the next few days, he remained in the intensive-care unit. The *Lexington Herald-Leader* editorialized that "Kentuckians have been encouraged this week by the improved medical condition" of Ed Prichard. Understanding that Prichard would require a substantial amount of time for recuperation, the paper nonetheless stated, "His many friends have been heartened by his improvement thus far."[33]

Notions that Prichard was improving were short-lived. On November 30, doctors reported that his condition had worsened due to undisclosed "additional medical complications." The following day, Prichard underwent his second major surgery in ten days, as doctors removed more bile from his abdominal cavity and added more drainage tubes. The surgeons were pleased that Prichard's body seemed to tolerate the additional surgery. As December approached, he was listed in "serious but stable" condition.[34]

But, again, Prichard's improvement stalled. For three weeks in December 1984, his ailing body could not completely recover, and doctors were frustrated to find more internal abdominal bleeding. Their best efforts failed to stop the bleeding, and Prichard's condition worsened. As Christmas approached, he was a dying man. The doctors saw the situation as hopeless. Shortly after 8:00 P.M., on December 23, 1984, the end finally came. Edward F. Prichard Jr. was dead. His death came one day after the thirty-fourth anniversary of his return to Paris from prison.

Upon hearing of his death, Prichard's many friends and colleagues eagerly spoke about his special life and legacy. Ned Breathitt said, "Kentucky has just lost one of its most treasured sons," and noted that Prichard "had the ability to walk with kings or the lowliest person with equal ease." Earle Clements stated that Prichard was "the richest and most exciting intellect I have ever met." John Kenneth Galbraith said, "He was the most brilliant lawyer I ever knew." Katharine Graham reminisced that "Prich was a great human being and a lifelong friend." The *New York Times* and the *Washington Post* ran extended obituaries of the New Deal savant who lived such a tortured life after 1949, and local newspapers treated Prichard's death as a major front-page story.[35]

Following the funeral in Lexington, Prichard's cremated remains were buried next to his parents in the Prichard family plot in the Paris cemetery. Dotted throughout the graveyard are a litany of Bourbon County notables who had played such prominent roles in Prichard's life—Pearce Paton, Lee Kirkpatrick, and Judge Ardery are buried nearby. Prichard's grave is only some thirty feet from that of Cassius Clay, the man who so diligently kept the 1948 voting scandal on the front pages, and about fifty yards from the remains of Billy Baldwin. Prichard's simple marker reveals nothing to the casual observer of his remarkable odyssey. A small stone, with Lucy's name next to his, reads merely: "Edward Fretwell, Jr., January 21, 1915–December 23, 1984."

Epilogue

Kentuckians today have only a vague memory of one of the Commonwealth's most remarkable sons. The memory that endures is not of one of his high-level positions in Washington or even of ballot boxes; rather, Prichard is associated with the educational reform committee that still bears his name, and his legend continues to grow.[1] Prichard left many friends who subsequently contributed to that legend. In their view, he was one of the most brilliant men of his time, destined for greatness if not for a temporary lapse in judgment. Had it not been for a harmless "prank" or Judge Ardery's "disloyalty," Ed Prichard would certainly have been governor, senator, or perhaps president.

Besides ignoring Prichard's own role in the ballot-box scandal, such conclusions miss a deeper point. Prichard had not the ambition or the personality for such posts. Putting oneself up for an elective office requires an ego of the sort Prichard did not possess. Rather, Prichard preferred the role of the trusted lieutenant, where he could be inside the room when important political decisions were made; among the daily, almost casual, contacts with the power brokers; and within earshot of gossip he could later dispense to other political animals and deferential journalists. This was an intoxicating world that had fascinated Prichard from his youth. Whether listening to the local politicians at the Bourbon County courthouse discuss local elections or writing a presidential speech, Prichard thrived in the political arena, but not at the level of running for office. Being fully engaged within the realm of power was what Prichard needed, not leading it.

That realm, whether in Bourbon County or Washington, lavished praise on Prichard's extraordinary gifts of intellect and oratory while ignoring his considerable flaws. Prichard felt right at home in the rarefied air of the Frankfurters and the Berlins. He was accustomed, at an early age, to considerable influence within the upper echelons of power. In time, he considered himself to be somewhat immune from the rules that applied to everyone else. After all, his life up to 1948 seemed to suggest that Prichard lived in a rather different world—he had conquered the Ivy League without strenuous effort; he had risen so fast in Washington that he perhaps came to believe all the things so many of his friends said about him; and, upon his return to Kentucky, he became a very successful lawyer, even though he cared little about the daily practice of law. His name was mentioned nationally as a future political star. Without having to pay his dues, Prichard had grown used to flouting the rules.

Prichard was also a product of a political culture that existed outside the world of the Frankfurters and the Grahams, a Machiavellian subworld where his father, Pearce Paton, Billy Baldwin, and Tommy Corcoran lived. They were all political animals who taught Prichard that he could thrive in a world where personal relationships mattered far more than ideology and where the ends ultimately justified the means. Their methods became his methods.

To his enemies, Ed Prichard was an unscrupulous rogue who bent the rules—personal, financial, and political—at will, and whose legendary status is wholly undeserved. There are elements of truth in this assessment, but it ignores the fact that Prichard was not without principles. After all, he consistently fought for civil rights, labor, full employment, environmentalism, a merit system for state employees, and education reform when such views were often considered politically foolhardy. He usually conducted this work without any financial compensation and, except for the education reform committee, with little, if any, public recognition. Despite his many weaknesses, Prichard's passionate brand of politics remained with him throughout his life.

The truth is that Ed Prichard was a man of enormous contradictions. While surrounded by devoted friends who admired and adored him, he spent most of his life desperately lonely. Although he was blessed with a brilliant intellect, he did not possess the discipline to focus that magnificent mind for a sustained time until shortly before his death. He could be arrogant and audacious, but he was also deeply insecure. Lastly, and most profoundly, while he was committed to the ideological thrust of democracy, he was also taught to view democracy with a certain contempt. This essential paradox involved the very nature of political power—whether it is sought for its ultimate ends in order to ensure equality and promote democracy or primarily for its own sake and to be used as a means to benefit those who wield it. Prichard expressed it best when he stated that he was divided between his love of tradition and his commitment to egalitarianism. This tension, like most personal paradoxes, was never fully resolved.

To those who knew the full story, Prichard's saga was more than rise and fall, hubris and humiliation. His story revealed how courage can emerge from the depths of tragedy. After the onslaught of blindness and kidney failure, Prichard discovered a resiliency, discipline, and inner peace that sadly took most of his life to find. Despite overwhelming financial and physical challenges, as well as his many personal faults, Prichard came back from the throes of self-pity and despair to build a life of considerable accomplishment. He may not have prevailed, but he endured.

Prichard's lasting legacy to his state was the education reform to which he devoted the last part of his life. The Prichard Committee continued, and its pioneering work was instrumental in passage of the Kentucky Education Reform Act (KERA) in 1990, one of the most sweeping and fundamental public education reforms in the nation. Educational advocates were eager to acknowledge Prichard's leadership in launching the movement that led to KERA—the same man who years before could not even appear on the same platform with a prominent politician without enduring stinging criticism.

In his hometown of Paris, the memory of "the trial" continues to divide the community, and hard feelings still resonate. There are those in Bourbon County who praise the Arderys for steadfastly refusing to be tarnished by the corrupt Prichards; and many others remain bitter that Bill and Phil Ardery betrayed their longtime friend. In Paris there are, of course, no statues or markers recognizing Prichard, no streets or schools named for him. In the courthouse square, the house on Houston Avenue, or at the cemetery where he is buried, there is no hint that a man once lived here who bedazzled elite audiences in Princeton, Cambridge, and Washington.

There is, however, one place in Bourbon County where one can find a certain monument to "Prich." In the new county historical museum, patrons place their donations inside a small, metallic box. Over the box is a simple notice that such devices were once used in county elections but were later replaced by voting machines. In faded letters, one can even make out the word "Clintonville."[2] Prichard's name is never mentioned, and the infamous voting scandal is never acknowledged. Most visitors casually dismiss the tattered box as simply a nostalgic relic from a long dead era. But the box recalls a cynical political culture that once seduced a young political prodigy and, in the end, sowed the seeds of his downfall.

Notes

Introduction

1. *Louisville Courier-Journal* (hereafter cited as *C-J*), Dec. 26, 1984; *Lexington Herald-Leader* (hereafter cited as *H-L*), Dec. 25, 1984; *New York Times* (hereafter cited as *NYT*), Dec. 25, 1984; *Washington Post*, Dec. 25, 1984.

2. *C-J*, Dec. 28, 1984; *Kentucky New Era*, Dec. 28, 1984.

I The Political Education of "Sonny" Prichard

1. *Fourteenth Census of the United States, 1920: State Compendium, Kentucky* (Washington, D.C., 1924), 73; John Ed Pearce, "Bourbon County: The Quintessence of Kentucky," *Louisville Courier-Journal Magazine* (hereafter cited as *C-J Magazine*), May 5, 1985.

2. Pearce, "Bourbon County"; *Fourteenth Census*, 13, 31, 73; *Fifteenth Census of the United States, 1930: Population, Part I*, 951; Keith C. Barton, "'Good Cooks and Washers': Slave Hiring, Domestic Labor, and the Market in Bourbon County, Kentucky," *Journal of American History* 84 (1997): 436-60.

3. John W. Carpenter and William B. Scott Jr., *Kentucky Courthouses* (London: John W. Carpenter, 1988), 188-89.

4. Neal R. Peirce, *The Border South States: People, Politics, and Power in the Five Border South States* (New York: Norton, 1975), 220.

5. Robert M. Ireland, *The County in Kentucky History* (Lexington: Univ. Press of Kentucky, 1976), 12-14; James C. Klotter, *Kentucky: Portrait in Paradox, 1900-1950* (Frankfort: Kentucky Historical Society, 1996), 195-98; Lowell H. Harrison and James C. Klotter, *A New History of Kentucky* (Lexington: Univ. Press of Kentucky, 1997), 78. An essay on the modern aspects of political corruption in Kentucky is Bobbie Ann Mason, "Doing the Boptrot," *New Yorker*, May 9, 1994.

6. Thomas D. Clark, *Kentucky: Land of Contrast* (New York: Harper and Row, 1968), 162-63; Harrison and Klotter, *A New History of Kentucky*, 274-76. For other examples of vote fraud in Kentucky, see Larry J. Sabato and Glenn R. Simpson, *Dirty Little Secrets: The Persistence of Corruption in American Politics* (New York: Times Books, 1996), 298-99, 401-2.

7. Ireland, *County in Kentucky History*, 82.

8. Mildred McDaniel, "The Evolution of a Ruling Class in Contemporary County Government," Master's thesis, Univ. of Kentucky, 1949, 54-57; confidential information.

9. Clark, *Kentucky*, 163.

10. Charles Kerr, ed., *History of Kentucky* (Chicago: American Historical Society, 1922), 6:311-12.

11. Ibid.; *Who Was Who in America, 1961-68* (Chicago: Marquis, 1968), 4:34; Philip Ardery, *Heroes and Horses: Tales of the Bluegrass* (Lexington: Univ. Press of Kentucky, 1996), 11-12; *Lexington Leader*, Dec. 8, 1935; *C-J*, July 27, 1967.

12. Clay Family Papers, box 79, Special Collections, M.I. King Library, Univ. of Kentucky; Mary Clay Berry, *Voices from the Century Before: The Odyssey of a Nineteenth-Century Kentucky Family* (New York: Arcade, 1997); Temple Bodley and Samuel M. Wilson,

eds., *History of Kentucky: The Blue Grass State* (Chicago: Clarke Publishing, 1928), 1048-49.

13. John Ed Pearce, "The Man Who Might Have Been President," *C-J Magazine*, Oct. 24, 1976.

14. Bodley and Wilson, *History of Kentucky,* 509; McDaniel, "Evolution of a Ruling Class," 126, 171.

15. McDaniel, "Evolution of a Ruling Class," 54.

16. *Kentucky Post,* July 10, 1982; Henry Prichard, interview by author, Lexington, May 4, 1995.

17. E. Polk Johnson, *A History of Kentucky and Kentuckians* (Chicago: Lewis Publishing, 1912), 3:1718-19; Henry Prichard interview.

18. 1920 Bourbon County Manuscript Census; Bourbon County Deed Book, 1919, 602; Deed Book, 1924, 77; Henry Prichard interview.

19. Naomi Isrig Brill, interview by Terry Birdwhistell, Nov. 8, 1984, Prichard Oral History Project (hereafter cited as POHP), Special Collections, Univ. of Kentucky; Johnson, *A History of Kentucky,* 1718; Pearce, "The Man Who Might Have Been President."

20. Frederick A. Wallis, ed., *A Sesquicentennial History of Kentucky* (Hopkinsville: Historical Record Assoc., 1945), 1020; confidential information.

21. Henry Prichard interview.

22. *Kentucky Post,* July 10, 1982.

23. Confidential information.

24. *Kentucky Post,* July 10, 1982.

25. Brill interview; Philip Ardery, interview by author, Louisville, Sept. 15, 1994.

26. Katherine Dryden, interview by Terry Birdwhistell, Aug. 15, 1984, POHP.

27. Amos Taylor, interview by Terry Birdwhistell, July 24, 1984, POHP; *Kentucky Post,* July 10, 1982.

28. Elizabeth Brent, interview by Terry Birdwhistell, Aug. 2, 1984, POHP.

29. Ibid.; Pearce, "The Man Who Might Have Been President."

30. Henry Prichard, interview by author, Lexington, March 28, 1995; Frank J. Sulloway, *Born to Rebel: Birth Order, Family Dynamics, and Creative Lives* (New York: Pantheon, 1996), 83-118, 353.

It is not surprising that Henry Prichard was drawn to music rather than politics. Sulloway notes that for later-borns such as Power, "their most pressing problem is to find a valued family niche that avoids duplicating the one already staked out by the parent-identified firstborn. Instead, they seek to excel in those domains where older siblings have not already established superiority" (353).

31. Speech given by Prichard at seminar on the Kentucky Constitution revision, July 12, 1966, oral history tape, Pogue Library, Murray State Univ.

32. *Paris Kentuckian-Citizen,* August 30, 1922; Marion Mitchell, interview by Terry Birdwhistell, July 31, 1984, POHP.

33. Mitchell interview.

34. Philip Ardery interview (Sept. 15, 1994).

35. Pearce, "Man Who Might Have Been President."

36. Ibid.

37. John Ed Pearce, "Adversity and Atonement," *C-J Magazine,* Oct. 31, 1976; *Boston Globe,* May 15, 1983.

38. Pearce, "Adversity and Atonement"; Pearce, "The Man Who Might Have Been President"; Brent interview.

39. Philip Ardery interview (Sept. 15, 1994).

40. Brent interview.

41. Brill interview.

42. Philip Ardery interview (Sept. 15, 1994).

43. Taylor interview; Pearce, "The Man Who Might Have Been President."

44. *H-L*, July 21, 1931; "Ardery File," Thomas R. Underwood Papers, Special Collections, Univ. of Kentucky; Philip Ardery interview (Sept. 15, 1994); *H-L*, July 21, 1931.

45. *Paris Kentuckian-Citizen*, May 6, July 22, 1931.

46. George T. Blakey, *Hard Times and New Deal in Kentucky, 1929-1939* (Lexington: Univ. Press of Kentucky, 1986), 10-11; Klotter, *Kentucky*, 245-49.

47. *H-L*, July 21, 1931.

48. Ardery, *Heroes and Horses*, 79.

2 Banishment to Paradise

1. Jamie Sayen, *Einstein in America: The Scientists' Conscience in the Age of Hitler and Hiroshima* (New York: Crown Publishers, 1985), 64.

2. Ibid., 219.

3. Pearce, "The Man Who Might Have Been President"; *Bourbon County Citizen*, Dec. 29, 1984; Arthur M. Schlesinger Jr., "'Prich': A New Deal Memoir," *New York Review of Books*, March 28, 1985.

4. *Daily Princetonian*, Feb. 10, 22, 23, 1932.

5. Ibid., March 3, April 5, 1932; Toynbee quoted in William E. Leuchtenburg, *The FDR Years: On Roosevelt and His Legacy* (New York: Columbia Univ. Press, 1995), 6.

6. *Daily Princetonian*, April 14, 1932.

7. Ibid., April 28, 1932.

8. Ibid., May 13, 14, 1932.

9. Ibid., Nov. 1, 1932.

10. Ibid., Oct. 27, Nov. 5, 1932; James Wechsler, *Revolt on the Campus* (New York: Covici Friede, 1935), 426.

11. *Daily Princetonian*, Nov. 3, 4, 1932.

12. Ibid., Nov. 2, 1932.

13. Ibid., Nov. 17, 1932.

14. Pearce, "The Man Who Might Have Been President."

15. *Daily Princetonian*, Feb. 2, 3, 4, 1933.

16. Ibid., Feb. 23, May 12, 1933; Gordon A. Craig, telephone interview with author, Dec. 2, 1994.

17. *Daily Princetonian*, Nov. 28, 1933.

18. Ibid., Oct. 25, 1933.

19. Richard Wightman Fox, *Reinhold Niebuhr: A Biography* (New York: Pantheon, 1985), 121, 129; Paul Merkley, *Reinhold Niebuhr: A Political Account* (Montreal: McGill-Queen's Univ. Press, 1975), 32-42; John Egerton, *Speak Now Against the Day: The Generation Before the Civil Rights Movement in the South* (New York: Knopf, 1994), 78, 126, 127.

20. *Daily Princetonian*, Dec. 13, 1933.

21. Ibid., Feb. 10, 1934.

22. Ibid., Feb. 21, 23, 1934; Craig interview.

23. *Daily Princetonian*, Feb. 24, March 3, 1934.

24. Ibid., March 10, 1934.

25. *Princeton Alumni Weekly,* Nov. 10, 1939; *Daily Princetonian,* March 24, April 21, 28, 1934.

26. *Daily Princetonian,* May 2, 1934.

27. Ibid., June 1, 1934.

28. Ibid., Aug. 29, 1934; *Princeton Alumni Weekly,* Oct. 12, 1934.

29. *Daily Princetonian,* Sept. 29, 1934.

30. Geoffrey C. Ward, *A First-Class Temperament: The Emergence of Franklin Roosevelt* (New York: Harper and Row, 1989), 311; *Daily Princetonian,* Oct. 10, 1934; *NYT,* Oct. 10, 1934. See also James C. Klotter, *The Breckinridges of Kentucky, 1760-1981* (Lexington: Univ. Press of Kentucky, 1986), 241-42.

31. *Daily Princetonian,* Oct. 11, 1934.

32. *NYT,* Oct. 11, 1934; *Cincinnati Enquirer,* Oct. 11, 1934.

33. *NYT,* Oct. 11, 1934.

34. Craig interview.

35. *NYT,* Oct. 11, 1934.

36. Ibid., Oct. 12, 1934; *The Daily Princetonian,* Oct. 12, 1934.

37. *Daily Princetonian,* Oct. 16, 1934.

38. Ibid., Oct. 18, 1934.

39. Ibid., Oct. 27, Nov. 7, 1934.

40. *Princeton Nassau Herald,* 1935; Robert Cohen, *When the Old Left Was Young: Student Radicals and America's First Mass Student Movement, 1929-1941* (New York: Oxford Univ. Press, 1993), 94-97.

41. *Daily Princetonian,* Nov. 13, Dec. 12, 1934.

42. Ibid., Jan. 14, 1935.

43. Ibid., Jan. 15, 1935.

44. Ibid., Feb. 6, 1935.

45. Edward Fretwell Prichard Jr. (hereafter cited as EFP) to Earle C. Clements, Sept. 28, 1978, in Earle C. Clements Papers, personal correspondence, box 5, Special Collections, Univ. of Kentucky; Thomas D. Clark, interview by author, Lexington, Dec. 29, 1994.

46. *Daily Princetonian,* April 12, 1935.

47. Ibid., April 16, 1935.

48. *Louisville Times,* Dec. 17, 1983; Prichard celebration, Louisville, 1979, videotape in possession of Sara Combs, Stanton, Kentucky; Frankfurter to Elizabeth Morris Graham, Nov. 5, 1964, File 59, Felix Frankfurter Papers, Library of Congress.

49. *Daily Princetonian,* May 3, 18, 20, 1935.

50. Ibid., May 9, 1935.

51. Edward F. Prichard Jr., "Popular Political Movements in Kentucky, 1875-1900" (senior honors thesis, Princeton Univ., 1935), 30-31.

52. Ibid., 74. For an extended analysis of the threads between Greenbackerism and American Populism, see Lawrence Goodwyn, *Democratic Promise: The Populist Moment in America* (New York: Oxford Univ. Press, 1976), 135-53, 565-81.

53. Prichard, "Popular Political Movements," 256.

54. Ibid.; *Daily Princetonian,* June 15, 1935.

55. In his bibliography, Woodward noted that Prichard's senior thesis "was helpful." See Woodward, *Origins of the New South, 1877-1913* (Baton Rouge: Louisiana State Univ. Press, 1951), 504.

56. Craig interview.

3 Harvard Law School

1. *Introductory Suggestions for Law School Work for the First-Year Students in the Harvard Law School, 1928-29* (Cambridge: Harvard Univ. Press, 1928), 5; Arthur E. Sutherland, *The Law at Harvard: A History of Ideas and Men, 1918-1967* (Cambridge: Harvard Univ. Press, 1967), 221-22; Sidney Post Simpson, "The New Harvard Curriculum," *Harvard Law Review* 51 (April 1938): 966-87; Philip Elman Oral History, Columbia Univ. For a modern perspective on the first year at Harvard Law School, see Scott Turow, *One L* (New York: Farrar Straus Giroux, 1988).

2. Harvard Law School Yearbook, vol. 2, 1938-39, Harvard Law School Archives; *Life*, Nov. 1, 1937; Edward H. Warren, *Spartan Education* (Boston: Houghton Mifflin, 1942), ix, 22, 24; John Houseman, *Unfinished Business: Memoirs, 1902-1988* (New York: Applause Theatre Books, 1989), 461.

3. John Ed Pearce, *Divide and Dissent: Kentucky Politics, 1930-1963* (Lexington: Univ. Press of Kentucky, 1987), 39.

4. *Paris Kentuckian-Citizen*, Aug. 21, 1935; Pearce, "Adversity and Atonement"; Blakey, *Hard Times and New Deal*, 177-79; Klotter, *Kentucky*, 304-6. Chandler, incidentally, had attended Harvard Law School himself in the early 1920s. Though he later claimed he left Cambridge because of money, the real reason Chandler left Harvard to attend the University of Kentucky Law School was provided by Erwin Griswold—Chandler flunked out. Erwin Griswold, interview by Terry Birdwhistell, Washington, D.C., March 21, 1986, POHP.

5. *Paris Kentuckian-Citizen*, Aug. 2, 1935.

6. *Time*, June 19, 1939; Philip Ardery, interviews by author, Louisville, July 26, Sept. 15, 1994; William K. Van Allen, interview by author, Charlotte, North Carolina, Sept. 27, 1994.

7. Griswold interview.

8. Ibid.; Robert Amory Jr. interview by Terry Birdwhistell, Washington, D.C., March 19, 1986, POHP; Brent interview.

9. Morton Holbrook, interview by author, Owensboro, Kentucky, June 16, 1995; Van Allen interview; Laura Kalman, *Legal Realism at Yale, 1927-1960* (Chapel Hill: Univ. of North Carolina Press, 1986), ch. 2; Donald A. Ritchie, *James M. Landis: Dean of the Regulators* (Cambridge: Harvard Univ. Press, 1980), 30-31.

10. Pearce, *Divide and Dissent*, 39.

11. "The Law School," *Harvard Law Review* 51 (Dec. 1937): 310; Philip Ardery interview (July 26, 1994); Philip P. Ardery, "Prich," *Filson Club History Quarterly* 68 (Oct. 1994): 503; Ardery, *Heroes and Horses*, 79-80; Van Allen interview.

12. *Princeton Alumni Weekly*, Nov. 6, 1936; Philip Ardery interview (Sept. 15, 1994); Van Allen interview; Holbrook interview.

13. Holbrook interview.

14. David Halberstam, *The Powers That Be* (New York: Knopf, 1979), 167.

15. Ibid.; Frankfurter to Elizabeth Morris Graham, Nov. 5, 1964, Frankfurter Papers.

16. Halberstam, *The Powers That Be*, 158-59; Joseph L. Rauh Jr., interview by Terry Birdwhistell, March 21, 1986, POHP.

17. Philip Ardery interview, Sept. 15, 1994; "Ames Competition Briefs," Harvard Law School, 1936-37, no. 63, Harvard Law School Archives.

18. Philip Ardery interview (July 26, 1994); Ardery, "Prich," 504.

19. EFP to A.B. Chandler, telegram, Dec. 19, 1936, box 13, Albert B. Chandler Papers, Special Collections, Univ. of Kentucky.

20. Bruce Allen Murphy, *The Brandeis/Frankfurter Connection: The Secret Political Activities of Two Supreme Court Justices* (New York: Oxford Univ. Press, 1982), 76.

21. Ardery, *Heroes and Horses*, 81.

22. Harvard Law School Yearbook, 318; Philip Ardery interview (Sept. 15, 1994).

23. EFP to editor, *NYT*, May 6, 1937.

24. Amory interview.

25. *Life*, Nov. 1, 1937. A poignant memoir of another Ivy League "wonder boy" who was featured in *Life* while in college and also later self-destructed is Calvin Trillin, *Remembering Denny* (New York: Farrar Straus Giroux, 1993).

26. Griswold interview. For a review of how the "court-packing" controversy resonated at the Harvard Law School, see Ritchie, *James M. Landis*, 82-84. Prichard later remarked that "Roosevelt's greatest political mistake was not his fight on the Supreme Court but in allowing Henry Morgenthau and his own inherent fiscal orthodoxy to lead him into the deflationary folly of 1937. It was the depression of 1937 which took the political bloom off of the New Deal and which led to the political reverses of 1938 . . . in many ways, the great tragedy of the New Deal was that Mr. Roosevelt never became a convinced New Dealer, at least in the Keynesian sense, until he had lost the political initiative." EFP to Arthur M. Schlesinger Jr., Sept. 13, 1960, Arthur M. Schlesinger Jr. Papers, John F. Kennedy Library, Boston.

27. Klotter, *Kentucky*, 310-15; Pearce, *Divide and Dissent*, 45.

28. *NYT*, April 15, 1938.

29. Rauh interview; Jerold S. Auerbach, *Labor and Liberty: The LaFollette Committee and the New Deal* (Indianapolis: Bobbs-Merrill, 1966); Hollinger F. Bernard, ed., *Outside the Magic Circle: The Autobiography of Virginia Foster Durr* (Tuscaloosa: Univ. of Alabama Press, 1985), 108-9; Katie Louchheim, ed., *The Making of the New Deal: The Insiders Speak* (Cambridge: Harvard Univ. Press, 1983), 67-68; Patrick J. Maney, *"Young Bob" LaFollette: A Biography of Robert M. LaFollette, Jr., 1895-1953* (Columbia: Univ. of Missouri Press, 1978), 212-13. Paul Y. Anderson, writing for *The Nation*, was not as impressed with LaFollette's questioning of Girdler as was Prichard. The "duel" between Girdler and LaFollette, Anderson thought, "turned out to be pretty much of a flop." *Nation*, Aug. 20, 1938.

30. See Henry M. Hart Jr. and Edward F. Prichard Jr., "The Fansteel Case: Employee Misconduct and the Remedial Powers of the National Labor Relations Board," *Harvard Law Review* 52 (June 1939): 1275-1329; Louchheim, *Making of the New Deal*, 68; William E. Leuchtenburg, *The Supreme Court Reborn: The Constitutional Revolution in the Age of Roosevelt* (New York: Oxford Univ. Press, 1995), 229. For Prichard's original manuscripts, see Henry M. Hart Papers, box 29, Harvard Law School Archives.

31. MacLeish to Frankfurter, Feb. 20, 1939, Frankfurter Papers; Felix Frankfurter, *Mr. Justice Holmes and the Supreme Court* (Cambridge: Harvard Univ. Press, 1939); Scott Donaldson, *Archibald MacLeish: An American Life* (New York: Houghton Mifflin, 1992), 290-91.

32. Halberstam, *The Powers That Be*, 168; Frankfurter to Philip Graham, Feb. 6, 1939, File 59, Frankfurter Papers.

4 An Extended Campus

1. Quoted in David Brinkley, *Washington Goes to War* (New York: Knopf, 1988).

2. Van Allen interview.

3. *Princeton Alumni Weekly*, Nov. 14, 1941; James McGlothlin, telephone interview with author, Feb. 1, 1995.

4. Van Allen interview; McGlothlin interview.

5. Katharine Graham, interview by author, Washington, D.C., June 9, 1995.

6. Katharine Graham, interview by Vic Hellard, July 26, 1983, POHP; McGlothlin interview; Katharine Graham, *Personal History* (New York: Knopf, 1997), 106-9.

7. Graham, *Personal History,* 109; EFP to Eugene Meyer, Jan. 10, 1940, box 39, Eugene Meyer Papers, Library of Congress.

8. Van Allen interview; Katharine Graham interview (Hellard); McGlothlin interview; Schlesinger, "'Prich'"; *Princeton Alumni Weekly,* Dec. 15, 1939; Louchheim, *Making of the New Deal,* 73; *Boston Globe,* May 15, 1983.

Prichard's personality shares many of the same qualities as described by British psychologist Hans Eysenck's definition of a "Typical Extrovert": he "is sociable, likes parties, has many friends, needs to have people to talk to . . . he often acts on the spur of the moment, and is generally an impulsive individual." Eysenck quoted in Sulloway, *Born to Rebel,* 173.

9. *Louisville Times,* Dec. 17, 1983; EFP to Eleanor Roosevelt, Jan. 8, 1940, box 1616, Eleanor Roosevelt Papers, Franklin D. Roosevelt Library.

10. *Fortune,* Aug. 1945.

11. Norman M. Littell, *My Roosevelt Years,* ed. Jonathan Dembo (Seattle: Univ. of Washington Press, 1987), 215-16; Graham, *Personal History,* 109; Kentucky Educational Television, "Distinguished Kentuckian," produced by O. Leonard Press, Sept. 18, 1974.

12. Schlesinger, "'Prich'"; Rauh interview.

13. Roger K. Newman, *Hugo Black: A Biography* (New York: Pantheon, 1994), 284; James F. Simon, *The Antagonists: Hugo Black, Felix Frankfurter, and Civil Liberties in Modern America* (New York: Simon and Schuster, 1989), 108-12.

14. *Minersville School District v Gobitis,* 310 US 586, 8 (1940).

15. On June 14, 1943—Flag Day—the Supreme Court reversed its decision in the *Gobitis* case by a 6-3 vote in *West Virginia State Board of Education v Barnette.* Despite the protestations of his new clerk, Philip Elman, Frankfurter issued a dissent in the case. Henry J. Abraham and Barbara A. Perry, *Freedom and the Court: Civil Rights and Liberties in the United States,* 6th ed. (New York: Oxford Univ. Press, 1994), 238-42; Kermit Hall, ed., *The Oxford Companion to the Supreme Court of the United States* (New York: Oxford Univ. Press, 1992), 551, 925-26.

16. Rauh interview; Simon, *The Antagonists,* 108-12.

17. In the Rauh interview, Rauh acknowledged that Prichard spoke with him on numerous cases while serving as Frankfurter's clerk, and that Prichard also discussed court matters with Phil Graham. Rauh felt that Frankfurter was aware Prichard discussed such sensitive matters outside the Court.

18. Gobitis draft, Frankfurter Papers; Simon, *The Antagonists,* 112-13; *Christian Century* quoted in Terry Eastland, ed., *Religious Liberty in the Supreme Court: The Cases That Define the Debate Over Church and State* (Washington, D.C.: Ethics and Public Policy Center, 1993), 37; Abraham and Perry, *Freedom and the Court,* 238-39; Melvin I. Urofsky, *Felix Frankfurter: Judicial Restraint and Individual Liberties* (Boston: Twayne, 1991), 50-52.

19. Prichard, "One-Man Army for Humanity," *Washington Post Book World,* Oct. 26, 1975.

20. Schlesinger, "'Prich'"; Rauh interview.

21. Louchheim, *Making of the New Deal,* 71.

22. Katharine Graham (author), June 9, 1995.

23. Katharine Graham (author); Graham, *Personal History,* 121-22; Rauh interview; Schlesinger, "'Prich.'"

24. Katharine Graham interview (author); Harold Ickes diary, May 3, 1942, Ickes Papers, Library of Congress; EFP to Philip Graham, December 20, 1942, in the private possession of Katharine Graham, Washington, D.C. (hereafter cited as Graham Papers); EFP to Arthur M. Schlesinger Jr., Sept. 13, 1960, Schlesinger Papers.

25. Arthur M. Schlesinger Jr., telephone interview with author, November 7, 1996; confidential information; Graham, *Personal History,* 127. Evangeline Bell later married David Bruce, who was ambassador to the Court of St. James's in the Kennedy and Johnson administrations.

She remained a close friend of Prichard's for the rest of his life. See also Nelson D. Lankford, *The Last American Aristocrat: The Biography of David K.E. Bruce* (Boston: Little, Brown, 1996), 169-72; *Look,* Aug. 13, 1963.

26. Meyer to EFP, n.d., EFP to Meyer, n.d., Meyer Papers; Graham, *Personal History,* 132-33.

27. Robert H. Jackson Oral History, Columbia Univ.; EFP to Robert H. Jackson, Feb. 5, 1941, Robert H. Jackson Papers, Library of Congress.

28. EFP to Francis Biddle, March 3, 1941, Jackson Papers.

29. Jackson Oral History; Jackson to Francis Biddle, March 7, 1941, Jackson Papers.

30. J. Edgar Hoover to Jackson, April 5, 1941, Jackson Papers; Athan G. Theoharis and John Stuart Cox, *The Boss: J. Edgar Hoover and the Great American Inquisition* (Philadelphia: Temple Univ. Press, 1988), 13. During this period, Jackson often defended the FBI against charges that it was becoming an "American Gestapo." Eugene C. Gerhart, *America's Advocate: Robert H. Jackson* (Indianapolis: Bobbs-Merrill, 1958), 190-212. See also Richard Gid Powers, *Not Without Honor: The History of American Anticommunism* (New York: Free Press, 1995), 161-64.

31. EFP to Francis Biddle, June 11, 1941, Jackson Papers. It is probable that Prichard had met Keynes in Washington, since the British economist was close friends with both Felix Frankfurter and Isaiah Berlin. For Keynes's relationships with some selected Washington insiders, see Roy Harrod, *The Life of John Maynard Keynes* (New York: Norton, 1951), 555-56, and Jordan A. Schwarz, *The New Dealers: Power Politics in the Age of Roosevelt* (New York: Vintage, 1993), 134-35.

32. *Fortune,* Aug. 1945.

33. *Boston Globe,* May 15, 1983; Prichard Personnel Report, Oct. 29, 1941, box 29, Oscar Cox Papers, Roosevelt Library.

34. Steven Fraser, *Labor Will Rule: Sidney Hillman and the Rise of American Labor* (New York: Free Press, 1991), 293-97, 460-61; James MacGregor Burns, *Roosevelt: The Soldier of Freedom* (New York: Harcourt Brace Jovanovich, 1970), 50-53; I.F. Stone, "Division in the OPM," *Nation,* March 8, 1941. Historian Alan Brinkley writes that because of accommodationists within the labor movement like Hillman, Labor's prospects diminished in the early 1940s. "Labor's own leaders," Brinkley argues, "were already gravitating . . . toward a new vision of political economy in which the idea of 'industrial democracy' played no important role." Alan Brinkley, *The End of Reform: New Deal Liberalism in Recession and War* (New York: Knopf, 1995), 224-25.

35. Schlesinger interview; Fraser, *Labor Will Rule,* 483; Paul A.C. Koistenen, "Mobilizing the World War II Economy: Labor and the Industrial-Military Alliance," *Pacific Historical Review* 42 (Nov. 1973): 447-48.

36. EFP to Hillman, Dec. 15, 1941, Sidney Hillman Papers, Labor-Management Documents Center, Cornell Univ.

37. Fraser, *Labor Will Rule,* 462-63, 645-56.

38. Drew Pearson, "Washington Merry-Go-Round," *C-J,* Jan. 19, 1942.

39. Robert Nathan, interview by author, Arlington, Va., June 9, 1995; Graham, *Personal History,* 136.

40. EFP to Hillman, Feb. 25, 1942, Hillman Papers.

41. Nelson Lichtenstein, *Labor's War at Home: The CIO in World War II* (Cambridge: Cambridge Univ. Press, 1982), 84; *Princeton Alumni Weekly,* Nov. 14, 1941; EFP to Wayne Coy, April 7, 1942, Wayne Coy Papers, Franklin D. Roosevelt Library. Keynes had proposed a program of compulsory savings and additional taxes in 1940. See William J. Barber, *Designs Within Dis-*

order: Franklin D. Roosevelt, the Economists, and the Shaping of American Economic Policy, 1933-1945 (Cambridge: Cambridge Univ. Press, 1996), 134-35.

42. EFP to Oscar Cox, Oct. 5, 1942; Cox to EFP, Oct. 6, 1942, Cox Papers; David Robertson, *Sly and Able: A Political Biography of James F. Byrnes* (New York: Norton, 1994), 318-20.

43. "Personnel Action on Edward F. Prichard, Jr.," packet 5, part 1, James F. Byrnes Papers, Clemson Univ.

44. *Newsweek,* Jan. 4, 1943.

5 The Wunderkind

1. Robertson, *Sly and Able,* 20-27, 298-300, 318-26.

2. FDR to Cohen, Sept. 4, 1941, box 12, Benjamin V. Cohen Papers, Library of Congress; Schwarz, *The New Dealers,* 143-45; Cabell Phillips, "The New Dealers—Where Are They Now?" *NYT Magazine,* Sept. 29, 1946.

3. Harold L. Ickes diary, Jan. 3, 1943, Ickes Papers, Library of Congress; Louchheim, *Making of the New Deal,* 72.

4. Robertson, *Sly and Able,* 184-85, 250, 256, 282; Thomas S. Morgan, "James F. Byrnes and Segregation," *The Historian* 56 (summer 1994): 646; Fraser, *Labor Will Rule,* 530-33.

5. *Fortune,* Aug. 1945.

6. Sir Isaiah Berlin, telephone interview with author, Feb. 12, 1995; Schlesinger, "'Prich.'"

7. Louchheim, *Making of the New Deal,* 73. This story has grown to somewhat apocryphal heights. Arthur M. Schlesinger Jr. wrote that Prichard was having his hair cut when the call came from FDR himself. The Knox scenario in Frankfurter's office was the version repeated by Prichard.

8. Jonathan Daniels, *White House Witness: 1942-1945* (Garden City, N.J.: Doubleday, 1975), 41-42, 115-16.

9. John Kenneth Galbraith, interview by William Cooper, Cambridge, Mass., June 9, 1987, POHP.

10. Galbraith interview; Eliot Janeway, *The Struggle for Survival: A Chronicle of Economic Mobilization in World War II* (New Haven: Yale Univ. Press, 1951), 295; Carl Hamilton Oral History, Columbia Univ.

11. Claude Wickard Oral History, Columbia Univ.; Chester C. Davis Oral History, Columbia Univ.

12. Jesse W. Tapp Oral History, Columbia Univ.

13. EFP to James F. Byrnes, May 26, 1943, RG 250, box 15, Office of War Mobilization records, National Archives. For a labor perspective on wartime wage and price issues, see Nelson Lichtenstein, *The Most Dangerous Man in Detroit: Walter Reuther and the Fate of American Labor* (New York: Basic Books, 1995), ch. 8.

14. James F. Byrnes, *All in One Lifetime* (New York: Harper, 1958), 198-99.

15. Samuel Bledsoe Oral History, Columbia Univ.; Hamilton Oral History. See also Roger J. Sandilands, *The Life and Political Economy of Lauchlin Currie: New Dealer, Presidential Adviser, and Development Economist* (Durham: Duke Univ. Press, 1990), ch. 4.

16. Studs Terkel, *The Good War: An Oral History of World War II* (New York: Pantheon, 1984), 321; see also Lash, *Dealers and Dreamers: A New Look at the New Deal* (New York: Doubleday, 1988).

17. Monica Lynne Niznik, "Thomas G. Corcoran: The Public Service of Franklin Roosevelt's 'Tommy the Cork,'" (Ph.D. diss., Univ. of Notre Dame, 1981), 1-18, 132, 234-

35, 380-85, 518-19; T.H. Watkins, *Righteous Pilgrim: The Life and Times of Harold L. Ickes, 1874-1952* (New York: Henry Holt, 1990), 693; Allan J. Lichtman, "Tommy the Cork: The Secret World of Washington's First Modern Lobbyist," *Washington Monthly*, Feb. 1987, 47.

18. Joseph C. Goulden, *The Super-Lawyers: The Small and Powerful World of the Great Washington Law Firms* (New York: Weybright and Talley, 1971), 153; Bob Woodward and Scott Armstrong, *The Brethren: Inside the Supreme Court* (New York: Simon and Schuster, 1979), 88-95; Corcoran to Hubert Humphrey, Aug. 31, 1956, "Corcoran File," Famous Names List, Johnson Library.

19. Rauh, interview by Paige Mulhollan, July 30, 1969, Oral History Collection, Johnson Library. On these years in Johnson's life before winning election to the Senate, see Robert A. Caro, *Means of Ascent: The Years of Lyndon Johnson* (New York: Knopf, 1990). Caro describes these years as "years of hopelessness and despair" for the ambitious Texan (xxviii).

20. Wickard Oral History; Thomas I. Emerson Oral History, Columbia Univ.; Graham, *Personal History*, 154.

21. Schlesinger, "'Prich'"; *Boston Globe*, May 15, 1983.

22. *Fortune*, 1945; Marvin Jones Oral History, Columbia Univ.; Daniels, *White House Witness*, 81.

23. John Morton Blum, *V Was For Victory: Politics and American Culture During World War II* (New York: Harcourt Brace Jovanovich, 1976), 122.

24. Bruce Catton, *The War Lords of Washington* (New York: Greenwood, 1948), 207.

25. Janeway, *The Struggle for Survival*, 317-22; Catton, *War Lords of Washington*, 204-7; Brinkley, *The End of Reform*, 195-98; Robert E. Sherwood, *Roosevelt and Hopkins: An Intimate History* (New York: Harper, 1948), 699-700. In his recounting of this event, Nelson wrote only that "one of my most trusted assistants" had tipped him off concerning Roosevelt's plan to fire Nelson and replace him with Baruch. See Donald Nelson, *Arsenal of Democracy: The Story of American War Production* (New York: Harcourt, Brace, 1946), 388-89.

26. Robertson, *Sly and Able*, 326-27; Personnel Memo, June 9, 1943, packet 5, Byrnes Papers; Nelson *Arsenal of Democracy*, 389. It is unknown whether Byrnes knew of Prichard's role in the Nelson episode.

27. *C-J*, Oct. 4, 1976; *C-J Magazine*, June 24, 1945.

28. Earle Clements to EFP, Aug. 16, 1978, Clements Papers.

29. *Fortune*, Aug. 1945; *C-J*, July 27, Aug. 6, 1943; *Newsweek*, Aug. 16, 1943; Janeway, *The Struggle for Survival*, 322.

30. EFP to Philip Graham, Sept. 16, 1943, Graham Papers; *H-L*, Feb. 21, 1979; Bourbon County Women's Club, "Bourbon County Men and Women Who Served in World War II," Kentucky Historical Society; Daniels, *White House Witness*, 41-42.

31. Daniels, *White House Witness*, 194-95.

32. Richard Hedlund, "The Most Hated Man in America: Fred Vinson and the Office of Economic Stabilization," *Filson Club History Quarterly* 68 (April 1994): 267-69.

33. Marvin Jones Oral History; Davis Oral History; EFP to Vinson, April 20, 1944, box 108, Frederick M. Vinson Papers, Special Collections, Univ. of Kentucky.

34. Thomas I. Emerson, *Young Lawyer for the New Deal: An Insider's Memoir of the Roosevelt Years* (Savage, Md.: Rowman and Littlefield, 1991), 267-77.

35. Burns, *Roosevelt*, 338; Joel Seidman, *American Labor from Defense to Reconversion* (Chicago: Univ. of Chicago Press, 1953), 122-23.

36. *C-J*, June 27, 1943.

37. *Boston Globe*, May 15, 1983.

38. *C-J*, Jan. 20, 1944.

39. *Fortune*, Aug. 1945; EFP to Vinson, April 28, 1944, box 51, Vinson Papers; Lichtenstein, *Labor's War at Home*, 208-9.

40. EFP to Vinson, July 17, 1944, box 112, Vinson Papers.

41. Donald A. Ritchie, "Alben W. Barkley: The President's Man," in *First Among Equals: Outstanding Senate Leaders of the Twentieth Century*, eds. Richard A. Baker and Roger H. Davidson (Washington, D.C.: Congressional Quarterly, 1991), 147; "Kentucky's New Dealer: Ed Prichard Remembers," produced by Britt Davis, Kentucky Educational Television, 1984; Alben W. Barkley, *That Reminds Me* (Garden City: Doubleday, 1954), 169-82; Samuel I. Rosenman, *Working with Roosevelt* (New York: Harper, 1952), 429; Byrnes, *All in One Lifetime*, 210-11; Burns, *Roosevelt*, 434-44; George W. Robinson, "Alben Barkley and the 1944 Tax Veto," *Register of the Kentucky Historical Society* 67 (July 1969): 205-7; Doris Kearns Goodwin, *No Ordinary Time: Franklin and Eleanor Roosevelt: The Home Front in World War II* (New York: Simon and Schuster, 1994), 486-87.

42. EFP to Eugene Meyer, Sept. 29, 1944, and EFP to Meyer, Nov. 10, 1944, box 39, Meyer Papers.

43. Katharine Graham interview (author); Graham, *Personal History*, 198.

44. EFP to Philip Graham, Sept. 8, 1944, Graham Papers; Wayne Coy to EFP, Sept. 12, 1944, box 39, Meyer Papers. Porter later formed one of Washington's most prestigious law firms, Arnold, Fortas, and Porter, with Thurman Arnold and Abe Fortas.

45. *Fortune*, Aug. 1945; *Firing Line with William F. Buckley*, #1218, produced by Warren Steibel, Oct. 27, 1982; 1983; Henry Prichard interview (March 28, 1995); EFP to Harold Ickes, Sept. 18, 1944, Harold Ickes Papers.

46. EFP to Frankfurter, Jan. 5, 1945, Frankfurter Papers; Cohen to Roosevelt, Jan. 16, 1945, box 12, Cohen Papers; FDR to Cohen, Jan. 20, 1945, Cohen Papers. When James F. Byrnes was named secretary of state by Harry Truman, one of his first appointments was to make Cohen the counselor of the State Department.

47. *Newsweek*, March 26, 1945.

48. Herman M. Somers, *Presidential Agency: The Office of War Mobilization and Reconversion* (Cambridge: Harvard Univ. Press, 1950), 78-82.

49. Theoharis and Cox, *The Boss*, 244-45; Theoharis, ed., *From the Secret Files of J. Edgar Hoover* (Chicago: Ivan R. Dee, 1991), 201-3. The files of the 1945 FBI "White House Survey" are, as of this date, still classified.

50. Somers, *Presidential Agency*, 84-86. See also Robert R. Nathan, *Mobilizing for Abundance* (New York: McGraw-Hill, 1944).

51. Alonzo L. Hamby, *Man of the People: A Life of Harry S. Truman* (New York: Oxford Univ. Press, 1995), 600.

52. *H-L*, Nov. 29, 1979.

6 "Corrective Steps"

1. *Public Papers of the Presidents of the United States: Harry S. Truman, 1945* (Washington: Government Printing Office, 1961), 48-49.

2. Theoharis, *Secret Files*, 203-4; Kai Bird and Max Holland, "The Tapping of 'Tommy the Cork,'" *Nation*, Feb. 8, 1986. A prescient editorial in *The Nation*, written in 1941, warned that considering the "generally anti-labor and reactionary personnel of the FBI," no real guarantees existed that the bureau would not use its wiretapping capability "against labor and against persons of suspected views." *Nation*, March 8, 1941.

3. FBI "technical log" on EFP (hereafter referred to as "PR Log"), May 8, 1945, Hoover Official and Confidential File, FBI Reading Room, Washington, D.C. (hereafter cited as HOCF). The original transcripts of the Prichard wiretaps are housed at the Truman Library.

4. M.E. Gurnea to Hoover, June 2, 1945, HOCF; Theoharis and Cox, *The Boss*, 244-45; Athan Theoharis, *Spying on Americans: Political Surveillance from Hoover to the Huston Plan* (Philadelphia: Temple Univ. Press, 1978), 160-62; Richard Gid Powers, *Secrecy and Power: The Life of J. Edgar Hoover* (New York: Free Press, 1987), 280-81. A recent Truman biographer notes that Truman "presumably" supported Attorney General Clark's refusal in 1945 to authorize FBI wiretaps. But in light of the Corcoran and Prichard taps, Truman's "civil liberties record is thus mixed." Robert H. Ferrell, *Harry S. Truman: A Life* (Columbia: Univ. of Missouri Press, 1994), 302-3.

General Harry Vaughan, Truman's FBI liaison, later said that when he arrived at the White House in 1945, the FBI "had about a dozen phone taps on various people in Washington." This account is exaggerated, as is Vaughan's memory of Truman's reaction to the first wiretaps brought to him—"He [Truman] said 'cut them off. Tell the FBI we haven't any time for that kind of shit.'" Ovid Demaris, *J. Edgar Hoover: As They Knew Him* (New York: Carroll and Graf, 1994), 109.

5. Theoharis, *The Boss*, 171; Theoharis, *Secret Files*, 203; D.M. Ladd to Hoover, June 5, 1950, HOCF; Clark Clifford with Richard Holbrooke, *Counsel to the President: A Memoir* (New York: Random House, 1991), 190; Alexander Charns, *Cloak and Gavel: FBI Wiretaps, Bugs, Informers, and the Supreme Court* (Urbana: Univ. of Illinois Press, 1992), 25-26; *Final Report of the Select Committee to Study Government Operations with Respect to Intelligence Activities*, book 2, 94th Congress, Report 94-755, 27-28, 37; Harry Truman later said that "any attempt to invade the privacy of a private citizen, doesn't matter what it is, is in violation of the Bill of Rights, and those who propose such a thing are more of a danger to the country than the ones they want to listen in on." Concerning the precise issue of wiretapping, Truman said, "I have always been against it, when I was in the Senate and when I was president." Merle Miller, *Plain Speaking: An Oral Biography of Harry S. Truman* (New York: G.P. Putnams, 1973), 413-14; William W. Keller, *The Liberals and J. Edgar Hoover: Rise and Fall of a Domestic Intelligence State* (Princeton: Princeton Univ. Press, 1989); Christopher Andrew, *For the President's Eyes Only: Secret Intelligence and the American Presidency from Washington to Bush* (New York: Harper Collins, 1995), 157-59. For the FBI's more extensive political surveillance, see Kenneth O'Reilly, *"Racial Matters: The FBI's Secret File on Black America, 1960-1972* (New York: Free Press, 1989) and Clayborne Carson, *Malcolm X: The FBI File* (New York: Carroll and Graf, 1991). A defense of both Hoover and the FBI's techniques is Cartha D. "Deke" DeLoach, *Hoover's FBI: The Inside Story by Hoover's Trusted Lieutenant* (Washington: Regnery, 1995).

In early 1941, Attorney General Jackson informed FDR that he was also aware that Navy Intelligence had wiretapped officials in the Office of Production Management. Although Jackson understood the desire "to get something on some of these labor leaders," he warned the president that the administration could ill afford "to become characterized as lawless." Robert H. Jackson to FDR, April 29, 1941, Frankfurter Papers.

6. PR Log, May 8, 1945.

7. *U.S. News and World Report*, Dec. 19, 1983; *C-J*, Dec. 15, 1983.

8. PR Logs, July 28, Aug. 20, 1945; Laura Kalman, *Abe Fortas: A Biography* (New Haven: Yale Univ. Press, 1990), 115.

9. PR Logs, July 28, 31, 1945.

10. Ibid., July 15, 1945.

11. Ibid., July 9, 1945.

12. Ibid., July 9, 30, 1945; *C-J*, Sept. 29, 1945.

13. PR Log, Aug. 16, 1945.

14. Ibid., Sept. 20, 1945.

15. *C-J*, Dec. 15, 1983.

16. Stephen Kemp Bailey, *Congress Makes a Law: The Story Behind the Employment Act of 1946* (New York: Columbia Univ. Press, 1950), 13-14, 41, 160; Brinkley, *The End of Reform*, 260-64; Fraser, *Labor Will Rule*, 559.

17. Bailey, *Congress Makes a Law*, 46, 110-16, 154; Brinkley, *The End of Reform*, 264.

18. EFP to Vinson, Aug. 27, 1945, box 1, Vinson Papers; Fortune, Aug. 1945; Bailey, *Congress Makes a Law*, 166-67, 228, 233; Brinkley, *The End of Reform*, 262-64; Byrd L. Jones, "The Role of Keynesians in Wartime Policy and Postwar Planning, 1940-1946," Working Papers, *American Economic Review* 62 (May 1972): 131; Barber, *Designs Within Disorder*, 161-68; Hamby, *Man of the People*, 366-67. The primary significance of the bill was in establishing a Council of Economic Advisors to the President.

19. Philip P. Ardery, interview by Terry Birdwhistell, Aug. 23, 1984, POHP; Ardery, "Prich," 507-9; PR Logs, Aug. 23, Sept. 20, 1945. Ardery's autobiographical account of his wartime exploits are covered in his book, *Bomber Pilot: A Memoir of World War II* (Lexington: Univ. Press of Kentucky, 1978).

20. EFP to Vinson, Sept. 29, 1945; Vinson to EFP, Sept. 29, 1945, "Prichard File," Vinson Papers.

21. *Time*, Oct. 8, 1945.

22. *Washington Post*, Sept. 30, 1945.

23. Pearce, "The Man Who Might Have Been President."

24. Nathan interview; Katharine Graham interview (author).

7 A Lukewarm Reception

1. Ardery, "Prich," 509.

2. EFP to Vinson, Oct. 8, 23, 1945, "Prichard Personal File," Vinson Papers.

3. Corcoran Log, Feb. 15, 1946, HOCF.

4. *C-J*, Jan. 23, 24, 1946; Alonzo L. Hamby, *Beyond the New Deal: Harry S. Truman and American Liberalism* (New York: Columbia Univ. Press, 1973), 81.

5. EFP to Katharine Graham, Dec. 22, 1945, Graham Papers; EFP to Frankfurter, June 29, 1946, Frankfurter Papers.

6. *C-J*, Jan. 27, 1946.

7. Ibid., Jan. 16, 1946.

8. Ibid., Jan. 17, 1946; T. Kerney Cole, interview by author, Frankfort, July 22, 1994.

9. *C-J*, Jan. 22, 1946.

10. Ardery, "Prich," 509.

11. EFP to Clements, May 1, 1946, box 210, Clements Papers; Barkley to *C-J*, July 20, 1946, box 22, Alben W. Barkley Papers, Special Collections, Univ. of Kentucky.

12. Corcoran summary, June 19, 1946, HOCF; EFP to LBJ, June 12, 1946, box 47, House of Representatives File, Lyndon Baines Johnson Library, Austin, Texas.

13. Philip Ardery interview (Sept. 15, 1994); Klotter, *Kentucky*, 326-27.

14. EFP to Frankfurter, June 29, 1946, Frankfurter Papers.

15. *C-J*, Dec. 11, 1946; Jacqueline Bull to EFP, Nov. 25, 1946, box 4, Kentucky Constitution Revision Assembly Records, Special Collections, Univ. of Kentucky; Edward T. Breathitt, interview by author, Lexington, June 22, 1994.

16. *Paris Kentuckian-Citizen,* May 3, 1946.

17. *H-L,* June 11, 1961.

18. Robert Houlihan, interview by author, Lexington, Dec. 27, 1996.

19. Houlihan interview; Pearce, "The Man Who Might Have Been President."

20. Lucy Prichard to Barry Bingham, Nov. 9, 1985, Barry and Mary Bingham Papers, Filson Club.

21. Houlihan interview; Corcoran Log, Jan. 10, Aug. 12, 1946, HOCF; EFP to Stewart B. Hopps, Sept. 19, 1946, Thomas G. Corcoran Papers, Library of Congress; EFP to Corcoran, July 1949, Corcoran Papers. Other New Deal attorneys found the immediate financial rewards of their years in Washington to be quite lucrative. Thurman Arnold, formerly head of the anti-trust division in the Justice Department, was promised $50,000 in retainers from various corporations before he ever started his own Washington law practice. See Arnold to J.R. Sullivan, June 26, 1945, in Gene M. Gressley, ed., *Voltaire and the Cowboy: The Letters of Thurman Arnold* (Boulder: Colorado Associated Univ. Press, 1977), 358-59.

22. EFP to Vinson, July 12, 1946, EFP to Vinson, telegram, June 24, 1946, Vinson Papers.

23. EFP to Frankfurter, June 29, 1946, Frankfurter Papers; Joseph P. Lash, *From the Diaries of Felix Frankfurter* (New York: Norton, 1975), 303.

24. Election Commissioners Record, Bourbon County Courthouse; *Paris Kentuckian-Citizen,* Nov. 8, 1946.

25. Vinson to EFP, Dec. 6, 1946, Vinson Papers.

26. *H-L,* Feb. 16, 1947; Lucy Prichard to Eugene Meyer, March 26, 1947, box 39, Meyer Papers; Houlihan interview.

27. W.S. Sherwood to Clements, April 5, May 19, 1946, box 210, Clements Papers.

28. *National Week,* Jan. 17, 1947.

29. Steven M. Gillon, *Politics and Vision: The ADA and American Liberalism, 1947-1985* (New York: Oxford Univ. Press, 1987), 4-40; Norman D. Markowitz, *The Rise and Fall of the People's Century: Henry A. Wallace and American Liberalism* (New York: Free Press, 1973), 222-25; Hamby, *Beyond the New Deal,* 161-63; *NYT,* March 30, 1947; Wilson Wyatt Sr., interview by author, Louisville, Sept. 15, 1994; Robert Nathan interview; Rauh to Wilson Wyatt, Sept. 29, 1947, box 4, Wilson W. Wyatt Papers, Special Collections, Univ. of Kentucky.

30. Pearce, *Divide and Dissent,* 47-48; Klotter, *Kentucky,* 330.

31. Marc Karnis Landy, *The Politics of Environmental Reform: Controlling Kentucky Strip Mining* (Washington: Resources for the Future, 1976), 57-61; Thomas Hamilton Syvertsen, "Earle Chester Clements and the Democratic Party, 1920-1950" (Ph.D. diss., Univ. of Kentucky, 1982), 80-84; William Clark Spragens, "The 1947 Gubernatorial Election in Kentucky" (master's thesis, Univ. of Kentucky, 1951), 66-71.

32. EFP to Clements, Sept. 28, 1978, personal correspondence, Clements Papers; Ardery, "Prich," 510.

33. Philip Ardery interview (Sept. 15, 1994); confidential information.

34. John A. Keck to EFP, telegrams, July 17, 19, 1947, box 224, Clements Papers; EFP to Clements, May 24, 1947, box 224, Clements Papers; EFP to Clements, March 26, 1947, box 218, Clements Papers; *Paris Kentuckian-Citizen,* July 18, 1947.

35. EFP to Clements, Aug. 25, 1947, box 218, Clements Papers; Tom Underwood to Paul A. Porter, Oct. 16, 1947, box 214, Clements Papers; Harrison and Klotter, *A New History of Kentucky,* 400-402.

36. EFP to Clements, Sept. 23, 1947, box 218, Clements Papers.

37. Clements to EFP, Nov. 11, 1947, box 312, Clements Papers; EFP to Clements, Nov. 29, 1947, box 312, Clements Papers.

38. Clements to EFP, Aug. 16, 1978, Clements Papers.

39. Bourbon County Deed Book, 123:260, 124:231, Bourbon County Courthouse; Bourbon County Mortgage Book, 81:417, 84:572, Bourbon County Courthouse; confidential information.

40. Catalog, Transylvania College, 1948-49.

41. James Loeb to EFP, Dec. 5, 1947, ADA Papers, State Historical Society of Wisconsin.

42. *C-J*, Dec. 11, 1947; James D. Squires, *The Secrets of the Hopewell Box: Stolen Elections, Southern Politics, and a City's Coming of Age* (New York: Times Books, 1996), 55.

43. Mark F. Ethridge to Maurice Rosenblatt, Sept. 2, 1952, Mark F. Ethridge Papers, Southern Historical Collection, Univ. of North Carolina at Chapel Hill; Egerton, *Speak Now Against the Day,* 470; Klotter, *Kentucky,* 333; *Lexington Leader,* May 4, 1949.

44. *Woodford Sun,* July 21, 1949; *Kentucky Post,* July 10, 1982.

45. EFP to Franklin Roosevelt Jr., April 1, 1948, box 4, Wyatt Papers; Markowitz, *Rise and Fall of the People's Century,* 281-83.

46. James Loeb, interview by Jerry N. Hess, Sept. 1971, Truman Library; Mary Sperling McAuliffe, *Crisis on the Left: Cold War Politics and American Liberals* (Amherst: Univ. of Massachusetts Press, 1978), 36-38.

47. *Democracy at Work: Official Proceedings of the Democratic National Convention, 1948; Firing Line with William F. Buckley Jr.,* #1218, produced by Warren Steibel, Oct. 27, 1982; Carl Solberg, *Hubert Humphrey: A Biography* (New York: Norton, 1984), 13-14; Irwin Ross, *The Loneliest Campaign: The Truman Victory of 1948* (New York: New American Library, 1968), 120-26; Egerton, *Speak Now Against the Day,* 495-97; William C. Berman, *The Politics of Civil Rights in the Truman Administration* (Columbus: Ohio State Univ. Press, 1970), 102-9; Numan V. Bartley, *The New South, 1945-1980* (Baton Rouge: Louisiana State Univ. Press, 1995), 74-103; *Woodford Sun,* Sept. 30, 1948.

48. Wilson W. Wyatt Sr., *Whistle Stops: Adventures in Public Life* (Lexington: Univ. Press of Kentucky, 1985), 49; H. Lew Wallace, "Alben Barkley and the Democratic Convention of 1948," *Filson Club History Quarterly* 55 (July 1981): 231-52.

49. Democratic National Committee News Release, Oct. 6, 1948, box 64, House of Representatives Files, Johnson Library.

50. Princeton *Alumni Weekly,* Oct. 11, 1963; Election Commissioner's Record, Bourbon County Courthouse.

51. *Paris Kentuckian-Citizen,* July 30, Aug. 13, 20, Oct. 29, 1948.

52. *Paris Daily Enterprise,* Nov. 2, 1948; *Paris Kentuckian-Citizen,* Nov. 5, 1948.

53. *H-L,* Nov. 3, 1948; *Paris Daily Enterprise,* Nov. 2, 1948.

54. Thomas Dewey to John Sherman Cooper, telegram, Nov. 2, 1948, box 916, John Sherman Cooper Papers, Special Collections, Univ. of Kentucky.

55. Schlesinger interview.

8 "Press Vigorously and Thoroughly"

1. Caro, *Means of Ascent,* xxxi.

2. *Paris Daily Enterprise,* Nov. 4, 1948; *Paris Kentuckian-Citizen,* Nov. 5, 19, 1948; *Frankfort State Journal,* Nov. 6, 1948.

3. *Paris Daily Enterprise,* Nov. 6, 1948; Richard Clayton Smoot, "John Sherman Cooper:

The Paradox of a Liberal Republican in Kentucky Politics" (Ph.D. diss., Univ. of Kentucky, 1988), 40-41.

4. Hoover to Alexander M. Campbell, Nov. 3, 1948, FBI 56-834-2, FBI File on Bourbon County Vote Fraud Investigation (hereafter referred to as "FBI File"). For Campbell's role in the Alger Hiss case, see Allen Weinstein, *Perjury: The Hiss-Chambers Case* (New York: Random House, 1997), 156-57, 162-65, 240-45.

5. "The Kansas City, Missouri, Primary Election of 1946," Tom C. Clark Papers, Harry S. Truman Library, Independence, Missouri; Caro, *Means of Ascent*, 384; Robert Dallek, *Lone Star Rising: Lyndon Johnson and His Times, 1908-1960* (New York: Oxford Univ. Press, 1991), 331; Ronnie Dugger, *The Politician: The Life and Times of Lyndon Johnson: The Drive for Power from the Frontier to the Master of the Senate* (New York: Norton, 1982), 339.

There had been a recent investigation of vote fraud following the 1942 general election in Harlan County, Kentucky. Ninety-nine individuals were indicted in federal court in the conspiracy, and after numerous trials covering three years, more than fifty people were convicted. For a recent congressional investigation of vote fraud, see "Hearing Before the Subcommittee on the Constitution of the Committee on the Judiciary: The Need for Further Federal Action in the Area of Criminal Vote Fraud," 98th Cong., 1st sess., 1984.

6. Squires, *Secrets of the Hopewell Box*, 66.

7. Teletype, Nov. 9, 1948, 56-834-3, FBI File; A. Rosen to D.M. Ladd, memo, Nov. 11, 1948, 56-834-4, FBI File.

8. Hoover to Clark, memo, Nov. 17, 1948, 56-834-7, FBI File.

9. Ardery, "Prich," 512; Philip Ardery interview (Sept. 15, 1994); *United States v Alvarado Erwin Funk and Edward Fretwell Prichard, Jr.,* RG 267, U.S. Supreme Court Appellate Case Files, #795, box 6121, National Archives (hereafter referred to as *U.S. v Funk and Prichard*), 347. In responding to the question of whether the visit to Judge Ardery was upon Prichard's request, Phil Ardery said (in 1949), "I can't say honestly whether I went at his suggestion or whether he went at my suggestion."

10. Ardery, "Prich," 512-13.

11. Ibid.; *U.S. v Funk and Prichard,* 349; Philip Ardery interview (Sept. 15, 1994).

12. Ardery, "Prich," 513; Philip Ardery interview (Sept. 15, 1994).

13. Ardery, "Prich," 517; John Ed Pearce, interview by author, Louisville, June 30, 1994.

14. *Paris Daily Enterprise,* Nov. 8, 9, 11, Dec. 9, 1948.

15. *Lexington Leader,* April 15, 1949; Clay Family Papers, box 79, Special Collections, Univ. of Kentucky; Rosen to D.M. Ladd, memo, May 2, 1949, 56-834-163, FBI File.

16. Preliminary report, 56-834-24, FBI File; Nichols to Tolson, memo, Dec. 16, 1948, 56-834-40, FBI File.

17. A. Rosen to M.D. Ladd, memo, Nov. 23, 1948, 56-834-26, FBI File; *Lexington Leader,* March 11, 1949. Clay's daughter, not knowing of the FBI's interest in the Prichard case, naturally gives her father primary credit for prosecuting Prichard: "It is a tribute to my father's persistence and sense of outrage that the vote fraud case was ever resolved." Berry, *Voices from the Century Before,* 442-43.

18. *Congressional Record,* 80th Cong., 2d Sess., vol. 94, pt. 1, 10259-60; *Lexington Leader,* Jan. 14, 1949.

19. Joseph Mooney, interview by author, Lexington, Oct. 12, 1994.

20. Pearce interview. Clay's daughter later recalled the stress that the case had on her family, specifically her mother, who throughout the investigation "was always in tears." Berry, *Voices from the Century Before,* 443.

21. *Lexington Leader,* Feb. 4, 15, 1949; A. Rosen to M.D. Ladd, memo, March 9, 1949,

56-834-94, FBI File; Report, 56-834-109, FBI File. Clay's efforts on behalf of prosecuting Ed Prichard were remembered by Prichard's colleagues years later. In the late 1950s, when Clay was in the Kentucky legislature, Edward Breathitt recalled that "a lot of us" in the General Assembly "didn't like him because of what he did to Prich . . . we didn't pay much attention to him." Edward T. Breathitt interview.

22. *C-J,* March 16, 1949.

23. *Paris Kentuckian-Citizen,* March 11, 1949.

24. Fred Hallford to Hoover, memo, April 8, 1949, 56-834-128, FBI File; Rosen to Ladd, memo, April 8, 1949, 56-834-130, FBI File; Hoover to Clark, April 11, 1949, 56-834-126, FBI File; teletype, April 15, 1949, 56-834-139, FBI File; *Lexington Leader,* March 30, 1949, Nov. 7, 1976; *Paris Daily Enterprise,* March 27, 1949.

25. Memo, 56-834-243, FBI File; Hoover to SAC, Louisville, Feb. 14, 1949, 56-834-75, FBI File; Mooney interview.

26. *H-L,* March 31, April 1, 9, 1949; *Lexington Leader,* April 8, 14, 1949.

27. *U.S. v Funk and Prichard,* 8-9.

28. Memo, SAC, Louisville to Hoover, April 19, 1949, 56-834-163, FBI File.

29. *U.S. v Funk and Prichard,* 9.

30. *U.S. v Funk and Prichard,* 10-12; A. Rosen to D.M. Ladd, memo, April 20, 1949, 56-834-154, FBI File.

31. *Lexington Leader,* April 15, 1949; *Paris Kentuckian-Citizen,* April 22, 1949.

32. Hallford to Hoover, May 24, 1949, 56-834-207, FBI File.

33. Susan M. Patten to Joseph Alsop, April 24, 1949; Lucy Prichard to Joseph Alsop, April 11, 1949, Joseph and Stewart Alsop Papers, Library of Congress.

34. Rosen to Ladd, memo, April 28, 1949, 56-834-149, FBI File; teletype, May 2, 1949, 56-834-151, FBI File.

35. *Paris Daily Enterprise,* May 4, 1949: Mooney interview; Ardery, "Prich," 514; confidential information; Pearce, "Adversity and Atonement."

36. *U.S. v Funk and Prichard,* "Grand Jury Charge," no. 7688. The author is grateful to William Stone of Louisville, Kentucky, for sharing his copy of the grand jury indictment.

37. *C-J,* May 5, 1949; *Lexington Leader,* May 4, 1949; *Paris Daily Enterprise,* May 4, 1949.

38. Brent interview.

39. *H-L,* May 5, 1949; Tyler Abell, ed., *Drew Pearson: Diaries, 1949-1959* (New York: Holt, Rinehart, and Winston, 1974), 46.

40. *H-L,* May 5, 1949; *Paris Daily Enterprise,* Jan. 7, 1951.

41. Pearce, "Adversity and Atonement"; State Department of Health of Kentucky, *Directory of Births and Deaths Registered in Kentucky,* 1046.

42. Vinson to Prichard, May 19, 1949, "Personal File," box 51, Vinson Papers. Prichard's firstborn, however, did not take his father's name. He would always be known by his middle name, Allen.

43. Rosen to D. M. Ladd, memo, May 11, 1949, 56-834-159, FBI File; Undated report, 56-834-238, FBI File.

44. Report, July 1, 1949, 56-834-283, FBI File.

45. Philip Ardery interview (Sept. 15, 1994). In this interview, Ardery could not remember being asked by Prichard to serve as his attorney. In court transcripts, Ardery stated that after the indictment, Prichard asked him to serve as his counsel, and Ardery refused. *U.S. v Funk and Prichard,* 351. Under the canons of professional ethics of the American Bar Association of the previous year, the ABA stated clearly: "It is the duty of a lawyer to preserve his client's confidences. This duty outlasts the lawyer's employment." American Bar Association, *Opinions of*

the Committee on Professional Ethics and Grievances, 1947, 35. For further elucidation on the attorney-client privilege, see 12 *Federal Procedure,* 1 Ed 33:275. An excellent legal summary is provided in "The Attorney-Client Privilege: Fixed Rules, Balancing, and Constitutional Entitlement," *Harvard Law Review* 91 (Dec. 1977): 464-87. For a recent inquiry into some of the investigatory methods of the FBI, see Ronald Kessler, *The FBI: Inside the World's Most Powerful Law Enforcement Agency* (New York: Pocket Books, 1993), 111-39.

46. William C. Stone, interview, Louisville, Oct. 13, 1994.

9 Playing for Keeps

1. Rauh interview (Birdwhistell).

2. Ibid.; EFP to Thomas Corcoran, Aug. 25, 1949, Corcoran Papers.

3. Berlin interview. After the war, Berlin returned to Oxford, where he became one of the most influential political philosophers of the century and was president of the British Academy in the 1970s. He died in 1997. For an analysis of Berlin's work, see John Gray, *Isaiah Berlin* (Princeton: Princeton Univ. Press, 1996).

4. *U.S. v Funk and Prichard,* 34-36; *C-J,* July 6, 1949.

5. *U.S. v Funk and Prichard,* 40-41.

6. *H-L,* July 7, 1949.

7. *Washington Post,* July 8, 1949; *H-L,* July 8, 1949.

8. *C-J,* July 27, 1967.

9. *U.S. v Funk and Prichard,* 340-52.

10. Ibid., 352-53.

11. *H-L,* July 9, 1949.

12. Hallford to Hoover, teletype, July 8, 1949, 56-834-279, FBI File.

13. *Cincinnati Enquirer,* July 9, 1949; Abell, *Drew Pearson,* 46.

14. EFP to Corcoran, July 11, 1949, Corcoran Papers. Another file in the Corcoran Papers, labeled "Legal File—Edward F. Prichard, Jr., 1946-51," is sealed until June 2008.

15. *U.S. v Funk and Prichard,* 356-60.

16. Ibid., 366-67; *Lexington Leader,* July 11, 1949; Houlihan interview.

17. Confidential information; Rauh interview (Birdwhistell).

18. Mooney interview; Rosen to Ladd, memo, July 13, 1949, 56-834-281, FBI File.

19. *Louisville Times,* July 12, 1949; *Lexington Leader,* July 12, 1949.

20. *U.S. v Funk and Prichard,* 379-95; *Lexington Leader,* July 12, 1949.

21. *U.S. v Funk and Prichard,* 403-8; *Lexington Leader,* July 12, 1949; *C-J,* July 13, 1949.

22. *U.S. v Funk and Prichard,* 439-41; *C-J,* July 14, 1949.

23. *C-J,* July 14, 1949.

24. *U.S. v Funk and Prichard,* 455-60; *C-J,* July 14, 1949.

25. *U.S. v Funk and Prichard,* 465-73.

26. Ibid., 492-93; *Louisville Times,* July 14, 1949; *C-J,* July 15, 1949.

27. *U.S. v Funk and Prichard,* 492-93; *Louisville Times,* July 14, 1949.

28. *Louisville Times,* July 14, 1949; *H-L,* July 15, 1949; *Cincinnati Enquirer,* July 15, 1949.

29. Houlihan interview (author); Houlihan to Arthur M. Schlesinger Jr., March 2, 1992, Graham Papers.

30. *Louisville Times,* July 14, 1949; *C-J,* July 15, 1949; *H-L,* July 15, 1949; *Woodford Sun,* July 21, 1949; confidential information.

31. *Washington Post,* July 15, 1949; *NYT,* July 15, 1949; *Paris Kentuckian-Citizen,* July 15, 1949; *C-J,* July 16, 1949; Mary Caperton Bingham, interview by author, Louisville, June 30,

1994; Pearce interview; Rauh to Wilson Wyatt, Nov. 17, 1949, Wyatt Papers. Barry and Mary's daughter, Sallie, later wrote her own bitter account of her family's history. Sallie remembered seeing Prichard at parties in the Binghams' Louisville home, but suddenly, in the 1950s, "he seemed to have been expunged." Sallie used the estrangement between Prichard and her parents as an example of her father's propensity to expel friends when they were no longer socially or politically useful. The Prichard example provides no such evidence. The separation, it is understood, was initiated by Prichard. Sallie Bingham, *Passion and Prejudice: A Family Memoir* (New York: Knopf, 1989), 276-77.

32. Peter H. Irons, *The New Deal Lawyers* (Princeton: Princeton Univ. Press, 1982), 298; Goulden, *Super-Lawyers*, 19; Gressley, *Voltaire and the Cowboy*, 345, 396; Rauh interview (Birdwhistell); Rauh interview (Mulhollan); *Frankfort State-Journal*, July 16, 1949.

33. Hoover to Campbell, memo, Dec. 21, 1949, 56-834-336, FBI File; Hallford to Hoover, July 20, 1949, 56-834-286, FBI File.

34. *C-J*, Dec. 3, 1949; *Paris Kentuckian-Citizen*, Dec. 9, 1949. Ardery's jurisdiction over Franklin County was eventually removed by the General Assembly in 1960 (see Pearce, *Divide and Dissent*, 114).

35. Pearce, "Adversity and Atonement."

36. Mooney interview; Ardery, "Prich," 517; Ardery, *Heroes and Horses*, 92-93.

37. Pearce, "Adversity and Atonement"; *Boston Globe*, May 15, 1983.

38. Berlin interview; Sir Isaiah Berlin, letter to author, June 25, 1994; Rauh interview (Birdwhistell); *Boston Globe*, May 15, 1983.

39. Lady Bird Johnson, letter to author, Aug. 17, 1993; Joseph Alsop to Averell Harriman, July 19, 1949, Alsop Papers.

40. Joseph Terry, interview by author, Lexington, Dec. 28, 1994.

41. David Curd, telephone interview with author, Feb. 24, 1995; *H-L*, March 3, 1953; confidential information; Charles Rosen, *Scandals of '51: How the Gamblers Almost Killed College Basketball* (New York: Holt, Rinehart and Winston, 1978), 170-71, 206-7; Russell Rice, *Kentucky Basketball's Big Blue Machine* (Huntsville: Strode, 1976), 226-29; Curd was once sued for hedging on a $2,500 election bet in 1944. The Kentucky Court of Appeals heard the case and decided that since election bets were illegal, the appellant had no legal capacity to sue in the first place. *Craig v Curd*, 218 SW 2d 395 (1949). The rumor of an election bet made its way around Bourbon County. In an interview on a completely different subject, a Frankfort woman recalled being told that Prichard made a bet on the 1948 election at a party held at the Paris Country Club. See Ruth Murphy, interview by Jeffrey Suchanek, Nov. 1994, Veterans of World War II Oral History Project, Univ. of Kentucky.

42. Berlin interview; John Kenneth Galbraith, interview by Bill Cooper, Cambridge, Mass., June 9, 1987, POHP.

43. *C-J*, July 17, 1949.

10   Ashland

1. *H-L*, July 22, 1949.

2. EFP to Corcoran, Aug. 25, 1949, Corcoran Papers.

3. Edward Burling to Corcoran, Aug. 23, 1949, Corcoran Papers.

4. EFP to Corcoran, Aug. 30, Nov. 10, 1949, Corcoran Papers.

5. *U.S. v Funk and Prichard*, 502-3; Katharine Graham interview (author).

6. *C-J*, Aug. 3, 1949; *Frankfort State-Journal*, July 19, 1949.

7. Stone interview; Hallford to Hoover, Feb. 3, 1950, 56-834-346, FBI File; *Lexington*

Leader, Dec. 6, 7, 11, 1949; *H-L,* Dec. 24, 1949; *Woodford Sun,* Oct. 20, 1949. For details of Funk's career in Middlesboro, see John Gaventa, *Power and Powerlessness: Quiescence and Rebellion in an Appalachian Valley* (Urbana: Univ. of Illinois Press, 1980), 132-39, 215, 219, 225-29, 240.

8. Katharine Graham interview (author). The canceled checks and lists of all donors to Prichard's fund are located in the private papers of Katharine Graham.

9. James Rowe to Frank Pace, Feb. 23, 1950, Corcoran Papers.

10. Bingham interview. Prichard's effect on various New Deal Washingtonians seems eerily similar to that of columnist Joseph Alsop, whose drinking and eccentric habits were also quietly tolerated by his Georgetown friends. See Robert W. Merry, *Taking on the World: Joseph and Stewart Alsop—Guardians of the American Century* (New York: Viking, 1996), 477-79.

11. *Paris Kentuckian-Citizen,* July 29, Aug. 12, 1949.

12. *Edward F. Prichard Jr. v United States of America,* United States Court of Appeals, 6th Cir., no. 10964, 2-10 (hereafter referred to as *Prichard v United States); H-L,* April 5, 1950.

13. *C-J,* May 5, 1950.

14. Crater, memo, phone conversation, April 28, 1950; Anonymous letter, n.d., Vinson Papers.

15. David Prewitt to Vinson, June 20, 1950, Vinson Papers.

16. *C-J,* June 3, 5, 1950.

17. *Prichard v United States; Washington Evening Star,* June 6, 1950.

18. *C-J,* June 17, 18, 19, July 4, 1950; *Christian Science Monitor,* July 8, 1950; EFP to Joseph Alsop, Aug. 23, 1949, Alsop Papers.

19. *C-J,* July 15, 1950.

20. Ibid., July 22, 1950.

21. Ibid., August 29, 1950.

22. EFP to Paul Porter, July 17, 1950, Graham Papers.

23. EFP to Philip Graham, Sept. 17, 1950, Graham Papers; Philip Graham to Lucy Prichard, Aug. 23, 1950, Graham Papers; Lucy Prichard to Philip Graham, n.d., Graham Papers; Graham, *Personal History,* 198-99.

24. EFP to Philip Graham, Aug. 23, 1950, Graham Papers.

25. EFP to Paul Porter, Dec. 8, 1950, Vinson Papers.

26. Berlin interview.

27. "Case of Edward F. Prichard, Jr.," Docket of Pardon Cases, Records of the Office of the Pardon Attorney, National Archives, 77:255; "Daily Presidential Appointments," box 5, Matthew J. Connelly Files, Truman Library; McGrath to Truman, Dec. 21, 1950, President's Official File, Truman Library.

28. Clements to Truman, Dec. 19, 1950, President's Official File, box 1303, Truman Library. Katharine Graham asserts that the central figure in obtaining Prichard's early release was John Sherman Cooper. No written validation of this assertion, however, exists. Graham, *Personal History,* 198.

29. Presidential warrant on Edward F. Prichard Jr., Dec. 21, 1950, Office of the Pardon Attorney.

30. *NYT,* Dec. 23, 1950; *Paris Daily-Enterprise,* Dec. 22, 1950.

31. Lucy Prichard to Truman, Dec. 22, 1950, President's Personal File, file 5654, Truman Library; Truman to Lucy Prichard, Dec. 29, 1950, President's Personal File, file 5654, Truman Library.

32. L.T. Mencke to Truman, telegram, Dec. 26, 1950, President's Official File, box 1303,

Truman Library; R.L. Price to Truman, telegram, Dec. 26, 1950, E.F. Prichard Cross-Reference File, Truman Library.

33. *Paris Daily Enterprise,* Jan. 2, 1951; EFP to Truman, Jan. 17, 1951, President's Personal File, file 5654, Truman Library.

11 New Trials

1. EFP to Philip Elman, Jan. 9, 1951, Philip Elman Papers, Harvard Law School Archives.

2. Richard Gilbert to EFP, July 17, 1951, Corcoran Papers; EFP to Philip Graham, March 6, 1951, Graham Papers.

3. Joseph Alsop to Averell Harriman, July 19, 1949, Alsop Papers.

4. EFP to Philip Elman, Feb. 9, 1951, Elman Papers; EFP to Philip Graham, March 6, 1951, Graham Papers.

5. EFP to Corcoran, Oct. 30, 1951, Corcoran Papers; Corcoran to E.E. Ruby, Nov. 16, 1953, Corcoran Papers; Corcoran to Cohen, Dec. 31, 1951, Corcoran Papers.

6. *Kentucky Post,* July 10, 1982. One example is that of the legendary James Curley, who recovered from a prison stay to win the post of Boston mayor and later governor of Massachusetts. See Jack Beatty, *The Rascal King: The Life and Times of James Michael Curley, 1874-1958* (Reading, Mass.: Addison-Wesley, 1992), 78-84, 499.

7. EFP to Arthur M. Schlesinger Jr., March 7, 1953, Schlesinger Papers; Pearce, "Adversity and Atonement."

8. *NYT,* Dec. 21, 1951.

9. EFP to Philip Graham, March 6, 1951, Graham Papers; EFP to Arthur M. Schlesinger Jr., April 26, 1952, Schlesinger Papers.

10. *C-J,* Nov. 5, 1951.

11. EFP to Arthur M. Schlesinger Jr., April 26, 1952, Schlesinger Papers.

12. EFP to Frankfurter, Dec. 8, 1951, Frankfurter Papers; Pearce interview.

13. *C-J,* June 24, 1952; *NYT,* June 24, 1952; Edward A. Farris, interview by author, Frankfort, Feb. 1, 1995.

14. James Loeb, interview by Jerry Hess, Truman Library; David McCullough, *Truman* (New York: Simon and Schuster, 1992), 888-89; Hamby, *Man of the People,* 600-601; Abell, *Drew Pearson,* 177.

15. *C-J,* July 15, 1952.

16. Ibid., July 26, 1952.

17. Schlesinger, "'Prich.'"

18. *NYT,* Sept. 20, 1952.

19. EFP to Joseph Alsop, Dec. 31, 1952, Alsop Papers.

20. Ibid., Feb. 1, 1953; Herbert Brownell with John P. Burke, *Advising Ike: The Memoirs of Attorney General Herbert Brownell* (Lawrence: Univ. Press of Kansas, 1993), 142, 152.

21. EFP to Truman, Feb. 23, 1953, Post-Presidential File, box 373, Truman Library; Truman to EFP, March 7, 1953, Post-Presidential File, Truman Library.

22. *C-J,* Feb. 10, June 6, 1953.

23. EFP to Frankfurter, March 9, 1953, Frankfurter Papers.

24. EFP to Corcoran, May 20, 1953, Corcoran Papers; EFP to Philip Graham, March 1, 1954, Graham Papers; EFP to Schlesinger, March 7, 1953, Schlesinger Papers.

25. EFP to Frankfurter, Feb. 15, 1954, Frankfurter Papers; Schlesinger, "'Prich.'"

26. *C-J,* April 1, 1954.

27. EFP to Corcoran, April 3, 1954, Corcoran Papers.

28. EFP to Frankfurter, April 11, 1954, Frankfurter Papers.

29. Berlin interview.

30. EFP to Frankfurter, April 11, 1954, Frankfurter Papers; Henry Prichard interview (March 28, 1995).

31. EFP to Cohen, June 3, 1954, box 4, Benjamin V. Cohen Papers, Manuscript Division, Library of Congress; EFP to Arthur M. Schlesinger Jr., Sept. 13, 1960, Schlesinger Papers. See also Watkins, *Righteous Pilgrim,* 951-52.

32. EFP to Cohen, June 19, 1954, Cohen Papers.

33. Henry Prichard interview (March 28, 1995); see also Judith Wylie-Rosett, "Obesity and Type II Diabetes," in Reva T. Frankle, ed., *Obesity and Weight Control* (Rockville, Md.: Aspen Publishers, 1988), 425-40; Stephen B. Levine, "Sexual Dysfunction and Diabetes," in *Behavioral and Psychological Issues in Diabetes* (National Institute of Health Publication #80-1993, 1979), 183-87.

34. Henry Prichard interview (March 28, 1995); see also *Diabetes and Your Eyes* (Bethesda: National Institute of Health, #83-2171, June 1983), 4.

35. EFP to Corcoran, Dec. 4, 1954, Corcoran Papers.

36. EFP to Corcoran, May 31, 1955, Corcoran Papers.

37. Rauh interview (Birdwhistell); Schlesinger, "'Prich'"; Pearce, "Adversity and Atonement."

38. EFP to Philip Graham, Jan. 1, 1955, Graham Papers.

39. Bourbon County Deed Book, 134:314, Bourbon County Courthouse; Bourbon County Mortgage Book, 81:417, 84:572; Woodford County Deed Book, 51:370, Woodford County Courthouse; Henry Prichard interview (March 28, 1995); *Princeton Alumni Weekly,* Jan. 24, 1958.

40. Berlin interview; Schlesinger interview; Chandler newsletter, box 39, Lawrence Wetherby Papers, Special Collections, Univ. of Kentucky.

41. Pearce, *Divide and Dissent,* 56-60; EFP, interview by George Robinson, Feb. 21, 1979, Bert Combs Oral History Project, Eastern Kentucky Univ.

42. Interview with Bert T. Combs, by Terry Birdwhistell, May 28, 1986, POHP.

43. Ibid.

44. Pearce, *Divide and Dissent,* 64-65; Harrison and Klotter, *A New History of Kentucky,* 403.

12 "Wandering in the Wilderness"

1. Frank Browning, "After the Scandal: Picking Up the Pieces," *Washington Monthly* 5 (Oct. 1973): 41.

2. Pearce, "Adversity and Atonement."

3. Combs interview (May 28, 1986, by Birdwhistell).

4. Pearce, "Adversity and Atonement."

5. Lyndon Johnson to EFP, Dec. 17, 1959, U.S. Senate Master File, Lyndon B. Johnson Library; Pearce interview.

6. Breathitt interview; Pearce, *Divide and Dissent,* 73.

7. Pearce, *Divide and Dissent,* 86-87; Harrison and Klotter, *A New History of Kentucky,* 406-7.

8. Pearce, *Divide and Dissent,* 91-95.

9. EFP to Clements, July 14, 1959, box 266, Clements Papers; Pearce, *Divide and Dissent*, 96.

10. Pearce, *Divide and Dissent*, 96-97.

11. For discussion of how unnamed politicians were "out to get Ardery" by removing Franklin County from his district shortly after the trial, see *Paris Kentuckian-Citizen*, Dec. 9, 1949.

12. C. Leslie Dawson, interview by author, Lexington, June 21, 1994.

13. Kentucky Educational Television, "Distinguished Kentuckian," produced by O. Leonard Press, Sept. 18, 1974.

14. Dawson interview.

15. *Official Report of the Proceedings of the 1960 Democratic National Convention and Committee* (Washington: National Document Publishers, 1964), 283; Katharine Graham interview (author). For Phil Graham's role in LBJ's selection, see Graham, *Personal History*, 259-67; Arthur M. Schlesinger Jr., *Robert Kennedy and His Times* (Boston: Houghton Mifflin, 1978), 1:215-21; Theodore H. White, *The Making of the President, 1960* (New York: Atheneum, 1961), 199-203; and *The Making of the President, 1964* (New York: Atheneum, 1969), 407-15, for the infamous "Graham memorandum." Dallek, *Lone Star Rising*, 574, 578-81.

16. *C-J*, July 1, Nov. 11, 1960. Ed Sr. paid off all of the personal tax liens against him in 1961. The liens on his property alone came to $352,057. Real Estate Encumbrance Book 2, Bourbon County Courthouse.

17. Federal Tax Lien Book 1, Woodford County Courthouse.

18. James Hudson, interview by author, Frankfort, July 24, 1994; Pearce, "Adversity and Atonement."

19. Pearce, *Divide and Dissent*, 138; Harrison and Klotter, *A New History of Kentucky*, 408-9.

20. Combs interview (May 28, 1986, by Birdwhistell).

21. Ibid.; *H-L*, Feb. 7, 1963.

22. Combs interview (May 28, 1986, by Birdwhistell).

23. Julius Rather, interview by author, Lexington, April 14, 1995; "KET's Distinguished Kentuckian Series."

24. EFP to Rauh, April 14, 1962, Rauh to EFP, April 20, 1962, and R.E. Corish to Rauh, May 15, 1962, Joseph L. Rauh Jr. Papers.

25. Pearce interview; Shelby Kinkead, interview by Terry Birdwhistell, Lexington, March 4, 1986, POHP.

26. Breathitt interview.

27. Pearce, *Divide and Dissent*, 189-98; EFP, interview by Barry Peel, Jan. 25, 1977, Robert R. Martin Oral History Project, Eastern Kentucky Univ.; Harrison and Klotter, *A New History of Kentucky*, 405.

28. William Greider, interview by author, Washington, D.C., June 24, 1993.

29. Browning, "After the Scandal."

30. Edward F. Prichard Jr., audiotape of speech at Hindman, Kentucky, May 24, 1963, in possession of Sara Combs, Stanton, Kentucky. There is also a copy in the University of Kentucky archives.

31. *H-L*, Dec. 24, 1984; Lucy Prichard to Barry and Mary Bingham, Nov. 9, 1985, Bingham Papers.

32. *C-J*, May 3, 13, 1963; Breathitt interview; Robert Bell, interview by author, Lexington, Feb. 22, 1995; Albert B. Chandler with Vance Trimble, *Heroes, Plain Folks, and Skunks: The Life and Times of Happy Chandler* (Chicago: Bonus Books, 1989), 268-69.

33. Pearce, *Divide and Dissent,* 89.

34. Chandler, *Heroes, Plain Folks, and Skunks,* 269.

13 Back in the Arena

1. A thorough analysis of the racial realities in Kentucky before World War II is George C. Wright, *Racial Violence in Kentucky, 1865-1940: Lynchings, Mob Rule, and "Legal Lynchings"* (Baton Rouge: Louisiana State Univ. Press, 1990). See also Marion B. Lucas, *A History of Blacks in Kentucky,* vol. 2 (Frankfort: Kentucky Historical Society, 1992).

2. Executive Order, June 26, 1963, Bert T. Combs Papers; Pearce, *Divide and Dissent,* 220-21. Although not as close to Prichard as Vice President Johnson, President Kennedy none-theless was familiar with him. On one trip to the Oval Office, Bob Bell, a member of Governor Combs's staff, recalled that before a meeting with a delegation of governors, Kennedy told Combs to send Ed Prichard his regards. Bell interview.

3. Pearce, *Divide and Dissent,* 221; Harrison and Klotter, *A New History of Kentucky,* 411-12; Breathitt interview.

4. *Woodford Sun,* Oct. 3, 1963; Bruce L. Felknor, *Political Mischief: Smear, Sabotage, and Reform in U.S. Elections* (New York: Praeger, 1992), 116.

5. Breathitt interview; George Robinson, ed., *Bert Combs: The Politician* (Lexington: Univ. Press of Kentucky, 1991), 149-50. For a stark comparison of how another Southern governor approached the divisive issue of civil rights, see Dan T. Carter, *The Politics of Rage: George Wallace, the Origins of the New Conservatism, and the Transformation of American Politics* (New York: Simon and Schuster, 1995).

6. Pearce, *Divide and Dissent,* 222-23.

7. Don Mills, interview by author, Lexington, Sept. 14, 1994; *NYT,* Aug. 4, 5, 1963; Chalmers M. Roberts, *The Washington Post: The First 100 Years* (Boston: Houghton Mifflin, 1977), 362-63; Graham, *Personal History,* 331-37; Carol Felsenthal, *Power, Privilege, and the Post: The Katharine Graham Story* (New York: G.P. Putnam's, 1993), 217-19, 224; Merry, *Taking on the World,* 332. See also *Time,* April 16, 1956.

8. *C-J,* March 6, 1964; Bell interview.

9. *H-L,* May 21, 1964; Cole interview.

10. Breathitt interview.

11. Kenneth E. Harrell, ed., *The Public Papers of Governor Edward T. Breathitt, 1963-1967* (Lexington: Univ. Press of Kentucky, 1984), 523-24; Breathitt interview.

12. Breathitt interview; Bell interview.

13. EFP to Lady Bird Johnson, Oct. 27, 1964, box 1701, Presidential "Social Files," Lyndon B. Johnson Library; Greider interview.

14. Jim Hudson and Marvin Coles, interview by author, Sept. 16, 1994.

15. Ibid.

16. Breathitt interview.

17. EFP to Clements, Feb. 21, 1964, Constitutional Revision Assembly File, Clements Papers.

18. Clements to EFP, Feb. 28, 1964, Clements Papers.

19. "The Proposed Revision of the Kentucky Constitution," box 5, Kentucky Constitutional Revision Assembly Records, Univ. of Kentucky.

20. Committee Assignments, box 31, Clements Papers.

21. Landy, *The Politics of Environmental Reform,* 170-71; *H-L,* Feb. 25, 1993.

22. Mills interview; Landy, *The Politics of Environmental Reform,* 171. The Widow Combs became a Kentucky legend and a symbol of anti-coal company sentiment. In 1977, President Jimmy Carter invited her to the White House to attend the signing of the federal strip mine bill. She died in 1993.

23. Gaventa, *Power and Powerlessness,* 132-35. For an extended study of the effects of strip mining on the economic, political, and social life of eastern Kentucky, see Harry M. Caudill, *Night Comes to the Cumberlands: A Biography of a Depressed Area* (Boston: Little, Brown, 1962). In 1974, Al Funk was interviewed by the BBC about the social costs of strip mining on the people of Middlesboro. When asked if he had any "moral responsibility to maintain the people who wish to stay in that area, and who have been working their fingers off to keep them in a reasonable condition of living," Funk replied, "No sir, these people don't work for us and never have worked for us—they're just people." The interviewer responded, "You mean they get in the way of strip-mining operations?" Funk answered, "Well, I don't say they get in the way, but they just don't add anything to the assets of the company." Gaventa, *Power and Powerlessness,* 135.

24. Landy, *The Politics of Environmental Reform,* 188-90. The broad-form deed was eventually prohibited by a constitutional amendment approved in 1987.

25. *H-L,* Jan. 5, 1966; *Louisville Times,* Jan. 18, 1966; Greider interview.

26. *Louisville Times,* Jan. 26, 27, 1966; Breathitt interview.

27. Breathitt interview; Pearce, "Adversity and Atonement."

28. Hudson interview.

29. *H-L,* Nov. 23, 1965.

30. Greider interview.

31. *H-L,* Dec. 3, 1965.

32. Transcript of the Proceedings of the Constitution Revision Assembly, Nov. 23, 1965, Constitution Revision Assembly Series, Clements Papers.

33. James F. Gordon to Rodgers Badgett, June 7, 1966, and EFP to Clements, June 15, 1966, Clements Papers.

34. Newspaper clipping, n.d, Clements Papers; Ben M. Johnson to Harry Lee Waterfield, March 9, 1964, Clements Papers.

35. Ken Toomey to W.C. Flannery, Sept. 30, 1966, and Flannery to Bill Pendleton, n.d., box 503, Chandler Papers.

36. "The Proposed Revision of the Kentucky Constitution," Kentucky Constitution Revision Assembly Records, box 5, Special Collections, Univ. of Kentucky.

37. Doris Bibb to Tommy Shirley, Nov. 30, 1966, box 510, Chandler Papers.

38. W.T. Pendelton Jr. to Chandler, Oct. 6, 1966, box 504, Chandler Papers.

39. Marion Vance newsletter, box 510, Chandler Papers.

40. Prichard Oral History, Pogue Library, Murray State Univ.

41. *C-J,* Sept. 18, 1966.

42. Downing to Breathitt, Oct. 13, 1966, Constitution Revision Assembly Series, Clements Papers.

43. *C-J,* Nov. 9, 1966. Although the state constitution of 1891 still stands, voters have subsequently approved several amendments since 1966 that have changed the state charter in ways that Prichard sought. The court system was overhauled to include a Supreme Court, and governors can now succeed themselves. On the other hand, the General Assembly still meets in biannual sessions of sixty days, and little has changed in the functioning dynamics of local government.

310NOTES TO PAGES 239-250

14 "Picking up the Pieces"

1. Federal Tax Lien Book 1, Woodford County Courthouse.

2. *C-J,* July 27, 1967; Coles interview.

3. Harrison and Klotter, *A New History of Kentucky,* 413-14.

4. EFP to Clements, March 6, 1968, "Prichard File," Clements Papers.

5. Henry Prichard interview (March 28, 1995).

6. Robinson, *Bert Combs,* 111.

7. Hudson interview.

8. Terry interview; Hudson interview.

9. EFP to Clements, March 6, 1968, "Prichard File," Clements Papers. For an example of the movement to "dump Johnson" in early 1968, see William H. Chafe, *Never Stop Running: Allard Lowenstein and the Struggle to Save American Liberalism* (New York: Basic Books, 1993), 262-75.

10. EFP to Clements, July 12, Aug. 5, 1968, Clements Papers. In the 1960s, Clements was back in Washington as president of the Tobacco Institute. For background on Clements in this new role as the nation's chief tobacco lobbyist, see Richard Kluger, *Ashes to Ashes: America's Hundred-Year Cigarette War, the Public Health, and the Unabashed Triumph of Philip Morris* (New York: Knopf, 1996), 270, 278-79, 288, 322.

11. EFP to Clements, Sept. 28, 1978, Clements Papers. By late 1966, Prichard's expressed doubts about the Vietnam War turned to outright opposition. Harvey Sloane, interview by author, Washington, D.C., June 8, 1995.

12. EFP to Clements, June 10, 1968, Clements Papers; *Diabetes and Your Eyes* (Bethesda: National Institute of Health, #83-2171, June 1983).

13. EFP to Clements, July 25, 1968, Clements Papers. See also Goulden, *Super-Lawyers,* 150-51.

14. EFP to Rauh, Sept. 6, 1968, Rauh Papers; EFP to Clements, Jan. 6, 1969, Clements Papers.

15. Federal Tax Lien Book 1, Woodford County Courthouse; Hudson interview; William Graham interview; Ardery, "Prich," 518-19. Ardery added that he refused to sue Prichard but advised the client to take his case to the state bar. From the time Prichard had his license renewed in 1954 to his death, the official proceedings of the Kentucky state bar do not reveal any official sanctions taken against Prichard for ethical violations.

16. Coles interview.

17. *Kentucky New Era,* Dec. 24, 1984; William Graham interview; Browning, "After the Scandal," 44.

18. *Goss v Personnel Board,* 456 SW 2d 819; *C-J,* June 27, 1970.

19. William Graham interview.

20. Ibid.; Hudson interview.

21. William Graham interview.

22. For a critical portrait of Combs's legal work on behalf of eastern Kentucky coal operators, see Harry M. Caudill, *Theirs Be The Power: The Moguls of Eastern Kentucky* (Urbana: Univ. of Illinois Press, 1983), 154-57.

23. Pearce, "The Man Who Might Have Been President"; Katherine Dryden interview; Hudson interview.

24. Lady Bird Johnson, letter to author; EFP to Breathitt, March 9, 1973, Edward T. Breathitt Papers, Pogue Library, Murray State Univ.

25. EFP to Clements, May 30, 1974, Clements Papers; Felsenthal, *Power, Privilege, and the Post,* 433.

26. Prichard's brother, Henry Power Prichard, spent most of his life after World War II in Hollywood, California, where he was a successful songwriter and musician. His most creative period was the 1940s. One of his compositions, "Take Care When You Say 'Te Quiero,'" was played by the Guy Lombardo orchestra. His most popular song, "Kentucky," topped the twenty leading songs list in Great Britain in 1946. Though not well known in his native state, Henry's compositions continue to generate royalties worldwide. Henry Prichard interview (March 28, 1995); *Paris Kentuckian-Citizen,* Oct. 19, 1945, March 8, 1946.

27. Schlesinger, "'Prich'"; *H-L,* Feb. 21, 1979; EFP to Clements, May 30, 1974, Clements Papers.

28. William Graham interview.

15 Twilight Renaissance

1. Browning, "After the Scandal," 39-44.

2. EFP to William Greider, Oct. 22, 1974, Bingham Papers.

3. Confidential information. Lucy Prichard not only refused to be interviewed for this book but also sealed over fifteen hours of oral history tapes by her husband housed at the University of Kentucky Library.

4. Pearce interview.

5. Greider to EFP, Sept. 30, 1974, Bingham Papers.

6. EFP to Greider, Oct. 9, 1974, Bingham Papers.

7. EFP to Barry Bingham, Oct. 23, 1974, Bingham Papers.

8. Katharine Graham to EFP, Oct. 15, 1974, and Barry Bingham to EFP, Oct. 30, 1974, Bingham Papers. Greider left the *Washington Post* and became a writer for *Rolling Stone.* He has also written three best-selling political books, *Secrets of the Temple: How the Federal Reserve Runs the Country* (New York: Simon and Schuster, 1987), *Who Will Tell the People?: The Betrayal of American Democracy* (New York: Simon and Schuster, 1992), and *One World, Ready or Not: The Manic Logic of Global Capitalism* (New York: Simon and Schuster, 1997).

9. EFP to Joseph Rauh, Oct. 24, 1974, Rauh Papers.

10. EFP to Katharine Graham, June 2, 1975, Graham Papers.

11. Greider interview. An intriguing book concerning Prichard was contemplated by Robert Penn Warren, who discussed with some friends the possibility of writing a fictional account of Prichard's life. According to R.W.B. Lewis, Warren "at one time had thought of basing a novel" on Prichard's saga, which had "many of the ingredients—drama, color, malfeasance, attractive personalities—that appealed to Warren as the makings of a novel." R.W.B. Lewis, letter to author, Sept. 28, 1992.

12. EFP to Katharine Graham, Jan. 20, 1975, Graham Papers.

13. *Kentucky Post,* July 10, 1982.

14. *H-L,* July 8, 9, 1975; *C-J,* July 8, 1975; *Mountain Life and Work* 51 (July-Aug. 1975).

15. Hudson interview; EFP to Benjamin V. Cohen, Dec. 7, 1973, Cohen Papers.

16. Peirce, *Border South States,* 223-25. See also an article by Peirce on Prichard's life that appeared in the *Washington Post,* Aug. 14, 1978, and the *Minneapolis Tribune,* Aug. 13, 1978.

17. William Graham interview.

18. EFP to Cohen, Dec. 7, 1973, Cohen Papers.

19. *C-J*, Aug. 12, 1976.

20. Pearce interview; confidential information.

21. Pearce interview.

22. Pearce, "Adversity and Atonement"; Pearce interview.

23. Pearce interview; James Rowe to Barry Bingham, Nov. 16, 1976, box 85, James Rowe Papers, Roosevelt Library.

24. *Lexington Leader*, Nov. 7, 1976; Pearce interview.

25. Confidential information; Pearce interview; Bingham interview.

26. EFP to Katharine Graham, Nov. 22, 1976, Graham Papers; EFP interview (Robinson).

27. Ardery wrote that "it was not the crime itself that caused our break. Until 1976, Prich had stoutly claimed innocence and by doing so put himself in the position of making my father . . . a liar." Ardery, "Prich," 500. This ignores, of course, the very public statement Prichard made following his last failed appeal in which he admitted his "mistakes" and in no way claimed innocence. To his friends and associates, Prichard never claimed innocence, only making veiled humorous comments about the Arderys, jail, and Bourbon County voting practices. To some of his closest friends, Prichard offered varying stories about his involvement, but in neither case did he attempt to portray himself as innocent.

28. *C-J*, Feb. 1, 6, 7, 8, 1977. Prichard was not, however, a one-man crusader against abuses of the merit system. Earlier, in 1972, he had defended the Ford administration of charges it had violated the system. When charges were brought that Democratic officials had interfered with the appointment, promotion, and dismissal of numerous state employees, Prichard represented the Economic Security commissioner who was being sued. Prichard won, when the State Personnel Board found that patronage "has been so long a congenial part of the political spectrum," and that under such circumstances, it was impossible "that principles of the merit system should be held inviolate by every commissioner . . . in the administration." *Frankfort State Journal*, Dec. 31, 1972.

29. Federal Tax Lien Book 1, Woodford County Courthouse; William Graham interview.

30. Henry Prichard interview (March 28, 1995).

31. St. John's Episcopal Church, Versailles, Kentucky, Canonical Register, 46, 64, Kentucky Historical Society; Henry Prichard interview (March 28, 1995).

32. Katharine Graham interview (author); Mills interview.

33. *H-L*, Feb. 21, 1979; Sloane interview; Berlin interview; Schlesinger interview.

34. Mills interview; Art Jester, interview by author, Lexington, Nov. 26, 1994.

35. *H-L*, Aug. 13, 1978; Browning, "After the Scandal," 44.

36. See form letter and guest list for the Prichard dinner in the "Prichard file," Bingham Papers; "Prichard Celebration," videotape, in the possession of Sara Combs, Stanton, Kentucky; *C-J*, Nov. 30, 1979.

16 The Final Struggle

1. Thomas Parrish, "The Prichard Committee for Academic Excellence: The First Decade, 1980-1990," Prichard Committee Files, Lexington.

2. Ibid.

3. John Stephenson, interview by author, Berea, Kentucky, June 24, 1994.

4. *C-J*, March 18, July 19, 1980.

5. Ibid., April 3, 1980; Daniel Reedy, interview by author, Lexington, Nov. 16, 1994. The following year, Prichard received an honorary Doctor of Humane Letters from Northern Kentucky University.

6. *C-J*, July 26, Oct. 27, 1980; Lucy Prichard to Ned Breathitt, Aug. 6, 1980, Breathitt Papers.

7. Schlesinger interview.

8. *C-J*, Feb. 4, 1981.

9. "Statement by Edward F. Prichard, Jr., Chairman, Committee on Higher Education in Kentucky's Future," March 3, 1981, Prichard Committee files; *C-J*, March 4, 1981.

10. "Discussion of 'Financial Condition of Higher Education,' Aug. 17, 1981," Prichard Committee Files.

11. *Wall Street Journal*, Aug. 26, 1981; confidential information; *College Heights Herald*, Sept. 22, 1981.

12. *In Pursuit of Excellence: The Report of the Prichard Committee on Higher Education in Kentucky's Future to the Kentucky Council on Higher Education* (Frankfort: Council on Higher Education, 1981), 15-18.

13. Parrish, "The Prichard Committee."

14. Stephenson interview; see foreword in James Still, *River of Earth: The Poem and Other Poems* (Lexington: King Library Press, 1982-83). The acknowledgment of the foreword did not, on the other hand, afford Prichard the recognition and respect he merited as a literary critic. The King Press even spelled his last name as "Pritchard."

15. *Bourbon County Citizen-Advertiser*, Sept. 9, 1981.

16. Reagan Walker, "The Legacy of 'Prich': Bluegrass-Roots Reform," *Education Week*, May 11, 1988.

17. Jester interview; Al Smith, interview by author, Lexington, June 5, 1996.

18. *Firing Line*, #1218, produced by Warren Steibel, Oct. 27, 1982.

19. Ibid.; Jester interview; Smith interview; *H-L*, Oct. 28, 1982.

20. Schlesinger, "'Prich.'"

21. *U.S. News and World Report*, Dec. 19, 1983; *C-J*, Dec. 15, 1983.

22. Terry interview; *C-J*, Jan. 4, 1983.

23. Federal Tax Lien Book 1; Woodford County Deed Book, 110:13, Woodford County Courthouse, Versailles. The mortgage was obtained from the Farmers National Bank in Danville, Kentucky, where Louis Prichard had started work on January 1, 1983, as an assistant vice president; Woodford County Mortgage Book, 89:675. For a brief background of Louis's career at the bank, see *Kentucky Advocate*, April 2, 1995.

24. Philip Ardery interview (Sept. 15, 1994); Bingham interview; James Rowe to EFP, Dec. 10, 1981, box 111, Rowe Papers; Amory interview.

25. Robert Sexton, interview by author, Lexington, Feb. 2, 1995. See also Bert T. Combs, "Creative Constitutional Law: The Kentucky School Reform Law," *Harvard Journal on Legislation* 28 (summer 1991): 367-78.

26. *H-L*, May 29, 1983; Harrison and Klotter, *A New History of Kentucky*, 417-18. Sloane later agreed with Prichard's postelection analysis; Sloane interview.

27. Walker, "The Legacy of 'Prich,'"; Sexton interview; Parrish, "The Prichard Committee"; *C-J*, June 4, 1984. The Berea degree was awarded posthumously to Lucy; Stephenson interview.

28. *H-L*, Nov. 10, 1984.

29. *C-J*, Sept. 5, 1984; Jim Oppel, "Ed Prichard on the High Cost of Running for Elective Office," *Louisville Magazine*, Dec. 1981.

30. William Graham interview.

31. Parrish, "The Prichard Committee."

32. *C-J*, Nov. 20, 22, 1984; Woodford County Will Book 42:15. As an indication of

Prichard's finances at the time of his death, in January 1985 the Woodford County Probate Court fixed a bond of Prichard's assets at $234,000. This included "stocks, bonds, corporate bonds or notes or other investments." Prichard did not die completely free from paying off all his IRS debts. He had retired twenty-six liens placed on him from 1960 to 1978, with the exception of one lien for $143.71 that remained unpaid at the time of his death; Federal Tax Lien Book 1, Woodford County Courthouse.

33. *C-J*, Nov. 24, 27, 1984; *H-L*, Nov. 28, 1984.

34. *C-J*, Dec. 1, 1984.

35. Ibid., Dec. 24, 25, 1984; See Richard Harwood's obituary in the *Washington Post*, Dec. 25, 1984.

Epilogue

1. The Prichard Committee for Academic Excellence is a nonprofit organization, headquartered in Lexington, that helps oversee the process of education reform in Kentucky. The primary occupation of the committee today is the implementation of the 1990 Kentucky Education Reform Act (KERA), which was passed in reaction to the 1988 Kentucky Supreme Court decision that found Kentucky's system of public education unconstitutional. The case was argued before the Court by former governor Bert T. Combs. See Harrison and Klotter, *A New History of Kentucky*, 391-99, 420.

2. The museum is located on Pleasant Street in Paris, just blocks from where Ed Sr. rented a home in the 1920s. The Clintonville ballot box located there, however, is an older version of the type used as evidence in Prichard and Funk's trial. Following Prichard's conviction, the ballot boxes were housed for years in the basement of the Bourbon County Courthouse but were removed when the building underwent renovation in 1995.

Sources

Manuscript Collections

Clemson University, Clemson, South Carolina
    James F. Byrnes Papers
Filson Club Library, Louisville, Kentucky
    Barry and Mary Bingham Papers
    Boyd F. Long Papers
Harvard Law School, Cambridge, Massachusetts
    Philip Elman Papers
    Henry L. Hart Jr. Papers
Lyndon B. Johnson Library, Austin, Texas
    Lyndon B. Johnson Papers
        House of Representatives Files
        LBJ Archives: Famous Names Records
        LBJ Archives: Senate Records
        President's Social Files
John F. Kennedy Library, Boston, Massachusetts
    Arthur M. Schlesinger Jr. Papers
Kentucky Historical Society, Frankfort, Kentucky
    St. John's Episcopal Church Canonical Records
University of Kentucky, Lexington
    Alben Barkley Papers
    Albert B. Chandler Papers
    Clay Family Papers
    Earle C. Clements Papers
    Constitutional Revision Assembly Records
    John Sherman Cooper Papers
    Thomas Underwood Papers
    Frederick M. Vinson Papers
    Lawrence Wetherby Papers
    Wilson Wyatt Papers
Labor-Management Documentation Center, Cornell University, Ithaca, New York
    Sidney Hillman Papers
Library of Congress, Washington, D.C.
    Joseph and Stewart Alsop Papers
    Benjamin V. Cohen Papers
    Thomas G. Corcoran Papers
    Felix Frankfurter Papers
    Harold L. Ickes Manuscript Diary
    Harold L. Ickes Papers

Robert L. Jackson Papers
Eugene Meyer Papers
Reinhold Niebuhr Papers
Joseph L. Rauh Jr. Papers
Murray State University, Murray, Kentucky
Edward T. Breathitt Papers
Harry Lee Waterfield Papers
National Archives, Washington, D.C.
Office of the Pardon Attorney Records
Office of War Mobilization and Reconversion Records, RG 250
U.S. Supreme Court Appellate Case Files, RG 267
Franklin D. Roosevelt Library, Hyde Park, New York
Francis Biddle Papers
Oscar Cox Papers
Wayne Coy Papers
President's Official Files
Eleanor Roosevelt Papers
Franklin D. Roosevelt Papers
James H. Rowe Jr. Papers
Southern Historical Collection, University of North Carolina, Chapel Hill
Mark Ethridge Papers
State Historical Society of Wisconsin, Madison
Americans for Democratic Action Papers
Harry S. Truman Library, Independence, Missouri
Tom C. Clark Papers
Matthew J. Connelly Files
Cross-Reference Files
Post-Presidential Official Files
President's Official Files
President's Personal Files
Harry S. Truman Papers

Government Collections

Bourbon County Courthouse, Paris, Kentucky
Bourbon County Deed Book
Bourbon County Mortgage Book
Election Commissioners Records
Real Estate Encumbrance Book
Federal Bureau of Investigation, Washington, D.C.
Thomas G. Corcoran Technical Surveillance
J. Edgar Hoover Official and Confidential Files
Louis B. Nichols Official and Confidential Files
Edward F. Prichard Jr. Technical Surveillance
Woodford County Courthouse, Versailles, Kentucky
Federal Tax Lien Book
Woodford County Will Book

Private Collections

Philip P. Ardery, Louisville, Kentucky
   FBI File on 1948 Bourbon County Vote Fraud Investigation
Sara Combs, Stanton, Kentucky
   Bert T. Combs Papers (now deposited at the University of Kentucky)
   "Prichard Celebration" videotape
Katharine Graham, Washington, D.C.
   Katharine Graham Papers
   Philip L. Graham Papers
Prichard Committee for Academic Excellence, Lexington, Kentucky
   Prichard Committee Clippings
William C. Stone, Louisville, Kentucky
   FBI File on Edward F. Prichard Jr.

Oral Histories

Columbia Oral History Collection, New York
   Samuel B. Bledsoe, Chester C. Davis, Philip Elman, Thomas I. Emerson, Carl Hamilton,
      Robert H. Jackson, Marvin Jones, Claude Wickard.
Eastern Kentucky University, Richmond
   Edward F. Prichard Jr. (1977/1979)
Lyndon B. Johnson Library, Austin, Texas
   Joseph L. Rauh Jr., James H. Rowe Jr.
Murray State University, Pogue Library
   Edward F. Prichard Jr (1966)
University of Kentucky, Lexington
   Edward F. Prichard Jr. Oral History Project
      Robert Amory Jr., Philip P. Ardery, Elizabeth Brent, Naomi I. Brill, Earle C. Clements,
      Elizabeth Clotfelder, Bert T. Combs, Katherine Dryden, Wendell Ford, John Kenneth
      Galbraith, Katharine Graham, Erwin Griswold, Betty Jo Denton Heick, Robert
      Houlihan, Shelby Kinkead, Marion J. Mitchell, Joseph L. Rauh Jr., Amos T. Taylor
Veterans of World War II Oral History Project
   Ruth Murphy
Harry S. Truman Library, Independence, Missouri
   James Loeb, Joseph L. Rauh Jr., Harry Vaughan

Interviews

The notes, transcripts, and original tapes of the following interviews by the author have been
   deposited in the Special Collections Department, University of Kentucky Library: Philip P.
   Ardery, Grover Baldwin, Robert Bell, Sir Isaiah Berlin, Mary Bingham, Edward T. Breathitt,
   Thomas D. Clark, T. Kerney Cole, Marvin Coles, Sara Combs, Gordon A. Craig, David
   Curd, Tom Davis, Debra Dawahare, C. Leslie Dawson, Edward Farris, Katharine Graham,
   William Graham, William Greider, Vic Hellard, Morton Holbrook, Robert Houlihan, James
   Hudson, Art Jester, Don Mills, James McGlothlin, Joseph Mooney, Robert Nathan, John
   Ed Pearce, Henry P. Prichard, Julius Rather, Daniel Reedy, Arthur M. Schlesinger Jr., Rob-

ert Sexton, Harvey Sloane, Al Smith, John Stephenson, James Still, William C. Stone, Joseph Terry, William Van Allen, Wilson Wyatt Sr.

Newspapers and Magazines

Boston Globe, Bourbon County Citizen, Christian Science Monitor, Cincinnati Enquirer, College Heights Herald, Daily Princetonian, Fortune, Frankfort State Journal, Kentucky Advocate, Kentucky Kernel, Kentucky New Era, Kentucky Post, Lexington Herald-Leader, Life, Look, Louisville Courier-Journal, Louisville Times, Mountain Life and Work, The Nation, Newsweek, New York Times, Paris Daily Enterprise, Paris Kentuckian-Citizen, Princeton Alumni Weekly, Time, U.S. News and World Report, Wall Street Journal, Washington Evening Star, Washington Post, Woodford Sun

Books

Abell, Tyler, ed. *Drew Pearson: Diaries, 1949-1959.* New York: Holt, Rinehart, and Winston, 1974.

Alsop, Joseph, with Adam Platt. *"I've Seen the Best of It": Memoirs.* New York: Norton, 1992.

Andrew, Christopher. *For The President's Eyes Only: Secret Intelligence and the American Presidency from Washington to Bush.* New York: Harper Collins, 1995.

Ardery, Philip. *Bomber Pilot: A Memoir of World War II.* Lexington: Univ. Press of Kentucky, 1978.

———. *Heroes and Horses: Tales of the Bluegrass.* Lexington: Univ. Press of Kentucky, 1996.

Auerbach, Jerold S. *Labor and Liberty: The LaFollette Committee and the New Deal.* Indianapolis: Bobbs-Merrill, 1966.

Bailey, Stephen Kemp. *Congress Makes a Law: The Story Behind the Employment Act of 1946.* New York: Columbia Univ. Press, 1950.

Barber, William J. *Designs Within Disorder: Franklin D. Roosevelt, the Economists, and the Shaping of American Economic Policy, 1933-1945.* Cambridge: Cambridge Univ. Press, 1996.

Barkley, Alben W. *That Reminds Me.* Garden City: Doubleday, 1954.

Bartley, Numan V. *The New South: 1945-1980.* Baton Rouge: Louisiana State Univ. Press, 1995.

Beatty, Jack. *The Rascal King: The Life and Times of James Michael Curley, 1874-1958.* Reading, Mass.: Addison-Wesley, 1992.

Berry, Mary Clay. *Voices from the Century Before: The Odyssey of a Nineteenth-Century Kentucky Family.* New York: Arcade, 1997.

Berman, William C. *The Politics of Civil Rights in the Truman Administration.* Columbus: Ohio State Univ. Press, 1970.

Bingham, Sallie. *Passion and Prejudice: A Family Memoir.* New York: Knopf, 1989.

Blakey, George T. *Hard Times and New Deal in Kentucky, 1929-1939.* Lexington: Univ. Press of Kentucky, 1986.

Blum, John Morton. *V Was for Victory: Politics and American Culture During World War II.* New York: Harcourt Brace Jovanovich, 1976.

Brinkley, Alan. *The End of Reform: New Deal Liberalism in Recession and War.* New York: Knopf, 1995.

Brinkley, David. *Washington Goes to War.* New York: Knopf, 1988.

Brownell, Herbert, with John P. Burke. *Advising Ike: The Memoirs of Attorney General Herbert Brownell.* Lawrence: Univ. Press of Kansas, 1993.

Burns, James MacGregor. *Roosevelt: The Soldier of Freedom.* New York: Harcourt Brace Jovanovich, 1970.

Byrnes, James F. *All in One Lifetime.* New York: Harper, 1958.

Caro, Robert A. *Means of Ascent: The Years of Lyndon Johnson.* New York: Knopf, 1990.

Catton, Bruce. *The War Lords of Washington.* New York: Greenwood Press, 1948.

Caudill, Harry M. *Night Comes to the Cumberlands: A Biography of a Depressed Area.* Boston: Little, Brown, 1962.

Chafe, William H. *Never Stop Running: Allard Lowenstein and the Struggle to Save American Liberalism.* New York: Basic Books, 1993.

Chandler, Albert B., with Vance Trimble. *Heroes, Plain Folks, and Skunks: The Life and Times of Happy Chandler.* Chicago: Bonus Books, 1989.

Chandler, David Leon. *The Binghams of Louisville: The Dark History Behind One of America's Great Fortunes.* New York: Crown, 1987.

Charns, Alexander. *Cloak and Gavel: FBI Wiretaps, Bugs, Informers, and the Supreme Court.* Urbana: Univ. of Illinois Press, 1992.

Clark, Thomas D. *Kentucky: Land of Contrast.* New York: Harper and Row, 1968.

Clifford, Clark, with Richard Holbrooke. *Counsel to the President: A Memoir.* New York: Random House, 1991.

Cohen, Robert. *When the Old Left Was Young: Student Radicals and America's First Mass Student Movement, 1929-1941.* New York: Oxford Univ. Press, 1993.

Dallek, Robert. *Lone Star Rising: Lyndon Johnson and His Times, 1908-1960.* New York: Oxford Univ. Press, 1991.

Daniels, Jonathan. *White House Witness, 1942-1945.* Garden City, N.J.: Doubleday, 1975.

Davis, Deborah. *Katharine the Great: Katharine Graham and the Washington Post.* New York: Harcourt Brace Jovanovich, 1979.

DeLoach, Cartha D. "Deke." *Hoover's FBI: The Inside Story by Hoover's Trusted Lieutenant.* Washington: Regnery Publishing, 1995.

Demaris, Ovid. *J. Edgar Hoover: As They Knew Him.* New York: Carroll and Graf, 1994.

Donaldson, Scott. *Archibald MacLeish: An American Life.* New York: Houghton Mifflin, 1992.

Dugger, Ronnie. *The Politician: The Life and Times of Lyndon Johnson: The Drive for Power from the Frontier to the Master of the Senate.* New York: Norton, 1982.

Egerton, John. *Speak Now Against the Day: The Generation Before the Civil Rights Movement in the South.* New York: Knopf, 1994.

Emerson, Thomas I. *Young Lawyer for the New Deal: An Insider's Memoir of the Roosevelt Years.* Savage, Md.: Rowman and Littlefield, 1991.

Everman, H.E. *The History of Bourbon County, 1785-1865.* Paris: Bourbon Press, 1977.

Felknor, Bruce L. *Political Mischief: Smear, Sabotage, and Reform in U.S. Elections.* New York: Praeger, 1992.

Felsenthal, Carol. *Power, Privilege, and the Post: The Katharine Graham Story.* New York: G.P. Putnam's, 1993.

Ferrell, Robert H. *Harry S. Truman: A Life.* Columbia: Univ. of Missouri Press, 1994.

Flynn, George Q. *The Mess in Washington: Manpower Mobilization in World War II.* Westport: Greenwood, 1979.

Fox, Richard Wightman. *Reinhold Niebuhr: A Biography.* New York: Pantheon, 1985.

Frankfurter, Felix. *Mr. Justice Holmes and the Supreme Court.* Cambridge: Harvard Univ. Press, 1939.

Fraser, Steven. *Labor Will Rule: Sidney Hillman and the Rise of American Labor.* New York: Free Press, 1991.

Gaventa, John. *Power and Powerlessness: Quiescence and Rebellion in an Appalachian Valley.* Urbana: Univ. of Illinois Press, 1980.

Gentry, Curt. *J. Edgar Hoover: The Man and His Secrets.* New York: Plume, 1991.

Gerhart, Eugene C. *America's Advocate: Robert H. Jackson.* Indianapolis: Bobbs-Merrill, 1958.

Gillon, Steven M. *Politics and Vision: The ADA and American Liberalism, 1947-1985.* New York: Oxford Univ. Press, 1987.

Goodwin, Doris Kearns. *No Ordinary Time: Franklin and Eleanor Roosevelt: The Home Front in World War II.* New York: Simon and Schuster, 1994.

Goulden, Joseph C. *The Super-Lawyers: The Small and Powerful World of the Great Washington Law Firms.* New York: Weybright and Talley, 1971.

Graham, Katharine. *Personal History.* New York: Knopf, 1997.

Gray, John. *Isaiah Berlin.* Princeton: Princeton Univ. Press, 1996.

Gressley, Gene M., ed. *Voltaire and the Cowboy: The Letters of Thurman Arnold.* Boulder: Colorado Associated Univ. Press, 1977.

Halberstam, David. *The Powers That Be.* New York: Knopf, 1979.

Hall, Kermit, ed. *The Oxford Companion to the Supreme Court of the United States.* New York: Oxford Univ. Press, 1992.

Hamby, Alonzo. *Beyond the New Deal: Harry S. Truman and American Liberalism.* New York: Columbia Univ. Press, 1973.

———. *Man of the People: A Life of Harry S. Truman.* New York: Oxford Univ. Press, 1995.

Harrell, Kenneth E., ed. *The Public Papers of Governor Edward T. Breathitt, 1963-1967.* Lexington: Univ. Press of Kentucky, 1984.

Harrison, Lowell H., and James C. Klotter. *A New History of Kentucky.* Lexington: Univ. Press of Kentucky, 1997.

In Pursuit of Excellence: The Report of the Prichard Committee on Higher Education in Kentucky's Future to the Kentucky Council on Higher Education. Frankfort: Council on Higher Education, 1981.

Ireland, Robert H. *The County in Kentucky History.* Lexington: Univ. Press of Kentucky, 1976.

Irons, Peter H. *The New Deal Lawyers.* Princeton: Princeton Univ. Press, 1982.

Janeway, Eliot. *The Struggle for Survival: A Chronicle of Economic Mobilization in World War II.* New Haven: Yale Univ. Press, 1951.

Jewell, Malcolm E. *Kentucky Votes.* Lexington: Univ. of Kentucky Press, 1963.

Kalman, Laura. *Abe Fortas: A Biography.* New Haven: Yale Univ. Press, 1990.

———. *Legal Realism at Yale, 1927-1960.* Chapel Hill: Univ. of North Carolina Press, 1986.

Keller, William. *The Liberals and J. Edgar Hoover: Rise and Fall of a Domestic Intelligence State.* Princeton: Princeton Univ. Press, 1989.

Kessler, Ronald. *The FBI: Inside the World's Most Powerful Law Enforcement Agency.* New York: Pocket Books, 1993.

Klotter, James C. *The Breckinridges of Kentucky, 1760-1981.* Lexington: Univ. Press of Kentucky, 1986.

———. *Kentucky: Portrait in Paradox, 1900-1950.* Frankfort: Kentucky Historical Society, 1996.

Lash, Joseph P. *Dealers and Dreamers: A New Look at the New Deal.* New York: Doubleday, 1988.

———. *From the Diaries of Felix Frankfurter.* New York: Norton, 1975.

Leuchtenburg, William E. *The FDR Years: On Roosevelt and His Legacy.* New York: Columbia Univ. Press, 1995.

———. *The Supreme Court Reborn: The Constitutional Revolution in the Age of Roosevelt.* New York: Oxford Univ. Press, 1995.

Lichtenstein, Nelson. *Labor's War at Home: The CIO in World War II.* Cambridge: Cambridge Univ. Press, 1982.

———. *The Most Dangerous Man in Detroit: Walter Reuther and the Fate of American Labor.* New York: Basic Books, 1995.

Littell, Norman M. *My Roosevelt Years,* edited by Jonathan Dembo. Seattle: Univ. of Washington Press, 1987.

Louchheim, Katie, ed. *The Making of the New Deal: The Insiders Speak.* Cambridge: Harvard Univ. Press, 1983.

Lucas, Marion B. *A History of Blacks in Kentucky.* Vol. 2. Frankfort: Kentucky Historical Society, 1992.

Maney, Patrick J. *"Young Bob" LaFollette: A Biography of Robert M. LaFollette, Jr., 1895-1953.* Columbia: Univ. of Missouri Press, 1978.

McAuliffe, Mary Sperling. *Crisis on the Left: Cold War Politics and American Liberals.* Amherst: Univ. of Massachusetts Press, 1978.

McCullough, David. *Truman.* New York: Simon and Schuster, 1992.

Merkley, Paul. *Reinhold Niebuhr: A Political Account.* Montreal: McGill-Queen's University Press, 1975.

Merry, Robert W. *Taking on the World: Joseph and Stewart Alsop—Guardians of the American Century.* New York: Viking, 1996.

Murphy, Bruce Allen. *The Brandeis/Frankfurter Connection: The Secret Political Activities of Two Supreme Court Justices.* New York: Oxford Univ. Press, 1982.

Nathan, Robert. *Mobilizing for Abundance.* New York: McGraw-Hill, 1944.

Nelson, Donald M. *Arsenal of Democracy: The Story of American War Production.* New York: Harcourt, Brace, 1946.

Newman, Roger K. *Hugo Black: A Biography.* New York: Pantheon, 1994.

Niebuhr, Reinhold. *Beyond Tragedy: Essays on the Christian Interpretation of History.* New York: Scribner's, 1937.

Osgood, Charles G. *Lights in Nassau Hall: A Book of the Bicentennial, Princeton, 1746-1946.* Princeton: Princeton Univ. Press, 1951.

Parris, Michael E. *Felix Frankfurter and His Times: The Reform Years.* New York: Free Press, 1982.

Pearce, John Ed. *Divide and Dissent: Kentucky Politics, 1930-1963.* Lexington: Univ. Press of Kentucky, 1987.

Peirce, Neil R. *The Border South States: People, Politics, and Power in the Five Border South States.* New York: Norton, 1975.

Powers, Richard Gid. *Not Without Honor: The History of American Anticommunism.* New York: Free Press, 1995.

———. *Secrecy and Power: The Life of J. Edgar Hoover.* New York: Free Press, 1987.

Ritchie, Donald A. *James M. Landis: Dean of the Regulators.* Cambridge: Harvard Univ. Press, 1980.

Roberts, Chalmers M. *The Washington Post: The First 100 Years.* Boston: Houghton Mifflin, 1977.

Robertson, David. *Sly and Able: A Political Biography of James F. Byrnes.* New York: Norton, 1994.

Robinson, George, ed. *Bert Combs: The Politician.* Lexington: Univ. Press of Kentucky, 1991.

Rosen, Charles. *Scandals of '51: How the Gamblers Almost Killed College Basketball.* New York: Holt, Rinehart and Winston, 1978.

Ross, Irwin. *The Loneliest Campaign: The Truman Victory of 1948.* New York: New American Library, 1968.

Sabato, Larry J., and Glenn R. Simpson. *Dirty Little Secrets: The Persistence of Corruption in American Politics.* New York: Times Books, 1996.

Sandilands, Roger J. *The Life and Political Economy of Lauchlin Currie: New Dealer, Presidential Adviser, and Development Economist.* Durham: Duke Univ. Press, 1990.

Schwarz, Jordan A. *The New Dealers: Power Politics in the Age of Roosevelt.* New York: Vintage, 1993.

Seidman, Joel. *American Labor from Defense to Reconversion.* Chicago: Univ. of Chicago Press, 1953.

Sherwood, Robert E. *Roosevelt and Hopkins: An Intimate History.* New York: Harper, 1948.

Simon, James F. *The Antagonists: Hugo Black, Felix Frankfurter, and Civil Liberties in Modern America.* New York: Simon and Schuster, 1989.

Solberg, Carl. *Hubert Humphrey: A Biography.* New York: Norton, 1984.

Somers, Herman M. *Presidential Agency: The Office of War Mobilization and Reconversion.* Cambridge: Harvard Univ. Press, 1950.

Squires, James D. *The Secrets of the Hopewell Box: Stolen Elections, Southern Politics, and a City's Coming of Age.* New York: Times Books, 1996.

Still, James. *River of Earth: The Poem and Other Poems.* Lexington: The King Library Press, 1982-83.

Sulloway, Frank J. *Born to Rebel: Birth Order, Family Dynamics, and Creative Lives.* New York: Pantheon, 1996.

Sutherland, Arthur E. *The Law at Harvard: A History of Ideas and Men, 1918-1967.* Cambridge: Harvard Univ. Press, 1967.

Terkel, Studs. *The Good War: An Oral History of World War II.* New York: Pantheon, 1984.

Theoharis, Athan, ed. *From the Secret Files of J. Edgar Hoover.* Chicago: Ivan R. Dee, 1991.

———. *Spying on Americans: Political Surveillance from Hoover to the Huston Plan.* Philadelphia: Temple Univ. Press, 1978.

———, and John Stuart Cox. *The Boss: J. Edgar Hoover and the Great American Inquisition.* Philadelphia: Temple Univ. Press, 1988.

Trillin, Calvin. *Remembering Denny.* New York: Farrar, Straus and Giroux, 1993.

Turow, Scott. *One L.* New York: Farrar Straus Giroux, 1988.

Urofsky, Melvin I. *Felix Frankfurter: Judicial Restraint and Individual Liberties.* Boston: Twayne, 1991.

Warren, Edward H. *Spartan Education.* Boston: Houghton Mifflin, 1942.

Watkins, T.H. *Righteous Pilgrim: The Life and Times of Harold L. Ickes, 1874-1952.* New York: Henry Holt, 1990.

Wechsler, James. *Revolt on the Campus.* New York: Covici Friede, 1935.

White, Graham, and John Maze. *Harold Ickes of the New Deal.* Cambridge: Harvard Univ. Press, 1985.

Woodward, Bob, and Scott Armstrong. *The Brethren: Inside the Supreme Court.* New York: Simon and Schuster, 1979.

Wyatt, Wilson W. *Whistle Stops: Adventures in Public Life.* Lexington: Univ. Press of Kentucky, 1985.

Articles

Ardery, Philip P. "Prich." *Filson Club History Quarterly* 68 (Oct. 1994): 499-520.

"The Attorney-Client Privilege: Fixed Rules, Balancing, and Constitutional Entitlement." *Harvard Law Review* 91 (Dec. 1977): 466-87.

Bird, Kai, and Max Holland. "The Tapping of 'Tommy the Cork.'" *The Nation,* Feb. 8, 1986.

Brinkley, Alan. "The Antimonopoly Ideal and the Liberal State: The Case of Thurman Arnold." *Journal of American History* 80 (1993): 557-79.

Browning, Frank. "After the Scandal: Picking Up the Pieces." *Washington Monthly* 5 (Oct. 1973): 41-44.

Combs, Bert T. "Creative Constitutional Law: The Kentucky School Reform Law." *Harvard Journal on Legislation* 28 (summer 1991): 367-78.

Hart, Henry M., Jr., and Edward F. Prichard Jr. "The Fansteel Case: Employee Misconduct and the Remedial Powers of the National Labor Relations Board." *Harvard Law Review* 52 (June 1939): 1275-1329.

Hedlund, Richard P. "The Most Hated Man in America: Fred Vinson and the Office of Economic Stabilization." *Filson Club History Quarterly* 68 (April 1994): 267-84.

Jones, Byrd L. "The Role of Keynesians in Wartime Policy and Postwar Planning, 1940-1946." Working Papers, *American Economic Review* 62 (May 1972): 125-33.

Koistenen, Paul A.C. "Mobilizing the World War II Economy: Labor and the Industrial-Military Alliance." *Pacific Historical Review* 42 (Nov. 1973): 443-78.

Lichtman, Allan J. "Tommy the Cork: The Secret World of Washington's First Modern Lobbyist." *Washington Monthly* (Feb. 1987): 41-49.

Mason, Bobbie Ann. "Doing the Boptrot." *New Yorker,* May 9, 1994.

Morgan, Thomas S. "James F. Byrnes and Segregation." *The Historian* 56 (summer 1994): 645-54.

Oppel, Jim. "Ed Prichard on the High Cost of Running for Elective Office." *Louisville Magazine,* Dec. 1981.

Pearce, John Ed. "Adversity and Atonement." *Louisville Courier-Journal Magazine.* Oct. 31, 1976.

———. "Bourbon County: The Quintessence of Kentucky." *Louisville Courier-Journal Magazine,* May 5, 1985.

———. "The Man Who Might Have Been President." *Louisville Courier-Journal Magazine,* Oct. 24, 1976.

Prichard, Edward F. Jr. "One-Man Army for Humanity." *Washington Post Book World,* Oct. 26, 1975.

Ritchie, Donald A. "Alben W. Barkley: The President's Man." In *First Among Equals: Outstanding Senate Leaders of the Twentieth Century,* edited by Richard A. Baker and Roger H. Davidson. Washington, D.C.: Congressional Quarterly, 1991.

Schlesinger, Arthur M., Jr. "'Prich': A New Deal Memoir." *New York Review of Books,* March 28, 1985.

Stone, I.F. "Division in the OPM." *Nation,* March 8, 1941.

Walker, Reagan. "The Legacy of 'Prich': Bluegrass-Roots Reform." *Education Week,* May 11, 1988.

Wallace, H. Lew. "Alben Barkley and the Democratic Convention of 1948." *Filson Club History Quarterly* 55 (July 1981): 231-52.

Television Programs

"Distinguished Kentuckian." Produced by O. Leonard Press. Sept. 18, 1974. Kentucky Educational Television.

Firing Line with William F. Buckley Jr. No. 1218. Produced by Warren Steibel. Oct. 27, 1982.

"Kentucky's New Dealer: Ed Prichard Remembers." Produced by Britt Davis. Kentucky Educational Television, 1984.

Unpublished Sources

McDaniel, Mildred. "The Evolution of a Ruling Class in Contemporary County Government." Master's thesis, University of Kentucky, 1949.

Niznik, Monica Lynne. "Thomas G. Corcoran: The Public Service of Franklin Roosevelt's 'Tommy the Cork.'" Ph.D. diss., University of Notre Dame, 1981.

Parrish, Thomas. "The Prichard Committee for Academic Excellence: The First Decade, 1980-1990." Paper for the Prichard Committee, Lexington, Kentucky.

Prichard, Edward F., Jr. "Popular Political Movements in Kentucky, 1875-1900." Senior honors thesis, Princeton University, 1935.

Smoot, Richard Clayton. "John Sherman Cooper: The Paradox of a Liberal Republican in Kentucky Politics." Ph.D. diss., University of Kentucky, 1988.

Spragens, William Clark. "The 1947 Gubernatorial Election in Kentucky." Master's thesis, University of Kentucky, 1951.

Syvertsen, Thomas Hamilton. "Earle Chester Clements and the Democratic Party, 1920-1950." Ph.D. diss., University of Kentucky, 1982.

Court Cases and Government Reports

Craig v Curd, 218 SW 2d 395 (1949).

U.S. Congress, Senate. *Final Report of the Select Committee to Study Government Operations with Respect to Intelligence Activities.* 94th Congress, 2d Sess. (1976), Rep. 94-755.

Goss v Personnel Board, 456 SW 2d 819 (1970).

Minersville School District v Gobitis, 310 US 586 (1940).

Edward Fretwell Prichard, Jr. v United States. R.G. 267, U.S. Supreme Court, Appellate Case Files, no. 795. National Archives.

United States v Alvarado Erwin Funk, Jr. and Edward Fretwell Prichard, Jr. R.G. 267, U.S. Supreme Court, Appellate Case Files, no. 795. National Archives.

United States v Peoples Deposit Bank and Trust. 112 F. Supp. 720.

Index

CPSIA information can be obtained
at www.ICGtesting.com
Printed in the USA
LVHW030136211222
735627LV00001B/77

9 780813 190969